Racial and Ethnic Politics in California

Racial and Ethnic Politics in California:
Continuity and Change

Sandra Bass and Bruce E. Cain, editors

2008
Berkeley Public Policy Press
Institute of Governmental Studies
University of California, Berkeley

Printed in the United States of America.

Library of Congress Cataloging-in-Publication Data

Racial and ethnic politics in California / Bryan O. Jackson, Michael B. Preston, editors.
p. cm.
Includes bibliographical references.
ISBN 9780877724285
1. Political participation—California. 2. Minorities—California—Political activity. 3. California—Politics and government—1951- I. Jackson, Byran O. II. Preston, Michael B.
JK87985.R33 1991
323'.042'09794—dc20 91-18676

Contents

POLICY

Chapter 1

Introduction: Toward Greater Pluralism?

Bruce E. Cain and Sandra Bass

In the first two decades after the 1965 U.S. immigration reform that ended discriminatory quotas, immigration visibly transformed America's southwestern states. The results were particularly dramatic in California. The state's non-Hispanic white population dropped from 77% to 48% between 1970 and 2000, due mostly to the growth of the Asian and Latino populations. As these immigrant populations have spread to other regions of the United States in recent years—the Northeast, mid-Atlantic, and South especially—some states are now experiencing the political and social repercussions that California and other southwestern states went through two decades ago. Many of the same questions Californians were asking themselves in the eighties are now on the political forefront in states like Virginia, Nebraska, and Illinois: Are new immigrants taking jobs away from U.S. citizens? Are undocumented residents a boon or a drain to the economy? Are Asians and Latinos assimilating as well or as quickly as the Irish and Italians in the early twentieth century?

Immigration, despite nearly three decades of public debate, is still politically salient in California, as the 2006 special election for Congressman Duke Cunningham's replacement amply demonstrated. Moreover, due to significant differences in white and nonwhite fertility rates, the demographic impact of immigration will be felt for some time to come even if the U.S. adopts more draconian immigration restrictions. As a consequence, California will continue to move further down the path towards multiracial/ethnic politics in the coming decades. The question is not whether, but at what rate, California and the rest of the country will become more multiracial and multiethnic. The demographic die has been cast.

The shift to a more multiracial and multiethnic landscape presents several institutional and political challenges. The civil rights revolution—the more aggressive application of the 14th Amendment and the Voting Rights Act to create more opportunities for minority participation and representation—was forged in a biracial context. That legal framework, which was so effective in the earlier era, has not always fit the new multiracial/ethnic circumstances as well. Asian-Americans, for instance, have not yet won any significant voting rights cases under either Sections 2 or 5 of the Voting Rights Act. Also, the old civil rights framework does not directly address some of the new election administration issues that have emerged since the 2000 election, such as whether poor nonwhite voters have a higher likelihood of casting a spoiled ballot or whether election administration problems are more frequent in less socio-economically advantaged areas.

Politically, there are challenges as well. The voting shares of California's Latino and Asian populations are growing, but those of the black and white populations are not. Areas that used to be represented by elected officials of one racial or ethnic group are now being challenged by candidates from another. The presence of new groups requires new coalitional strategies and partnerships. But can these groups forge these political alliances, or is the gulf between their interests too wide?

Then there is the question of whether the new multiracial and multiethnic politics will be more or less "pluralist" than the old biracial division. In the pluralist, neo-Madisonian ideal, groups should form many fluid, temporary coalitions that vary with the issues at stake and political circumstances. By avoiding permanent winners and losers and promoting many temporary alliances, a pluralist democracy theoretically diminishes social tensions and enhances systemic legitimacy. Of particular concern to pluralists is whether there is a pernicious overlap between class and race, creating a nonwhite underclass with fewer economic and political resources and experiencing higher levels of personal and occupational discrimination. Pluralists fear that the cumulative gap in advantages between white and nonwhite populations could create a permanent and potentially destabilizing cleavage in American politics.

What do the following chapters have to say about these questions? Are groups adapting to the new multiracial, multiethnic circumstances? Is the result something closer or further from the pluralist ideal?

Characteristics of the New Multiracial, Multiethnic Politics

Some, but not all, of the facts about multiracial, multiethnic politics in California lend themselves to pluralistic optimism. As the Ali Modarres essay repeatedly points out, there is tremendous diversity in the ranks of the emerging nonwhite population. From the pluralist perspective, diversity of circumstances is a good thing, because it often leads to a corresponding diversity of interests and perspectives, lessening the chances of a hardened bipolar, white-nonwhite political cleavage.

The influx of new immigrants has added linguistic, occupational, religious, and cultural differences into the population mix. There are significant differences both across and within different ethnic and racial groupings. As Modarres explains: "By the late seventies, the picture of immigration to the state had become more complex. Highly educated, middle-class immigrants mixed with laborers and refugees from Southwest Asia. Californians could no longer speak of a prototypical immigrant."

As we see in Chapter 2, many Asian immigrants (especially Chinese and Korean) are more highly educated than their Latino counterparts, but at the same time, some Asians (e.g., Cambodian, Laotian, and Vietnamese) are more similar to Latinos in socio-economic profile. In short, there is socio-economic diversity both across and within racial and ethnic categories. And unlike Europe, where many of the immigrants share a common religion (i.e., Muslim), there is no clear faith divide between California's immigrant and native populations, and, certainly, nothing like the tensions between Christians and Muslims in France, Britain, Germany, Denmark, and Holland. These are important facts to a pluralist, because class and religion have historically been important and enduring sources of political polarization. Heterogeneity across immigrant groups in these dimensions helps the pluralist cause.

Another good demographic fact from a pluralist perspective is that the level of overall segregation in California is still moderate. Immigration seems to be creating multi-ethnic neighborhoods in urban areas especially. Modarres finds that "two thirds of all census tracts fall within the range of moderately segregated to moderately integrated" and the urban areas that have received the greatest numbers of immigrants display the greatest amount of integration.

If geographic patterns reveal anything about relationships between racial groups—which they do when individuals have the ability to vote with their feet and move to neighborhoods of their choosing—then the fact that the new immigrants live in integrated areas would seem to be a sign of positive race relations. However, if the scarcity of low-priced housing stock or other adverse economic circumstances is forcing disadvantaged groups to live in proximity to one another, the integrated pattern tells us little about how groups actually perceive one another. There is no way to tell from Modarres's data which is the case. And the fact that whites are less integrated with the new immigrant groups than the immigrant groups are with one another and the black population is an important caveat to any racial optimism.

The racial picture in California at the moment seems to be mixed between the pluralist and hard cleavage models. The presence of new nonwhite groups living in proximity to one another in urban areas is offset by the more segregated situation of suburban and rural whites. Inner-city black and Latino populations provide a core of politically liberal representatives to the legislature while the white rural and suburban areas are more likely to produce conservative, Republican-elected officials. Latinos, as Kim Geron reminds us in her essay, are growing in numbers and making inroads in the Central Valley in terms of electing Latino officials even though the overall pattern in California is blue on the coasts and red in the inland areas. The ability of Latino candidates like Bonnie Garcia and Abel Maldonado to get elected as Republicans in rural areas illustrates further the emerging diversity of Latino interests in California.

Redistricting can marginally lessen or enhance the natural concentrations of populations, but even with a reformed redistricting system, the state will still on average produce 75-80% safe seats. Unless redistricting disregards communities of interest and compactness, the patterns of residential segregation of white versus nonwhites will continue to produce safely liberal and conservative seats. In so far as this contributes to legislative polarization, the prognosis has to be for more of it to occur in the future unless redistricting norms change dramatically.

The future of ethnic relations in California is also very much tied to national and state economic trends. Across the country, income disparities have increased since the seventies. The economy is changing: skilled blue-collar jobs are on the decline, unions are less powerful, and many immigrants, Latinos especially, find themselves in low-paying service and manufacturing jobs. If whites and more affluent Asians increasingly choose to cohabit in suburban areas while blacks and Latinos live in concentrated urban areas, this will further the current disparities in socio-economic resources across local communities. In Chapter 10, Manuel Pastor reminds us that California went from fifteenth to fourth in the national rankings of economic disparity between the top and bottom fifths of the income distribution. At the same time, there is a trend toward localizing public spending, which exacerbates the impact of unequal community resources. Wealthier communities can pass bond measures to upgrade school facilities or upgrade infrastructure. Poorer communities are less able to do the same. Growing economic disparities imbedded in a system of more decentralized government services could create a deeper divide in the future between the white haves and the nonwhite have-nots, strengthening social and political polarization.

Ethnic Networks

Breaking through the barriers to elected office is the foremost challenge for any new political group. Running for office can be expensive, time consuming, and require a broad base of support. This is especially true in California, with its large state Senate and Assembly districts, expensive media markets, and a highly professionalized political class. The paths that different ethnic and racial groups follow to achieve political influence are in large measure dictated by each group's size and resources. Looked at this way, there is a clear divide between the groups that can pursue overt ethnic candidacies and those that cannot.

Ethnic candidacies are campaigns that rely on core voter support from their ethnic/racial group, appealing directly to them with group-oriented issues and themes. Latinos provide the best example of this strategy in California. As Ricardo

Ramírez and Luis Fraga show, the probability of electing a Latino candidate is strongly related to the density of Latino registered voters in a given area. Districts in which 40% or more of the registered voters are Latino are virtually certain to elect a Latino candidate.

Ethnic or racial groups that want to pursue this strategy must meet certain conditions. First, they must be sufficiently numerous to be able to elect a candidate from their community if they vote as an ethnic bloc. Given high rates of non-citizenship, lower levels of education and much residential mobility, population density per se does not always translate into immediate political power, as Latinos in downtown L.A. discovered in the 1980s and 1990s. Even now, Latinos are a third of California's population but only 16% of it voters.

The second condition for a successful ethnic candidacy is sufficient cohesion among the group's voters. In the seventies and eighties, Latino leaders were sometimes frustrated by the ability of white or black incumbent legislators to win Latino voters over with superb constituency service, or by hiring Latino staff members and championing local causes. Over time, the argument that Latino elected officials would better understand and represent Latino voters became more prevalent.

However, the experience of California's African-American community is instructive here because after its initial successes in electing black elected officials, some members of the black community began to question whether they were as well served as others. As Melina Abdullah and Regina Freer put it, initially black voters trusted black officials to take care of their interests, but over the years working-class and poor blacks began to question whether black officials attended to their interests as well as they did to the black middle class. This was certainly a theme in Tom Bradley's career as mayor of Los Angeles. Until the Rodney King riots refocused Bradley's attention on the plight of poorer downtown black constituents, the primary beneficiaries of city hiring and contracts were the black middle class. In recent years, African Americans have lost control of state legislative and city mayoral positions, in part because a significant bloc of black voters no longer believed that descriptive representation necessarily equated to material and policy benefits. This may happen to Latino voters over time as well.

Thirdly, electoral success requires finding candidates who have the resources, support, and credibility to run competitive campaigns. This also takes time to develop as Latinos first had to establish themselves at the local government level or serve time in the legislature as staffers. The pool of potential Latino candidates at all levels is much deeper today than it was 25 years ago. Term limits have opened up more opportunities sooner for Latinos than would have been the case before 1990. This and a favorable redistricting by the Court Masters in 1991 helped to increase Latino membership in the state Senate from 3 in 1990 to 10 in 2004, and in the Assembly from 4 to 20.

While the ethnic candidate strategy fits the resources and capacities of the Latino community well, it does not work as well for Asian-American candidates. To begin with, there are currently no majority Asian-American state legislative or congressional districts in California. Moreover, even if there were, given historical differences among Asian nationalities, the various Asian nationalities cannot be counted on to vote as a cohesive bloc. As a consequence, Asian-American candidates have been most successful running as nonethnic candidates, that is to say, running on general appeals to party and policy and not on ethnic specific issues or themes.

As Wendy Tam Cho's essay explains, while their electoral appeals may be nonethnic, ethnic networks nonetheless play an important role in helping Asian candidates to find the resources and support to run for office. In this way, Asian candidates are following the well-worn path of Jewish, Armenian, and Greek candidates in California. None of these communities is large enough to elect their own representatives without significant support from other ethnic and racial groups, but they have the resources to provide critical early money and support. The pattern for Robert Matsui and Norm Mineta is no different than for George Deukmejian, Phil Angelides, or Howard Berman.

Partly due to the fund-raising scandals in the Clinton administration, there are some common misunderstandings about Asian campaign finance. The stereotype is that Asians give strategically to maximize influence in the manner of interest groups trying to win favorable legislation or access to powerful legislators. But overwhelmingly, most Asian contributors are actually donating along ethnic lines and across geographic boundaries to help Asian candidates in the early stages of their careers. Over time, Asian candidates then become less dependent on ethnic money. This then represents a second path to political influence: leveraging money instead of population to jump start ethnic candidates running nonethnocentric campaigns.

Does one strategy dominate the other? Possibly not: the ethnic candidate strategy works well at the district level, but when ethnic candidates run for statewide offices, their records can look parochial to those who do not belong to that group. Latinos have done well inside the legislature, winning the Assembly Speaker position three times since 1990, in part because their caucus is so large. But to date, they have been less successful running statewide, including the ill-fated attempt by Cruz Bustamante to run in the recall against Arnold Schwarzenegger. Asians have seen their numbers grow to a handful in the legislature, but they have not clearly defined and executed an Asian-American agenda. In the end, groups pursue the political paths that are open to them whatever the relative advantages and disadvantages of that route. Latinos, because of their numbers and relative lack of wealth, will continue to pursue the ethnic candidate strategy. Asians, for the opposite reasons, will not.

It is worth remembering that political influence is not merely expressed and practiced through the party system and elected office. An emerging characteristic of contemporary democracy is advocacy through nonprofits and grassroots. Both the Els de Graauw and Abdullah/Freer essays remind us that ethnic networks operate in this informal political sector as well. Nonprofits in San Francisco have effectively advocated for language rights and improved city services. Their ability to mobilize and energize citizens at the grassroots gives them leverage over elected officials. In San Francisco, some of these groups rival the political parties and trade unions in their influence.

California's trade unions, though diminished in membership numbers, reasserted themselves as an electoral force in recent years. Campaign finance reform laws have created an opportunity for PACs of all sorts, including labor, to finance political candidates. In addition, as Kenneth Burt points out, they have recruited candidates out of their ranks, and provided manpower for related campaign activities such as registration drives and get-out-the-vote efforts. Forced into the political arena by initiatives that would have threatened their ability to organize, labor's more aggressive strategy included reaching out to minority communities. In Burt's words, "Labor came to view minority communities as a political partner" with Latino leaders such as Miguel Contreras and Joe Nunez symbolizing "that Labor had become an organization increasingly representative of, and at times led by, minorities." A number of prominent minority legislators came out of the ranks of labor over the last 20 years, including Antonio Villaraigosa, Fabian Núñez, Judy Chu, and Gil Cedillo.

Policy Outcomes and Minority Power

There are characteristic advantages and disadvantages for minorities operating in the highly decentralized and fractured California system of local and state government. The chief advantage is that there are so many points of entry into elected offices—special governments, city councils, school boards, county boards, the state legislature, etc.—that it is possible for relatively small groups to obtain representation at some level of government fairly quickly. If instead California had a European style democracy with only a few elected offices and strong party discipline, the threshold size and level of resources needed to participate effectively in policymaking would be much higher.

At the same time, the disadvantages of the California system are the problems of multiple veto points and alternative policy venues. Multiple veto points means that decision-making is often fractured over several branches and levels of government at the same time. Think of education, for instance. At the state level, the governor and legislature control the budget, and in shortfall years, they have the ability to override even constitutional limitations such as Proposition 98, the minimum funding guarantee for public education. Then there is the state superintendent of schools and the state board of education. At the local level, there are school boards, and sometimes local mayors, such as Antonio Villaraigosa in Los Angeles, to contend with. This in effect means that efforts at one level can be counteracted at another. For instance, state-level funding aims for equality as mandated by the Serrano decisions, but local schools can undermine the equality goal by funding school operations through private foundations and passing local bond measures.

The other problem with the California system is the existence of alternative policy venues. The most important are direct democracy mechanisms: the initiative, referendum, and recall. If a policy stalls in the state legislature, where minorities have made significant gains in terms of representation and leadership positions, the effort can be redirected into an initiative measure. As discussed in earlier editions of *Racial and Ethnic Politics in California*, the arenas of representative government and direct democracy are racially distinct: the statewide electorate is more white, middle class, and conservative on certain issues. As Terry Christensen and Larry Gerston remind us in Chapter 6, a number of measures opposed by a majority of Latinos have passed as initiative measures, most dramatically Propositions 187 and 209, which sought to deny public services to illegal immigrants and to dismantle affirmative action at public institutions, respectively. The initiative operates as a statewide at-large election in which the predominantly white majority prevails. Since white voters are overrepresented and nonwhite voters are underrepresented in that total, nonwhite groups are at a disadvantage when the venue shifts from representative to direct democracy and they disagree with the white majority. Conversely, given that district lines observe racial communities of interest and also that districts are based on total population not registered voters, the legislative arena tends to be more favorable to Latinos and other minorities.

Belinda Reyes points out that a similar dynamic occurs in some communities that have held on to at-large election systems for school board races. Latinos and blacks continue to have higher drop-out rates and lower levels of education. To the degree that school policies can break cycles of cumulative disadvantage, she argues that more diversified representation is part of the answer. But clearly if basic differences in underlying wealth and socio-economic advantage persist, they will limit what even fully diversified school boards can do. This returns us to the theme earlier about economic and racial clumping in California: If the current trends persist, disparities in local resources could create even more significant disparities in opportunities for children in different areas of the state.

Racially or ethnically descriptive representation can sometimes be the answer to community issues, but the African-American example is illuminating. Despite getting electoral gains much earlier than the new minority groups, blacks still lag behind other groups in educational achievement and, according to Elsa Chen, in equal treatment in the criminal justice system. Indeed, despite impressive gains at all levels of elected government in the seventies and eighties, the fundamental problems of poverty and violence persist in the black community. Descriptive representation does not always translate into better substantive representation, and even when it does, solutions to the broadest and most important problems often require having partners from other ethnic and racial groups, including white Californians.

The disillusionment among white liberals with solving urban poverty and racism has left minority legislators to their own devices. The enclave pattern of white migration represents a serious obstacle to recreating the progressive agenda of the sixties and seventies. Increasingly ensconced in white suburbs while ceding troubled urban areas to nonwhites in a decentralized governmental context promotes a perverse Tiebout world in which the haves vote with their feet to live with other largely white haves, and minorities are trapped in communities without the benefit of middle-class leadership and resources. Whites and some Asians, in their enclaves, get better schools, safer neighborhoods, and nice amenities such as parks and attractive retail areas. Nonwhites are trapped in resource poor communities.

This scenario, if it develops further, is far from the pluralist model. Rather than entering into flexible coalitions, racial and economic sorting could remove opportunities to work together by a process of separation into relatively homogeneous local communities. The freedom of some to move where they like could limit opportunities for others. Representation alone will not solve the most critical economic and social problems for minorities in the future if California's white population continues to separate itself and its resources from nonwhite minority communities.

Chapter 2

California in Flux: Demographic Trends in the State

Ali Modarres

Introduction

Little can be said about politics and policy in California without an overt reference to demography. The rapidity with which demographic shifts, changes, or flux occur profoundly alters the sociopolitical landscape every few years, demanding our ongoing attention. This is particularly true in a representative democracy, in which geography plays an important role. The Golden State's population trajectory is fundamentally oriented toward growth and multiculturalism: change is the constant for California. Therefore, the future of our democracy relies heavily upon a deeper appreciation of demographic dynamics and the importance of creating a mode of decision-making that is inherently adaptive to change and willing to accommodate new Californians and their choices of political representation.

Few states rival California in terms of demographic dynamism, and interstate and international migrations are, in essence, the greatest forces that have and will continue to reshape this state.[1] It is therefore important to afford these demographic factors the largest space for discussion, underlining the fact that while certain regions in the U.S. have witnessed a population decline (due to out-migration and the absence of discernable immigration), states such as California and their growing metropolitan areas have remained viable due to their continuing attractiveness as a destination for the foreign-born population.[2]

In this chapter, I will explore demographic dynamics in the state during the last few decades. I hope to illustrate how current and future demographic processes may continue to create a multifaceted California that will require innovative governance and a responsive policymaking environment. To that end, the roles of gender, nativity, and the changing labor market will be highlighted.

Peopling the State

California has always been promoted by its admirers, from miners to ranchers and industrialists and financiers to movie tycoons. The peopling of California has been done through some economic heavy lifting and environmental magic, but mostly through an active imagination that gives the state its capitalist bohemianism. From the late 19th century to the WWII era, people rushed to this land for its alluring gold mines, agricultural abundance, blue skies, and the unending promise of progress, prosperity, and a healthy environment. People from all walks of life populated the state to achieve here what they could not have in other places. The state's population grew to seven million by 1940—more than doubling its 1920 and tripling its 1910 figures (see Figure 1),[3] but this growth was spatially uneven. By 1940, close to half of all Californians resided in Los Angeles and San Francisco counties alone (see Table 1). However, by WWII, Los Angeles County had become a major population magnet and was substantially larger than San Francisco, a pattern that would be sustained throughout the 20th century. This uneven distribution in 1940 meant that close to one hundred years of the American "rush" to the West had produced two types of urban

---

[1] Selected recent publications on the dynamics of population growth in California include Hans P. Johnson, "A State of Diversity: Demographic Trends in California's Regions," *California Counts, Population Trends and Profile* (Public Policy Institute of California, May 2002); William H. Frey, *Metro America in the New Century: Metropolitan and Central City Demographic Shifts Since 2000* (The Brookings Institution, September 2005); William H. Frey, *Metropolitan Magnets for International and Domestic Migrant* (The Brookings Institution, October 2003).

[2] See Table 3 and Figure 4 in Hans P. Johnson, "A State of Diversity: Demographic Trends in California's Regions," *California Counts, Population Trends and Profiles* (Public Policy Institute of California, May 2002), 7. Also see: Bruce Katz and Andy Altman, "An Urban Renaissance in a Suburban Nation," *Ford Foundation Report*, Vol. 36 Issue 2 (Spring 2005): 36–37.

[3] California Department of Finance. *REPORT I 47–69: 1940, 1950, 1960, and 1970 CENSUS COUNTS.* http://www.dof.ca.gov/HTML/DEMOGRAP/I47-69.htm.

Figure 1. Population Growth

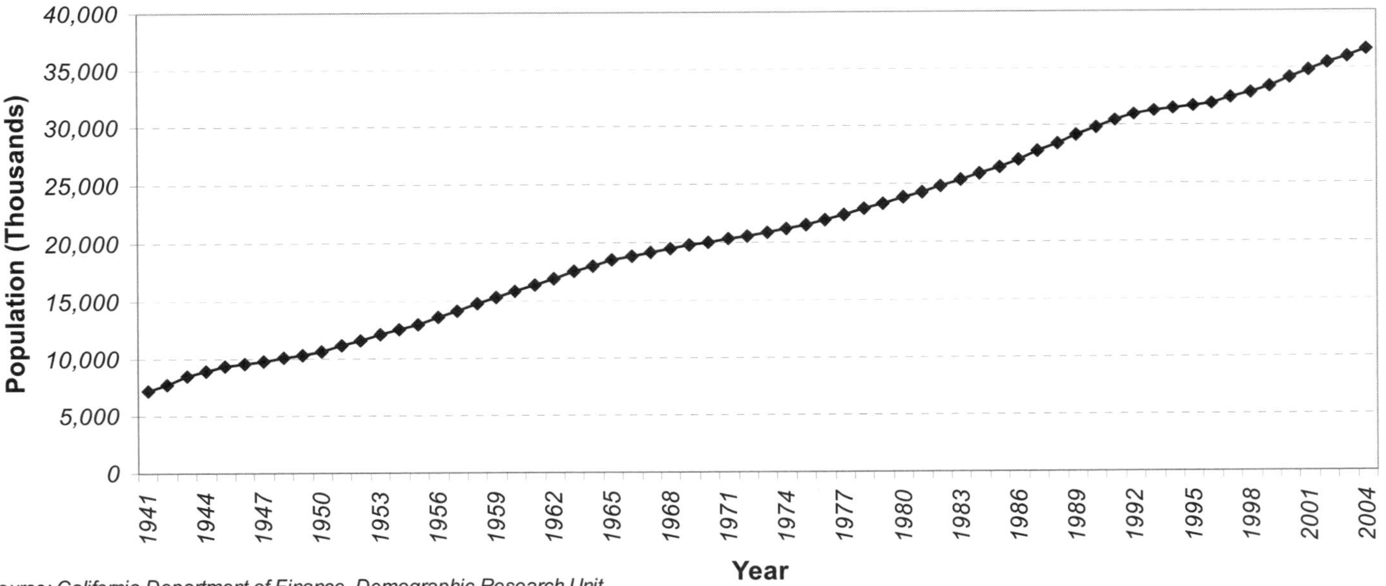

Source: California Department of Finance, Demographic Research Unit

Table 1. Population Trajectory from 1940 to 1970 by County

Rank	County	4/1/1940	County	4/1/1950	County	4/1/1960	County	4/1/1970
1	Los Angeles	2,785,643	Los Angeles	4,151,687	Los Angeles	6,038,771	Los Angeles	7,032,075
2	San Francisco	634,536	San Francisco	775,357	San Diego	1,033,011	Orange	1,420,386
3	Alameda	513,011	Alameda	740,315	Alameda	908,209	San Diego	1,357,854
4	San Diego	289,348	San Diego	556,808	San Francisco	740,316	Alameda	1,073,184
5	Fresno	178,565	Contra Costa	298,984	Orange	703,925	Santa Clara	1,064,714
6	Santa Clara	174,949	Santa Clara	290,547	Santa Clara	642,315	San Francisco	715,674
7	Sacramento	170,333	San Bernardino	281,642	San Bernardino	503,591	San Bernardino	684,072
8	San Bernardino	161,108	Sacramento	277,140	Sacramento	502,778	Sacramento	631,498
9	Kern	135,124	Fresno	276,515	San Mateo	444,387	Contra Costa	558,389
10	San Joaquin	134,207	San Mateo	235,659	Contra Costa	409,030	San Mateo	556,234
	Total population	5,176,824		7,884,654		11,926,333		15,094,080
Top 10 counties	Proportion of California Population	0.75		0.74		0.76		0.76
	California	**6,907,387**		**10,586,223**		**15,717,204**		**19,953,134**

Source: California Department of Finance. REPORT I 47–1940, 1950, 1960, and 1970 Census Counts.

places: those that grew from the gold rush and those that were built upon a land rush. As the case of Los Angeles illustrates, it was the latter that proved to be more successful in the long run. From 1940 to 1970, the state prospered from the economic boom of the postwar era, and the increasing numbers of southern Californians testified to the state's continued popularity. By 1960, when the state surpassed a population of 15.7 million (more than double the 1940 population), San Diego ranked second in population and Orange County moved to the fifth position (see Table 1). A decade later, Los Angeles, Orange, and San Diego counties housed close to 10 million people (half of the state population), while San Francisco, Alameda, and Santa Clara counties had grown to 2.7 million, collectively. In other words, between 1940 and 1970, the three counties in the south grew more than three times larger in population, whereas the Bay Area counties barely doubled their populations.[4] By 1970, southern California had formed the basis of an urban complex, stretching hundreds of miles from Ventura County to the California-Mexico border. With the establishment of accessible water, a viable higher education system, and an extensive road network, the state, especially its southern region, could grow in economic stature and population.[5] However, as Figure 2 illustrates, at no point in these two decades did migration rates match those of the 1940s. In fact, migration declined in importance from the mid-1950s to the late 1960s.

The 1965 Immigration Act changed that picture. Whereas California had always benefited from immigration and interstate migration, the end of national-origin quotas and changing tides of immigration shaped the future of the state. By the early 1970s, the impact of the Immigration Act was felt as more immigrants from Pacific Rim countries found their way to the U.S. And in this new era of immigration, California, especially Los Angeles, was becoming the new Ellis Island of the late 20th century.

Another dimension of the changing immigration laws in the 1960s was a unilateral end to the Bracero program, a guest-worker policy that had helped the American labor market during the postwar years. The suspension of this program produced significant changes in the nature of immigration from Mexico. The late 1960s and the early 1970s witnessed a growing number of undocumented immigrants from Mexico who were attracted to the agricultural industry of California, especially in the face of inadequate native-born farm laborers in the state.[6]

---

[4] It should be noted that the northern counties, including San Mateo, are smaller in total land area than the three in the south. However, the southern counties also contain large areas of uninhabited land. Regardless, despite their lower numerical growth, population densities in the northern counties are larger.

[5] See the following edited volume on the details of how California infrastructure investments translated to a population boom: Martin Schiesl, *Responsible Liberalism* (Edmund G. "Pat" Brown Institute of Public Affairs, 2003).

[6] See the following book for a detailed discussion of how the agricultural industry purposefully focused on California and its potential Mexican labor population. Ronald Takaki, *A Different Mirror: A History of Multicultural America* (Boston: Back Bay Books, 1993).

Figure 2. Components of Population Change

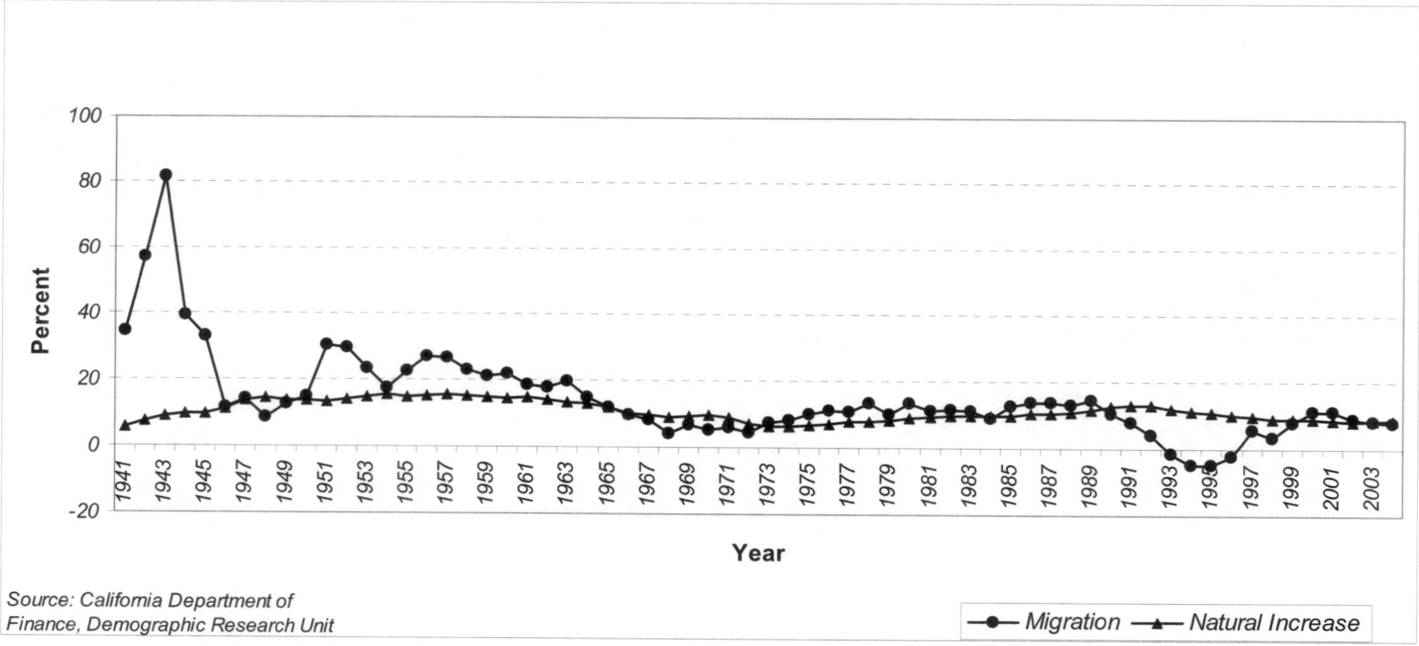

Source: California Department of Finance, Demographic Research Unit

As the number of documented immigrants grew under the 1965 Immigration Act, which brought a larger number of highly skilled immigrants to the U.S. and California, the number of less well-to-do farm laborers increased as well. By the late 1970s, the picture of immigration to the state had become more complex. Highly educated, middle-class immigrants mixed with laborers and refugees from Southwest Asia. Californians could no longer speak of a prototypical immigrant. In the 1980s and the 1990s, when the largest wave of immigration to the U.S. since the turn of the 20th century arrived in the country, California's national share translated to one in four immigrants. These new Californians were poised to change the demographic landscape of the state and its metropolitan areas. In Los Angeles County, California's sprawling metropolis, the foreign-born population grew from 11% in 1970 to over 36% in 2000.[7]

During the last two decades of the 20th century, Californians witnessed the burgeoning of their multi-ethnic cities and observed the growth of cultural particularism, which was fueled by the presence of a diverse population with differing cultural expectations and requirements. This particularistic approach to the definition of rights and sociopolitical discourse had to be reconciled with the universalistic nature of citizenship, which attempts to de-emphasize differences. Governance in the postimmigration era meant that immigration itself would become a topic of debate and contention (e.g., Prop. 187) and political representation would move beyond the traditional African-American and white issues and coalitions. In a state with large Latino and Asian populations, a multivocal political coalition would be challenging at best. Since the 1970s, California has given birth to a deeper meaning of an inclusive form of governance. In redefining the nature of this multi-ethnic governance, it is natural that the tendency is to either long for a return to an imaginary era with a functioning political hegemony or to hope for the magical appearance of a manageable diversity—all voices present, everybody heard, and compromises easily achieved. Of course, if none of this can be achieved, the next best thing is to turn to Hollywood in order to imagine a populist governance structure interpreted by actors and screenwriters. To adapt to the changing demography of California, we need the imagination, but not a nostalgia seeking to recapture the so-called "greatness" of the past. We need to invent a government that can adapt to the realities of change; one that runs the scale of local to global. Migration is a growing reality all over the globe. For California to erect metaphoric and physical walls to prevent change suggests that the ideal has been to stop time and turn back the clock. If progress is the goal, walls and exclusionary practices are not viable solutions. Governance in California has to be about the future—a future in which demographic shifts are inseparable from public policy, political representation, and the economy.

---

[7] Census Bureau, SF3A.

Immigration and the Future of California

Figure 3 provides a summary of documented immigration to California. In this state, no other county has received as many immigrants as Los Angeles. The large volume of immigration to this county over the last two decades translated to a total foreign-born population of 3.4 million (i.e., 36.2% of the total population) in 2000.[8] This demographic characteristic provides a unique perspective on the future of the state and some of its major urban centers. For example, in Los Angeles County, no single racial group (this excludes Latinos) matches the foreign-born population in magnitude. Non-Hispanic white, African American, and API (Asian Pacific Islander) groups were individually smaller, which suggests that if the foreign-born population voted as a political bloc, the fate of politics and public policy would be different. Of course, that kind of change at the polls is not going to occur, since the foreign-born population is politically diverse and many of its members are not citizens. In fact, an important subtext of debates on the foreign-born population is the large number of people with Mexican ancestry. It should be remembered, however, that Asians do make up a significant portion of the foreign-born population and their immigration patterns dramatically affected the demographic landscape of the state throughout the 1990s. This issue will be discussed further when the social geography of the state is analyzed.

An interesting change in California's net migration in the 1990s reveals the importance of immigration in understanding the demography. From 1993 to 1996, California witnessed a negative net migration for the first time since 1940, despite the large levels of immigration to the state in the 1990s (see Figure 3). Had it not been for immigration, California's population would have likely declined, as seen in other states where immigration levels are low.[9] Comparing Figures 2 and 3, we can conclude that, at least since the 1990s, California's population growth has relied on immigration and its demography reflects its ability to do so. If this trend continues, in all likelihood, the state will house an even larger multi-ethnic and foreign-born population in the future. This means that political incorporation of the new Californians will have to rely on expanding citizenship and structural integration. For that to take place, however, we need to become more knowledgeable about immigration patterns and the social and economic dynamics that affect the foreign-born population, and to focus on alternative means of multicultural collaborations. Beyond the white-African-American and Latino-African-American dialogues, we need to understand the growing importance of the Asian population, not as a monolithic group, but as an internally diverse group of various ethnonationals. For example, the Chinese and Filipinos are important and growing

---

[8] The 2005 American Community Survey (from the Census Bureau) estimates a foreign-born population of 3,510,827 (+/-33,016) for Los Angeles County. This suggests that the proportion of the foreign-born population has remained about 36%.

[9] Michael T. Maley, *Beyond Segregation: Multiracial and Multiethnic Neighborhoods in the United States* (Philadelphia: Temple University Press, 2005).

Figure 3. Documented Immigration to California 1984-2005

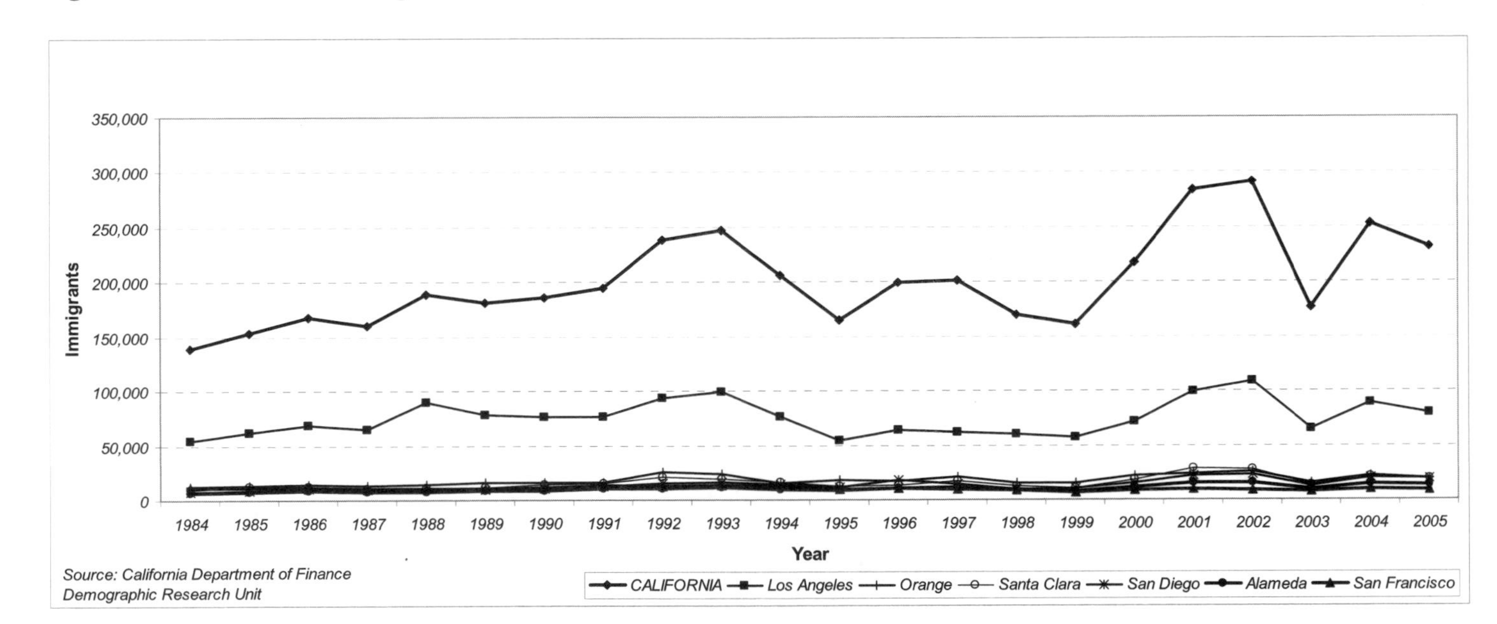

Figure 4. Age Cohorts by Gender (California 1990-2001)

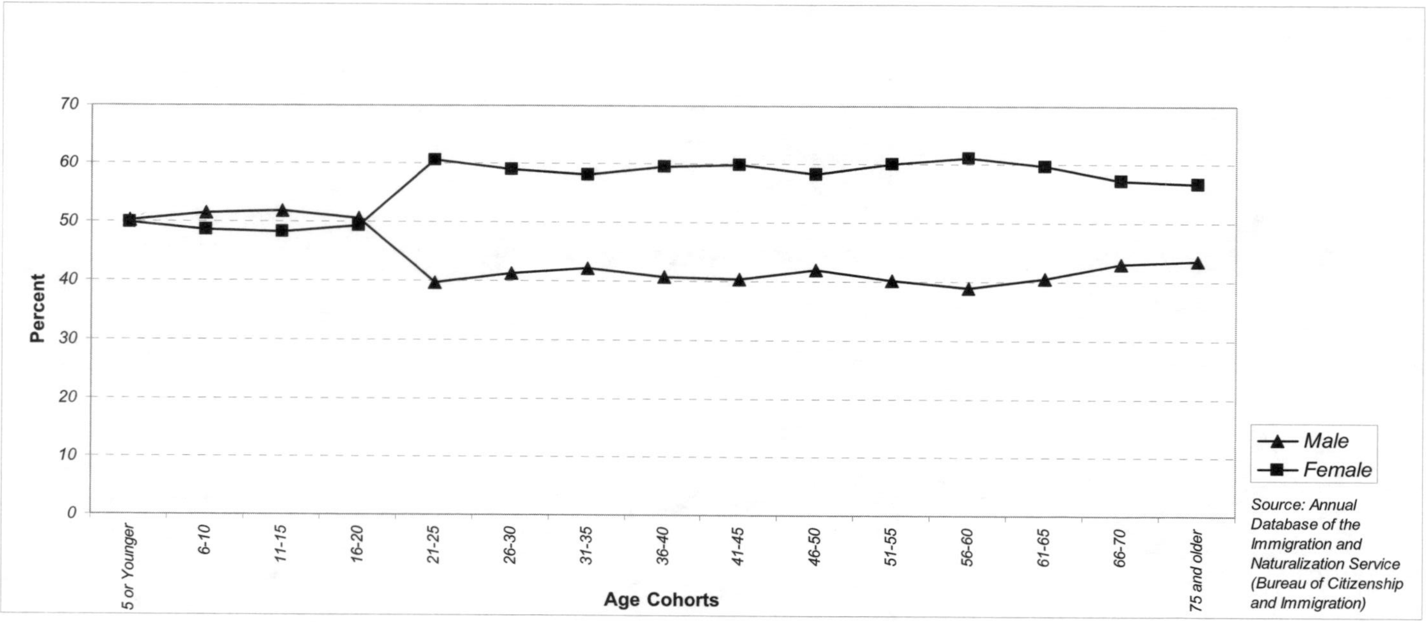

70
60
50
40
30
20
10
0
Percent
5 or Younger
6-10
11-15
16-20
21-25
26-30
31-35
36-40
41-45
46-50
51-55
56-60
61-65
66-70
75 and older
Age Cohorts
Male
Female
Source: Annual Database of the Immigration and Naturalization Service (Bureau of Citizenship and Immigration)

populations in the state and their political incorporation may produce a significant increase in the number of eligible voters and expand their political participation.

As Table 2 illustrates, four Asian countries were prominent among the top five countries of birth for immigrants to California in the 1990s. Collectively, these countries provided a larger number of immigrants in the 1990s than Mexico. This change in immigrants' country of origin, combined with the lower net migration from other states in the country, means that while we should be cognizant of the Latino immigrants and their needs, advocacy for further political incorporation of the Asian populations must continue and grow. The 2005 American Community Survey estimated that while Chinese and Filipinos (under racial and ethnic classification categories) exceeded one million each, Asian Indians (455,000), Koreans (413,000), and Vietnamese (540,000) groups have a significant presence as well.[10] A striking change in the demographic landscape of California is the arrival of a large number of Asian and South-Asian populations. In 2005, nearly 20% of all Asian-Indian populations,[11] 39% of Chinese, 48% of Filipinos, 33% of Koreans, and 38% of Vietnamese in the U.S. resided in the Golden State. The degree to which California can accommodate (i.e., structurally integrate) these new immigrants will determine the future of its economy, politics, and social structure.

California's immigrants will pose a challenge to every arena of public policy in the years to come for reasons that go beyond nationality and culture. For example, demographically speaking, the new immigrants differ significantly from their predecessors. While a majority of people, including the anti-immigrant contingent, imagine the average immigrant to be a young Spanish-speaking male, the reality of immigration is different. Throughout the 1990s, women outnumbered men and were older than their male counterparts (see Figures 4 and 5). While many have come as dependents, through family reunification, the number of highly skilled female immigrants has also increased. As the number of female-headed households increases among immigrants, public policy debates on housing and other urban issues will become more important and will require a gendered focus. Historically, female immigrants have been more likely to become citizens, and they are more likely to stay in the U.S. even after facing divorce. California, as a major gateway for the current swells of U.S. immigration, and its economic, social, and political future are undoubtedly tied to immigrants. Attention to the specific needs of immigrant populations (in their diversity and plurality) will have to form the basis of political incorporation debates and public service. To avoid current and

---

[10] U.S. Census Bureau. http://factfinder.census.gov/servlet/ADPTable?_bm=y&-geo_id=04000US06&-context=adp&-ds_name=ACS_2005_EST_G00_&-tree_id=305&-_lang=en&-_caller=geoselect&-format=

[11] In the case of Asian Indians, a striking geographic distribution has been formed. According to the 2005 estimate from the American Community Survey, nearly 21% of all Asian Indians reside in a geographically contiguous area that extends from Union City in the Bay area to Santa Clara and the San Jose region. Los Angeles and San Diego appear to be secondary areas of concentration for this population.

Table 2. Annual Immigration to the State, Top Five Countries of Birth, 1990–2001

Country of Birth	1990	1991	1992	1993	1994	1995
Mexico	56,549	52,866	91,332	109,027	106,995	86,960
Philippines	54,907	55,376	59,179	63,189	53,501	50,962
China	28,746	31,699	38,735	65,552	53,976	35,459
Vietnam	48,662	55,278	77,728	59,613	41,344	41,752
India	28,679	31,165	34,629	40,021	34,873	34,715

Country of Birth	1996	1997	1998	1999	2000	2001	Total
Mexico	159,967	144,826	130,884	147,569	173,587	206,216	1,466,778
Philippines	55,855	49,094	34,463	31.026	42,473	53,153	603,178
China	41,725	41,147	36,883	32,204	45,651	56,426	508,203
Vietnam	42,067	38,519	17,649	20,393	26,747	35,531	505,283
India	44,848	38,061	36,481	30,237	42,044	70,289	466,042

Source: Annual Data of Immigration and Naturalization Services (Bureau of Citizenship and Immigration).

Figure 5. Immigration by Gender - California 1990-2001

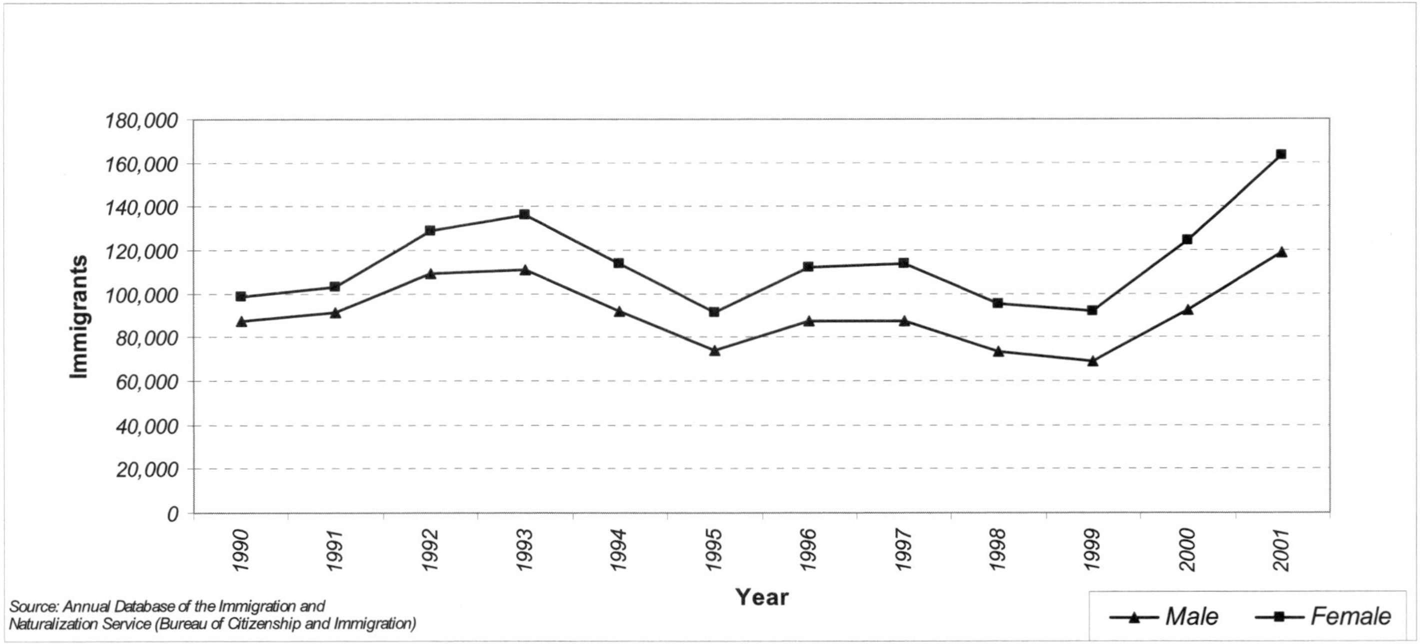

Source: Annual Database of the Immigration and Naturalization Service (Bureau of Citizenship and Immigration)

future inequities, a heightened attention to immigrants and their needs will be necessary.

On the Geography of Race and Ethnicity

By 2005, the non-Hispanic white population was still the racial/ethnic majority in the state, making up close to 43% of the population.[12] This group was followed in size by Latinos (35.5%), Asians (12.2%) and African Americans (5.9%). Compared to the racial and ethnic composition in 1980 and 1990, the state had become home to more Latinos, but also and more importantly, to Asians (see Figures 6 and 7). The latter group grew from about 3% of the population in 1970 to nearly 12% in 2000. This translated to an increase of close to 3.5 million Asians, from 671,000 in 1970 to over 4.1 million in 2000 (and 4.3 million in 2005). Though a significant majority of this growth was fueled by immigration, secondary migrations from other states into California are important as well.

While Latinos are a clear majority in cities such as Los Angeles, the numerical majority of non-Hispanic whites, and occasionally Asians, in other urban settings requires us to give special attention to the geographic distribution of these populations. This is especially important in a political process that is closely tied to the geography of electoral districts and the battles fought to draw them. Though it would be impossible to provide a comprehensive discussion of this topic within the confines of this chapter, it is crucial to highlight some of the more significant aspects of racial and ethnic geography in the state.

Remembering that "communities of interest" became the operating phrase of the last reapportionment efforts, perhaps the most appropriate way to begin any conversation on this topic is to present two sets of interrelated information and analyze them simultaneously. These are the geography of integration patterns (as opposed to segregation, which is often the mode of analysis) and the spatial structure of socio-economic indicators in the state. The following provides a quick overview of both, followed by an analysis of the relationship between integration and socio-economic indicators in California.

Residential Integration Pattern

In a political world in which minority rights are still under attack, it is natural that we would seek to draw political boundaries in a manner that protects racial and ethnic voices—i.e., based on race, ethnicity, or other indicators of likeness. Translated into reality, this means that we attempt to draw boundaries around

---

[12] See footnote 10.

Figure 6. Racial and Ethnic Shifts in California

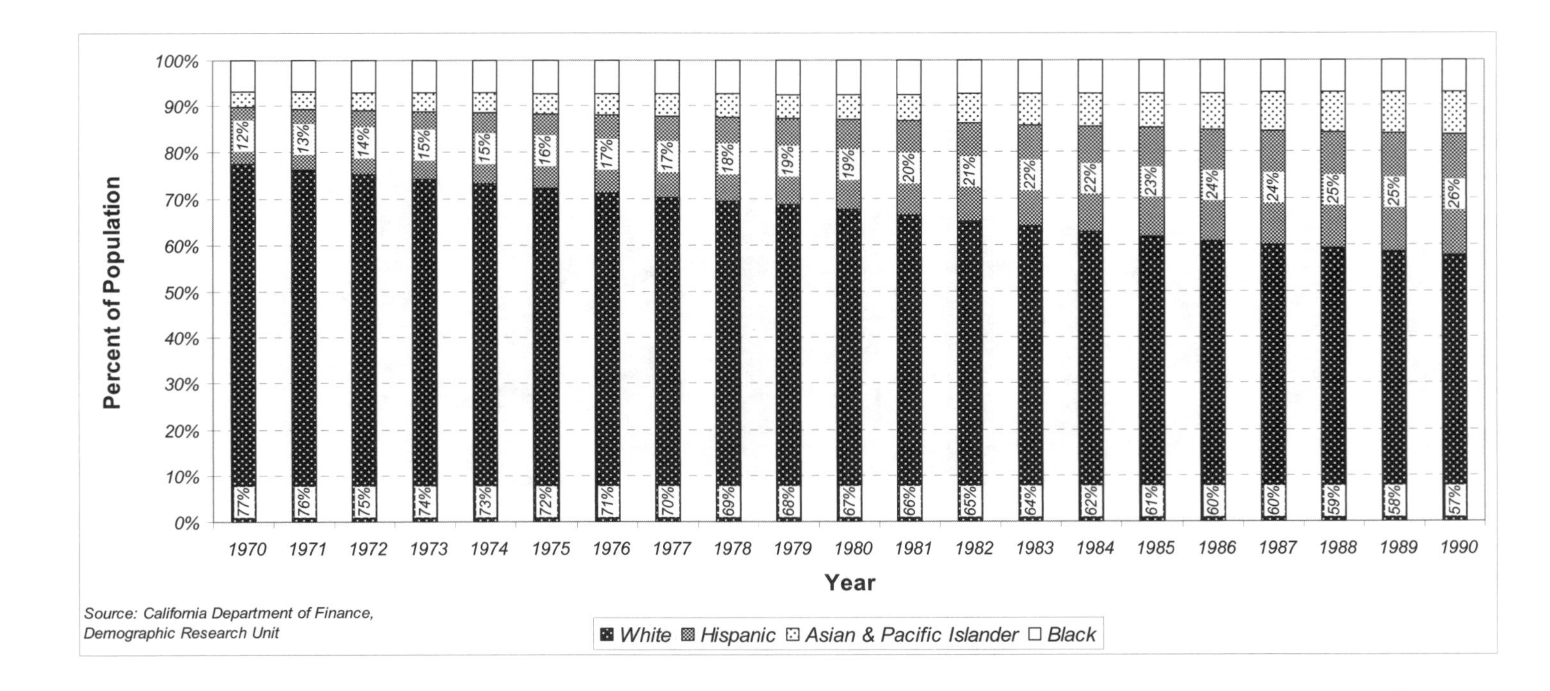

Figure 7. Racial and Ethnic Shifts in California 1990-2000

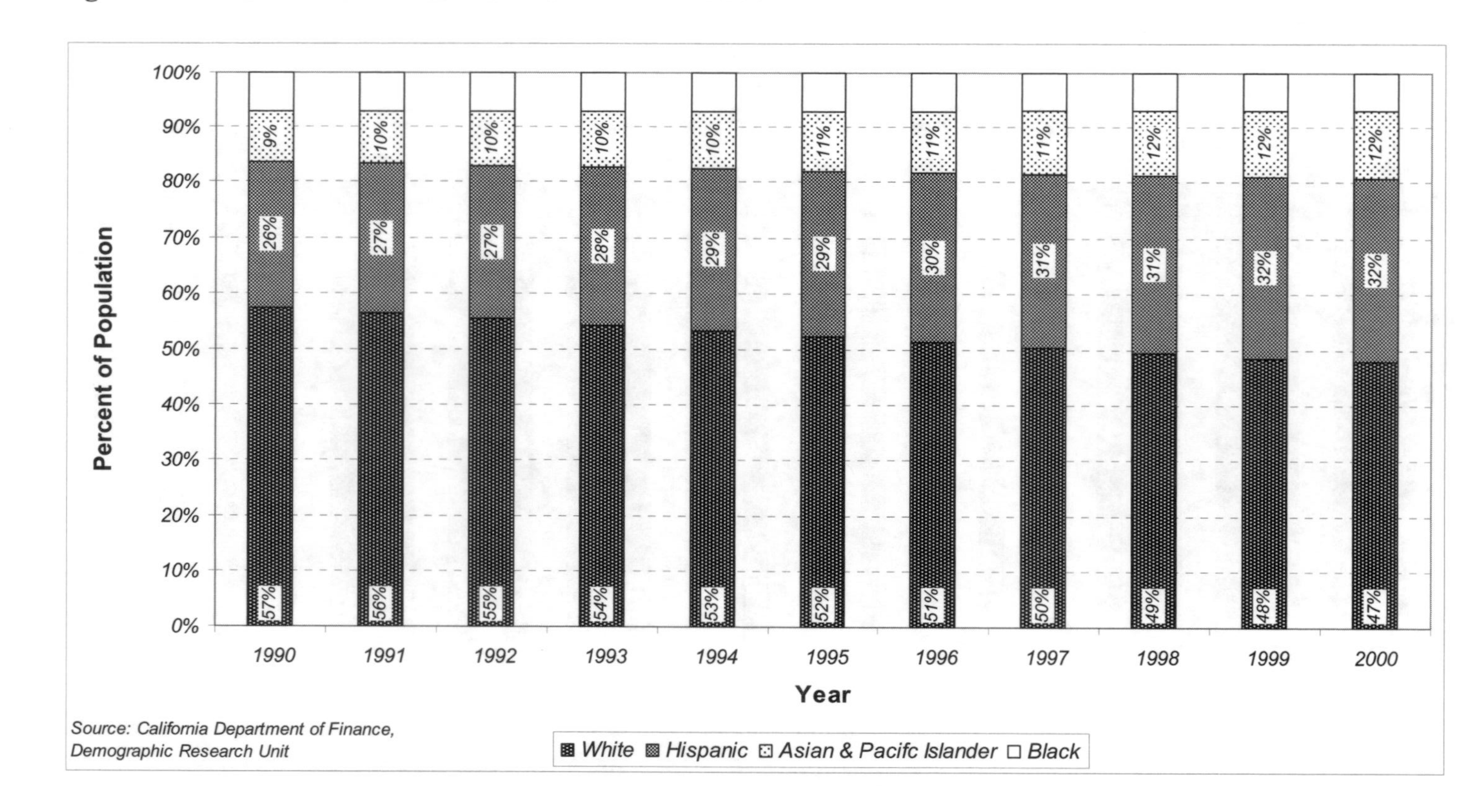

highly concentrated minority populations and hope that, as the majority voice within these proscribed geographies, they can make their concerns heard. As such, advocates for elevating the voice of minorities seek to identify geographically segregated places and assure that the powers-that-be do not dilute the voting power of the minority by mixing such geographies with those of the majority. Practically, it means that as long as the fear of a noninclusive majority exists, the protection of minority rights translates to protecting, and by extension maintaining, segregated neighborhoods. A political system that has equated democracy with the tyranny of the majority is naturally faced with this reciprocal, Catch-22 dilemma. From a demographic perspective and a fundamentally utopian aspiration, though, we continue to search and hope for racially stable and integrated places, where spatial coexistence translates to better group/social relationships.

Smith, Ellen, Maly, Frey et al., and Modarres, among many others have written extensively about the topic of integration and its stability over time.[13] However, little has been done to bring this research to the arena of racial/ethnic politics, especially as it relates to political redistricting. This means that the driving force for determining the geography of electoral politics is our basic assumptions regarding concentration (or more aptly segregation) patterns by race and ethnicity. While it is important to avoid any dilution of minorities' votes, it is equally important to recognize that in urban areas such as Los Angeles and San Francisco, the growing number of integrated neighborhoods requires us to rethink our conceptions of political redistricting, as far as its relationship to homogenous racial and ethnic neighborhoods is concerned. In the first half of the 21st century, we will face a fundamental question: how will we preserve minority rights in a changing world of socio-demographic urban landscapes? The emergence of stable integrated neighborhoods may exclude the presence of the white population. In such a case, how can we reconceptualize a civil society that, despite its geography of diversity, may be facing discernable discriminatory practices from systematic structural inequities?

---

[13] Richard A. Smith, "Creating Stable Racially Integrated Communities: A Review," *Journal of Urban Affairs*, Vol. 15, Issue 2 (1993): 115–40; Richard A. Smith, "Discovering Stable Racial Integration," *Journal of Urban Affairs*, Vol. 20, Issue 1 (1998): 1–25; Ingrid Gould Ellen, "Stable Racial Integration in the Contemporary United States: An Empirical Perspective," *Journal of Urban Affairs*, Vol. 20, Issue 1 (1998): 27–42; Ingrid Gould Ellen, *Sharing America's Neighborhoods: The Prospects for Stable Racial Integration* (Cambridge, Mass.: Harvard University Press, 2000); Michael T. Maly, "The Neighborhoods Diversity Index: A Complementary Measure of Racial Residential Settlement," *Journal of Urban Affairs*, Vol. 22, Issue 1 (2000): 37–47; Michael T. Maly, *Beyond Segregation; Multicultural and Multiethnic Neighborhoods in the United States* (Philadelphia: Temple University Press, 2005); William H. Frey and Reynolds Farley, "Latino, Asian, and Black Segregation in U.S. Metropolitan Areas: Are Multi-Ethnic Metros Different?" *Demography*, Vol. 33, Issue 1 (1996): 35–50; Ali Modarres, "Neighborhood Integration: Temporality and Social Fracture," *Journal of Urban Affairs*, Vol. 26, Issue 3 (2004): 351–77.

In order to bring the discussion on California's demography somewhere between the two extremes, we must develop more sophisticated measurements of integration and relate them to socio-economic status and racial and ethnic characteristics. To illustrate the importance of this process, I will employ a modified entropy index analysis, the use of which I have previously argued for in a longitudinal study of Los Angeles County, [14] and will examine the geography of integration in the state.

This methodology relies on the well-known entropy formula ($E=-\Sigma P_i * \text{Log } P_i$);[15] however, it employs central tendency statistics to classify each area according to its entropy value on a scale that varies from segregated to integrated. While full integration would require the presence of all groups, for an area to approach integration, it would simply require the presence of two or more groups in sufficient numbers. In a multi-ethnic and multiracial setting, it would be nearly impossible to achieve a complete presence of all groups, and as such, this methodology simply accounts for that reality.

I have chosen seven racial and ethnic groups for my analysis of California. This means that any one census tract can have an entropy value between 0, which is the highest level of segregation and log (7), which is the highest level of integration. With a mean of 0.41 and a standard deviation of 0.13 for California in 2000, entropy values for all census tracts can be divided into four categories: segregated (i.e., less than one standard deviation from the mean), moderately segregated (i.e., within one standard deviation below the mean), moderately integrated (i.e., within one standard deviation above the mean), or integrated (i.e., larger than one standard deviation above the mean).

Table 3 provides a summary of all census tracts in California, divided into these four categories. This table suggests that more than two-thirds of all census tracts fall within the range of moderately segregated to moderately integrated, with integrated census tracts approaching 17% of all tracts in California. This is significant, since most analyses of segregation have ignored these integrated (or, more accurately, "approaching integration") tracts. As Maps 1 and 2 illustrate, a significant majority of these census tracts occur in highly urbanized places. It appears that as these places have become more multi-ethnic, they have become more integrated. In other words, immigration may have contributed to the growth of integrated communities in California. In order to understand the mechanism of integration or at least its socio-economic explanation, it is important to pay attention to some of the interesting nuances of this pattern. Table 4 offers a glimpse into some of the possible explanations for the observed patterns of integration. Clearly, the negative correlation with the non-Hispanic white population suggests that more integrated neighborhoods occur in the absence of this group. As expected, however, the presence of Asian/Pacific Islanders and multiracial populations provides the highest level of correlation. This means that immigration, especially from

---

[14] Modarres, 2004.

[15] Where i = 1, . . . , number of groups in the analysis.

Table 3. Integration Status

	Number of Tracts	Percent of Tracts
Segregated	1,215	17.2
Moderately Segregated	2,112	30.0
Moderately Integrated	2,517	35.7
Integrated	1,192	16.9
Total	7,036	99.8

Note: Thirteen census tracts were excluded due to missing data.
Source: Census Bureau, SF3, 2000.

Asia, has contributed to a growing number of integrated neighborhoods in California. For Latinos, the situation is reversed. This means that as Latinos have grown in population, it is more likely that their neighborhoods have shifted to a more homogenous/segregated condition. Therefore, immigration alone cannot be seen as the driving force of a growing integration pattern; instead, a specific subset within this population is the crucial factor. In addition to the importance of Asian immigration, for example, the time of arrival in the U.S. is an important factor. Statistically speaking, neighborhoods with the highest number of immigrants who have arrived since 1980 have the highest positive correlation with integration level (see Table 4).

The positive correlation between integration and time of arrival in the U.S., especially for those who arrived over two decades ago, suggests that integration may be shifting from a temporary to a more permanent status. Higher correlations with citizenship status and the female presence in the labor force do suggest that these communities consist of working families who have permanently settled in the U.S. The only concern we may have to face is the observed correlation between integration and the number of renter-occupied housing units. Despite their socioeconomic status, the foreign-born populations are spatially mobile and, therefore, the integrated communities that they help create can diminish quickly if housing market dynamics change. Given the current geography of renter-occupied housing units, which is driven by regional land-use planning decisions, the likelihood of losing these integrated neighborhoods overnight is minimal. However, as a matter of public policy, the negative correlation of owner-occupied housing units with integration, albeit at a small but significant level, should be taken as the sign that integration is not occurring as a social process that affects all areas, but is instead affected by housing availability and affordability patterns. For many lower middle-class immigrants, this translates to the emergence of integrated neighborhoods.

This appears to occur more prevalently among the Asian/Pacific Islander population. The irony of this process, however, is that it leaves no room for intervention and sustainability, which are required in creating stable integrated com-

Map 1. Integration Pattern in 2000, the Bay Area

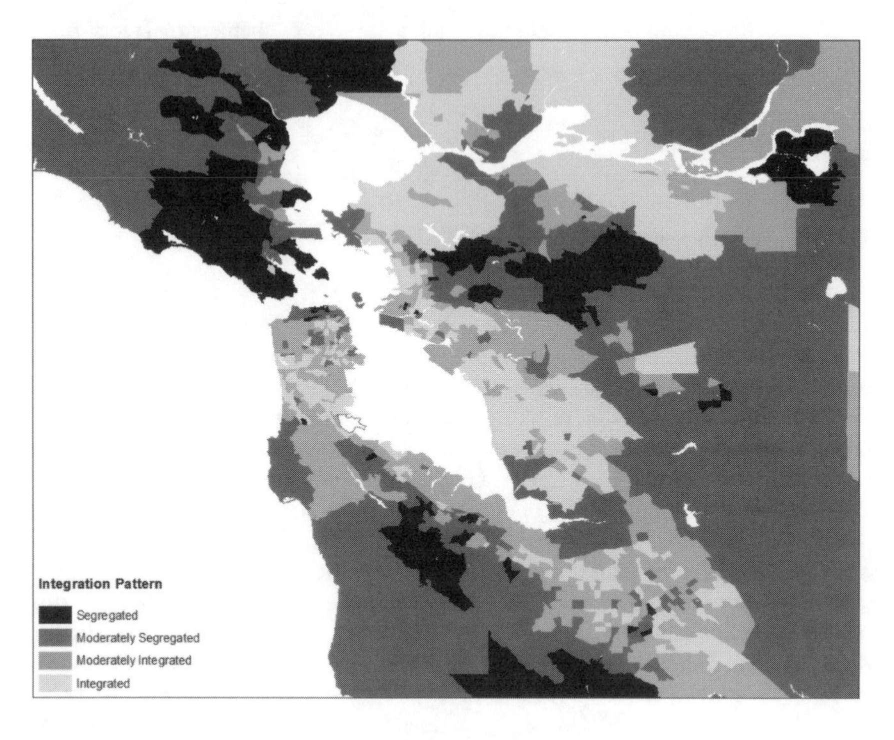

Source: Census Bureau, SF3, computations by the author.

munities.[16] This has remained a concern in integration patterns in American cities. As a state with a large share of immigration in the last three decades, therefore, we should expect a higher level of integration, and statistically speaking, we observe that pattern already. But, to sustain this pattern, we will need proactive policies and community activism, the likes of which were documented by Maly and others.[17]

---

[16] Michael T. Maly, *Beyond Segregation: Multiracial and Multiethnic Neighborhoods in the U.S.* (Philadelphia: Temple University Press, 2005).

[17] *Ibid.*; Ingrid Gould Ellen, *Sharing America's Neighborhoods: The Prospects for Stable Racial Integration* (Harvard University Press, 2000).

Map 2. Integration Pattern in 2000, Southern California

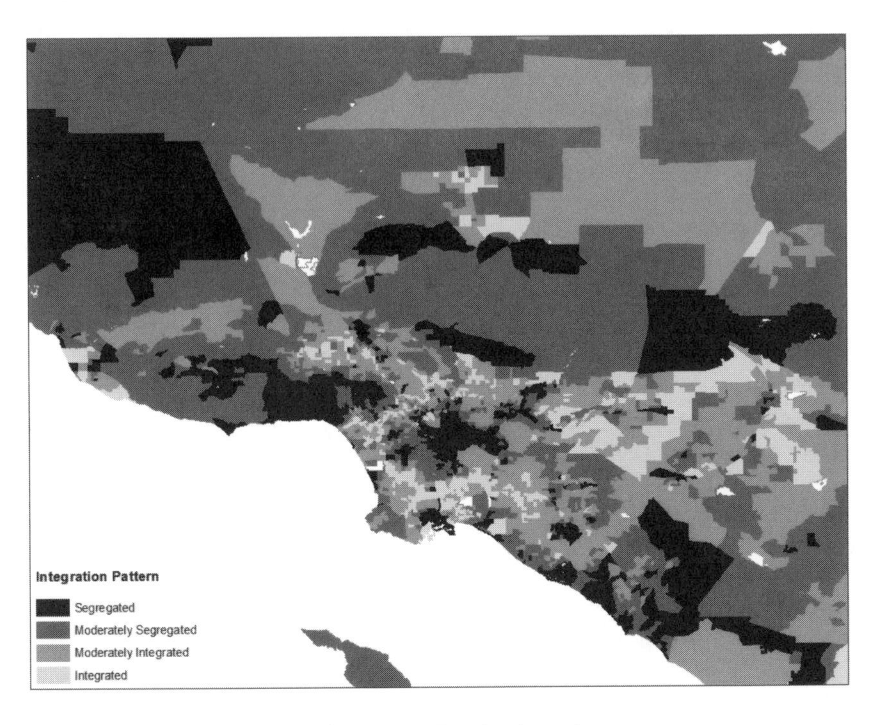

Source: Census Bureau, SF3, computations by the author.

Integrated Neighborhoods and the Fate of Political Redistricting

Regardless of their stability pattern and where they occur, integrated neighborhoods are numerous enough to require our attention. As Table 3 illustrates, close to 17% of census tracts in California are integrated and another 35.7% are approaching integrated status. This means that, with the expected rise in immigration, the number of integrated neighborhoods will continue to grow. From a democratic perspective, these neighborhoods will be the best testing grounds for creating political districts that cater to the notion of "communities of interest." Table 4 suggests that these are multiracial/multi-ethnic communities that house working families with high levels of female participation in the labor market. In other words, residents of integrated communities may be better served if seen as working families whose interests are driven by their stage-in-life issues and socio-economic status, as opposed to the ethnic or racial group to which they belong. Equitable access to education, the job market, and housing would most likely be of primary interest to them. Their shared socio-economic and demographic character-

Table 4. Correlation between Entropy and Selected Variables

	Pearson Correlation	Sig. (2-tailed)	N
Proportion of Non-Hispanic White Population	-0.22	0.00	7036
Proportion of Non-Hispanic African-American Population	0.27	0.00	7036
Proportion of Non-Hispanic Native-American Population	0.02	0.15	7036
Proportion of Non-Hispanic Asian/Pacific Islander Population	0.44	0.00	7036
Proportion of Non-Hispanic Other Population	0.09	0.00	7036
Proportion of Non-Hispanic Multiracial Populations	0.49	0.00	7036
Proportion of Latino Population	-0.14	0.00	7036
Year of Entry 1995 to March 2000	0.12	0.00	7036
Year of Entry 1990–1994	0.14	0.00	7036
Year of Entry 1985–1989	0.11	0.00	7036
Year of Entry 1980–1984	0.20	0.00	7036
Year of Entry 1975–1979	0.10	0.00	7036
Year of Entry 1970–1974	0.01	0.47	7036
Year of Entry 1965–1969	0.04	0.00	7036
Year of Entry before 1965	-0.06	0.00	7036
Foreign Born – Naturalized Citizen	0.28	0.00	7036
Foreign – Not a Citizen	0.03	0.03	7036
Native	0.08	0.00	7036
Owner Occupied Housing Units	-0.05	0.00	7036
Renter Occupied Housing Units	0.20	0.00	7036
Median Contract Rent	-0.02	0.12	7036
Median Value for Specified Owner Occupied Housing Units	-0.16	0.00	7036
Poverty Rate	-0.01	0.40	7022
Median Household Income	-0.10	0.00	7036
Female not in Labor Force	0.01	0.49	7036
Female in Labor Force	0.20	0.00	7036
Male not in Labor Force	0.07	0.00	7036
Male in Labor Force	0.13	0.00	7036

*Correlation is significant at the 0.05 level (2-tailed).
**Correlation is significant at the 0.01 le3vel (2-tailed).

istics, despite their cultural differences, should be considered a strong factor for their geographic grouping into specific legislative districts. Integrated neighborhoods are perhaps the most intriguing places for building issue-oriented community-based coalitions, from which a new generation of political leadership can grow.

Over the next four decades, California is expected to increase its population by another 25 million people.[18] There is no doubt that this growth will be racially and ethnically uneven. For example, while the white population is expected to decline by four million between 2000 and 2050 (from 16 to 12 million), the number of Latinos is projected to grow from 11 to 29 million. During the same period, the Asian population is expected to grow from three to four million. This means that in the year 2050, California will house over 36 million nonwhite residents, whose internal diversity and multi-ethnic/multiracial characteristics will not lend themselves to geographies of segregation, as observed in the 20th century. The new California will be more spatially integrated by race and ethnicity and not necessarily by socio-economic class. However, integrated communities will not be limited to lower socio-economic groups. From inner-city neighborhoods to the suburbs, integrated neighborhoods will become an important feature of major cities in California.

For spatial integration and social integration to converge, however, we need to consider the existing exclusionary practices that perpetuate differences. The process of political redistricting must be re-examined so that the ghosts of racial and ethnic politics are exorcised. While keeping an eye on minority rights, we have to learn a new language and develop a methodology that transcends segregation considerations and incorporates integration potentials. This means that in the years to come, we must develop acceptable techniques for identifying communities of interest and elevate sociodemographic factors into our geographic notions of representation. This requires a political will and a societal readiness to envision a new era in which public policy will transcend concerns for desegregation and begin to articulate steps that will allow new Americans and minorities to construct their civic identity through the ideals of, and first-hand experience with, equity, equality, and social justice. Without structural integration, economic, social, and political integration can hardly occur. And without the necessary sense of equality that can only occur through the process of integration, race and ethnicity can become self-perpetuating phenomena, whose existence will parallel our uneven socio-economic landscape. Of course, with the emerging patterns of spatial integration discussed in this chapter, California is facing a golden opportunity to achieve social integration, embedding its multicultural and demographic dynamism into its economic, social, and political structures. If we fail to realize this opportunity, the transformative power of integration in building an equitable civil society will be either lost or greatly postponed.

---

[18] State of California, Department of Finance, *Population Projections for California and Its Counties 2000–2050*, Sacramento, California, July 2007.

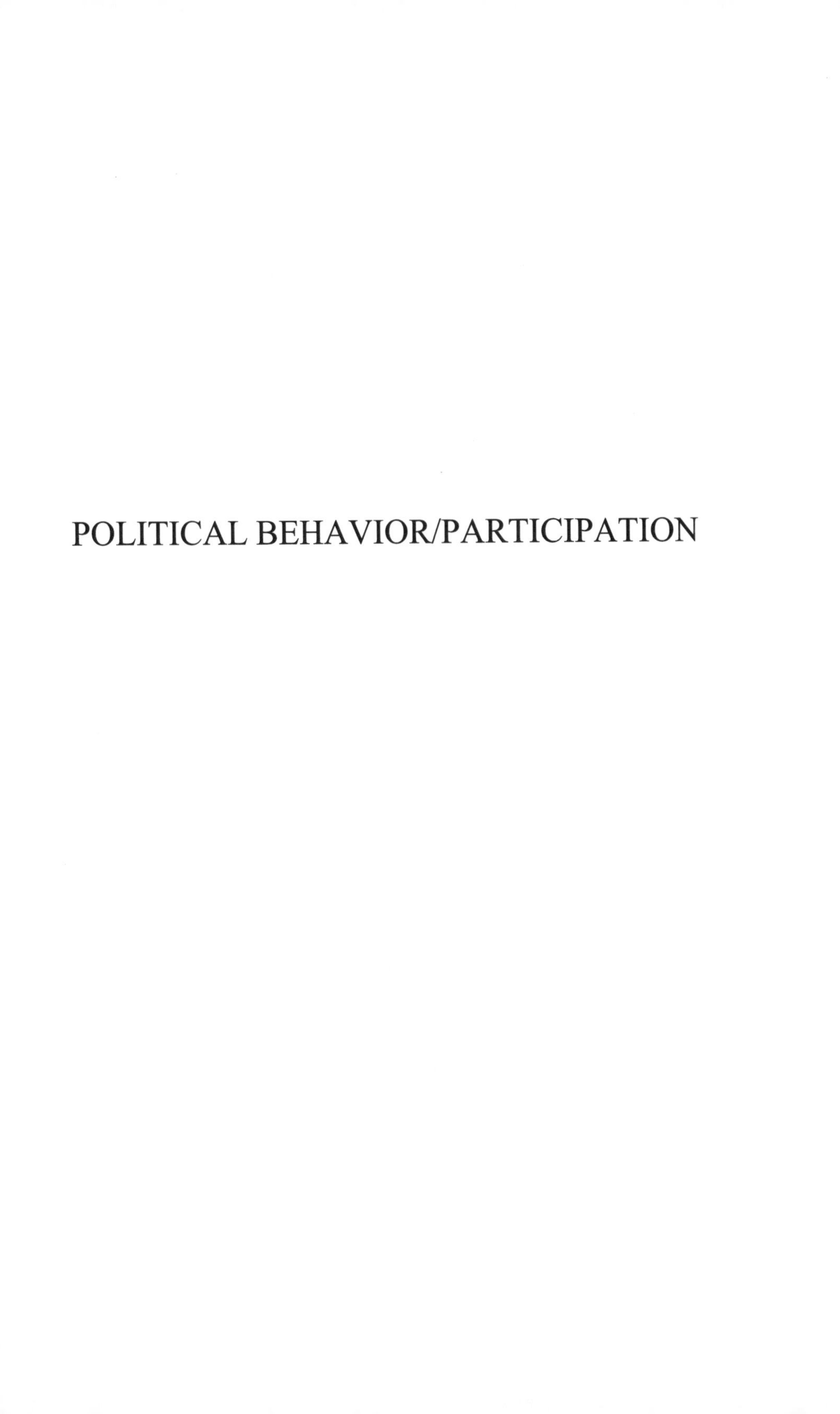

POLITICAL BEHAVIOR/PARTICIPATION

Chapter 3

Demythicizing the Asian-American Campaign Contributor

Wendy K. Tam Cho

However one would like to portray or interpret the 1996 campaign finance scandals, there is no dispute that Asian Americans were clearly central figures. And although the public is rarely interested in the role of Asian Americans in American politics, in this instance, this group of contributors attracted considerable attention from the media. This attention, albeit negative, cast the connection between Asian Americans and campaign finance into the limelight, highlighting for average Americans what political activists have been claiming for some years, that Asian Americans have become major-league contributors. Indeed, because of the voluminous media attention, we believe that we know something about the behavior of this group despite the lack of scholarly research. There is now a fairly large received wisdom about Asian Americans and campaign finance. For instance, it is now widely believed that Asian Americans are unique political animals because they combine general political apathy with generous campaign giving. Moreover, their contributions are believed to be significant and disproportionately large in relation to the size of their population. Indeed, while Asian Americans have been arriving in droves only since 1965, some now claim that Asian Americans have, in this short time span, become disproportionately influential with respect to financial campaign contributions.[1] The broad understanding is that Asian Americans favor activism not on the front lines, but from the sidelines. As Conservative Ron Unz pithily puts it, Asians are on the verge of becoming "Republican Jews" since Americans of Asian descent have deep pockets, "without the liberal guilt."[2]

Moreover, this insider's conventional wisdom, that Asian Americans cannot be expected to turn out to vote in large numbers, but that they can be induced to make large campaign contributions, is certainly not lost on politicians and fundraisers.[3] The late Robert Matsui (D–CA), former Democratic National Committee (DNC) treasurer, said that "[i]n 1976 there was one Asian at the Democratic National Committee who worked the [Asian-American] community. In a few weeks, he had a million dollars."[4] The clout and dollar amounts have only risen since the 1970s. In 1996, the DNC collected a record-breaking $5 million from John Huang's efforts. Though over $1 million was eventually returned to donors in an attempt to correct ethical lapses,[5] the dollar amounts are noteworthy, nonetheless. The Republicans, as well, have recognized the large potential source of funds. After Matt Fong introduced Bob Dole at a rally of ethnic supporters in California, Roy Wong, the Asian-American get-out-the-vote director concluded "this is the first time the Asian community has been reached out to so aggressively."[6] Clearly, both parties have come to view Asian ethnic communities as a rich source of financial support, still largely untapped. Despite the recent immigrant status of Asian Americans, party leaders believe that "the economic success of many Asian immigrants should soon make them a major source of politi-

---

[1] See, e.g., William Wong, "Asian Americans Shake Off Stereotypes, Increase Clout as Political Activism Grows," *Los Angeles Times*, February 23, 1988; Carole J. Uhlaner, Bruce E. Cain, and D. Roderick Kiewiet, "Political Participation of Ethnic Minorities in the 1980s," *Political Behavior* 11 (1989): 195–221; Yen Le Espiritu, *Asian American Panethnicity* (Philadelphia: Temple University Press, 1992); Alethea Yip, "A Taste of Political Power: APAs Enjoy Increasing Political Clout," *AsianWeek*, August 9–15, 1996; Pei-te Lien, *The Political Participation of Asian Americans* (New York: Garland; Nakanishi, 1997), Don Nakanishi, "When Numbers Do Not Add Up: Asian Pacific Americans and California Politics," in *Racial and Ethnic Politics in California, Volume 2,* ed. Michael B. Preston, Bruce E. Cain, and Sandra Bass (Berkeley: IGS Press, 1997).

[2] Ron Unz, "Why National Review is wrong: Value added" *National Review* 46, 21 (November 7, 1994): 56–58.

[3] Peter Kwong and JoAnn Lum, "A Silent Minority Tests Its Clout," *The Nation*, (January 16, 1988): 50–52; Judy Tachibana, "California's Asians: Power from a Growing Population." *California Journal* (November 1986): 535–43.

[4] Thomas Massey, "The Wrong Way to Court Ethnics." *The Washington Monthly*, May 1986, 21–26.

[5] Alan C. Miller, "Democrats give back more disputed money," *Los Angeles Times*. November 23, 1996.

[6] Sam Chu Lin, "Optimism on Both Sides: Campaigns Look to APAs as Swing Votes in 10 States," *AsianWeek*, October 11, 1996.

cal funding."[7] Candidates are starting to work San Francisco's Chinatown the way they have long worked Miami's Jewish donor circuit. Fred Fujiota, president of the Japanese-American Democratic Club of San Francisco told the *San Francisco Chronicle* that he gets "approached by everybody from all over the country. They want an introduction to the club. They send appeals for money." In 1990, a columnist for *AsianWeek* wryly observed, "members of the Chinatown and greater Asian-American communities don't need a calendar to see that there are some elections coming. They can just tell by the huge volume of mail inviting them to candidates' fundraisers."[8]

Despite the emerging folklore and obvious potential impact on American politics, there has not yet been a systematic study of financial contributions to political campaigns by Asian Americans.[9] What is the exact pattern of Asian-American campaign contributions? To whose campaigns are they contributing money? Why do they contribute? Do they contribute money in order to influence politicians? Are they successful in pushing their favorite policy issues? Or, are they merely symbolic contributors—that is, do they contribute only to other Asian candidates as a gesture of ethnic pride or solidarity? Instead of basing our knowledge in scholarly work, our impressions of Asian-American contributions are shaped largely by fast and loose commentary glibly put forth and then recirculated amongst politicians, activists, pundits, and journalists. Beyond the many casual statements lacking hard evidence, we know little about the patterns of Asian-American campaign contributions. Perhaps part of the problem is that there is a mistaken notion that the data are not available. Espiritu states that "Although comprehensive data are not available, Asian Americans are believed to be the second most generous political donors after Jewish Americans."[10] However, the claim that comprehensive data are not available is plainly mistaken. Much of the relevant data exist in public archives. It is simply the sheer volume and structure of the data that make it difficult, but not impossible, to parse manageably. Though it is cumbersome to rake through years of campaign contribution records documenting millions of contributors and contributions, this task is essential to establishing an understanding of Asian-American political participation in this realm.[11] Our un-

[7] Ron Unz, "Why National Review is wrong: Value added" *National Review* 46, 21 (November 7, 1994): 56–58.

[8] Grace Siao, "Feinstein Meets with 40 LA Asian Leaders," *AsianWeek*, February 23, 1990.

[9] Some cursory studies have been conducted. Fugita and O'Brien (1991, 151–52) commented on Japanese-American contributions on the basis of a survey. Espiritu examined the 1985 campaign contributions of Michael Woo and the 1987 campaign contributions of Warren Furutani, candidates in Los Angeles city elections. Tachibana reports on the funding of a few candidates by Asian-American donors.

[10] Yen Le Espiritu, *Asian American Panethnicity* (Philadelphia: Temple University Press, 1992).

[11] The full collection of FEC individual contribution reports is very large. There were 341,237 records in 1980, 168,383 in 1982, 260,581 in 1984, 274,635 in 1986, 436,294 in 1988, 530,328 in 1990, 888,224 in 1992, 838,212 in 1994, 1,229,605 in 1996,

derstanding in this area should not be confined to anecdotal evidence when the hard facts are accessible.[12]

This chapter sets out to subject a growing consensus about Asian-American political behavior to empirical tests. In doing so, I aim to demonstrate that the common understanding of Asian-American campaign contributors is largely a myth, perpetuated by journalists and pundits. I proceed by first describing the Federal Election Commission (FEC) data and then providing an overview of the data extraction process. Second, I argue that Asian-American contributors to federal campaigns are primarily symbolic contributors, i.e., their main objective is not to gain influence from members of Congress but to contribute to campaigns in a more symbolic manner. Third, I note the surprisingly strong and unexpected patterns that are evident from the data to support the claim that many of the contributions from Asian Americans are symbolic in nature. Lastly, I expound on the implications of these results on our overall understanding of the dynamics behind campaign contributing.

---

and 1,005,184 in 1998. Overall, then, there are about 6 million records to parse for these 10 election cycles.

[12] Even surveys, often the best sources of individual-level data, seem to be of limited usefulness, since they conflict markedly in their accounts of campaign contribution levels. For instance, Rosenstone and Hansen (1993) examined data from the National Election Studies (1952–1990). In this time period, they report, the percentage of people who contributed to campaigns peaked in 1960 at 11.6%. The average for the time period was 8.84%. Steven J. Rosenstone and John Mark Hansen, *Mobilization, Participation, and Democracy in America* (New York: Macmillan Publishing Company, 1993), 61. However, other surveys report much higher numbers. For instance, in a 1993 *Los Angeles Times* Poll of six southern California counties, 12% of Asian Americans, 21% of whites, 9% of blacks, and 5% of Latinos reported that they had contributed to a campaign. Pei-te Lien, *The Political Participation of Asian Americans* (New York: Garland, 1997). These numbers are significantly higher than those reported in the NES data set. Moreover, a 1984 statewide California poll detected even higher numbers. In that poll, 18% of Asians, 20% of whites, 17% of blacks, and 12% of Latinos reported that they had contributed to a campaign. Carole J. Uhlaner, Bruce E. Cain, and D. Roderick Kiewiet, "Political Participation of Ethnic Minorities in the 1980s," *Political Behavior* 11(1989): 195–221. Within the Asian-American subcategory, 15% of the Chinese, 26% of the Japanese, 16% of the Koreans, 14% of the Filipinos, and 18% of other Asians reported that they had donated money. Lastly, a 1996 Texas statewide poll reported that 19% had contributed to a campaign. The breakdown for ethnicities has 15% of Asians, 17% of Latinos, 20% of blacks, and 24% of whites contributing money to campaigns. The reports from different surveys are clearly discrepant. More to the point, the inconsistency in numbers across polls is strikingly irreconcilable. Further, all of the polls report numbers that seem to be too high to be plausible given what we can glean from objective records.

The Federal Election Commission Data

Instead of relying on questionable surveys, pundits' accounts, or journalistic news stories to lend insight into the questions of campaign finance, a more reliable method is to examine the actual contribution records. The best source of objective data to answer these questions comes from the Federal Election Commission (FEC). Candidates running for federal office are required to file records of their contributions with the FEC. A downside of the FEC data is that candidates must report only the names of individual contributors who contribute more than $200.[13] Since this clearly excludes some contributors, this bias against the small contributors should be noted. In addition, the FEC began collecting data only during the 1978 elections, following the 1974 amendments to the Federal Election Campaign Act (FECA).[14] Hence, we are unable to undertake a long historical study of campaign finance. Fortunately, this time period excludes very few Asian-American candidates since, outside of Hawaii, few Asians ever sought office until quite recently.[15]

The FEC data are limited in scope. For each donation, in addition to the amount, date, and recipient of the donation, we know, at most, the name, address, and occupation of the donor. Given the lack of personal information about each donor, it is difficult, then, to relate much of the campaign contribution dynamic to

---

[13] While campaigns are not required to report contributions under $200, many campaigns do report these contributions. Hence, many of these contributions are included in the data set.

[14] The Federal Election Campaign Act (FECA) was originally passed by Congress in 1971. In response to revelations from Watergate that large amounts of campaign funds were being "laundered" through secret foreign bank accounts, Congress passed amendments to FECA in 1974. FECA, the most sweeping campaign reform legislation in U.S. history, required federal candidates to disclose fully their contributions and expenditures, established campaign expenditure limits, and set limits on contributions.

[15] There are a few exceptions, including two victorious candidates. From 1956 to 1960, Democrat Dalip Singh Saund won three primary elections (one uncontested) and three general elections in California's 29th district. Following redistricting, he won the primary but lost the general for the 38th district in 1962. In 1976, S. I. Hayakawa won a four-way Republican primary and then triumphed in the general election as well to represent California in the U.S. Senate. In 1906, Benjamin Chow ran as a Socialist candidate in Massachusetts's 1st district. He received only 3.87% of the vote. In 1950, Democrat Charles Komaiko lost the general election for the 12th district of Illinois. Kirpal Singh contested but lost Republican primaries for California's 2nd district in 1962 and 1964. In 1972, Benjamin Chiang and Richard Kau won Republican primaries in California's 2nd and 41st districts, respectively, but both lost their general election contests. Jesse Chiang lost the 1974 Republican Senate primary in Washington. In 1976, Melvin H. Takaki won the Republican primary but lost the general election in Colorado's 3rd district. That same year, Edward Aho won a few hundred votes in Michigan's 11th district, running as the Human Rights candidate. In 1978, Democrat Rajeshwar Kumar (a write-in candidate in the primary) lost Pennsylvania's 19th district in the general election to Republican William F. Goodling.

individual characteristics. Despite this unfortunate situation, an insight into how to utilize the FEC records is that one group—exactly one group—can be reasonably identified on the basis of name alone, Asian Americans.[16] In this study, four different ethnic name dictionaries were used to identify Asian contributors, one each for the Chinese, Japanese, Korean, and Vietnamese groups.[17] Each contributor's name was checked against these dictionaries for a match to one of the Asian ethnic names. This amounts to checking each of the 6,085 names in the dictionaries against each of 6 million contributions. Hence, to create a data set for examining Asian-American contributions, a minimum of 36.5 billion comparisons need to be performed.[18] The final data set includes only Asian-American contributors (over 60,000 contributions). This data set is difficult to cull, but rich indeed, and invaluable for researchers interested in Asian-American campaign finance behavior.

Motives behind Campaign Contributions

One especially interesting aspect of Asian-American campaign finance behavior is the dynamic behind the contributions. That is, why do Asian Americans contribute money? Are they trying to influence politicians in the manner that has been popularized as a result of the campaign finance scandals? Or is there little

---

[16] This procedure is more accurate than one might initially guess. For Koreans, for instance, Kim is by far the most common surname. Twenty-two percent of the Korean population has this surname. In addition, because Kim is a surname not found outside Korea, it is safe to assume that anyone with the surname is of Korean descent. It is followed by Yi (also Lee), which accounts for 15% of the population. Following Yi, are Pak (9%) and Choe or Choi (5%). Together, these four surnames account for about half of all Koreans. The next most common names are Chong, Kang, Cho, Yun, Chang, Im (also Lim), Shin, Han, O, So, Ryu, Kwon, Hwang, An, Song, and Hong. Each of these names accounts for about 1% of the Korean population. Intermarriage obviously produces some complications in this scheme. However, people with clearly ethnic first names can be identified through name matching.

[17] The Chinese dictionary includes 521 names. The Japanese dictionary includes 4,818 names. The Korean dictionary includes 334 names. The Vietnamese dictionary includes 63 names.

This is not an exhaustive list of the Asian nationalities. Other groups were left out for practical, not substantive, reasons. For instance, the Filipino group is a very substantial component of the Asian-American group. However, their surnames closely resemble Latino surnames, so it is virtually impossible to obtain an accurate count of Filipino contributors. Hence, candidates such as Gloria Ochoa, who ran in the 22nd House District in California in 1992, and A. R. "Cecy" Groom, a Democrat who ran for the 39th House District in California in 1998, are left out of the analysis.

[18] Only a decade ago, a task this large would have been prohibitively complicated for readily available computers. However, the revolution in the PC market now makes seemingly gargantuan sorting and comparing tasks feasible with typical desktop computer.

evidence of such motivations? Although the campaign finance scandals focused primarily on figures such as John Huang and Charlie Trie and their connection to party organizations such as the DNC, their behavior and the motivations that underlie their behavior have clearly been transferred to the individual Asian-American contributor. Because the media portrayed their actions as politically strategic, all Asian Americans are now viewed as behaving in the same light. Here, I do not explore Asian-American contributions to party organizations or to Political Action Committees (PACs). Instead, my analysis is limited to individual contributions to federal elections. The implication from the scandals is that the strategic influence-buying behavior is ubiquitous across contribution types.

In general, there seem to be two main reasons why people contribute to campaigns. They may do so symbolically, that is, they support a candidate they admire, often because the candidate is in some way similar to themselves. This type of contribution is not strategic in the sense that the potential of the candidate to win the election is not a primary concern and is not heavily weighted in the decision to contribute. Contributions to ethnic candidates could certainly fit this description. The other motivation behind campaign contribution is strategic and falls under the rubric of an investment. These contributions are given with the expectation of some future benefit. This type of giving is strategic in that the contribution is directed toward one's own interest, and so relies on an assessment of a "reasonable" chance of "paying off." The anticipated return may be as direct as a personal kickback or as indirect as expecting the representative to cast roll call votes of which one approves. Certainly, the idea that cash contributions might be used as a vehicle for peddling influence is obvious from the various limitations that have been suggested in the provisions to FECA and the concerns raised in *Buckley v. Valeo*.[19]

The origins of a contributor's actions are, of course, known only to himself. However, some insight into the psyche of the contributor can be gained by observing the pattern of the contributions. For instance, if Asians give predominantly to Asian-American candidates, then this would provide evidence of symbolic giving. Moreover, this evidence would be bolstered if we further found that many of these Asian-American candidates were never serious contenders. It is hard to argue that Asians are being strategic if they are donating predominantly to Asian-American

---

[19] Indeed, Congress has attempted on several occasions to curb the disproportionate influence of the wealthy. In 1907, a federal law was passed to prohibit direct contributions from corporations. In 1925, after the Teapot Dome scandal over cabinet-level bribery, the Corrupt Practices Act was passed. The act required disclosure of campaign funds. In 1943, labor unions were prohibited from direct contributions. In 1971, FECA was passed. In 1974, after the Watergate scandal, FECA was amended. In 1976, the Supreme Court in *Buckley v. Valeo* overturned key aspects of FECA because they were violations of First Amendment free speech rights. Congress then rewrote FECA to preserve most of its features. Many individuals, however, still attempt to bypass these limitations as is evident from the savings and loan scandal in the 1990s and the Clinton/Gore campaign finance scandals.

candidates who have little chance of attaining political office. If, however, contributors primarily donated to their own representative or to candidates who seem likely to be able to return favors to them, then this would appear to be strategic investment.

There are two questions at hand: whom do Asian Americans contribute to? And, why do they contribute? While we cannot determine, with certainty, why Asian Americans contribute, whom they contribute to provides insight into their motives. Ascertaining who Asian Americans financially support is a large but feasible task.

Assessments of Campaign Contributions

To assess Asian campaign contributors, I first examine the types of contribution received by two sets of candidates. The first set is comprised of candidates who are Asian American, those who, if elected, would provide descriptive representation. Most people, politicos included, probably could not name more than a handful of Asian-American candidates. This is not surprising since the majority of Asian-American candidates for the U.S. Congress have been low-profile candidates who lost their campaign bids and thus never served in Congress. Few Asian Americans have won House elections, or even garnered a significant proportion of the vote.[20] The second set of candidates is comprised of representatives whose districts have relatively high proportions of Asian Americans, those who are in a position to provide substantive representation. For present purposes, the threshold for "relatively high" is more than 10% of the constituency being Asian American. Across the country, there are 23 of these congressional districts.[21] These representatives are the most likely to provide substantive representation for Asian Americans. Because of their unique position, they are also likely to receive campaign contributions from Asian Americans. We are comparing, then, the contributions to the two groups that are most likely to provide either substantive or descriptive representation to the Asian-American community.

Certainly, Asian Americans have reasons to contribute to both sets of candidates, though the reasoning differs. One set offers an outlet for symbolic contribut-

[20] Appendix A lists some of the most low-profile Asian American campaigns. Table A-1 lists Asian American candidates who ran for federal office, but did not report or did not receive any campaign contributions. Table A-2 lists Asian-American candidates who received donations, but never actually mounted a candidacy.

[21] Most of these districts are in California, though there are three in New York, one in Illinois, and one in Washington. Twenty-two of these districts are listed in Table 3. Robert Matsui's district is 13% Asian but is not listed in Table 3, since he is covered Table 2. There are three additional districts that are approximately 10% Asian (districts 27, 37, and 41 in California). Thanks to Okiyoshi Takeda for pointing out this distinction. See also Takeda (n.d.).

ing while the other offers an outlet for strategic contributing. In addition, both sets of candidates have justifications for courting Asian-American contributors, though their modal appeals differ. One set purports to provide substantive representation while the other set would provide descriptive representation. A few can offer to provide both types of representation. In general, symbolic contributions are given to achieve descriptive representation while strategic contributions are intended to lead to substantive representation. These two styles are not mutually exclusive since Asian Americans may contribute to a viable Asian-American candidate running for office in their own district. Given that all of these candidates have incentives to court Asian-American contributors, I proceed now to detail whose appeals are heeded with the most enthusiasm.

Asian-American Candidates

Tables 1 and 2 summarize campaign contributions for the first set of candidates described, Asian Americans who ran for federal office in the 20-year period 1978–1998. Table 1 is divided into two parts, Table 1A and Table 1B. Both Table 1A and 1B provide the same information, but Table 1A is a summary of campaign contributions given to Asian-American candidates who ran for office in California while Table 1B covers all other states except Hawaii.[22] Table 2 is devoted to the careers of Robert Matsui (D–CA–5) and Norman Mineta (D–CA–15) since they had the two longest-standing careers of any (non-Hawaiian) Asian American in the House.

A brief look at Table 1 reveals several overwhelming characteristics of the campaigns of Asian-American candidates. First, Asian-American candidates generally do not run for office in districts with particularly high proportions of Asian constituents. It seems counter to initial expectations that of the districts where Asian Americans ran for office, the average percentage of the constituency that is Asian American would be relatively low (7.0% with a standard deviation of 5.0). There are certainly districts with much higher percentages of Asian Americans. California districts, for instance, top out at 28%. In another four districts, Asian Americans comprise over 20% of the constituency. While districts with high percentages of Asian Americans do attract some Asian-American candidates, they do not attract many. These districts are all represented by non-Asian representatives. This pattern contrasts sharply with the patterns found among blacks and Latinos.

---

[22] For an analysis of the Hawaii data, see Cho (2001). Since Hawaii is a majority-Asian environment, it is clearly a special case, and I have excluded all Hawaiian candidates from the analysis in this chapter.

Table 1A. Individual Campaign Contributions to Asian-American Congressional Candidates in California, 1978–1998

			Contributions					Primary Election		General Election	
Candidate	Race	Year	N	Amount	Asian	Ethnic	Ethnicity	Vote %	Major Opponent	Vote %	Major Opponent
Rose Ochi (D)*	CA–30	1982	25	$17,500	84%	67%	Japanese	14%	Matthew Martinez		
Dan Wong (R)*	CA–34	1982	9	$5,100	100%	100%	Chinese	46%	Paul R. Jackson		
Lily Chen (D)*	CA–30	1988	137	$112,548	96%	98%	Chinese	26%	Matthew Martinez		
Sang Korman (R)*	CA–21	1988	121	$99,000	99%	100%	Korean	14%	Elton Gallegly		
___*	CA–21	1990	281	$172,800	99%	99%	Korean	32%	Elton Gallegly		
___*	CA–24	1992	112	$75,600	96%	100%	Korean	24%	Tom McClintock		
___*	CA–24	1994	68	$46,800	96%	100%	Korean	16%	Rich Sybert		
Jay Kim (R)+	CA–41	1992	644	$319,590	85%	85%	Korean	30%	Charles Bader	60%	Bob Baker
___+	CA–41	1994	740	$374,258	85%	85%	Korean	41%	Valerie Romero	62%	Ed Tessier
___+	CA–41	1996	635	$361,340	81%	93%	Korean	58%	Bob Kerns	58%	Richard Waldron
___*	CA–41	1998	351	$235,182	89%	94%	Korean	26%	Gary Miller		
Albert C. Lum (D)*	CA–30	1992	263	$172,588	86%	96%	Chinese	16%	Xavier Becerra		
Elsa Cheung (R)**	CA–8	1994	13	$5,000	92%	85%	Chinese	100%	Uncontested	18%	Nancy Pelosi
Doris Liu (R)*	CA–15	1994	3	$1,750	33%	33%	Chinese	34%	Robert Wick		
Peter Mathews (D)*	CA–38	1992	30	$14,771	83%	100%	Indian	26%	Evan A. Braude		
___**	CA–38	1994	542	$270,219	85%	100%	Indian	100%	Uncontested	37%	Steve Horn
___*	CA–38	1996	80	$34,931	66%	100%	Indian	49%	Rick Zbur		
___**	CA–38	1998	156	$67,969	88%	100%	Indian	100%	Uncontested	44%	Steve Horn
Mark Takano (D)+	CA–43	1992	137	$72,926	65%	82%	Japanese	29%	Raven L. Workman	46%	Ken Calvert
___+	CA–43	1994	262	$120,405	53%	37%	Japanese	70%	Raven L. Workman	38%	Ken Calvert
Kyo Paul Jhin (R)*	CA–24	1996	60	$31,850	93%	89%	Korean	22%	Rich Sybert		
Matt Fong (R)+	CA Senate	1998	11,171	$7,995,453	27%	89%	Chinese	45%	Darrell Issa	43%	Barbara Boxer

Reported Asian Contribution Percentages are Percentages of Total N Contributions. Reported Ethnic Contribution Percentages are Percentages of the Total Asian N Contributions. Federal election data compiled from FEC reports. Other data compiled from the *Almanac of American Politics* (1980–1998), *America Votes* (1980–1998), and Congressional Directories. Reported opponent in primary elections reflects the candidate who received the most votes. Primary Vote Percentages reflect the percentage of the candidate's "own-party" vote.

* Candidate lost his/her primary election. **Candidate was unopposed in his/her party's primary. + Candidate ran in contested primary and general election.

Table 1B. Individual Campaign Contributions to Asian-American Candidates outside California, 1978–1998

			Contributions					Primary Election		General Election	
Candidate	Race	Year	*N*	Amount	Asian	Ethnic	Ethnicity	Vote %	Major Opponent	Vote %	Major Opponent
Jesse Chiang (I)***	WA Sen.	1982	1	$500	0%	0%	Chinese			1%	Henry Jackson
Soleng Tom (D)*	AZ-5	1982	4	$3,000	100%	100%	Chinese	17%	Jim McNulty		
Tom Shimizu (D)+	UT-2	1986	99	$72,570	11%	91%	Japanese	62%	Douglas Bischoff	44%	Wayne Owens
S. B.Woo (D)+	DE Sen.	1988	1287	$1,063,158	93%	93%	Chinese	74%	Ernest Ercole	43%	Michael Castle
___+	DE-AL	1992	994	$485,366	93%	92%	Chinese	50%	Samuel Beard	38%	William Roth, Jr.
D. Bhagwandin (R-C)**	NY-6	1992	39	$16,375	85%	100%	Indian	10%	Uncontested	19%	Floyd Flake
Jay W. Khim (R)*	VA-11	1992	40	$23,150	60%	96%	Korean	16%	Henry Butler		
Glenn Sugiyama (D)*	IL-9	1992	50	$28,851	28%	79%	Japanese	23%	Sidney Yates		
Esther Lee Yao (R)*	TX-25	1992	206	$108,732	91%	99%	Chinese	45%	Dolly Madison McKenna		
Neil Dhillon (D)*	MD-6	1994	496	$263,038	86%	99%	Indian	18%	Paul Muldowney		
Binh Ly (R)*	FL-19	1994	31	$20,860	62%	89%	Vietnamese	40%	Peter Tsakanikas		
Puall Shin (D)*	WA-2	1994	193	$125,985	77%	97%	Korean	18%	Harriet A. Spanel		
Ram Uppuluri (D)*±	TN-3	1994	261	$94,771	77%	74%	Indian	20%	Randy Button		
Nimi McConigley (R)*	WY Sen.	1996	79	$42,750	72%	100%	Indian	7%	Michael Enzi		
Yash Aggarwal (D-L)+	NY-20	1996	184	$79,034	90%	100%	Indian	67%	Ira Goodman	38%	Benjamin Gilman
Cheryl Lau (R)*	NV-2	1996	168	$85,805	83%	96%	Chinese	24%	Jim Gibbons		
J. Misir (R-C-I-FR)**	NY-6	1996	12	$5,950	83%	100%	Indian	100%	Uncontested	15%	Floyd Flake
Paul Park (D)*	IL Sen.	1996	53	$20,400	98%	100%	Korean	1%	Richard Durbin		
John Lim (R)+	OR Sen.	1998	428	$302,406	93%	91%	Korean	63%	John M. Fitzpatrick	34%	Ron Wyden
R. Nag. Nagarajan (D)*	IN-6	1996	18	$6,676	100%	100%	Indian	19%	C. J. Dillard-Trammell		
___*	IN-6	1998	1	$500	100%	100%	Indian	24%	Bob Kern		
David Wu (D)+	OR-1	1998	1388	$672,293	35%	92%	Chinese	52%	Linda Peters	55%	Molly Bordonaro

Reported Asian Contribution Percentages are Percentages of Total *N* Contributions. Reported Ethnic Contribution Percentages are Percentages of the Total Asian N Contributions. Federal election data compiled from FEC reports. Other data compiled from the *Almanac of American Politics* (1980–1998), *America Votes* (1980–1998), and Congressional Directories. Reported opponent in primary elections reflects the candidate who received the most votes. Primary Vote Percentages reflect the percentage of the candidate's "own-party" vote.

* Candidate lost primary election. ** Unopposed primary. *** No primary. + Contested primary and contested general election.

±Ram Uppuluri is Japanese and Asian Indian, but received little support from the Japanese community. See Shankar and Srikanth (1998).

Table 2. Campaign Contributions for Robert Matsui and Norman Mineta

			Contributions				Primary Election		General Election	
Candidate	Race	Year	*N*	Amount	Asian	Japanese	Vote %	Major Opponent	Vote %	Major Opponent
Norman Mineta (D)*	CA–13	1978	178	$43,245	30%	94%	100%	Uncontested	59%	Dan O'Keefe
___	CA–13	1980	109	$23,875	35%	97%	100%	Uncontested	59%	W. E. (Ted) Gagne
___	CA–13	1982	40	$27,746	28%	73%	100%	Uncontested	66%	Tom Kelly
___	CA–13	1984	50	$33,220	24%	58%	100%	Uncontested	65%	John D. Jack Williams
___	CA–13	1986	72	$43,450	33%	92%	100%	Uncontested	70%	Bob Nash
___	CA–13	1988	120	$74,965	33%	72%	100%	Uncontested	67%	Luke Sommer
___	CA–13	1990	346	$151,193	31%	81%	100%	Uncontested	58%	David E. Smith
___	CA–15	1992	575	$266,401	31%	61%	100%	Uncontested	64%	Robert Wick
___	CA–15	1994	603	$279,023	25%	60%	100%	Uncontested	60%	Robert Wick
Robert Matsui (D)	CA–3	1978	563	$157,561	36%	76%	36%	Eugene T. Gualco	53%	Sandy Smoley
___	CA–3	1980	54	$26,875	35%	84%	89%	Ivaldo Lenci	71%	Joseph Murphy
___	CA–3	1982	54	$33,546	15%	88%	100%	Uncontested	90%	Bruce A. Daniel
___	CA–3	1984	23	$15,953	13%	100%	92%	Bill Watkins	100%	Uncontested
___	CA–3	1986	92	$61,991	15%	86%	100%	Uncontested	76%	Lowell Landowski
___	CA–3	1988	212	$135,743	16%	73%	100%	Uncontested	71%	Lowell Landowski
___	CA–3	1990	653	$328,700	34%	80%	100%	Uncontested	60%	Lowell Landowski
___	CA–5	1992	186	$88,300	20%	76%	100%	Uncontested	69%	Robert S. Dinsmore
___	CA–5	1994	283	$146,539	20%	74%	100%	Uncontested	68%	Robert S. Dinsmore
___	CA–5	1996	254	$136,000	26%	77%	100%	Uncontested	70%	Robert S. Dinsmore
___	CA–5	1998	167	$76,700	10%	71%	100%	Uncontested	72%	Robert S. Dinsmore

Federal election data compiled from FEC reports. Other data compiled from the *Almanac of American Politics* (1980–1998) and *America Votes* (1980–1998). Reported Asian Contribution Percentages are Percentages of the Total N Contributions. Reported Ethnic Contribution Percentages are Percentages of the Total Asian Contributions.

* First elected in 1974.

Black and Latino districts are overwhelmingly comprised of minority voters and nearly always elect a black or Latino representative.[23]

Second, of the total number of contributions that Asian-American candidates receive, the percentage that comes from Asian-American contributors is very high. On average, Asian-American contributors account for 59.3% (with a standard deviation of 32.9) of the total number of contributions. This number is even higher (79.2%) with a smaller standard deviation (23.5) when the Japanese candidates' contributions are left out of the computation. For the Japanese candidates, the average drops to 27.2% with a standard deviation of 15.9%. Neither of these percentages is even remotely close to the much-lower percentage of Asian Americans that comprise the respective districts. On average, the difference in percentages of Asian-American contributors and Asian-American constituency is 52.4. Evidently, Asian-American candidates are able to garner support from many Asian Americans outside of their own districts. Consider, for example, S. B. Woo's contributions. He received over 93% of his contributions from Asian Americans while Asian Americans comprise only 1.4% of his constituency.

The support that the broad Asian-American community provides for Asian-American candidates is further evidenced in the numbers of in-district contributions. "In-district" contributions are contributions that are given to campaigns in a contributor's own district. Of the Asian Americans who contributed to S. B. Woo's campaign, for instance, only 3.5% lived in his state. Indeed, on average, only 24.4% of the contributions that Asian candidates receive from Asian Americans are from their own constituents. Asian Americans are clearly willing and even happy to support Asian candidates regardless of whether the candidate will be their own representative or even a representative from their own state! This pattern is not evident among candidates of other ethnicities. As we can see from Table 3, candidates generally receive more money from their own constituency.[24]

This broad support from the Asian-American community is broad only in the geographical sense. That is, while Asian Americans will cross districts, counties,

---

[23] Bernard Grofman and Chandler Davidson, eds., Controversies in Minority Voting: The Voting Rights Act in Perspective (Washington, D.C.: The Brookings Institution, 1992); David Lublin, The Paradox of Representation: Racial Gerrymandering and Minority Interests in Congress (Princeton: Princeton University Press, 1997).

[24] In-district contributions are determined by examining the zip code of the contributor. This method is not entirely accurate since some contributors do not list their zip codes and none of the contributors lists the four-digit extension for their zip code. Since some congressional districts include only parts of some zip codes, not having the four-digit extension leaves one unable to determine if some contributors should be included in a congressional district that does not include that entire zip code. In these calculations, if a zip code was partially included in a certain district, the contribution was counted as an in-district contribution. This results in an overcounting. Hence, the percentage of contributions that have come from outside the district is a conservative estimate. Lastly, though some contributors did not list a zip code, the number of these was small and does not account for much error in the estimates.

and states to lend support to a fellow Asian-American candidate, they generally will not cross ethnicities. Indeed, Table 1 provides strong evidence against the notion of Asian-American pan-ethnicity. Though journalists and activists virtually always speak of "Asian-American politics" and an "Asian-American identity," with regard to campaign finance, these concepts remain abstract and lack concrete and widespread evidence. Contributions to Asian-American candidates come predominantly from Asian Americans of the same ethnicity. To use S. B. Woo as an example again, note that over 92% of his "Asian-American donations" were specifically from Chinese Americans. Evidently, Asian-American candidates do not try or are not able to tap the campaign chests of the other Asian-American communities. On average, 84.6% of the Asian campaign contributions come from contributors of the same ethnicity.

Several contribution patterns have already emerged. The patterns for Asian-American candidates stand in stark contrast to the contributions that other candidates receive. Consider the numbers in Table 3 that summarize contributions to candidates who have represented areas with comparatively high concentrations of Asian Americans in the 1990s. The patterns that were so clear in Tables 1 and 2 are not evident in Table 3. They are not absent, but rather now appear in an intriguingly opposite manner. These non-Asian candidates receive less money from Asian Americans than one well-versed in journalistic accounts would have expected. The percentage of their funds received from Asian Americans is far less than the comparable Asian percentage of their constituencies. The sole exception to this rule is Representative Gary Ackerman (D–NY–5). He received over 18% of his donations from Asian Americans even though Asian Americans make up only 11% of his constituency. The average, however is 5.2% (4.6% without Ackerman) while the average percentage of the constituency that is Asian American is 16.3%. Contrary to initial expectations, then, Asian-American campaign donations do not figure prominently in "Asian-American districts."

We have already seen from Tables 1 and 2 that Asian Americans do, as the pundits report, contribute significant amounts of money to political campaigns. Hence, lack of resources is not the problem. Nor is the problem a lack of efficacy. The pundits' reports are misleading, however, in that while Asian Americans do have money and they do contribute, they do not contribute much to their *own* representatives. Instead, they choose disproportionately to fund Asian-American candidates of their own ethnicity running in other areas. They are not, as previous accounts imply, a source of funds for all candidates. Initial assessments seem to indicate that Asian Americans are less interested in establishing influential channels to their own legislators than they are in contributing symbolically. Apparently, the determining trait is not the district composition but the race of the candidate. The preliminary evidence is that Asian-American candidates are anomalies because the patterns of their contributions run counter to those expected from a "strategic contributor."

Table 3. Campaign Contributions to Candidates Who Represent Areas with Comparatively High Concentrations of Asians, 1990s

				Total Contributions		Asian Contributions			In-District Contributions		
Candidate	Race	State	Year	N	Amount	N	Amount	Percent	% Total	% Asian	% Asian in District
Xavier Becerra (D)	House	CA-30	1992-1996	166	$82,285	8	$3,958	4.8%	10.99%	11.43%	21%
Tom Campbell (R)	House	CA-15	1996	2378	$1,695,340	69	$47,400	2.9%	10.54%	23.53%	11%
Ron Dellums (D)	House	CA-9	1992-1996	305	$176,569	45	$37,467	13.9%	27.17%	26.71%	16%
Robert Dornan (R)	House	CA-46	1992-1994	766	$282,179	7	$3,700	0.9%	3.11%	26.67%	12%
David Dreier (R)	House	CA-28	1992-1996	427	$194,847	15	$10,083	3.6%	30.27%	42.86%	13%
Anna Eshoo (D)	House	CA-14	1992-1996	548	$278,388	20	$7,795	3.8%	54.18%	42.65%	12%
Bob Filner (D)	House	CA-50	1992-1996	621	$293,053	11	$5,267	1.7%	16.96%	19.92%	15%
Jane Harman (D)	House	CA-36	1992-1996	1104	$594,197	15	$9,083	1.3%	11.27%	18.58%	13%
Tom Lantos (D)	House	CA-12	1992-1996	155	$78,337	7	$4,950	4.1%	19.00%	42.06%	26%
Zoe Lofgren (D)	House	CA-16	1994-1996	381	$202,492	29	$14,495	7.1%	36.07%	53.29%	21%
Matthew Martinez (D)	House	CA-31	1992-1996	55	$34,911	6	$3,050	11.1%	24.73%	73.33%	23%
George Miller (D)	House	CA-7	1992-1996	167	$93,439	2	$617	1.1%	21.44%	22.22%	14%
Nancy Pelosi (D)	House	CA-8	1992-1996	346	$223,417	22	$12,867	6.3%	56.61%	76.30%	28%
Richard Pombo (R)	House	CA-11	1992-1996	554	$228,643	14	$4,475	2.4%	80.22%	83.99%	12%
Dana Rohrabacher (R)	House	CA-45	1992-1996	280	$144,147	29	$17,683	9.7%	28.53%	24.17%	11%
Ed Royce (R)	House	CA-39	1992-1996	489	$197,203	46	$17,174	9.2%	26.07%	21.56%	14%
Pete Stark (D)	House	CA-13	1992-1996	150	$96,472	3	$1,917	1.8%	1.17%	6.67%	19%
Sidney Yates (D)	House	IL-9	1992-1996	219	$135,892	1	$167	.13%	3.15%	0.00%	10%
Gary Ackerman (D)	House	NY-5	1992-1996	731	$496,635	141	$100,804	18.2%	42.65%	26.17%	11%
Thomas Manton (D)	House	NY-7	1992-1996	267	$138,059	15	$8,850	5.1%	20.41%	37.66%	11%
Nydia Velazquez (D)	House	NY-12	1992-1996	296	$128,563	7	$2,433	2.1%	10.20%	16.68%	19%
Jim McDermott (D)	House	WA-7	1992-1996	46	$20,731	2	$950	2.9%	41.28%	11.11%	11%

Federal election data compiled from FEC reports. Other data compiled from the *Almanac of American Politics* (1980–1998). Reported Asian Contributions Percentages are Percentages of the Total *N* Contributions. Numbers reflect a rounded, nonweighted average of the indicated time span.

Patterns among the Contributions

Thus far, we have examined only two types of candidacies, Asian-American candidates, and candidates for election in districts with a high percentage of Asian constituents. The following analysis includes all campaigns that received at least 25 contributions from Asian Americans. This set of campaigns is somewhat eclectic, but it is a good choice for examining the issues at hand, since including all congressional races in the data set is clearly not optimal, and excluding races where Asian contributors have given a sizeable number of contributions would be even odder. This is the set of races where Asian Americans contributed money, and my goal is to determine if there are characteristics that define the candidates that they chose to support. If there is some pattern of contributions among this set, it should give us an indication of where Asian Americans prefer to contribute.

In the search for patterns of contributions in this data, I examine two different but related aspects of donation rates. In particular, I am interested in campaigns that mobilize Asian Americans as well as campaigns in which Asians provided a high percentage of the funds and thus are arguably in an influential position. Mobilization and influence are defined by observing that campaigns that receive a large *number* of contributions (or dollars) from Asian Americans are clearly able to mobilize the Asian-American contributor, and campaigns that receive a large *percentage* of their funds from Asian Americans can be characterized as the campaigns where Asian Americans exert the greatest degree of influence. These two sets of campaigns need not be identical.

One pattern that is immediately evident is that serious candidates (those with a reasonable chance of running a victorious campaign) receive a lesser percentage of their funds from Asians. This tendency seems clearly unstrategic. Asian money flowed to low-profile, often less-than-serious and not hotly contested races. In this respect, Asian contributions seem to be primarily symbolic rather than successful strategic investments. There are few reasons, other than the symbolic ones, to fund these hopeless candidates. While Asians may not have known which candidates were the best investments, the presence of safe seats, incumbents, and low-quality challengers made them high information situations; the eventual victor of these races was not surprising.

If we compare Asian-American campaigns to the campaigns of candidates of different ethnicities, we note that the Asian-American campaigns receive the bulk of the Asian funds. This finding strikes at the foundation of journalists' and pundits' claims that Asian Americans are a source of funding for all. Instead, the evidence points to Asian groups behaving in a much more ethno-centric fashion. Although Asians do fund other candidates, their influence is greatest and most evident in Asian-American campaigns. The only exception appears when we examine the ethnicities separately. The Japanese support for Japanese-American candidates is not as strong or evident. Much of this effect can be attributed to the cases of Norman Mineta and Robert Matsui, congressional incumbents who were able to procur funds from a wide array of sources. However, one should note that this effect is not a general incumbency effect, since there are several other Japanese candidates in the data set.

Lastly, when we examine only Asian-Americans candidates, other patterns emerge that lay further claim to the conjectures that have been offered. In particular, the proportion of funds received from Asian Americans *increases* as the seriousness of the candidate's bid *decreases*. "Hopeless" candidates receive the most funding (proportionally) from Asians while the most competitive candidates received the lowest proportion of their funds from Asians. Apparently, competitive candidates need additional funding and a broader base of support than the Asian-American community can provide. Moreover, part of the reason why they are competitive is because they are able to solicit money (and, one assumes, other support, including votes) from a broader base of voters. Hopeless candidates, on the other hand, are unable to find many sources of money. Strategic contributors are not willing to invest in a hopeless candidate, so the only source of funds for these losing, long-shot candidates is nonstrategic/symbolic contributors.

If we examine the dollar amounts, instead of the percentage of funds, the story is unchanged. Asian-American candidates mobilize the Asian contributor, with Japanese candidates again being the only serious exception. Some other, not very surprising, patterns are evident as well. Senate races garner more contributions, and candidates who lose in the primary bring in fewer contributions than candidates who go on to run in the general election.

These data provide considerable insight into Asian campaign contributors, and the findings differ significantly from the story that circulates in the popular press. It is evident that Asian contributors do not fit the image of the classic investor contributor, or at minimum, are extremely unsuccessful in trying to fill that role. That is, it is possible that they are attempting to be strategic, but are failing miserably. Instead, Asian money generally seems to flow into the coffers of Asian-American campaigns, which rarely seem likely to succeed. On average, they are less influential in their own representative's bid and in the campaigns of successful candidates. And Asian-American campaigns are the ones that are most successful in mobilizing Asian contributors.

The Timing of Contributions

Notwithstanding the evidence thus far that Asians seem to be more symbolic than strategic in their contributions, note that the observed patterns may be consistent with a strategic motive that has not been examined yet. In particular, strategic motivations may be evident in the timing of the contribution. That is, a good strategy for Asian-American contributors is to provide the seed money for a campaign by giving money early in the campaign with the purpose of inducing further contributions from other potential contributors. Contributing in this manner, could be strategic rather than symbolic, but ultimately unsuccessful. That is, Asian donors may be choosing long-shot candidates, but trying to boost their odds by making early donations. This is quite different behavior from donating to plainly hopeless candidates as an act of ethnic solidarity.

The strategic timing of contributions can be seen in both a short-term as well as a long-term context. The short-term context occurs within an election period. Here, contributors would try to induce other contributors to give before the election occurs. In contrast, the long-term context spans several years. The strategy is to get a candidate elected, and then to shift attention elsewhere; once the candidate is in office, he can rely more on his incumbency advantage and less on support from a particular ethnic group. American candidates rely less on Asian-American contributors when they are established politicians. If this were true, Asian-American contributors would constitute a large proportion of contributions in the first few elections, but after the candidate becomes an incumbent, this type of seed money would diminish.

In the long-term context, there are only two candidates to observe, Norman Mineta and Robert Matsui. The plot in Figure 1 shows the pattern of their contributions beginning in 1978. Lines are fitted to the observations. From the plots, it appears that the proportion of their Asian contributions coming from Japanese donors decreased with time. Asian-American contributions, while largely stable, had been on a slight decline as well. While the lines slope downward, statistical tests indicate that this trend is not significant; the trend is not steep enough to provide evidence that Asian contributions changed over time. However, there is statistical evidence of a declining reliance on Japanese contributions over time. Hence, there is some evidence that Asian-American candidates tend to rely less on contributors of their own ethnicity over time. However, there is no evidence that reliance on the broad Asian-American group declines over time. The claim that there is no pan-ethnicity among Asian Americans, then, may be premature. Indeed, based on these results, the conjecture that a pan-ethnic identity is emerging cannot be discounted.

To explore whether Asian Americans employ the "seed money strategy" in the short-term context, we consider the candidates listed in Table 1. For some of these candidates, this timing strategy is either not evident or not successful. Thus, a number of candidates listed in Table 1 can be safely excluded from the analysis. First, we can exclude from this analysis candidates who do not receive some threshold number or amount in contributions. Here, this threshold number of contributions is somewhat arbitrarily set at 60. Since we are interested only in whether candidates benefit from receiving money from Asian Americans early in their campaign, the candidates who receive few contributions clearly belong outside the analysis. This leaves 27 races to consider. Second, of the remaining candidates, the candidates who receive at least 85% of their funds from Asian Americans are also excluded. Certainly, the money that these candidates have received from Asian Americans has not successfully been deployed as seed money. This leaves just 10 races to consider.

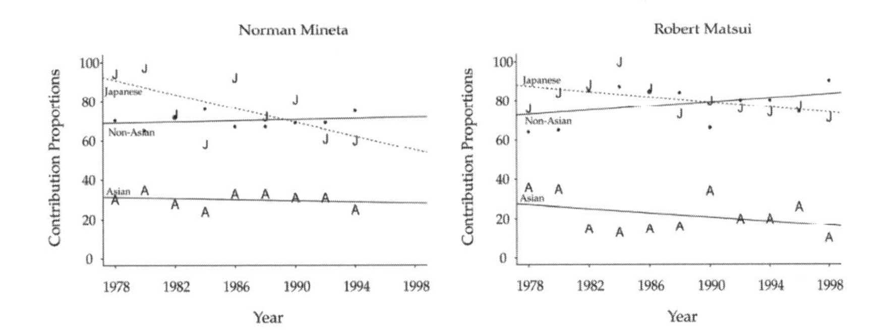

Figure 1. Regression lines for the proportion of contributions from different groups to Norman Mineta and Robert Matsui. The "A" indicates the proportion of contributions from Asians. The "J" indicates the proportion of Asian contributions from Japanese. The dots indicate the proportion of funds from non-Asian contributors.

Since there are so few races to consider, we can look at the contribution patterns for each race in some detail. An examination of each of the 10 races reveals that Asian Americans were not strategic or unsuccessfully deployed the seed money strategy. There is not a single case where we can statistically reject the hypothesis that proportions do not change over time. Hence, in the short-term context, there is little evidence of a successful "seed money" strategy. Asian-American contributions are not heavily weighted toward the beginning of the campaign but are dispersed evenly throughout the campaigning season. In most cases, they account for most of the contributions in any given week. That is, the money does not seem to induce very many non-Asian contributors. By and large, Asian-American contributors bear the brunt of funding Asian-American candidates and are unsuccessful in inducing others to take up their charge. Their giving is not front-loaded, as we would expect if there were a concerted effort to push candidates into the spotlight with an early burst of cash.

Conclusion

This examination of the behavior of Asian-American campaign contributors reinforces a key finding about voting and Asian Americans, that they do not act politically as a monolithic bloc. Instead, the interests of the different ethnic groups diverge on a number of political issues (Tam 1995). There is some evidence that the different Asian-American groups may coalesce as future generations come of age, but there is no certainty that this unity will emerge (Cho

1999). Despite the evidence, journalists and activists continue to trumpet "Asian Americans" as a force to be reckoned with today, claiming that those who court the Asian-American campaign donor will reap great rewards. Media accounts almost always slip into unbridled use of the umbrella term "Asian American." The popular media aside, a little thought and analysis lead one to conclude that many barriers must still be overcome before the notion of pan-Asian ethnicity becomes anything more than a favored and desired moniker among activists. Instead, the patterns of campaign contributions mirror voting trends by displaying few traces of pan-ethnic solidarity.

The journalistic accounts are more correct, however, when they speak of Asian Americans as potentially active and influential political participants. Asian Americans do contribute to campaigns and often contribute significant amounts, showing that they can and do have political causes to support. The media image, nonetheless, exaggerates the depth of Asian pockets and overplays the expansiveness of their interests. With regard to the funding of congressional candidates, Asian Americans are nationalist and nonstrategic in their expression. There is every reason to believe that many campaign contributors use cash to try to gain influence on policy. Since Asian Americans appear not to be strategic backers of plausible winners, the desire to buy influence cannot be generalized to them. In fact, when we examine the set of individuals who contribute to Asian-American campaigns, the evidence runs strongly to the contrary. Even in districts where Asian-American influence is presumably the highest, i.e., districts where they command a significant proportion of the electorate, the desire to buy influence through campaign contributions seems almost nonexistent. Rather, Asian Americans appear to be more concerned with expressing ethnic solidarity.

In this respect, the widely publicized 1996 campaign finance scandal involving John Huang and Charlie Trie further twisted an already distorted image. There is, to be sure, evidence that Asian-American donors do try to influence politicians through campaign contributions. While there continues to be widespread dissatisfaction with how the 1996 events and commentary unfolded, there is little debate that large sums of money and Asian Americans were involved. These sums are outside the scope of this paper since they primarily involved donations to presidential campaigns and the Democratic National Committee. It may be that an elite group of Asian Americans is very strategic in these more national situations, or that various Asian-American elites who participate at this level are more sophisticatedly strategic political actors than the individual contributors we have examined. This claim remains to be tested. My point is that donors at the congressional level are a large and significant group, and that their actions fall squarely within the realm of symbolic expression, and not strategic investment. Overlooking this fact would be a serious oversight. Allowing the media to distort the image of Asian-American contributors is unwarranted and unsupportable by the hard facts.

Appendix

In the course of compiling the data for this project, I came upon a couple of other categories of Asian-American candidates. There is some argument to be made for including these candidates in the data set. However, the arguments against including them are more compelling. Table A-1 and A-2 list the campaigns of these Asian-American candidates who were left out of the analysis. Table A-1 lists Asian-American candidates who ran for office but did not report or did not receive any campaign contributions. As we can see from the elections results, none of these candidates was a very serious contender. Hence, there may be a separate story to be told, and an intriguing dynamic to unfold, but these candidates should not be considered as part of the main data set.

Table A-2 lists another set of candidates who are Asian American, but were also left out of the analysis. The candidates in Table A-2 differ from those in Table A-1 in two important ways. First, all of the candidates in Table A-2 received and reported campaign contributions. In some cases, the money raised was significant and far more than was raised by some of the candidates that were included in the analysis. However, these candidates were not included because of the second important difference that these candidates exhibit, that is, unlike the candidates in Table A-1, none of these candidates actually ran in an election. Hence, there is little reason to include the candidates listed in Table A-2 in the analyses. However, to be complete, I do list, in this appendix, both the aborted Asian American campaigns and the campaigns that did not raise any money.

Table A-1. Asian-American Candidates with No Reported Contributions

Candidate	Race	District	Year	% Asian In District	Primary Election Major Opponent	Vote %	General Election Major Opponent	Vote %
Homer Cheung (R)	House	GA-4	1978	1%	Uncontested	100%	Elliot H. Levitas	19.0%
Milton S. Takei (P&F)	House	CA-19	1978	3%	Uncontested	100%	Robert Lagomarsino	4.0%
Khushro Ghandi (Labor)	House	NY-37	1978	0.1%	Uncontested	100%	Henry J. Nowak	0.3%
Tod Hiro Mikuriya (Lib.)	House	CA-8	1980	8%	Uncontested	100%	Ronald Delums	5.0%
Echo Goto (R)	House	CA-29	1984	1%	Uncontested	100%	Augustus F. Hawkins	13.0%
Mas Odoi (R)†	House	CA-31	1984	8%	Henry C. Minturn	40.6%		
Ronald T. Shigeta (R)*	House	CA-31	1986	8%	Jack McMurray	31.3%		
Stephen P. Shao (I)	House	VA-2	1986	2%	None		Owen Pickett	8.6%
Eunice Sato (R)	House	CA-31	1990	11.5%	Uncontested	100%	Mervyn M. Dymally	33.0%
Elizabeth A. Nakano (P&F)+	House	CA-30	1992	21%	Maria Munoz	52.0%	Xavier Becerra	7.39%
Dianand Bhagwandin (R-C)	House	NY-6	1994	6%	Uncontested	100%	Floyd Flake	19%
John A. Furutani (R)	House	CA-26	1994	7%	Gary E.Forsch	15.6%		
Emma Wong Mar (P&F)*	House	CA-9	1994	16%			Ron Dellums	5%
Linh Dao (I)	House	CA-15	1995	11%	None		Tom Campbell	5%
Gene Hsiao (I)+†	House	TX-7	1996	6%‡	Robert R. "Randy" Sims, Jr.	58.9%	Bill Archer	2.1%
Norio Kushi (Natural Law)	House	VT-AL	1996	1%	Uncontested	100%	Bernie Sanders	0.3%
Lih Young (D)*	House	MD-8	1996	8%	Donald Mooers	7.5%		
Linh Dao (R)*	Senate	CA	1998	9.1%	Matt Fong	0.4%		
Krista Lieberg-Wong (Green)	House	CA-31	1998	22%	Uncontested	100%	Matthew Martinez	5.0%
Long Pham (R)*†	House	CA-45	1998	11%	Dana Rohrabacher	8.4%		

Data compiled from the *Almanac of American Politics* (1980–1998) and *America Votes* (1980–1998).
† Candidate contributed to his own campaign.
Linh Dao ran in a special election to fill the seat left vacant by Mineta's resignation.
* Candidate lost his/her primary election.
‡ 1994 figure. The 1996 figure was unavailable due to redistricting.

Table A-2. Aborted Campaigns of Asian-American Candidates

Candidate	Race	District	Year	Total Contribution		Asian Contribution			Ethnic Contributions			% Asian
				N	Amount	*N*	Amount	Percent	*N*	Amount	Percent	in district
Norman Mineta (D)	House	CA-15	1996	211	$49,358	123	$16,933	34.3%	103	$12,775	75.4%	11%
Lily Chen (D)	House	CA-30	1992	7	$5,800	7	$5,800	100%	6	$5,500	85.7%	21%
Michael Woo (D)		CA	1988	4	$2,700	1	$700	25%	1	$700	100%	
S. I. Hayakawa (R)	Senate	CA	1980	3	$650	0	0	0	0	0	0%	5%
———	Senate	CA	1982	78	$59,521	11	$9,500	14.1%	11	$9,500	100%	5%
S. B. Woo (D)	Senate	DE	1990	68	$32,945	66	$31,945	97.1%	66	$31,945	100%	1%
March Fong Eu (D)	Senate	CA	1988	214	$154,950	175	$125,950	81.78%	149	$107,950	85.1%	5%
Alfred Lui (I)	House	NY-12	1992	16	$6,116	15	$5,916	93.75%	15	$5,916	100%	20%
Chung Nguyen (D)	House	CA-46	1994	8	$8,000	8	$8,000	100%	8	$8,000	100%	12%

Data compiled from FEC records, the *Almanac of American Politics* (1980-1998) and *America Votes* (1980-1998).

Chapter 4

Continuity and Change: Latino Political Incorporation in California Since 1990[1]

Ricardo Ramírez and Luis Fraga

The increased presence of Latinos in the politics of California is undisputed. Major newspapers, important journals focusing on statewide politics, and scholarly analyses suggest that the most significant change in the politics of California since 1990 has been the importance of Latinos in their roles as residents, voters, and elected officials.[2] Latinos are now estimated to make up 35% of the

---

[1] This chapter is a much revised version of "Latino Political Incorporation in California, 1990–2000," which appeared in David López and Andrés Jiménez, eds., *Latinos and Public Policy in California: An Agenda for Opportunity* (Berkeley: Institute for Governmental Studies, 2003).

[2] See, for example, the range of issues covered by the following articles in *The California Journal*: James Carroll, "Courting California: Both Parties Lust after Those Golden Electoral Votes," *California Journal*, Vol. 23, No. 9 (September 1992): 433–36; Dale Maharidge, "Did 1992 Herald the Dawn of Latino Political Power?" *California Journal*, Vol. 24, No. 1 (January 1993): 15–18; Elizabeth López, and Eric Wahlgren, "The Latino Vote: The Lure of Four Million Ballots," *California Journal*, Vol. 25, No. 11 (November 1994): 29–31; and Sherry Bebitch Jeffe, "Year of the Latino?" *California Journal*, Vol. 27, No. 10 (October 1996): 20. See also: Byran O. Jackson and Michael B. Preston, eds., *Racial and Ethnic Politics in California* (Berkeley: Institute of Governmental Studies, University of California, Berkeley, 1991); Aníbal Yáñez-Chávez, ed., *Latino*

California population, and it is estimated that they will be the largest ethnic and racial group in the state by 2016.[3] Exit polls conducted by the Cable News Network (CNN) estimate that Latinos constitute 19% of all Californians who voted in 2006, three times the percentage of Asian Americans and nearly five times the percentage of African-American voters.[4] Latino elected officials currently constitute 22.5% of all members of the state Assembly and 25% of the state Senate. Until recently, Cruz Bustamante, a Latino, was the two-term lieutenant governor. The current Speaker of the California State Assembly is Fabian Núñez. He is the longest-serving speaker since term limits took effect and is the third Latino to hold the post since 1996. These accomplishments are dramatic.

The changing nature of Latino politics in California gives rise to a number of important questions. Does the increased Latino presence reflect a fundamental shift in the distribution of political influence in California? What is the likelihood that the almost three-to-one disparity between population percentage and voter turnout in Latino communities will continue into the next decade? Has Latino nonelectoral civic participation increased at rates similar to increases in the likelihood of Latinos to vote? More Latinos are elected to state and local offices than ever before. How likely is it that this increased presence in state and local governments will translate into public policy that will serve the identified interests of Latino communities?

These questions have been the focus of much attention from journalists and scholars. Interestingly, both sets of analysts have reached similar conclusions regarding the electoral influence, representation, and policy benefits attained by Latinos during the period since 1990. Our review of major findings reveals the following:

- Latinos will continue to grow in their share of the California population.
- It is likely that this increased population growth, in combination with a sizeable increase within the next decade in the portion of the Latino population above age 18, will lead to Latinos continuing to grow as a major segment of the statewide electorate.
- Latinos are still substantially underregistered when compared to African-American and non-Latino white voters.

Politics in California (San Diego: Center for U.S.-Mexican Studies at the University of California, San Diego, 1996); Michael Preston, Bruce E. Cain, and Sandra Bass, eds., *Racial and Ethnic Politics in California* (Berkeley: Institute of Governmental Studies, University of California, Berkeley, 1998); and especially Harry P. Pachón, "Latino Politics in the Golden State: Ready for the 21st Century?" In *Racial and Ethnic Politics in California*, Volume Two, ed. Michael B. Preston, Bruce E. Cain, and Sandra Bass (Berkeley: Institute of Governmental Studies, University of California, Berkeley, 1998), 411–38.

[3] State of California, Department of Finance, Demographic Research Unit (http://www.dof.ca.gov/HTML/DEMOGRAP/Data/RaceEthnic/Population-00-50/RaceData_2000-2050.asp), last visited 08/25/07.

[4] Cable News Network, Voter News Service, 2006 Exit Poll Data (http://www.cnn.com/ELECTION/2006//pages/results/states/CA/S/01/epolls.0.html), last visited 08/25/07.

- Despite some contrary public comment, Latinos' propensity to register and vote as Democrats has grown since 1994.
- Of 17 statewide races for president, U.S. senator, and governor since 1990, Democrats have won 13. In seven of these races (54%) the racial and ethnic vote was the margin of victory. In two of seven races (28%), the Latino vote alone was the margin of victory.
- The increased presence of Latinos since 1990 in both houses and major parties of the state legislature has been consistent.
- Although Latinos now exercise a greater level of electoral and legislative influence than at any time in the history of the state, it is unclear whether public policies have been enacted that directly benefit Latino communities. These findings suggest a number of strategies that should be pursued by those interested in increasing the political incorporation of Latinos in California:
- Campaigns must be conducted to encourage noncitizen Latinos to naturalize as soon as they are eligible.
- Every effort must be made to encourage Latinos over age 18 to register and vote.
- Youth between the ages of 14 and 17 are an extremely important subset of the California Latino population that should be the focus of much political socialization. By 2015, this segment of the Latino population is likely to represent the largest percentage increase in the Latino electorate ever.
- Latino legislators must continue to maximize their influence within their respective parties. Such influence may be key to developing the necessary coalition support to enact legislation favorable to Latino communities.
- The magnitude of Latino legislative influence at state levels must be used to leverage state resources to better serve local governments and to leverage collaborative relationships with major holders of private capital at both state and local levels.

To examine systematically the available literature on Latino politics in the last decade, we organize this chapter into three parts. First, we outline a multidimensional model of political incorporation that distinguishes among electoral influence, representation, and policy benefit. In this model we use the analytical dimensions of access, opportunity, and institutionalization to examine the evolution and current state of Latino political incorporation. Second, we review published research, essays presented at major academic conferences, and original data to determine the empirical evidence of the increased presence of Latinos in California politics. We are able to assess the current state of knowledge regarding Latino politics. We find some major omissions in our understanding of Latino politics in the state. Primary among them is the linkage of increased political incorporation to the enactment of public policy favorable to Latino communities. Third, we suggest areas of future research and possible strategies to further enhance the political incorporation of Latinos in the state.

Conceptualizing Political Incorporation

Before summarizing major findings and conclusions, we develop a multidimensional conceptualization of political incorporation to serve as a guide in assessing the changing nature of Latino politics in California. This conceptual framework provides a way of deepening our understanding of the progress made by Latinos over the past 10 years.

Political incorporation can be defined as the extent to which self-identified group interests are articulated, represented, and met in public policymaking.[5] Political incorporation has three *descriptive* dimensions: electoral, representational, and policy-based. The electoral dimension captures the presence and potential influence of Latinos in affecting politics through their increased proportion of the general population, of U.S. citizens, of registered voters, of voters who turn out, and of bloc voters. The representational dimension, by comparison, focuses on the presence of Latinos in elected positions in state and local governments, their presence within majority and minority legislative delegations, and their presence in positions of formal policymaking, such as Assembly speaker, committee chairs, and partisan leadership. The policy dimension refers to the extent to which Latinos receive specified benefits from public policy. Although the policy dimension can be understood largely in procedural terms, such as policies giving greater access to educational or job opportunities, we suggest that this dimension must also include indicators of material condition such as median income, poverty rates, educational levels, and homeownership rates.[6]

Analytically, it is necessary to know the precise sources of increases in electoral influence. For example, increased presence in the population can lead to increased voter registration. This direct relationship, however, very much depends upon whether the population increase is due to immigration or birth of native citizens. If it is due to immigration, the increased presence in the population will translate into increased voter registration only as mediated through the processes of naturalization. Relatedly, even if most of the population increase is due to native births, it is important to know when substantial numbers of youth are likely to be age 18 and thus eligible to register and vote.

Similar questions can be posed regarding the increased representation of Latinos in legislative arenas. Although numbers have increased dramatically, are these representatives members of the majority party in legislatures? Have these Latino elected officials been chosen from districts where Latinos comprise majorities of

---

[5] This definition is based upon Rufus P. Browning, Dale Rogers Marshall, and David H. Tabb, *Protest Is Not Enough: The Struggle of Blacks and Hispanics for Equality in Urban Politics* (Berkeley: University of California Press, 1984), 25. They state: "The concept of political incorporation concerns the extent to which group interests are effectively represented in policymaking."

[6] For a more extended discussion of policy responsiveness, see Luis Ricardo Fraga, "Racial and Ethnic Politics in a Multicultural Society," Charles E. Gilbert Lecture, Swarthmore College, Swarthmore, Pennsylvania, November 16, 2000.

the population or the electorate? Are more of these public officials male or female?

Specifying increases in electoral influence and representation is, in and of itself, important. It is even more important, however, to know if such increases have translated into policy benefits for Latino communities. Has the increased presence of state legislators led to the making of public policy favorable to Latino communities at state levels? Has the increased presence of city council members and members of school boards led to policy that serves the self-identified interests of Latino communities? Understanding policy benefits is an analytical task fraught with challenges. Which policy areas should be examined? How should the analyst distinguish among potential benefits in issue articulation, agenda setting, and gains in laws and ordinances that are formally enacted? How does one distinguish analytically between policy benefits in legislatures and benefits made though the statewide referendum process? To address these and related questions we specify three distinct *analytical* dimensions of political incorporation in each of the arenas of electoral influence, representation, and policy benefit. The three analytical dimensions are access, opportunity, and institutionalization.[7]

In electoral influence, access refers to the extent to which Latinos are a potential component of the electorate. This potential can be driven by population growth and by naturalization of immigrants. A low level of access would occur when the population growth of the native-born is small or declining, or when naturalization rates are low. High levels of access would be obtained through high birth rates of the native-born and high naturalization rates among immigrants. Opportunity, by contrast, is more directly related to acquisition of the franchise. High levels of opportunity to influence the electoral process occur when the percentages of Latinos eligible to register are high or when actual registration rates grow substantially. The most important indicator of high electoral opportunity exists when Latinos constitute sizeable portions of the statewide electorate. Institutionalization at the electoral level occurs when Latinos vote together as a sizeable bloc for successful candidates and positions on statewide referenda. High rates of population growth, naturalization, registration, and voting do not necessarily translate into increased electoral influence if Latino voters do not vote as a sizeable bloc that is able to influence the outcome of elections at state and local levels. Among the primary determinants of the influence of the Latino vote is the extent to which

[7] This analytical framework builds upon Hero's concept of "two-tiered pluralism." See Rodney E. Hero, *Latinos and the U.S. Political System* (Philadelphia: Temple University Press, 1992). Hero distinguishes between political gains and material gains. Our framework more precisely specifies the nature of political gains and material gains. We suggest that it is important to distinguish the precise levels of gain in each of the three descriptive dimensions of electoral, legislative, and policy influence. These three dimensions can be mutually reinforcing. They can, however, also be quite independent of one another.

other major segments, especially non-Latino whites,[8] vote as a bloc in opposition to Latino preferences. High levels of electoral institutionalization occur when Latino voters vote as a bloc, vote for winning candidates and issues, and do both with consistency over time.

Representation can also be understood in terms of the three analytical dimensions. Access occurs to the extent that there are open or competitive seats in state and local government that Latino candidates have a reasonable chance of winning. High levels of opportunity exist when Latinos win elective office in substantial percentages relative to the number of other candidates. These high levels of opportunity are especially apparent when these officials are elected from constituencies where Latinos constitute a sizeable component, if not majority, of the population and/or electorate and cast most of their votes for the victorious candidate. Legislative institutionalization occurs when Latinos constitute a sizeable portion of a legislature, when they constitute a sizeable portion of the majority party, and when they hold influential positions in the larger legislative process such as Assembly Speaker, committee chairs, and party positions.

Policy benefit can also be understood in terms of access, opportunity, and institutionalization. Greater access in policy gains occurs when issues of concern to Latino communities are addressed with greater frequency and consistency in legislative arenas. This articulation of issues is most likely to come from newly elected Latino officials whose electoral constituencies include sizeable numbers of Latino voters. Policy opportunity exists to the extent that laws and ordinances are enacted that seriously consider the needs and interests of Latino communities. These laws and ordinances can deal with any of a number of issues ranging from employment to education to health care. Such legislation need not target Latinos explicitly. A broad program to increase access to health care for all uninsured Californians, for example, can especially help Latinos, who constitute a very large percentage of the uninsured in the state. Policy institutionalization occurs to the extent that Latinos experience an improvement in their material well-being as a result of enacted policies. These gains must not be temporary, and the policies that directly contribute to these gains must have a high likelihood of not being removed by subsequent legislatures.

Our model of political incorporation suggests that electoral influence, representation, and policy benefit can exist in a direct positive relationship. A gain in the first dimension can lead to gains in the other two. However, the model does not require that this be the case and is designed, in fact, to allow us to identify various patterns of clustering among the three dimensions. Although electoral influence may be considerable, the election of public officials who are the first choice candidates of Latino voters may not result. Gains in legislative representation, by contrast, can occur without a sizeable increase in Latino voters. This can happen, for example, as a result of changes in the boundaries of representational

---

[8] Non-Latino whites refers to voters who choose to identify themselves as non-Latino whites. Throughout the remainder of this essay, "white" will be used to refer to non-Latino whites.

districts. Latino candidates might also be more competitive in open seats created by term limits. Similarly, increases in electoral influence and representation need not lead to policy benefits. Increased representation can lead to the development of diverse coalitions of popular and legislative support for a specific proposal. The key to such support, however, is likely to be the identification of mutual self-interest more than legislative influence alone. What, then, are the patterns of electoral influence, representation, and policy benefit for Latinos from since 1990?

The Growing Presence of Latinos in California Politics

The academic research devoted to the growing presence of Latinos in California politics is not extensive. In this work, emphasis is placed on systematically examining population growth, naturalization, voter registration, and turnout. Most work focuses on Latino political influence at the statewide level. Only a few studies examine their presence in local governments. No research systematically examines the influence that Latino legislators have on enacting public policy at any level.

Electoral Influence

The substantial population growth of Latinos is often noted as one of the major changes in California since 1990. As Figure 1 demonstrates, the California Department of Finance estimates that the Latino population grew from 26% of the state's population in 1990 to 35.4% in 2006. By comparison, the Asian population grew from 9% to 12% over the same time period and the African-American population has declined slightly over this period. Of special note, the white population declined from 57% of the population in 1990 to an estimated 43.9% in 2006. Over the period 1990–2006, Latinos experienced the largest growth in the California population of any major racial and ethnic group.

More recently the California Department of Finance estimates that the net increase in the Latino population from 2000 to 2006 (i.e., natural births plus migration, minus deaths) was 2,169,580. Of this number, however, 1,898,275 were from births, and only 271,305 were from migration or immigration.[9] There is a consensus among demographers and social scientists that most of the Latino population growth since 1990 can be attributed to births, not immigration.[10] The implications

---

[9] Authors' estimates based on Department of Finance population and net birth estimates. (See http://www.dof.ca.gov/HTML/DEMOGRAP/ReportsPapers/Projections/Births/NetBirth.asp), last visited 08/25/07.

[10] David Hayes-Bautista, *La Nueva California: Latinos in the Golden State* (Berkeley: University of California Press, 2004); Roberto Suro and Jeffery Passel, *The Rise of the Second Generation: Changing Patterns in Hispanic Population Growth* (Washington

Figure 1. California Population Distribution 1990–2006

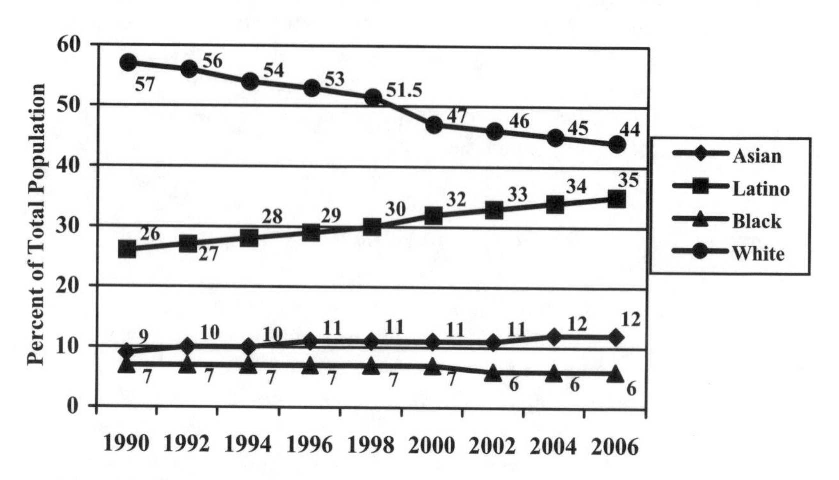

Source: California Department of Finance.

for the California electorate are clear. When these younger Latino Californians reach age 18, they could represent a sizeable increase in the voting-age population. Given the above population projections, a key year may be 2016, when many of these youth will reach voting age.

According to the Current Population Survey, there are 8,127,000 Latino adults in California. Of these, 4,433,000 (55%) were citizens. Latino registered voters totaled 2,455,000 (55%) of all adult Latino citizens. If all Latino adult citizens registered to vote, they could constitute as much as 31% of all registered voters in the state. While the percent of Latino registered voters is not equal to their share of the population, there has been a noticeable increase in the number of Latinos registered to vote, and this gained the media's attention in the recent years. A study by the Field Institute reported that between 1990 and 2000, there was an increase of one million Latino registered voters in California.[11] This increase accounts for just over 90% of all newly registered voters in the last 10 years. During the same period of time there was a net decrease in white non-Hispanic registered voters of about 100,000. Whites now constitute 63% of the state's registered voters, down from 79% in 1990.

D.C., The Pew Hispanic Center, 2003; Dowell Myers, *Immigrants and Boomers: Forging a New Social Contract for the Future of America*; Michael Alvarez and Tara L. Butterfield, "Citizenship and Political Representation in Contemporary California," Social Science Working Paper 1041, California Institute of Technology, Pasadena, July 1998.

[11] "California's Expanding Latino Electorate," *California Opinion Index*, Volume 1, 2000. The calculations in this paragraph are derived from estimates in Table 1, p. 2.

Figure 2 provides estimates for Latino voter registration and turnout from 1990 to 2004. Interestingly, patterns of voter registration reveal that although the total number of Latinos registered to vote has increased, the percent of Latino citizens who are registered fluctuates from just over 50% to 60% with registration rates in the mid-50% range for most of these years. What has dramatically increased, and been sustained since 1992, is a very high percentage of Latino registered voters reporting having voted on Election Day. From a low of 69% of Latino registered voters turning out in 1990 to a high of 85% of registered voting having cast ballots in 2004. 2002 is clearly an anomaly; this was a year when there were downturns in voting among all groups.

What is the percentage of the overall electorate in California represented by Latino voters? These data are critical for understanding whether changes in rates of turnout disrupt the overall patterns of Latino presence in the electorate. According to the Current Population Survey voter supplements from 1990 to 2004, the Latino share of the California electorate varied from 9% in 1990 to 16% in 2004. Using these estimates and 2006 exit polls conducted by the *Los Angeles Times* and CNN, Figure 3 provides estimates for 1990 to 2006. Latino voters nearly doubled their percentage of the California electorate from 9% in 1990 to 16% in 2004 and 2006. It is apparent that this trend has been gradual and consistent. The trend for African-American voters is distinct. They have remained relatively stable at 5–8% of the California electorate from 1990 to 2006. Asian-American voters have increased their percentage of the statewide electorate. They were 4% of the statewide electorate between 1990 and 1994 and more than doubled to 9% in 2002 and 2004, but saw a slight drop in 2006 to 7%. These changes are mirrored by a sizeable decrease in the presence of the white electorate over the same period. In 1990, they constituted 80% of the California statewide electorate. In 2004, they represented 65%, with a slight recovery to 69% in 2006. The overall decrease, nevertheless, has been gradual and sustained.

Not only is it important to note the increase in Latino voters but more notably that the majority of California's current Latino voters registered after 1994. There is evidence that this mobilization of voters was spurred by the contentious political context when three race-targeting initiatives were passed. The profile of those who registered between 1994 and 2000 is distinct. The Field Poll noted that the profile of new Latino voters from the mid 1990s to 2000 were distinct from voters before that time period. Of particular significance was that 50% were under the age of 30, 44% were born outside of the United States, 42% resided in Los Angeles County, 38% had less than a high-school education, and 34% had incomes of less than $20,000 per year. While the socio-economic profile of these voters was indeed younger, with lower levels of education and income and increased rates of registration by naturalized citizens, it is important to note that there were some significant similarities. It is estimated that 59% of these recently registered voters registered as Democrats, and only 18% registered as Republicans. This pattern is similar to that of Latinos who registered prior to 1994, of whom 61% registered as Democrats and 24% as Republicans.

Figure 2. Latino Registration and Turnout, 1990–2004

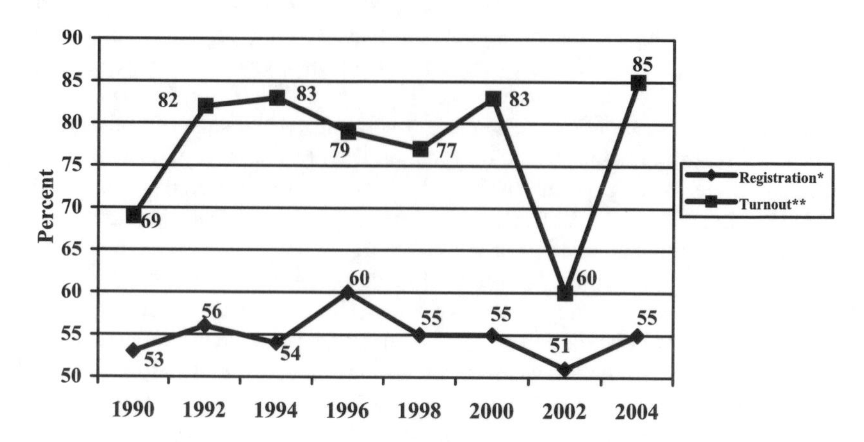

Source: Current Population Survey 1990–2004.

*Latino voter registration is the number of Latinos registered to vote divided by the total number of citizen voting-age Latinos eligible to vote.

** Latino voter turnout is calculated by dividing the total number of Latinos who voted by the total number of eligible Latino citizens.

Figure 3. Share of California Electorate, 1990–2006

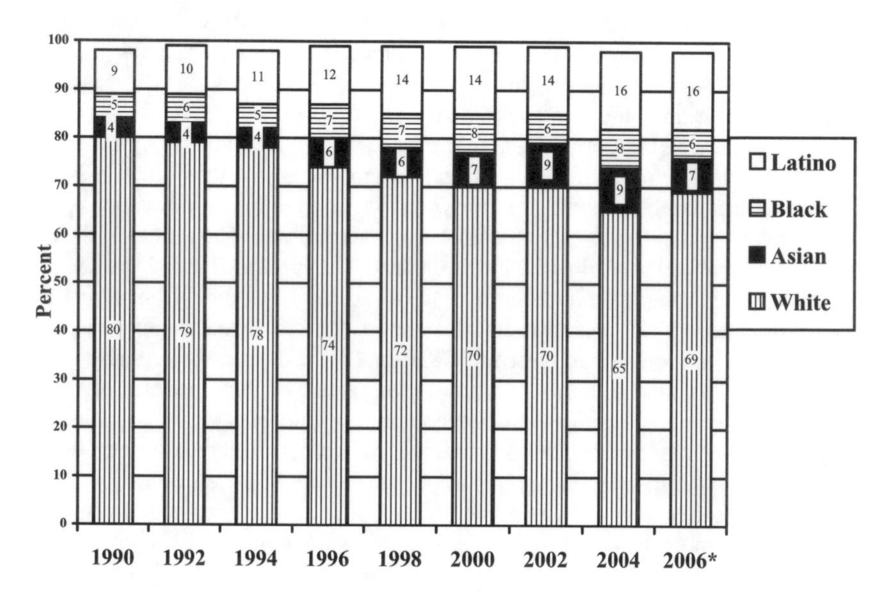

Source: CPS Voter Supplements, 1990–2004.

* Authors' estimates based on 2006 CNN and *Los Angeles Times* exit polls.

Since 2000, there has been an additional increase in Latinos registering to vote. Recent evidence suggests that indeed the profile of the Latino electorate is not static; it has changed since 2000. A comparison between those who first registered to vote before and those who registered after 2000 reveals some interesting differences. While Latino men were only about 44% of the Latino electorate who registered before 2000, there is now a near 50–50 split between Latino men and Latinos who first registered to vote after 2000. (Other notable distinctions are that just under 22% of those registered before 2000 are currently single, but 50% of those who registered since 2000 are single. The influence of immigrants is noticeable. While 72% of those who first registered to vote before 1994 were born in the U.S. or Puerto Rico, only 43% of those who first registered to vote between 1994 and 1999 were U.S.-born. Similarly, only 47% of those who first registered to vote since 2000 were born in the U.S. Interestingly, even though there is a continued preference for the Democratic Party among the most recently registered, the partisan advantage by Democrats that was noted by the Field Poll in 2000 appears to be fading. Fifty-nine percent of those who registered to vote before 2000 indicate that they are registered as Democrats. This has dropped significantly among those who registered since 2000 to 42.5%. The gains were not necessarily witnessed by the Republican Party, as only 18% registered Republican. Instead, 39.6% of the most recent registration cohort either picked a third party or no party at all.[12] At present, 58.2% of all registered Latinos are registered as Democrats and 22.1% as Republicans.[13] This is in contrast to the overall California population; in 2006, 42.5% of the state's electorate was registered as Democrat and 34.3% as Republican.[14] Thus, the newest cohort of Latino voters has not drastically changed the aggregate partisan registration patterns, but there is a potential that the once reliable advantage by Democrats, may be less reliable. Much of this will depend on the voting preferences of "independents" and those who decline to register with a political party.

The growth in the Latino population is significant and is likely to continue to increase. Similarly, as demonstrated in Figure 2 there is a consistent trend of Latinos registering and turning out to vote. This trend contributed to the fact that Latinos constituted a larger share of the California electorate in the last election than ever before. Given the partisan preferences of Latinos, does this suggest that Latinos have become an increasingly significant vote in determining the outcome of statewide elections?

In 1996, Guerra and Fraga developed a model of the "conditions for an effective statewide Latino electorate."[15] These authors argued that the influence of the Latino electorate would be enhanced to the extent that a set of contextual and strategic conditions were met. Contextual conditions referred to circumstances that

---

[12] Authors' calculations based on the Latino National Survey (2007).

[13] NALEO Election Handbook 2006.

[14] California Secretary of State. Statement of the Vote 2006.

[15] Fernando Guerra and Luis Ricardo Fraga, "Theory, Reality, and Perpetual Potential: Latinos in the 1992 California Elections," in *Ethnic Ironies: Latino Politics in the 1992 Elections*, ed. Rodolfo O. de la Garza and Louis DeSipio (Boulder, Colo: Westview Press, 1996), 132.

were not in the direct control of Latino voters and leaders. Among these conditions were competitive elections, the minimization of backlash, opportunities to elect Latino candidates, and the presence of ballot issues of particular concern to Latino voters (pp. 132–33). Strategic conditions are much more in the control of Latino voters and their leaders. These conditions are subdivided into those that are voter-focused and those that are elite-focused. Voter-focused conditions include voting as a bloc and effective voter-mobilization strategies on Election Day. Elite-focused conditions include voter registration and naturalization drives, substantive advocacy for Latino interests during campaign strategy sessions, "unity and intensity of endorsement by Latino political elites, organizations, and media," and community-based "organizational development and coordination" (pp. 134–37).[16]

The data in Figure 4 show the varying role Latinos have had in affecting major elections for president, U.S. senator, and governor from 1992 to 2004. These data specify the percentage of the statewide vote represented by each racial and ethnic partisan voting block. This method combines the size of a group of voters in the statewide electorate, based on Current Population Survey estimates, with the extent to which that vote is cast as a bloc for each candidate according to the *Los Angeles Times* Poll. How often were Latinos an effective statewide electorate since 1990?

An interesting pattern emerges in the cases when Latinos were critical in determining the outcome of statewide elections during this period. For example, Latinos were an essential component of Barbara Boxer's senatorial election in 1992. Boxer, the Democratic candidate, lost the white vote to her opponent. She would not have been elected senator in 1992 if it were not for the vote provided by Latino, African-American, and Asian-American voters. [17] The situation was repeated in Senator Feinstein's 1994 re-election campaign. White voters split in favor of her opponent. Voters of color represented 29% of her statewide total. Latinos comprised 15.7% of Feinstein's statewide support, more than the combined support by African Americans and Asian Americans (12.9%); Feinstein would not have won her re-election without the support of Latino voters.

This pattern of Latino voters representing the largest bloc of voters of color for successful Democratic candidates appears in the presidential election of 1996 and in both the senatorial election of 1998. Because of the split in the white vote, Clinton would not have won California in 1996 without the support of communities of color. Latino voters provided President Clinton with 18.2% of his statewide vote; African Americans provided him with 12.3%; and Asian Americans provided 6.44%. By comparison, white voters provided him with 63% of his vote.

[16] Guerra reclassifies a number of these conditions as external and internal in Fernando Guerra, "Latino Politics in California: The Necessary Conditions for Success," in *Racial and Ethnic Politics in California*, Volume Two, ed. Michael B. Preston, Bruce E. Cain, and Sandra Bass (Berkeley: Institute of Governmental Studies, University of California, Berkeley, 1998), 439–52.

[17] In the cases of both Bill Clinton and Dianne Feinstein, they each received such an overwhelming share of the white vote that the votes of communities of color were insignificant in determining the outcome of their respective elections.

Figure 4. Electoral Influence in California Races, 1990–2004

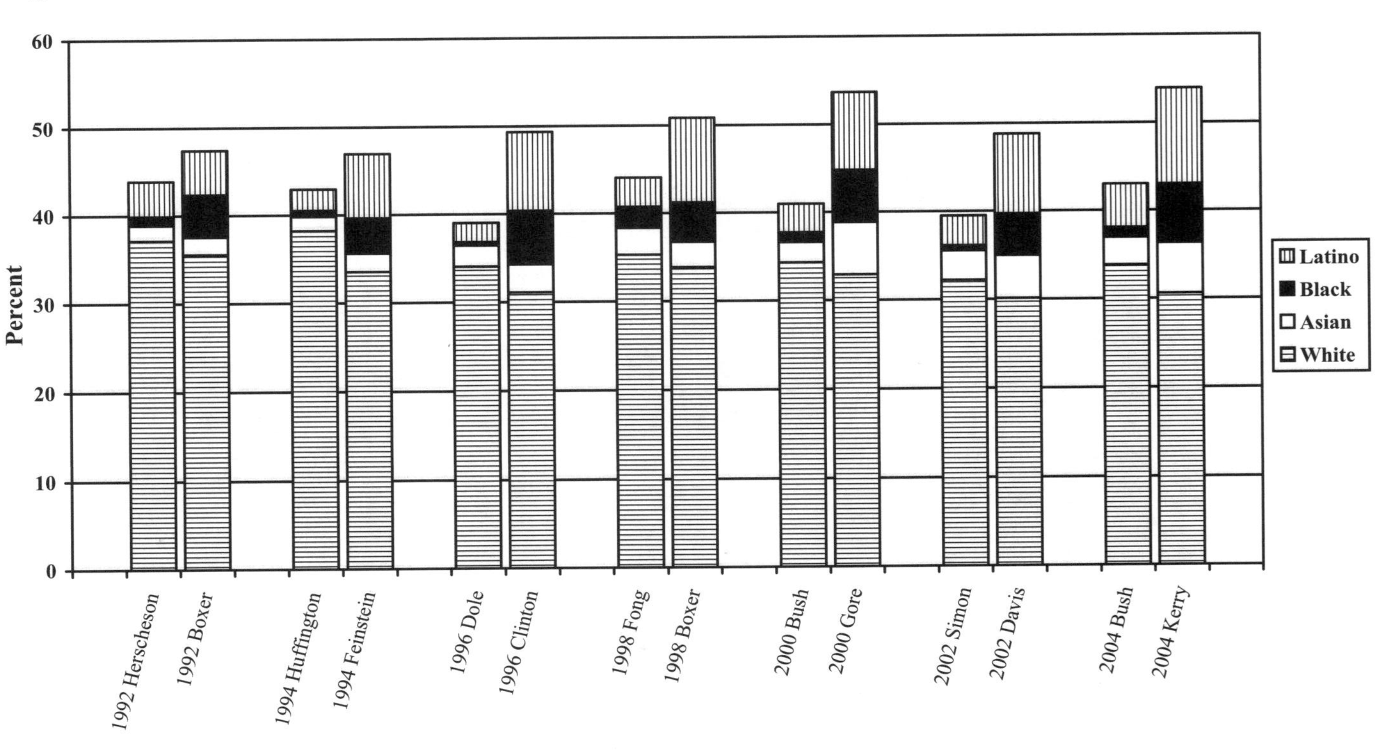

Source: *Los Angeles Times* Exit Poll, 1992–2004 and CPS Voter Supplements 1992–2004.

This was the first time that racial and ethnic minorities have comprised at least one-third of the winning candidate's support. Similarly, in 1998, voters of color provided incumbent Senator Barbara Boxer with important components of their margins of victory. Boxer won a majority of the votes of all racial and ethnic segments of the California electorate, but would have lost the election without the support from communities of color.[18] Latinos provided her with a full 19% of her statewide vote.

The pattern of Latinos comprising the largest portions of the votes from communities of color for successful Democratic candidates statewide was again evident in 2000. The votes of communities of color were critical to Al Gore's margin of victory in the presidential race. As stated earlier, Gore did not receive a majority of the votes cast by whites, but he did receive a majority of the votes cast by Asians, African Americans, and Latinos. Of these groups, Latinos comprised the largest percentage of the statewide total: a full 18.3%.

From 1990 to 2006, 17 elections were held for governor, U.S. senator, and president. Democrats have won 13 of these races. In seven of these 13 (54%) Latino voters were significant contributors to the winning Democratic candidates. Three of these nine successful Democratic candidates (i.e., one-third) would not have won without the Latino vote. Since 1990 Latino voters utilized their role as the largest bloc of communities of color and growing percentage of the California electorate to vote consistently as a majority bloc in favor of Democratic candidates. The report by the Field Institute in 2000 confirms estimates that the "net edge Latinos gave Democrats in overall vote" grew from +0.3% of the overall statewide vote in 1990 to +8.5% in the 1998 gubernatorial election.[19]

To summarize major research findings regarding access, opportunity, and institutionalization of electoral influence will synthesize our argument: Latinos steadily increased their electoral influence from 1990 to 2006. Population growth continued, and although immigration and migration continue to be important factors contributing to population growth, most of the increase in the Latino population since 1990 was due to native births. This fact bodes well for the Latino electorate. Younger Latinos, already citizens, can constitute a sizeable portion of the statewide electorate. These Latinos will not have to go through the complex processes of naturalization. Access by Latinos to electoral influence has grown over this 10-year period. In a similar fashion, the number of Latinos who are eligible to vote, who register, and who vote has increased considerably. Nonetheless, only half of eligible Latino citizens are registered to vote. Although Latino eligibility, registration, and turnout rates are still below those of whites, the magnitude of the difference has decreased significantly. Opportunity to influence elections, therefore, has increased substantially. Last, the institutionalization of electoral influence, when understood as the propensity of Latino registered voters not only to turn out, but to vote as a bloc, is increasingly critical to statewide Democratic mar-

---

[18] Communities of color provided Boxer with just over one-third of the statewide vote that she received.

[19] "California's Expanding Latino Electorate," Field Institute, Volume 1, 2000, p. 6.

gins of victory. Despite the increasing diversity within the Latino community represented by differences in country of origin, naturalization compared to native birth, and growing numbers of Latinos becoming more educated and middle class, Latinos still vote for major Democratic candidates in substantial numbers. For all of these candidates, Latino voters represent the largest portion of the margin of victory received from communities of color.

The growing institutionalization of Latino statewide electoral influence, however, has had its limits. A consistent white bloc vote against the preferences of overwhelming majorities of Latino voters was the primary reason that Proposition 187 was approved in 1994, as were Propositions 209 in 1996 and Proposition 227 in 1998. Each of these propositions affected Latino communities directly.[20] The data in Table 1 demonstrate the support ethnic and racial subgroups of the California electorate provided for these propositions. Figure 5 displays the way in which the combination of the size and preferences of the white vote led to the enactment of each proposition. Interestingly, the block vote by white voters on these propositions is similar to the distribution that gave Pete Wilson his gubernatorial re-election victory in 1994 and elected and re-elected Arnold Schwarzenegger in 2003 and 2006 respectively.[21] Tolbert and Hero, in "Race/Ethnicity and Direct Democracy: An Analysis of California's Illegal Immigration Initiative," point to the importance of an ethnic and racial context at the county level in understanding the magnitude of white support for Proposition 187. Ramírez improves upon this contextual analysis by focusing at the level of Assembly districts in his examination of voting on Proposition 209.[22] These contextual factors enrich our understanding of how a consistent white bloc vote limited the statewide electoral influence of Latinos.

Unfortunately, research examining the electoral influence of Latinos in local elections is scant. Although it is well-known that more Latinos serve in city coun-

---

[20] Proposition 187 limited the access that undocumented workers had to public education, social services, and health care. It also imposed state penalties for the use, forging, and distribution of false residency documents. Proposition 209 severely limited the use of affirmative-action programs. It outlawed the use of race and ethnicity in admissions to state colleges and universities, as well as in the awarding of contracts by state agencies and substate governments. Proposition 227 effectively eliminated the use of bilingual instruction in California public schools. Under this law, bilingual instruction was limited to one year for all students, regardless of language ability. Parents could petition for exceptions.

[21] Tolbert and Hero report that the correlation between county-level support for Proposition 187 and vote for Governor Pete Wilson was .85 (Caroline J. Tolbert and Rodney E. Hero, "Race/Ethnicity and Direct Democracy: An Analysis of California's Illegal Immigration Initiative," *The Journal of Politics*, Vol. 58, No. 3 (August 1996): 806–18.

[22] Ricardo Ramírez, "The Changing Landscape of California Politics, 1990–2000," unpublished doctoral dissertation, Stanford University, 2002.

Table 1. Support for Statewide Propositions, 1992–98

	Proposition 187		Proposition 209		Proposition 227	
	Yes	No	Yes	No	Yes	No
Latinos	23	77	24	76	37	63
Black	47	53	26	74	48	52
Asian	47	53	39	61	57	43
White	63	37	63	37	67	33
All	57	43	54	44	61	39

Source: *Los Angeles Times* Poll 1994–98.

Figure 5. Latino Electoral Influence in Statewide Ballot Propositions, 1992–98

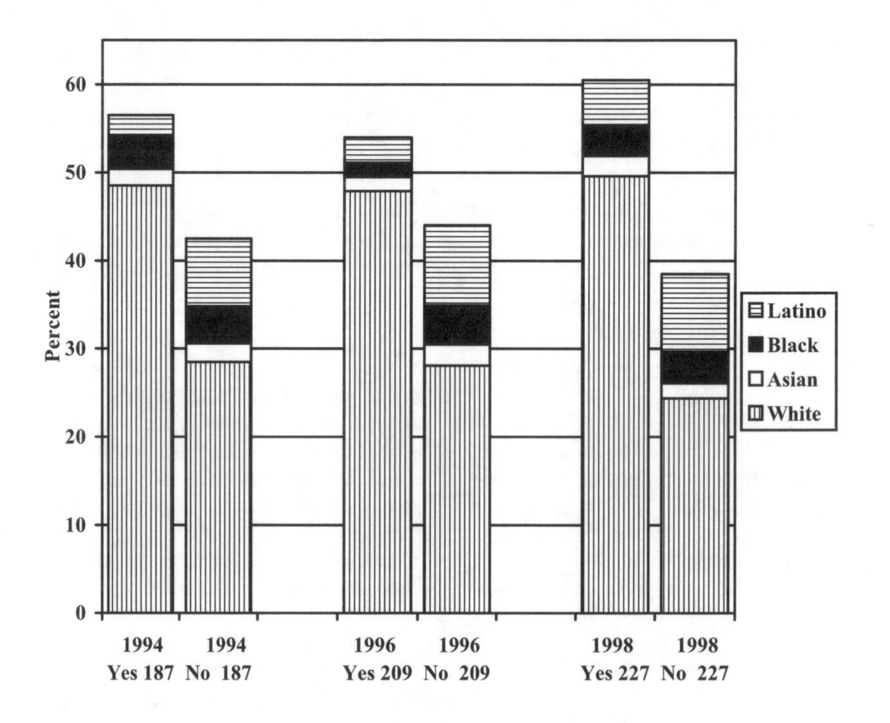

Source: *Los Angeles Times* exit polls 1992 and CNN exit polls 1994–1998.

cils, county boards of supervisors, and school boards than ever before,[23] no one study has examined systematically the longitudinal patterns of voting, and resulting legislative representation, in substate levels of government. This is a glaring omission in the scholarly and other analytical literature.

Representation

The legislative reapportionment and related redistricting that followed the 1990 and 2000 U.S. Censuses provided new opportunities for Latinos to elect representatives to Congress, the state Senate, and the state Assembly. Guerra and Fraga in "Theory, Reality, and Perpetual Potential: Latinos in the 1992 California Elections," note that throughout the 1980s, Latinos were able to elect three members of the U.S. Congress, three state senators, and four members of the state Assembly (p. 139). By the year 2000 the California congressional delegation added two additional Latinos and as of 2006 there are now seven Latinos members of Congress from California. In other words, since 1990, the number of Latinos in the California congressional delegation has more than doubled from three to seven.

The reapportionment of the state legislature in 1992 and 2002 has also led to more opportunities for Latino representation through the creation of more majority Latino population seats in the state the Senate and the Assembly to reflect the state's demographics. Examination of Figure 6 reveals that the number of Latinos in the state Senate increased from three in 1990 to four in 1996. This increased to seven in 1998, nine in 2002, and 10 in 2004. At present, Latinos comprise 25% of the state Senate, with the largest percentage increase occurring between 1996 and 1998. The increases in the number of Latino representatives in the state Assembly have been impressive since 1990. As indicated in Figure 6, four Latinos were elected to the state Assembly in 1990, seven in 1992, 10 in 1994, 14 in 1996, 17 in 1998, and 20 in 2000.[24] There are currently 18 Latinos in the state Assembly. They comprise 22.5% of the members of the state Assembly. This represents a 450% increase in the presence of Latinos in the state Assembly. How likely is it that this level of Latino representation in the Assembly will be maintained? What explains the drop in the number of elected officials from the 20 in 2000 to the current 18?

These questions are partly answered by examining levels of Latino voter registration in all 80 Assembly districts since 1992. We classify Assembly districts into three categories: "safe Latino," "Latino opportunity," and "occasional Latino." This classification was determined by the percent of Latino voter registra-

[23] Fernando Guerra, "Latino Politics in California: The Necessary Conditions for Success," in *Racial and Ethnic Politics in California*, Volume Two (Berkeley: Institute of Governmental Studies, University of California, Berkeley, 1998), 442–43.

[24] The total number of Latinos elected to the Assembly in 2000 was 20 but soon after dropped to 19. In a special election held March 6, 2001, Assemblywoman Gloria Romero was elected to the state Senate seat formerly held by Hilda Solis, who won election to the U.S. Congress in 2000. Romero's former Assembly district was filled by Judy Chu.

Figure 6. Latinos in the State Legislature, 1990–2006

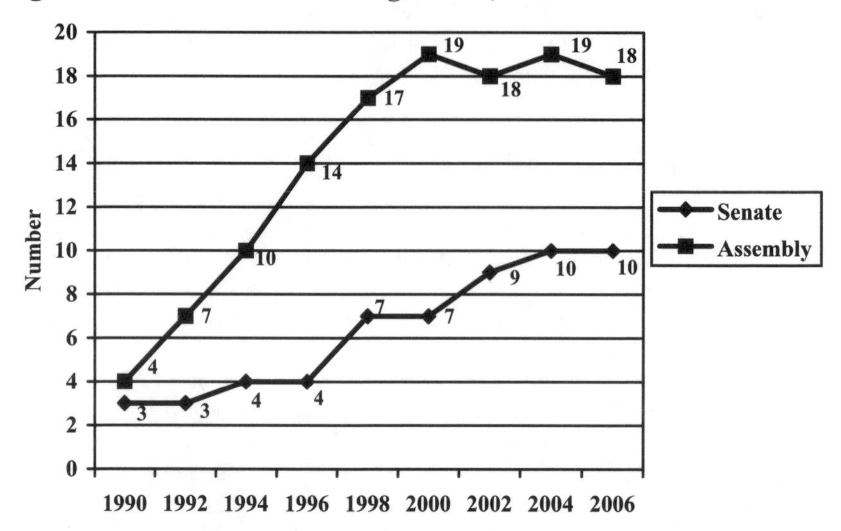

Source: California Secretary of State, Elections Division.

tion in each district. Figure 7 displays the number of "safe Latino" districts, or those with percentages of Latino voter registration at 40% and above of all registered voters in the district. Not surprisingly, a Latino member of the assembly was elected from all four such districts in 1992 and 1994. A similar pattern appears in 1996 where all eight 40%-and-above districts elected a Latino, as did all nine such districts in 1998. However, in 2000, this semblance of institutionalization of Latino representation in "safe Latino" districts changed. Antonio Villaraigosa endorsed outgoing Los Angeles City Councilwoman Jackie Goldberg for his former district. Rather than see this as a loss of a Latino seat, the Latino political elite recognized that while Latino descriptive representation would be one less, the Latino constituency in the district would still have substantive representation, given Goldberg's reputation. This sign of political maturity among Latino political elite was repeated shortly after the 2000 election. When Assemblymember Gloria Romero was victorious in her bid to fill the senate seat formerly held by Hilda Solis she endorsed a non-Latino, Judy Chu. In a special election to fill this vacancy, Chu was victorious in a district with over 40% Latino registered voters. Again, the political maturity of Latino political elite was evident in that it was understood that the Latino constituency would be well served by Chu, given her track record.[25]

[25] Interestingly, Judy Chu's district witnessed a reduction in Latino registered voters to somewhere in the mid 30% range. Since 2002, this district is no longer classified as a "Safe Latino" district because of the lower number of Latino registered voters.

Figure 7. Representation in "Safe Latino" Assembly Districts* by Election Year, 1992–2006

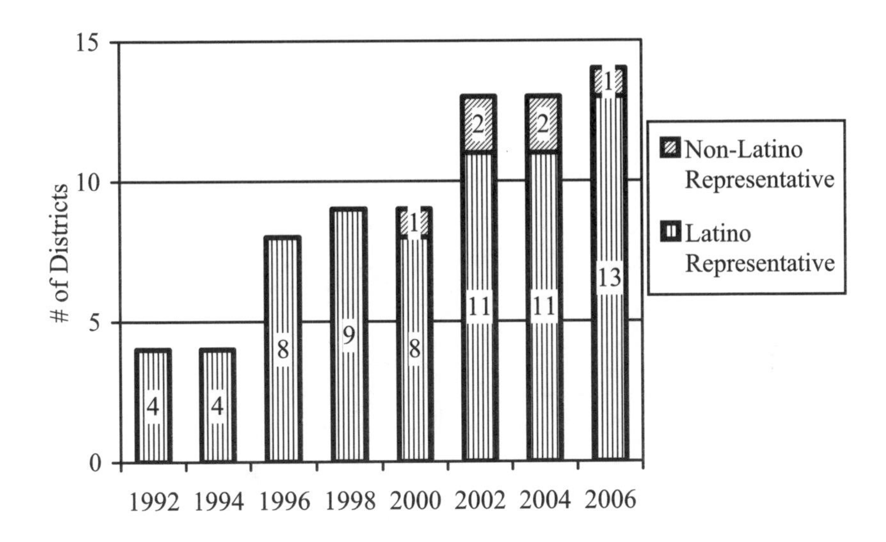

* Where Latinos comprise at least 40% of the registered voters.

In 2002, there was an increase in the number of "safe Latino" seats to 13 and 14 in 2006. The patterns of registration and representation displayed in Figure 7 suggest that 40% and above Latino registration in an Assembly district virtually guarantees the election of a Latino to office; near institutionalization of Latino representation follows. In 2004, two "safe Latino" seats were represented by non-Latinos and in 2004, there is only one of these seats that is not represented by a Latino.[26] Moreover, to date, all representatives in the "safe Latino" assembly districts have been Democrats.

As illustrated in Figure 8, there were 13 "Latino opportunity" Assembly districts, or those with 20–39% Latino voter registration, from 1992 to 1994, 12 such districts in 1996–1998, 17 in 2000, and 13 from 2002 to 2006. The number of

[26] Jackie Goldberg was re-elected in 2004, and a non-Latino was elected to fill the vacancy of Lou Correa's former assembly seat in Orange County when he was elected to serve in the county board of supervisors. Both seats are now represented by Latinos. The lone "Safe Latino" seat represented by a non-Latino is in the Inland Empire. Joe Baca, Jr., left his assembly seat after only one term in his unsuccessful bid to move up to the state senate. His brother, Jeremy Baca, lost the primary race to Wilmer Carter, former Rialto School Board member and longtime staffer for the late Congressman George Brown.

Figure 8. Representation in "Latino Opportunity" Assembly Districts* by Election Year, 1992–2006

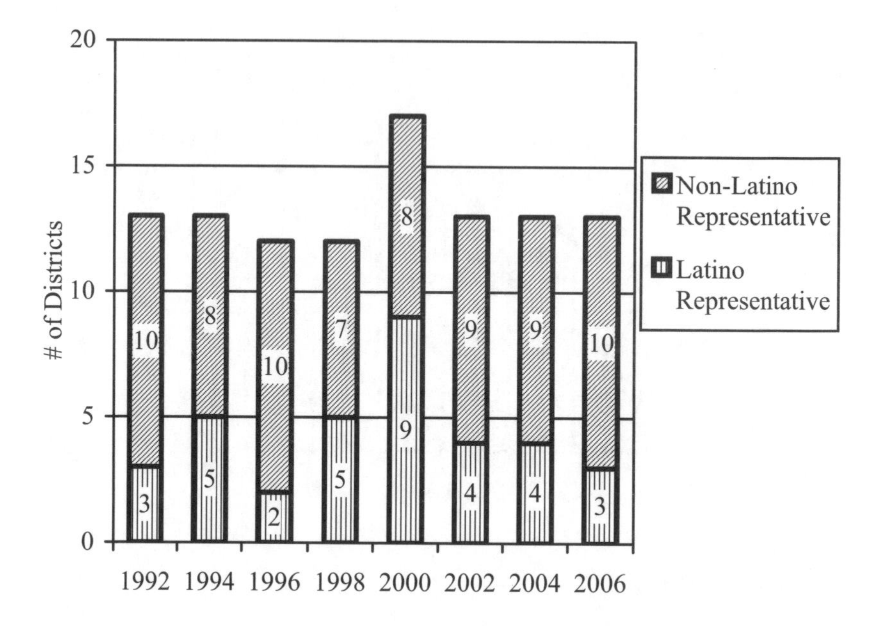

* Where Latinos comprise between 20 and 39% of the registered voters.

Latinos elected from such districts, however, has varied. Three Latinos were elected from these districts in 1992. Although five Latinos were elected from such districts in 1994, the number of Latino representatives from such districts dropped to two in 1996, and increased again to five in 1998.[27] In 2000, there were nine Latinos elected to these districts. This is the only time when more Latinos than non-Latinos have been elected to "Latino opportunity" districts. In 2002 and 2004 there were four Latinos elected to such districts, and in 2006 this dropped to three. There are two reasons why the number of Latinos elected to such districts varies. First, the loss of Latino descriptive representation in these districts is due to the inability of termed out Latinos to be replaced by a fellow Latino. However, some of the districts that were classified as "Latino opportunity" were re-classified as "safe Latino" districts as the percent of registered voters in the district who are Latino increased. Unlike "safe Latino" districts, "Latino opportunity" districts do not exhibit any clear pattern as to where Latinos will be successful. In fact, some

[27] One of the five in 1998 and two of the nine elected in 2000 were Republicans; all the others were Democrats. Since 2002 only one of the Latinos elected to these districts has been Republican.

of these districts have successfully replaced termed out Latinos with another Latino.

The pattern in "occasional Latino" Assembly districts, or those with 19% or less Latino registration, is distinct. No Latinos were elected from such districts in 1992, and only one was elected in 1994. Four were elected from such districts in 1996, three from 1998 through 2002, four in 2004, and two in 2006. One consistent pattern emerges in these "occasional Latino" districts: none of the Latino representatives has been replaced by another Latino after he or she left office. There is another significant point that should be raised. It initially appeared that Latino Republicans were more likely than Latino democrats to succeed in these districts as evidenced by the fact that all three of the Latinos in this district type were Republicans. However, upon close inspection we find that there have been a total of 12 different Latinos elected to these districts between 1992 and 2006; of these eight were Democrats and four were Republican.

Clearly Latinos can get elected from districts with noticeably lower rates of Latino registration than 40%, but it is unclear if such districts will continue to elect Latinos to the Assembly. "Latino opportunity" districts do seem more fertile for the election and re-election of Latinos than "occasional Latino" districts. However, only time will allow us to determine if these representational gains can be maintained once incumbents are required to leave office due to term limits.

These above described patterns reveal that Latinas have been elected in increasing numbers as well. In 1992, of all seven Latinos in the Assembly, four were Latinas. Five of 10, seven of 14, and six of 17 were Latinas in 1994, 1996, and 1998 respectively. From 2000–2006, only six of 18–20 Latinos during this time period in the Assembly were women. Stated differently, since 2000, 30–33% of all Latinos in the Assembly were women. By comparison, in this same time period 26 to 31% of all members of the Assembly were women. The increased presence of Latinas within the state legislative delegation may suggest that issues of special significance to Latino youth, increases in the feminization of poverty, and concerns regarding spousal abuse, especially as it relates to immigrant women, may have a greater voice in the legislature than ever before. Unfortunately, there is only one longitudinal study of the role of Latinas in the California Legislature.[28] In "Gender and Ethnicity: Patterns of Electoral and Legislative Advocacy among Latina and Latino State Officials in Four States," Fraga, Lopez, Martinez-Ebers, and Ramírez find that Latina presence within the Latino delegation has noticeably increased in the four states considered between 1990 and 2004. They find that the rate in California outpaces the increase in other states and the increase in women in the legislatures overall. More importantly, their analysis of survey data and elite interviews "reveals that Latinas place greater emphasis on representing the inter-

[28] Luis Fraga, Linda Lopez, Valerie Martinez-Ebers, and Ricardo Ramírez, "Gender and Ethnicity: Patterns of Electoral and Legislative Advocacy Among Latina and Latino State Officials in Four States," *Journal of Women, Politics, and Policy*, Vol. 28, No. 3 (2006): 121–45.

ests of multiple minority groups, promoting conflict resolution and building consensus in both the legislature as a whole and within the Latino caucus" (p. 122). A careful examination of the career paths, policy agendas, committee assignments, and participation within the Latino Caucus of the state legislature would be most revealing.

As stated previously, most Latinos elected to the Assembly and the Senate have been Democrats. This has provided them the opportunity to exercise considerable influence in the selection of party leaders. For example, the 13 Latino Democrat members of the Assembly in 1996 comprised 60% of the 22 votes then needed to select party leaders. Democrats held 43 of the 80 seats in the Assembly. This helped Latinos be elected to the positions of Speaker of the Assembly, Majority Leader of the Assembly, and numerous committee chairs (Guerra 1998, 446–47). The pattern of Latino representational institutionalization was again apparent in 1998. Latino Democrats constituted 54% (13 of 24)[29] of the majority necessary to select party leaders in the Assembly and 54% (7 of 13)[30] of the majority necessary to select party leaders in the Senate. This undoubtedly helped elect Rep. Antonio Villaraigosa as the second Latino Speaker of the Assembly. In effect, since 1996, Latinos have consistently comprised more than half of the majority needed to elect party leaders in the Assembly and Senate.[31] In 2004, only a year after being elected to the state Assembly, Fabian Núñez became the third Latino to be elected Speaker of the Assembly. There are two noteworthy elements to his election: the only two other viable candidates being considered for the post were two Latinos: Dario Frommer and Jenny Oropeza; and Núñez is now the longest serving Speaker of the Assembly since term limits took effect.

Our findings with regard to representation demonstrate that considerable gains in access, opportunity, and institutionalization have been made since 1990. Access was enhanced through the drawing of majority Latino population districts at congressional and state Assembly levels as a result of the 1990 and 2000 censuses. Majority-minority population districts have directly helped expand the number of Latino representatives. Due to the increased registration and turnout rates among Latinos, there has been a constant presence of Latino representatives from non-"safe Latino" districts. Opportunity for enhancing legislative influence has similarly increased with the election of increasing numbers of Latinos to these seats. This has occurred despite most of these districts not having a majority of registered voters who are Latino. In many state Assembly districts, however, Latinos are the plurality of registered voters. It is in the area of institutionalization of

[29] There was a total of 47 Democrats in the House in 1998.

[30] There was a total of 25 Democrats in the Senate in 1998.

[31] In 2000, there were 49 Democrats in the Assembly and 25 Democrats in the Senate. Additionally, it will not be surprising if Latino Republicans are also provided opportunities to hold important positions should the Assembly have Republicans as the majority party in the future. This, of course, depends upon Latino Republicans continuing to get elected to these offices. In 2004, Abel Maldonado became the first Latino Republican to have ever been elected to the Senate.

legislative influence where, somewhat counter-intuitively, Latinos have made the greatest gains. They represent sizeable portions of the majority party in both the state Senate and the state Assembly. Three Latinos have gained the powerful position of Speaker of the Assembly. Much less is known about the patterns of access, opportunity, and institutionalization of Latino representation in cities, counties, and other substate levels of government. Guerra estimates that as of 1997 there were 300 Latino city councilmembers in the state (p. 442) with over 100 in the 88 incorporated municipalities in Los Angeles County. In 17 of these, Latinos are in the majority (p. 442). There is much less representation at the county level, and "there [was] not a single Latino elected district attorney or sheriff in the 58 counties of California [in 1997]" (p. 443). There is no systematic study of Latino representation on school boards. Although more Latino representatives are serving in substate levels than ever before, no data exist on the patterns of representation over time. It is, therefore, difficult to assess whether representation at the substate level can be characterized as attaining access, opportunity, or institutionalization.

Policy Benefit

It seems reasonable to expect that the purpose of increasing electoral influence and representation is to serve Latino communities better through the enactment of public policies that serve their interests. Unfortunately, we found no existing study of policy accomplishments by Latino legislators, whether in terms of interest articulation, agenda setting, or legislative enactment. The scholarly community has not enhanced our understanding of whether increases in access, opportunity, and institutionalization in electoral influence and representation have led to any policy benefit for Latino communities.[32]

Although it may be unwise for scholars and other analysts to stray into the world of policy influence, the absence of such research should not inhibit them from pushing their research to directly inform policy proposals. It will be unfortunate if scholars and analysts of Latino politics criticize public officials for not serving more successfully the constituents who helped put many of them in office. Although such critiques can be useful, it is important that these scholars and analysts hold their own scholarship to the same standards, relative to enhancing policy gain, to which they hold public officials.[33] In this area of Latino politics, opportu-

---

[32] The only study of Latino state legislative influence we found was an analysis of Chicano legislators in Texas during the 67th session (1981) of the legislature. This excellent study deserves updating and replication across a number of states. See Tatcho Mindiola, Jr., and Armando Gutiérrez, "Chicanos and the Legislative Process: Reality and Illusion in the Politics of Change," in *Latinos and the Political System*, ed. F. Chris García (Notre Dame, Ind.: University of Notre Dame Press, 1988), 349–62.

[33] See for example: David Hayes-Bautista and Gregory Rodríguez, "Winning More Political Offices But Still No Agenda" (www.med.ucla.edu/cesla/oped/2-11-96.htm, last

nities for information sharing should be maximized. Such sharing could increase the range of strategies to increase the policy benefits received by Latinos in the state. Fraga suggests that the future attainment of policy gains by Latino communities could rest upon the capacity of Latino elected officials to link the interests of Latino communities to the broader public interest.[34] He terms the strategy to attain such linkages as the need for Latino public officials and their supporters to attain an *informed public interest.* Among the dimensions of this informed public interest are contingent color consciousness, opportunity and resource enhancement, self-determination, consensus building through the identification of mutual self-interest across diverse sets of legislative and popular stakeholders, and the acknowledgement of strategic roles.[35] Fraga's theory could be applied within the context of Latino policy benefit in California. Interestingly, several journalists have noted that a number of Latino legislators in California prefer to limit the extent to which they are known primarily as advocates for Latino interests. They see themselves as not just Latino politicians. In "Did 1992 Herald the Dawn of Latino Political Power," Maharidge states, "They [several newly elected Latino legislators] are a diverse group, but among those interviewed, one commonality emerged: All strove to distance themselves from being seen strictly as Latino politicians" (p. 17). Maharidge quotes newly elected state Assemblyman Louis Caldera as saying, "'I do not see myself as a Latino politician in that this is the only community I represent. You're only going to be relevant if you address issues of all Californians, not just one community'" (p. 17). State Assemblywoman Martha Escutia stated:

> I came from a very conservative family. My family always told me, "You're not Chicana, you're not Mexican American. If you have to identify yourself as something, don't hyphenate yourself: You're either American or you're Mexican but you can't be both." So I never related to the so-called Chicano movement, the *Movimiento*. When I was in college I was frankly too busy trying to do well academically and hold down 45 hours worth of jobs. I just had a different agenda. The agenda was I had to build the foundation in order to be successful, and after that I could become an activist (p. 18).

---

visited 5/24/00), 1996; and Dion Nissenbaum, "Assembly Speakers Set State for Power," *San Jose Mercury News*, April 10, 2000, A1.

[34] Luis Ricardo Fraga, "Self-Determination, Cultural Pluralism, and Politics," *The National Political Science Review*, Vol. 3 (1992a): 132–36; Luis Ricardo Fraga, "Latino Political Incorporation and the Voting Rights Act," in *Controversies in Minority Voting: The Voting Rights Act in Perspective*, ed. Bernard Grofman and Chandler Davidson (Washington, D.C.: The Brookings Institution, 1992b), 278–82.

[35] Fraga's "Racial and Ethnic Politics in a Multicultural Society" and Luis Ricardo Fraga and Jorge Ruiz-de-Velasco, "Civil Rights in a Multicultural Society," in *Legacies of the 1964 Civil Rights Act*, ed. Bernard Grofman (Charlottesville: University Press of Virginia, 2000), 190–209.

In April 2000, Assembly Speaker Villaraigosa resigned his position in order to run for mayor of Los Angeles. In reflecting upon the transfer of legislative power to incoming Speaker Bob Hertzberg, both Villaraigosa and Lieutenant Governor Bustamante commented on their strategy of integrating Latino interests with those of the entire state. Nissenbaum, in "Assembly Speakers Set State for Power," quotes Villaraigosa, "I think that the strength of my leadership is I've transcended the issue of race and ethnicity. It doesn't mean I don't fight—of course I fight for those [Latino] issues. But there are very few that are uniquely ethnic." Nissenbaum quotes a similar statement from Bustamante:

> I'm an advocate on behalf of the Latino community. But for us to be leaders of an entire category, or of an entire state, or of an entire region, you have to be a leader of all people, not just a few.

As an example of the recent pursuit of legislation that served many Latinos in California, but was not presented as a "Latino" program, some point to the "Healthy Families Initiative" that provided access to health care for many of California's poorest children. Nissenbaum quotes Villaraigosa:

> I knew going in that 50% of the 7 million uninsured were Latinos. But I would have been the author of Healthy Families if all 7 million had been white. It is one example where public policy was for everyone, but it particularly impacted Latinos.

Villaraigosa pursued a similar approach in supporting more minority outreach programs at the University of California after the passage of Proposition 209. According to Nissenbaum in "Assembly Speakers Set State for Power," he also pushed for a portion of a recently enacted $2 billion parks bond to be targeted for building playgrounds in poorer urban areas.

Areas of Future Research

There are several additional areas of future research where scholars and other analysts can contribute to a more comprehensive understanding of the current state of political incorporation of Latinos in California politics. One that should be explored is nonelectoral organizational participation, which has often been an area where communities of color have gained initial training and experience that can later be transferred to electoral politics. It is apparent that an increasing number of Latino community-based organizations have developed in several urban centers. Among the most prominent are those designed to serve the needs of immigrants, especially regarding the protection of their legal rights. Another is the activities of a variety of labor unions to better organize Latino citizen and immigrant workers. How successful are these organizations in serving Latino communities? Are there major differences in their membership and leadership across distinct Latino subgroups? What types of relationships do such organizations have to Latino elected officials? Do these organizations exercise any explicit influence in electoral politics?

A second area in need of research is bureaucratic representation. As we stated previously, Latinos have made great inroads in increasing their numbers in the state legislature and in a number of local governments. Has this increase led to the appointment, especially at more senior levels, of an increased number of Latinos in administrative positions? It is well known in the social sciences that those responsible for implementing public policy are often the most critical actors in determining the street-level consequences of legislative goals. It is also the case that they often outlive the terms of office of elected officials. This can be the case especially in California, where legislative term limits are prevalent.

A third area that needs further study is the selection of two successive Latinos to serve as Speaker of the California state Assembly in the late 1990s, the selection of Fabian Núñez as the Speaker only a year after being elected to the Assembly, and the election of Cruz Bustamante as lieutenant governor. The first two were major accomplishments, given that the speakership is one of the most powerful positions in the state legislative process. Despite the symbolic significance of the selection of Bustamante as the first Latino Assembly Speaker in 1996, there is no scholarly examination of his attainment of this position or of his accomplishments in office. The selection of Antonio Villaraigosa as the second Latino Assembly Speaker has also not been studied by scholars. In 1998, Bustamante was the first Latino candidate to win statewide office. What was the process whereby he became the strongest Democratic candidate for this position? How distinctive was his vote distribution as compared to other successful statewide candidates? Answers to these questions would contribute greatly to our understanding of the likelihood that these accomplishments can be replicated in the future.

Latino Political Incorporation 1990 to 2010

We began this chapter by developing a model of political incorporation. Three distinct dimensions of political incorporation were specified: electoral influence, representation, and policy benefit. We can now return to the model to assess how much progress Latinos have made since 1990. Figure 9 diagrams the evolution of this progress.

Our review suggests that Latinos made only marginal gains in electoral influence representation from 1990 to 1994. Although gradual increases in naturalization, registration, voting, and representation appeared, they were not substantial. The re-election of Pete Wilson as governor and the passage of Proposition 187 clearly signaled how much progress Latinos still had to make in exercising electoral influence. They were, however, a critical component of the winning coalition that put Dianne Feinstein back in the U.S. Senate. By 1994, Latinos were winning

Figure 9: Latino Political Incorporation, 1990–2010

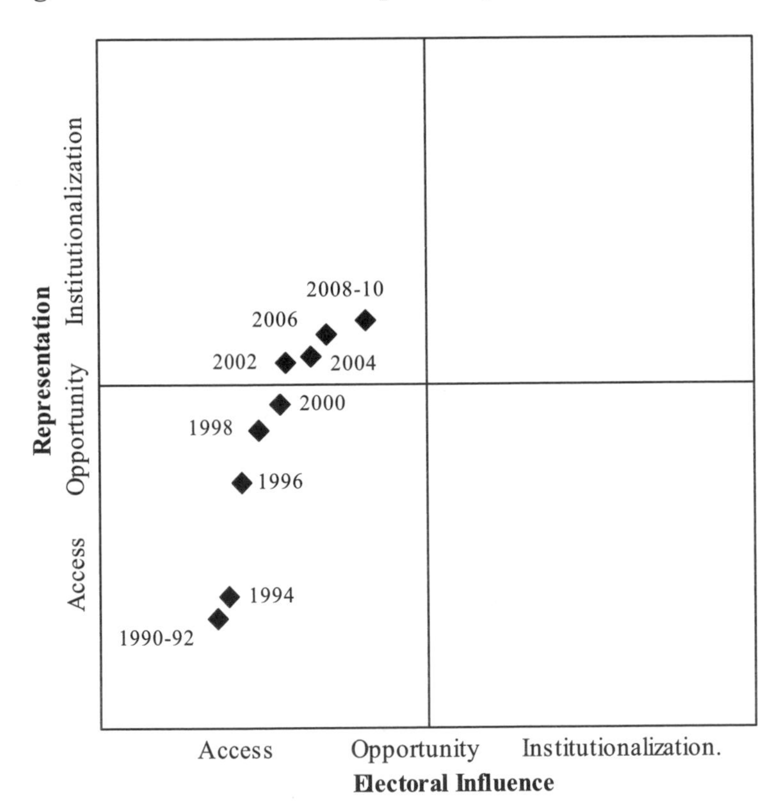

seats in both the state Assembly and the state Senate with regularity. These representatives now had new opportunities to advocate on behalf of their constituents.

In 1996, substantial gains occurred in representation but because the size of the Latino electorate did not increase substantially, there was very little change with respect to electoral influence. Latino registration went up considerably in that year, but Latinos still only represented 12% of the statewide electorate. Latinos, in combination with African Americans, were critical components of the winning coalition that gave California's 54 electoral votes to President Bill Clinton. In 1996, Latinos maintained their considerable presence in the state Senate and increased their representation in the Assembly. After 1996 the Assembly chose its first Latino speaker and elected Latinos to other influential positions in the majority Democratic legislature.

In 1998, Latinos built upon the gains described above. Registration and, especially, turnout rates increased, and Latinos continued to vote overwhelmingly Democratic. They were critical players in the electoral majority that returned Barbara Boxer to the U.S. Senate. Cruz Bustamante was elected lieutenant governor; he is the first Latino elected to statewide office in well over 100 years. Positions in the state legislature were further maintained and institutionalized. As a result of this election there were now more Latinos in the state Assembly and Senate than ever before. They were influential components of the Democratic majority in both chambers. Four Latino Republicans were also now in the state Assembly. As Figure 8 demonstrates, these gains in electoral influence and representation grew slightly in the 2000 election. Latino voters were the largest bloc of ethnic voters who guaranteed that Al Gore would receive California's 54 electoral votes. The gains were again noticeable in representation in 2002 as Latinos increased their presence in the Senate. In 2004 Fabian Núñez took the reins as the Speaker of the House and Latinos saw more gains in the Senate. The pattern that emerges is that the gains in representation have outpaced those in electoral influence. In the future, it is likely that there will be slower gains in representation, while the gains in electoral influence continue to be witnessed.

Despite these gains, however, it is still the case that only 55% of otherwise qualified Latino adult citizens in California are registered to vote. Targeted naturalization and voter-registration campaigns are still necessary. Other efforts to increase registration should be considered as well. It is likely, for example, that same-day registration would increase the number of Latinos registered to vote. Including instructions in civic participation, and especially the responsibilities of citizenship, as part of the standard curriculum of adult education classes, might socialize Latinos further in the importance of participating in politics. Such instruction could be included more explicitly in history and government classes for youth in high school as well. Because a higher percentage of Latinos are under the age of 18 compared to other subgroups, these youth could constitute a sizeable component of the future Latino electorate. Latino electoral influence could increase if noncitizens were allowed to vote in certain local elections. Although this has been limited to school board elections, one can imagine the growth in Latino electoral influence that would occur if permanent residents were allowed to vote for some local officials. This would be the case especially in major urban areas where noncitizen, permanent residents are concentrated. Aspects of Los Angeles politics could be very different if noncitizens were allowed to vote in local elections, for example.

The key to Latinos continuing to exercise considerable influence in statewide elections rests upon both a sizeable turnout and consistent bloc voting. Latinos have demonstrated their capacity to do this in selected elections since 1990. It is important to recognize, however, that this propensity of Latinos to support Democratic candidates can have costs. A consistent and predictable Latino bloc vote can be taken for granted by the Democratic Party. However, to the extent that Latinos split their votes between Democrats and Republicans, the likelihood of their influencing the outcome of an election decreases. This conundrum in which Latino voters find themselves rests, of course, upon the recent pattern of whites splitting their votes evenly between Democratic and Republican candidates. Whites still represent about two-thirds of the voters on Election Day. An overwhelming white vote for a candidate, as occurred in the 1994, 2003, and 2006 gubernatorial elections, can still overshadow any competing Latino vote. This suggests that any efforts to rally Latino voters cannot come at the expense of alienating a sizeable segment of the white electorate.

In 1992, Bruce Cain noted this vulnerability of Latinos to a white bloc vote in statewide referenda.[36] In assessing the ways in which the Voting Rights Act allowed for the assessment of majoritarian electoral institutions to make sure that they treated ethnic and racial voters equally, he noted that "this effort may be undercut by the majoritarian techniques of new populism" (p. 275). He was referring specifically to the possibility that the referendum process in California could be used as a way to limit the increased success Latinos and other ethnic groups might have in electing their first-choice candidates to public office as a result of the effective enforcement of the Voting Rights Act. The votes on Propositions 187, 209, and 227 reflected this vulnerability of Latinos to a white bloc vote very clearly.

Increasing the representation of Latinos can occur along two dimensions. One, the reapportionment that will occur as a result of the 2010 census, will largely determine both the incumbency advantages for current Latino elected officials and the likelihood that more Latinos will get elected to Congress, the state legislature, and local governments from districts where Latinos represent a sizeable segment of respective constituencies. Assembly and Senate Democratic majorities should serve Latino interests well, but several of the bills that have been approved by both the Assembly and the Senate have been vetoed by the current Republican governor. If more Latino Democrats are elected to the state legislature as a result of reapportionment, the influence of Latinos within the Democratic Party should be substantial. Reapportionment enhances access and opportunity for Latinos in a variety of legislative arenas. Institutionalization should continue to occur to the extent that greater inroads are made to positions of party leadership.

Changes in the Supreme Court's view of the role that race and ethnicity should play in reapportionment and redistricting could prove challenging to Latino interests. In *Shaw v. Reno* (1993) the Court severely questioned the constitutionality of using race to draw district boundaries designed to increase the representation of minority interests. In subsequent decisions the Court also outlawed the use of race when it could be identified as the "predominant factor" in drawing districts. These rulings could limit the capacity of Latinos to receive a substantial increase in the number of majority or plurality (influence) districts. It is unclear how the current Roberts Court will vote in redistricting cases, but given the recent vote that largely gutted *Brown v. Board*, the strategy among the Latino political elite will likely focus on maintaining current levels of representation by Latinos, under the

---

[36] Bruce E. Cain, "Voting Rights and Democratic Theory: Toward a Color-Blind Society?" in *Controversies in Minority Voting: The Voting Rights Act in Perspective*, ed. Bernard Grofman and Chandler Davidson (Washington, D.C.: The Brookings Institution, 1992), 261–77.

guise of incumbency protection, as opposed to pushing for more districts where Latinos are viable candidates. It certainly behooves Latinos to pursue a variety of both legal and political strategies to maximize their interests in reapportionment, and thus increase the institutionalization of Latino representation. Among ideas to consider in developing such strategies are: (1) demonstrating that current Latino officials who represent majority or plurality Latino districts do not represent only Latino concerns, (2) using criteria other than race or ethnicity, such as sociodemographic criteria like education and income, to draw district boundaries, and (3) minimizing the extent to which Latino interests are seen as competitive to the interests of African Americans and Asian Americans.

In Figure 9 we focus on representation and electoral influence since 1990. The question that remains is Latinos are approaching the ideal point to which Latino political incorporation should strive—the receipt of policy benefit. As stated earlier, it is more complicated to measure policy outcomes as they relate to Latinos. The current practice of a number of Latino elected officials to present themselves as representatives of both Latino interests and, at the same time, the larger public interest of the state, may be most critical to benefit being attained. Even though Latinos may become the majority population in the state within the next 20 years, it is very unlikely that they will possess the quantities of private investment capital that many business firms, and whites, generally enjoy. Coalition building across diverse interests may be the key to future Latino policy benefits.

Let us assume that Latinos become the largest segment of the California population and electorate. Let us also assume that they hold a majority of seats in both the Assembly and the state Senate. Let us further assume that there is a Latino governor and a Latino Assembly speaker. Last, let us assume that these public officials have as one of their concerns the enhancement of policy benefits, such as greater educational attainment and material well being, for their Latino constituents. Despite the apparent institutionalization of electoral influence and representation, the attainment of policy benefit over the long term will very much depend upon the successful negotiation of the mutual self-interest of Latinos with that of holders of major private capital. Economic growth and the resulting benefits of an expanded tax base rest squarely upon the propensity of holders of private capital to invest in California. Institutionalizing policy benefit for Latinos may rest, in large part, on the effectiveness of Latino elected officials in using public authority to serve a variety of the interests that comprise California.

The primary task of governance is the development of policy consensus, across a variety of issue areas that can be maintained over the long term. That task is the same whether Latinos or others hold the reins of public power. With full political incorporation comes a great deal of responsibility to those who put one in office, and to building a larger informed public interest. This review of Latinos as voters, elected representatives, and policy decision-makers suggests that they will continue to have the chance to undertake this most important task in California's future.

References

Alvarez, Michael, and Tara L. Butterfield. 1998. "Citizenship and Political Representation in Contemporary California." Social Science Working Paper 1041. California Institute of Technology, Pasadena, Calif., July.

Berg, Larry. 1995. "California, Progress or . . . . " *California Journal*. Vol. 26, No. 1 (January): 51–52.

Browning, Rufus P., Dale Rogers Marshall, and David H. Tabb. 1984. *Protest is Not Enough: The Struggle of Blacks and Hispanics for Equality in Urban Politics*. Berkeley: University of California Press.

Cable News Network, Voter News Service, 2006 Exit Poll Data (http://www.cnn.com/ELECTION/2006//pages/results/states/CA/S/01/epolls.0.html), last visited 08/25/07.

Cain, Bruce E. 1992. "Voting Rights and Democratic Theory: Toward a Color-Blind Society?" In *Controversies in Minority Voting: The Voting Rights Act in Perspective*, ed. Bernard Grofman and Chandler Davidson. Washington, D.C.: The Brookings Institution, 261–77.

California Department of Finance, Demographic Research Unit. (http://www.dof.ca.gov/Research/Research.php), last visited 10/01/07.

California Public Sector, 1991–95 Directories. California Public Sector Publications, Sacramento, California.

California Secretary of State, Elections Division Homepage, (http://www.ss.ca.gov/elections/elections.htm), last visited 10/01/07.

Carroll, James. 1992. "Courting California: Both parties lust after those golden electoral votes." *California Journal*, Vol. 23, No. 9 (September): 433–36.

Fraga, Luis Ricardo. 1992a. "Self-Determination, Cultural Pluralism, and Politics." *The National Political Science Review*, Vol. 3: 132–36.

———. 1992b. "Latino Political Incorporation and the Voting Rights Act." In *Controversies in Minority Voting: The Voting Rights Act in Perspective*., ed. Bernard Grofman and Chandler Davidson. Washington, D.C.: The Brookings Institution, 278–82.

———. 1999. "Racial and Ethnic Politics in a Multicultural Society." Lecture presented at the Metropolitan Research and Policy Institute, University of Texas at San Antonio. April 7.

Fraga, Luis Ricardo, and Jorge Ruiz-de-Velasco. 2000. "Civil Rights in a Multicultural Society." In *Legacies of the 1964 Civil Rights Act*, ed. Bernard Grofman. Charlottesville: University Press of Virginia, 190–209.

Guerra, Fernando, and Luis Ricardo Fraga. 1996. "Theory, Reality, and Perpetual Potential: Latinos in the 1992 California Elections." In *Ethnic Ironies: Latino Politics in the 1992 Elections*, ed. Rodolfo O. de la Garza and Louis DeSipio. Boulder, Colo.: Westview Press, 131–45.

Guerra, Fernando. 1998. "Latino Politics in California: The Necessary Conditions for Success." In *Racial and Ethnic Politics in California, Volume Two*, ed.

Michael B. Preston, Bruce E. Cain, and Sandra Bass. Berkeley, Calif.: Institute of Governmental Studies, University of California, Berkeley, 439–52.

Hayes-Bautista, David. 2004. *La Nueva California: Latinos in the Golden State.* Berkeley: University of California Press.

Hayes-Bautista, David, and Gregory Rodriguez. 1996. "Winning More Political Offices But Still No Agenda." (http://www.cesla.med.ucla.edu/Documents/oped/2-11-96.htm), last visited 10/1/07.

Hero, Rodney E. 1992. *Latinos and the U.S. Political System*. Philadelphia: Temple University Press.

Jackson, Bryan O., and Michael B. Preston, eds. 1991. *Racial and Ethnic Politics in California*. Berkeley, Calif.: Institute for Governmental Studies, University of California, Berkeley.

Jeffe, Sherry Babitch. 1996. "Year of the Latino?" *California Journal*, Vol. 27, No. 10 (October): 20.

Lopez, Elizabeth, and Eric Wahlgren. 1994. "The Latino Vote: The lure of four million ballots." *California Journal*, Vol. 25, No. 11 (November): 29–31.

Maharidge, Dale. 1993. "Did 1992 herald the dawn of Latino political power?" *California Journal*, Vol. 24, No. 1 (January): 15–18.

Mindiola, Tatcho, Jr., and Armando Gutiérrez. 1988. "Chicanos and the Legislative Process: Reality and Illusion in the Politics of Change." In *Latinos and the Political System*, ed. F. Chris Garcia. Notre Dame, Ind.: University of Notre Dame Press, 349–62.

Myers, Dowell. 2007. *Immigrants and Boomers: Forging a New Social Contract for the Future of America.* New York: Russell Sage Foundation.

NALEO Education Fund. 2007. *Latino Election Handbook.* Los Angeles: National Association of Latino Elected and Appointed Officials (NALEO).

Nissenbaum, Dion. 2000. "Assembly Speakers Set State for Power." *San Jose Mercury News*, April 10, A1.

Pachón, Harry P. 1998. "Latino Politics in the Golden State: Ready for the 21st Century?" In *Racial and Ethnic Politics in California, Volume Two*, ed. Michael B. Preston, Bruce E. Cain, and Sandra Bass. Berkeley, Calif.: Institute of Governmental Studies, University of California, Berkeley, 411–38.

Preston, Michael, Bruce E. Cain, and Sandra Bass, eds. 1998. *Racial and Ethnic Politics in California*. Berkeley, Calif.: Institute of Governmental Studies, University of California, Berkeley.

Ramírez, Ricardo. 2002. *The Changing Landscape of California Politics, 1990–2000.* Unpublished doctoral dissertation, Stanford University.

Rodriguez, Gregory. 1998. "Antonio Villaraigosa: The Assembly's new leader may have an historic opportunity to become an ethnic politician who transcends ethnicity." *California Government and Politics Annual 1998–1999*, 34–35.

State of California, Department of Finance, Demographic Research Unit (http://www.dof.ca.gov/HTML/DEMOGRAP/Data/RaceEthnic/Population-00-50/RaceData_2000-2050.asp), last visited 08/25/07.

Scott, Steve. 1997. "New Legislature: The Assembly's first Latino speaker confronts a caucus full of rookies, a lame-duck governor, and an ascendant state Senate, all with one eye on the term-limit clock." *California Journal*, Vol. 28, No. 1 (January): 6–11.

———. 1998. "Reality votes: California's political demographics are slowly growing more in sync with its overall demographics. How will this change affect the way election are run—and won—in 1998 and beyond?" *California Journal,* Vol. 29, No. 1 (January): 24–30.

Suro, Roberto, and Jeffery Passel. 2003. *The Rise of the Second Generation: Changing Patterns in Hispanic Population Growth*. Washington D.C: The Pew Hispanic Center

Starkey, Danielle. 1993. "Immigrant-bashing: Good policy or good politics?" *California Journal*, Vol. 24, No. 10 (October): 15–20.

Statewide Database, UC Berkeley Institute of Governmental Studies (swdb.berkeley.edu/), last visited 10/01/07.

Yáñez-Chávez, Aníbal, ed. 1996. *Latino Politics in California*. San Diego, Calif.: Center for U.S.-Mexican Studies at the University of California, San Diego.

York, Anthony. 1999. "Latino Politics." *California Journal*, Vol. 30, No. 2 (April): 26–34.

Chapter 5

Towards a Womanist Leadership Praxis: The History and Promise of Black Grassroots/Electoral Partnerships in California

Melina Abdullah and Regina Freer

Introduction

The 1982 governor's race is often viewed as a zenith moment for Black political power in California. Tom Bradley, then mayor of Los Angeles, stood a very good chance of becoming the first Black governor in the nation. His gubernatorial candidacy affirmed that significant progress toward Black political incorporation was underway, in California and across the nation.[1] Further, the small 8% Black population in the state that coincided with the zenith of the early 1980s

[1] Bradley's gubernatorial candidacy did not stand in isolation, but came as a part of several steps toward Black electoral incorporation, including the election of Wilson Riles as state school superintendent in 1970, Bradley's own election as the first Black mayor of a major city in 1973, Mervyn Dymally's 1974 election as lieutenant governor, Lionel Wilson's election as mayor of Oakland in 1977, and Willie Brown's ascent to Speaker of the California Assembly in 1980 along with eight state legislative seats and four members in California's congressional delegation. As went California, so too the rest of the country—with Jesse Jackson entering the presidential race in 1984 (*The Black Scholar* 1984).

indicated that demography was not necessarily destiny. Fast forward to the 2006 statewide election and many surmised that it represented a renaissance of Black political incorporation (Vogel 2006; Miller et al. 2006).[2] After a period of gradual slippage in representative numbers and disappearance from statewide elected office, the number of Blacks in the state legislature reached a historic peak with nine members,[3] the four-member Black congressional delegation was maintained, and Oakland once again elected a Black mayor.[4] However, the larger demographic context in California changed significantly from 1982 to 2006 as Latino population and political incorporation numbers soared. For Blacks, the celebratory moment of the 2006 election was almost immediately tempered by the anxiety that arose in 2007 with Black and Latina candidates in a head-to-head race for the 37th District congressional seat, a historically Black district encompassing Long Beach and Compton. Was demography, in fact, destiny in the new California? A collective sigh of relief echoed through the Black community when the recently elected Black Assemblymember Laura Richardson, with multiracial support, defeated state Senator Jenny Oropeza, her Latina opponent (Mitchell 2007). This sense of relief was enhanced by the ascent of Karen Bass, an African-American woman, to Assembly speaker in 2008 in spite of a bevy of Latino legislators vying for the position, but the success of these two Black women belied continuing disquiet. The periodic speculation and anxiety over the state of Black incorporation overlays a deeper and in many ways more complex concern with larger Black empowerment that goes beyond mere numbers. Whether or not we view the current state of Black electoral politics in California as a new high or a last hurrah, questions of sustainability and possibilities for improved conditions for Black Californians remain. This concern suggests that there is a need for an examination of the larger relationship between incorporation and empowerment.

Within the context of a winner-take-all, majority rule system, electoral numbers are imperative to political power. However, numbers alone do not necessarily translate into collective empowerment. Thus, this work seeks to look beyond the numbers by examining ways in which wins at the polls can be tied to substantive gains on the ground. Progressive leadership models among elected officials are paramount to such a correlation. Thus, the central focus of this work is to flesh out a model of leadership that connects electoral incorporation with community empowerment. Utilizing historical analysis and contemporary case study we weigh

---

[2] See official 2006 primary election results at www.ss.ca.gov.

[3] Assemblymembers Wilmer Amina Carter from San Bernadino, Laura Richardson representing Long Beach, and Sandre Swanson of Oakland all won districts that had previously been occupied by nonBlack members. They joined newly elected Assemblymembers Mike Davis and Curren Price, along with incumbent Assemblymembers Karen Bass and Mervyn Dymally and Senators Ed Vincent and Mark Ridley-Thomas—who moved from the Assembly to the Senate following the 2006 election.

[4] Former Congressman Ron Dellums was inaugurated as mayor in January 2007, succeeding Jerry Brown, who was elected to attorney general of the state of California.

predominant leadership models and assert that a womanist leadership model, one rooted in community organizing, group-centered leadership, coalition-building, and an insider/outsider strategy, offers promise for future Black political empowerment.[5]

Towards a Womanist Leadership Praxis

Womanism, first introduced by Alice Walker, is a concept that has been fleshed out largely in terms of theory, with applications generally limited to literary analysis, personal and collective ideology, and pedagogy (Walker 1983). For women of color, a womanist framework offers a foundation through which intersectional identities of race, class, gender, and other positions of oppression can be addressed simultaneously without the requirement that one be given primacy over the other or that identities be falsely separated out and examined individually. Further, womanism stands not only as theory, but also as a movement, or praxis, which requires that those who define themselves as womanists not only ascribe to theory, but engage in actions that work to dismantle oppression in all its forms.

What, then, does womanist praxis mean in terms of leadership? We assert that womanist leadership praxis incorporates both womanist theory—which is inherently progressive in that it requires its adherents to commit themselves to a position of resistance—and leadership approaches that support transformational goals. Our examination here focuses primarily on those leadership strategies that Black elected officials who are womanists and/or adherents to womanism incorporate. At the center of a womanist model is the concept of group-centered leadership that requires the "leader" to see herself or himself as a part of a movement, rather than the movement itself; as a result, womanist leaders are community-connected and tend to see their formal positions as extensions of grassroots movements.

Womanist leadership praxis stands in contrast to more traditional approaches to electoral politics that seek incorporation. While, by definition, Black electoral politics requires an approach that sees electoral success as one goal, for womanists, the central goal is larger—centering on broader Black political empowerment, which cannot be measured by incorporation alone.

---

[5] Womanist theory, as coined by Alice Walker (1983) and developed by Black feminist/womanist scholars Patricia Hill-Collins (2000), Kimberle Crenshaw (1995), and others, asserts that empowerment for one group of oppressed people is dependent on the empowerment of all oppressed people. The application of this theory to Black political empowerment will be developed in the forthcoming analysis.

Dilemmas of Incorporation

While political incorporation, or the integration of Blacks into the existing systems and structures, has long stood as a liberal goal, for most of the history of Blacks in this country, the pursuit of power was consigned to an outside, insurgent approach because of rigid racial exclusion. Institutional authority was targeted but could not generally be exercised by Blacks themselves.

Blacks did occasionally run for and win elections in the pre-Civil Rights era,[6] but these were isolated victories. Those who viewed the electoral arena as viable terrain did so strategically. Adherents to this strategy did not measure victory solely in electoral terms, but included consciousness-raising, movement-building, and mass politicization as key goals. As the Progressive Party platform for Vice-Presidential candidate and Black Los Angeles resident Charlotta Bass asserted, "Win or lose, we win by raising the issues" (Freer 2004, 609).

As the Civil Rights Movement, rooted in the South, won major victories, including the passage of the Voting Rights Act of 1965, calls for economic justice were not far behind—especially coming from the urban North and West. President Lyndon Johnson was pressured to respond to the growing demands of the increasingly urbanized Black population and did so through his Great Society programs. With new resources at their disposal, Black people confronted the dilemma of how best to engage for purposes of empowerment—through inside participation, outside agitation, or some combination.

Electoral Engagement

After the attainment of voting rights, Blacks began to elect African-American representatives to office, with an initial surge in the 1960s. Many African Americans began to tether their hopes to emerging Black elected officials. It was assumed that once elected, Blacks would be the truest of democratic representatives, serving as delegates for not only the constituency that elected them, but to the larger, attentive Black citizenry. Having spent so long as outsider critics, surely Blacks would act differently from whites once elected. The pressure to serve in this role was heightened by the small size of the contingent of Black elected officials (BEOs) who were initially expected to bear such a burden.

For the African-American electorate, many of whom had been entrenched in the protest movement that brought about this new access to electoral politics, their role as engaged citizens became a question. Conversely, BEOs were attempting to negotiate relationships with the public that made their election possible in the con-

[6] Fred Roberts was the first Black elected to the Assembly in 1918. See Anderson, 1996.

text of a larger winner-take-all electoral system predicated on compromise and incremental change.[7]

In determining roles, both electorates and elected officials were charged with the task of defining representation. For some, a trustee model—one that entrusted the elected with representing the interests of his or her constituency with little or no consultation—was seen as the most efficient and preferred form, with effectiveness being measured in the voting booth. Others defined authentic Black leadership in terms of community-connectedness; this required that BEOs not only share descriptive traits with constituencies or simply profess like ideologies, but also be entrenched in the community helping to organize and regularly consulting with the group. This delegate style falls in line with a womanist model elaborated here and requires representatives to advance collective interests in the formal political sphere.

In California, BEOs could be found in both camps. Elihu Harris, California state assemblymember from 1978 to 1990 and mayor of Oakland from 1991 to 1999, embraced the trustee model. According to Harris "[t]he primary role of Black leadership is to *set the agenda*, to *determine direction*, to articulate the needs of the Black community" [emphasis added] (Covin 1993, 25). Harris represented the cadre of Black leadership who saw themselves as empowered to determine community needs. While this position does not require that BEOs be divorced from the communities that they serve, grassroots mobilization and the connectedness of elected leaders to outside movements is not considered to be central to effective leadership.

Those elected officials who embraced what we term a womanist leadership model reflect the centrality of community-connectedness. For Diane Watson, who was first elected to the Los Angeles School Board in 1975, went on to serve in the state Senate from 1978 to 1998 and is currently U.S. representative for the 33rd Congressional District, Black leaders were to be "instruments" of change, coming out of "the movement at the grassroots" (*ibid.*, 26). This womanist approach was not confined to Black women, as State Senator Bill Greene, who served in the state Assembly from 1966 to 1975 and state Senate from 1975 to 1992 concurred with Watson's approach to leadership. "Black leadership should get political direction *primarily* from their interpretation of the wishes of their constituents. Leaders have to understand the need, the want, the station, the right of the people they represent. The constituency is necessary for everything the leader produces. Political thinking is collective. It is not individual" (*ibid.,* 31).

---

[7] Kweisi Mfume discusses the limitations that he faced during his early years as a radical Baltimore city councilman. The system is structured to allow for only limited reform, as a majority of the electoral body must support proposed legislation (Mfume 1998). Lani Guinier asserts that the required majority support especially restricts the ability of Black legislators to propose more transformative policy solutions, since they must gain the support of a significant number of white colleagues for bills to pass (Guinier 1994).

On the other side of the Black leadership dyad, Black constituents who worked tirelessly to win the vote and elect African Americans to office were largely willing to entrust newly elected representatives to pursue their interests. Thus, the role of the Black populace became one of mobilizing to elect additional Black leaders and support those who were in office when called upon. This meant that the election of those who were descriptively Black was central. "For most Black voters, the symbolic significance of the potential to elect a Black [to office] tended to override concerns for the specifics of issue positions. . . . Most Black voters have understandably automatically associated descriptive representation . . . with substantive representation" (Persons 1993, 46).

Such an association between descriptive and substantive representation was particularly common among those who were poised to take advantage of the limited tangible benefits that BEOs had the discretion to dole out—namely the burgeoning middle class. For them, collective mobilization often fell to the wayside in favor of individual improvement through education and economic development. It was their line of reasoning that such solitary investments would enable the Black populace to take advantage of new opportunities that their representatives in office would carve out.

However, the diverse experiences and positions of the Black community informed divergent visions of progress. While incorporation was clearly the preferred pathway to advancement for the Black middle class and a majority of African Americans in the South, many working-class and poor Blacks, especially in urban centers, chose to challenge existing structures and advocate more radical goals.

Alongside questions of how to interact with the electoral system were concerns about how to engage new programs and accompanying public agencies. For some, federally sponsored programs and bureaucracies were viewed as addressing the poverty and social isolation of the Black community. For others, agencies served to quell the possibility of growing revolutionary sentiments that were beginning to take hold.

The hesitancy among urban working-class and poor Blacks to wholly entrust BEOs with representing their interests was indicative of a general skepticism of liberal strategies that stress incorporation as the most viable path to empowerment and ignore the systemic causes of poverty and exclusion. This divide reflects a historic tension in Black political thought between those who prioritize individually centered social mobility and those who seek revolutionary systemic change (Gaines 1996).

The growing divide between Black middle-class and working-class/poor populations was further illustrated by community responses to Great Society programs. War on Poverty initiatives became springboards for those with political and bureaucratic ambitions (Reed 1999, 131). With mayors selecting the administrative leaders of programs, those Blacks who embraced the liberal ideologies that were consistent with program visions were quickly put in charge (Self 2003, 198–205). This sort of Black middle-class entitlement exacerbated tensions between

Black liberals and the grassroots by distancing poor and working-class Blacks from decision-making.

With limited input from the masses themselves, programmatic responses to inequality were often viewed as a form of mass pacification—seen as providing crumbs to the working class with the greatest incentives reserved for the middle class in the form of positions in the growing governmental bureaucracy. While the mounting discontent stopped short of calling for an end to the War on Poverty programs, what became evident is that governmental programs could not and would not fully address the needs of the masses of Black people. Hence, the inside methods endorsed by government had to be balanced with an outside strategy of grassroots activism.

Strategies of outside agitation not only served to politicize the grassroots, but sometimes led to tangible policy outcomes. For example, heeding activists' demands for self-determination, some War on Poverty programs required citizen participation in program administration. The Community Action Program (CAP), in particular, served as a training ground for grassroots organizers. Jobs provided through these War on Poverty programs eliminated many of the financial barriers that had previously limited the degree to which would-be activists had committed themselves to community organizing. Recognizing the potential that CAP provided to foster radical activism among urban communities, policymakers would eventually eliminate community participation requirements, both through defunding and in concept (Walters and Smith 1999, 114). However, the program's ultimate elimination could not undo the significant groundwork laid among the urban grassroots.

The CAP example highlights both the possibilities and limitations of utilizing government programs as a strategy. While such programs offered vital resources, the ultimate control over program administration and purse strings held by policymakers affirmed that governmental programs alone could not be depended upon as the singular strategy for empowerment, but could serve as a launching board for more radical agendas that would move forward outside the confines of governmental control.

With the realization that existing systems will never give marginalized groups access to revolutionary tools, more militant strategies for grassroots empowerment became an increasingly viable option. By the late-1960s the pendulum began to swing back from an incorporative model to one that reintroduced the possibility of revolutionary transformation through outside strategies. "Put simply, the conceptualization of Black political strategies designed to achieve favorable public policy must be comprehensive in character by utilizing both institutional and noninstitutional methods" (*ibid.*, 138).

Transformation versus Incorporation: California-Based Black Power and Revolutionary Movements

The move towards more radical grassroots transformation can be characterized as the Black power era. With the 1965 Watts revolt as a symbolic marker, the period is distinguished by its broad-based working-class engagement, the intensity with which participants dedicated themselves to activism, long-term empowerment goals, heightened commitment to move beyond liberal reform, and interconnected ideology and approach.

In stark contrast to the two major Civil Rights victories, the passage of the Civil Rights Act of 1964 and the Voting Rights Act of 1965, stood the very real repression experienced by urban Blacks at the hands of the state. The 1965 Watts revolt in Los Angeles and the activist response to the murder of Denzil Dowell in the San Francisco Bay Area[8] signaled an end to the illusion of state neutrality and fairness. Key in the development of the Black power movement was a migration in the base of the movement, from the southern United States to the urban North and West, with California taking on particular prominence. This move shifted the focus of Black political empowerment to growing Black urban populations whose racial experiences intersected with their economic realities in very clear ways. A surge of Black consciousness rooted in nationalist and revolutionary sentiment began to emerge among the Black masses (Brown 1992, 55).

Black Power and Inside/Outside Strategies

Rather than working within the confines of a restrictive system, Black power organizers made demands and issued expectations for expedient governmental responses. The tactics used to challenge the existing structures stood along a continuum ranging from armed revolution to working in collaboration with elected leaders.

A core strength of Black power movements was the linkage between theory and practice. The development of an underlying theory enabled movement members to organize around a united vision for the world rather than being limited to a response mode.[9] What made the theoretical framework especially strong was the

---

[8] The murder of African-American teenager Denzil Dowell in Richmond, California, at the hands of the Martinez sheriff's department in 1967 brought a tremendous activist response, including organizing and protests led by the Black Panther Party (Smith 1999, 35–38).

[9] The cultural nationalist agenda that informed the U.S. Organization and the Black Marxist perspective that formed the base for Black Panther Party organizing enabled activists to work toward this common world vision.

ever-evolving nature of it; theory was constantly reshaped by practical experience. Similarly, as the theory evolved so did practices.[10]

While key to the movement's sustainability and level of collective ownership, such ideological visions could not stand in isolation. Organizations gained legitimacy by meeting the immediate needs of the community. For the Black Panther Party (BPP), as well as US, it was often their responses to crises that drew membership, but it was their world vision that sustained it.[11]

Existing conditions tempered the ability of Black power organizations to immediately translate revolutionary ideals into practice. To be relevant to the lives of the working class, organizations could not simply espouse grand ideology, but were compelled to respond to immediate community needs. As such, avenues afforded through existing social, economic, and political structures often counterbalanced more revolutionary tactics. While it was recognized that electoral politics alone could not bring true community empowerment, the grassroots could not afford to completely disengage as electoral outcomes impacted their lives. However, rather than entrusting traditional BEOs to represent the interests of the Black masses or pushing for greater political incorporation, Black power organizers placed demands on Black elected officials to push progressive agendas and some, including the Panthers, even ran their own candidates for office.[12]

Like Charlotta Bass and the Progressive Party in the 1950s, the BPP viewed the foray of leaders Bobby Seale and Elaine Brown into the electoral arena as a part of a larger strategy, not an end unto itself. The decision to have the two run for mayor and city council respectively was part of a long-term strategy to capture power in Oakland and then gradually spread a revolutionary model of governance to other urban areas. As Elaine Brown explained, "The Survival Programs had accomplished a great deal by involving masses of Black people in revolution at the primary level of raising consciousness. Casting a vote for a Black party candidate would be the first concrete expression of that consciousness."[13] She goes on, "when Bobby Seale and I launched our campaign on the streets of West Oakland I could see on the faces of our constituents . . . a resurgence of hope. Whatever the outcome of the campaign, that alone gave it worth. . . . Large pockets of Oakland's Blacks who had not voted in years were registering. . . . They were becoming citizens, ready to change the nature of things."[14] The inside/outside strategy undergirded the Panther campaign.

As Elaine Brown observed:

---

[10] An illustration is the Black Panther Party's move of their core efforts from an armed revolution approach to a social services approach, including a reexamination of the role that electoral politics would play in Black empowerment.

[11] For the BPP, their free breakfast program was key in generating community buy-in.

[12] The Black Panther Party ran Elaine Brown for Oakland City Council in 1973 and Bobby Seale ran for mayor—winning 40% of the vote (Brown, 327).

[13] Elaine Brown, 313–14.

[14] *Ibid.*, 322–24.

> When the final results were tallied, we did not take seats in the house of the Establishment. But we did win. We won the votes of approximately 40 percent of the electorate. We won the solid support of Black people in Oakland. The Panther constituency had indeed expanded. We had planted our ideas a little deeper. We had established foundation.[15]

In addition to massive voter registration drives, the party informed and facilitated other types of political participation. As an example, in an effort to effect change in the Oakland public school system, party members began attending every school board meeting, criticizing the board for meeting at a time and place that made them inaccessible for most of the city's Black residents. The party "provided buses and free meals to people who would join us at board meetings. Eventually we forced the board to change its schedule to accommodate mass participation."[16] This activism was eventually directed at removing the superintendent of the school district, who was Black, thus demonstrating a commitment to substantive representation that went beyond supporting officials because they were Black.

Importantly, the BPP's efforts were centered on mobilization. Black residents were being actively connected to the formal political system and becoming a force to be reckoned with in the process.

Brown ran again for city council in 1975. By this time her connections extended beyond the BPP mobilization apparatus as she displayed keen coalition building skills linking the Black working class, the larger liberal-progressive political network, and the Black businesses and middle class. Though she again lost, her campaign forged new ground. According to historian Robert Self, it represented:

> the best of the decades-long grassroots and Black power movements in Oakland. She ran as the candidate of "multi-ethnic Oakland," promising the city's African American, Latino, Asian, and white voters "a new day in Oakland." She also drew large numbers of women into the campaign, breaking the Panther gender division of labor by selecting women for the top strategy positions on her team.[17]

Brown's leadership style could be described as womanist, not only in its obvious prioritization of women's perspectives, but in its adherence to collectivism.[18] Her various runs for office were group processes driven by collective, not individual advancement. In fact, she balked at the first suggestion that she run for city council on a ticket with Seale and only did so upon the urging of others in the BPP.[19]

---

[15] *Ibid.*, 327.

[16] *Ibid.*, 326.

[17] Self. 310.

[18] Despite Brown's rise to leadership of the BPP, the organization and others like US still reflected patriarchy of the larger society. See Davis (1984) for an analysis of the intricacies of race and gender in Black power organizations.

[19] *Ibid.*, 314–15.

Elaine Brown's two campaigns and the BPP's ability to mobilize Black citizens proved key to the 1977 electoral victory of Lionel Wilson, Oakland's first Black mayor. The Panthers registered thousands of Black Democrats and undertook a massive get-out-the-vote drive on Election Day. Panther support for Wilson was predicated on the assumption that their participation in his electoral coalition would translate into a pivotal role in his governing coalition. As former BPP Chair Elaine Brown, explained:

> I had certain expectations about his role in the future of Oakland. I was guaranteeing him our party's support in becoming mayor of Oakland. I only had three requests. I wanted to replace the police chief of Oakland with a Black who would assume that position with the clear understanding that I—in the Panther sense—had put him in office. Secondly, I wanted to be a silent partner in his selection of a new city manager. Finally, I wanted him over the years to support my recommendations for vacancies on the port board. He said it was the least he could do (Brown 1992, 327).

Inner turmoil within the party, transitions in leadership and focus, and government-sanctioned efforts to disrupt party activities greatly limited the Black Panthers' ability to hold the newly elected mayor to his promises. Wilson ultimately reneged on his commitment, shifting his focus from mobilizing an electoral coalition rooted in the Black community to crafting a governing coalition that often took Blacks, especially the Black working class, for granted, while prioritizing corporate interests.[20] In the face of deindustrialization and globalization, Wilson sought to woo corporations through his downtown development plan, which included the construction of a convention center and other publicly financed projects. While the motives were economic growth and job creation, little benefit reached the population of Black poor and working class as their ranks began to swell (Bush 1984, 319). Some in the Black middle class did benefit through employment and contracting opportunities, but overall, dreams of a revitalized downtown as a source of collective advancement did not come to pass (Mollenkopf 1983). Instead of building a base of mobilized community support to counterbalance demands of corporate constituents, Wilson and other Black politicians of the era largely mobilized for their own reelection and even then, did so in limited fashion, as electoral success meant relying on just enough of an appeal to racial symbolism to appease the Black public's demand for representation.

To be sure, Black mayors like Wilson faced serious challenges in seeking local solutions to national and international economic challenges. Likewise, few could have been elected with Black support alone. Wilson-style Black elected officials may have initially approached elected office with a goal of making policy changes that were beneficial to the larger Black community, but without community engagement to provide pressure from the outside, they would ultimately suc-

---

[20] See Clarence Stone (1989) for a discussion of the tension between electoral and governing coalitions of Black mayors.

cumb to institutional limitations. Despite their inability, and at times unwillingness, to maintain a sense of community connectedness, such politicians generally enjoyed long-term electoral success.

The prioritization of electoral success was not unique to Wilson; in fact, it was also key for one of the most enduring Black political figures in California history—Tom Bradley. The election of Tom Bradley to the 10th City Council District seat and ultimately the mayoralty of Los Angeles preceded Wilson's election and is often held up as a key turning point for the city's African Americans. In essence, Bradley's election as mayor of the nation's second largest city meant, for many, that Blacks had finally "arrived." Hence, a great deal of stock was placed in his ability to move the collective Black agenda forward.

Though both Bradley and Wilson represented a renewed incorporative strategy, there were important distinctions. While Wilson initially aligned himself with, then gradually moved away from radical grassroots constituents, Bradley made a concerted effort to distance himself from such groups early on. This distancing from the Black power movement was due, in part, to his more reformist political ideology, but it also responded to accusations and campaign strategies introduced by opponent Sam Yorty that would play on white fears by drawing links between Bradley and the Black Panther Party during the 1969 election (Sonenshein 1993, 91). In a calculated effort to maintain his coalition, Bradley drew clear boundaries between himself and radical movements (Halisi 2006).

For Bradley, whose base was the largely Black, but still diverse 10th Council District, the decision not to draw support from radical grassroots organizers was also reached out of a pragmatic decision rooted in the city's demographic make up. Where in Oakland, Wilson was running for mayor of a city with a majority Black population, the Black voting population in Los Angeles was 18% during Bradley's first run (Sonenshein 1993, 22). This demographic reality, in a sense forced Bradley's strategy of coalition building and encouraged his distancing from radical Black movements that might make non-Black coalition partners uncomfortable.

Despite Bradley's distancing from radical Black organizations, he relied heavily on a mobilized, largely Black middle-class, community base—especially in his initial run for mayor. While he continued his relationship with community members in the 10th district in his second, and ultimately successful 1973 mayoral bid, the way in which community members were utilized shifted.

> The Bradley organization had changed internally in preparation for the 1973 campaign. It had become both more professional and less ideological. The emphasis would be on mass media, backed by a grass-roots campaign, rather than the other way around. These changes reduced the crusade atmosphere that had made the 1969 campaign so appealing at the street level. To the Tenth District loyalists, however, the change was essential; after all, they had begun in 1973 with the intent to win, not to crusade (*ibid.,* 105).

While such a strategy might have proven successful in winning a citywide post, this was not the only strategy that worked. In fact, also in Los Angeles, Mervyn Dymally—a member of the state Assembly[21]—found a close relationship with working-class grassroots organizers was essential. While ideology accounts for some of this difference, both Bradley and Dymally were very pragmatic in their quests for office. The growing Black middle-class population set the tenor of Bradley's 10th district base (Sonenshein 1993, 55–56). In contrast, Dymally's strategy was successful in districts that were more heavily working class and poor and were more aligned with radical callings rather than being fully vested in the reformist agenda (*ibid.*, 56–57). Dymally nurtured relationships with leaders on the ground and remained active in grassroots organizations.[22] In his work *The Black Politician*, Dymally often references "the community" as a necessary driving force for Black elected officials (Dymally 1978), with an emphasis on the collective that evidences a womanist approach. Thus, where Bradley saw partnerships with radical organizers as a detriment, Dymally—during the same period and in the same city—saw their full participation as essential.

While Dymally's initial base of working-class grassroots support was, no doubt, key to his 1962 Assembly win, it was likely less contributory in his election to statewide office in 1974. Dymally maintained a level of community connectedness throughout his political career and enjoyed success as both a district-level and statewide candidate demonstrating that his behavior went beyond mere pragmatism.

For both Dymally and Bradley, the emphasis on electibility is distinct from the approach of womanist leaders Charlotta Bass and Elaine Brown who both asserted that winning was not the core focus of their candidacies. While such an outcome was, of course, desirable, their central focus was bringing the issues generated by their grassroots involvement to the fore.

The Wilson, Bradley, and Dymally examples, along with the candidacies of Elaine Brown and Bobby Seale illuminate the range of approaches and forms of leadership adopted by political insiders (and prospective insiders). While Brown and Seale saw elective office as a viable tool for an ultimately grassroots agenda, Dymally, and to a lesser degree Wilson, approached the insider/outsider relationship as a partnership. Even Bradley, who worked to distance himself from radical grassroots forces, utilized the mobilized Black middle class as a base and saw the need to bring services home.

---

[21] Dymally was first elected to the Assembly in 1962. He served in that post until 1966, when he was elected to the state Senate—becoming the first Black state senator in California. In 1974 he became the first Black lieutenant governor in the state and from there was elected to U.S. Congress where he served until 1992. He returned to elected office in 2002 when he ran for and won a seat in the state Assembly and is currently a candidate for state Senate (California State Assembly 2007).

[22] Including the Black Congress, a collective of Black radical organizations, which included both the Black Panther Party and US, that came together under the principle of "operational unity."

However, relationships between the Black grassroots and BEOs were not maintained wholly by elected officals or candidates. In 1972, a three-day Black leadership summit held at the University of Southern California included members of Congress along with key members of the Los Angeles's BEO contingent, including Mervyn Dymally and Yvonne Brathwaite Burke (Brown 2005, 81; Halisi 2006). Grassroots organizers viewed such interactions as an opportunity to challenge Black elected officials to translate community calls for action into policy. The participation of elected officials served as a general acknowledgement that outside forces were a critical component to broader Black empowerment. This meeting recalls similar constellations taking place throughout the country. Adolph Reed notes:

> [I]nto the early 1970s radicals, who were by and large veterans of Black power community organizing, typically had credible claims to a grassroots political base —often institutionalized through the organizational spinoffs of antipoverty initiatives. Therefore, through that period at least mainstream Black politicians felt a need to maintain communication and visible contact with radical activists. This was evident in Black officials' attendance and participation at the 1970 Congress of African Peoples and the National Black Political Conventions at Gary, Indiana, in 1972 and Little Rock, Arkansas, in 1974 (Reed 1999, 133).

As the Black power era wound down, the pressure exerted by grassroots mobilized Black constituents receded. Instead of "taking it to the street," the electoral arena was thought to carry the greatest promise and came to dominate Black political engagement. This demobilization may explain the apparent conundrum of increasing Black representation occurring simultaneous to the deterioration of conditions for large portions of the Black community.[23] As more Blacks were elected, and with a diminished cadre of grassroots leaders to hold them accountable, BEOs became brokers for "politics as usual," and the pendulum swung strongly in the direction of incorporative inside approaches.

Renewal of an Outside Strategy—1992

The 1992 civil unrest was a watershed moment in Los Angeles history, but it also serves as an important marker in the development of Black leadership and political incorporation. The fact that one of the most prominent Black mayors in the country presided over the city during this cataclysmic rebellion suggests some of the limits of Black electoral leadership. Though he was routinely reelected with unrivaled support from the Black community, Bradley was clearly not able to balance the needs and demands of Black working-class constituents with those who made up his corporate dominated governing coalition. Responding to BEO failures and a greater sense of discontent and rage, a previously si-

---

[23] See Reed (1999, 117–59) for a discussion of demobilization and Black politics.

lent poor and working-class majority forcefully and destructively swung the pendulum back to the outside.

Along with mounting alleged financial scandals, the 1992 civil unrest spelled the end of Bradley's reign. His own rise and fall coincides with the tide of BEOs' power in California more broadly. But this landmark moment was significant not only in its tragedy, as there was hope born in the aftermath. Some Black leaders seemed to understand the tragedy as a wake-up call for a return to mobilization. Grassroots activism took on renewed fervor in Los Angeles as police brutality, educational inequity, absence of jobs and economic opportunity, neighborhood nuisance abatement, and other concerns galvanized community attention.[24] Two key figures associated with this resurgence, Mark Ridley-Thomas and Karen Bass, represent a womanist leadership style that once again married insider and outsider approaches.

Contemporary Womanist Leadership Models

Womanist leadership is rooted in womanist praxis—a theory and set of practices that center the overlapping identities that oppress women of color as the quintessential "other" (Hill-Collins 2000, 70–72). Black women leaders, both in the sphere of formal politics—and perhaps more abundantly as outside agitators—have pioneered the leadership that manifests through womanist praxis. Women like Ida B. Wells, Mary Church Terrell, the Black clubwomen of the early 20th century, Lugenia Burns Hope, and Ella Baker began to shape a womanist model of leadership that works toward societal transformation through a community-connected, group-centered coalitional praxis. The reigns of womanist leadership were later picked up by Black women like Shirley Chisholm and Elaine Brown (Abdullah 2003 and 2007; Smooth 2002). While standpoint is central to womanist identity in that women of color view the world through a unique lens of overlapping oppressions (namely racism and sexism, with classism a likely additional axis), ascription to womanist praxis and leadership is not confined to women of color. Historically, while not often stated and sometimes contrary to conflicting sexist practices, progressive men have found womanist leadership models to be the most effective in moving agitational efforts beyond reformist goals.

Black leadership can be viewed as falling along a continuum ranging from traditional to womanist. Rather than serving as a measure of political ideology, womanist categorization stands to affirm the degree to which they are rooted in the sort of community-connected leadership model that is central to womanist praxis. (Although womanist leaders tend to be of the most progressive political leanings.) On the ground, the following measures illustrate movement along the continuum: (1) trajectory to political office, with those who have a history of community con-

[24] See Gottlieb et al. (2005) for a discussion of renewed social activism in Los Angeles post-1992.

nection and entrenchment through grassroots efforts being more aligned with womanist praxis than those who have adopted traditional paths to elected office (such as political staffers, attorneys, etc.); (2) active membership in community-based organizations, with womanist leaders being more likely to be actively involved in one or more grassroots organizations, often initiating the organizations as a means through which they might ensure their community connectivity; (3) primary motivation for seeking office, with womanist leaders being recruited to run for office rather than taking the initiative to run out of some sense of personal ambition; and (4) relationships with community organizations and/or grassroots leaders as a part of their campaign strategies, with community organizations/grassroots leaders invested in their candidacies rather than simply being solicited to endorse their candidacies.[25]

Both men and women can be found on either end of a womanist/traditional leadership continuum. California Black elected officials like Byron Rumford and Bill Greene found community-connected models to be especially useful (Self 2003). Mark Ridley-Thomas stands as a contemporary example of a Black leader who not only draws from womanist models, but embraces womanist theory.

First elected to office as Los Angeles 8th District City Councilman to replace the outgoing Robert Farrell in 1991, one of Ridley-Thomas's early efforts was the development of a comprehensive strategy to address the root causes of the uprisings following the Rodney King verdict. Working in partnership with Empowerment Congress—a group of grassroots leaders in the district that came together at Ridley-Thomas's urging to serve as a true community voice with a mission to "educate, engage, and empower"—he developed a plan that was aimed at providing long-term resources to the community, focusing primarily on "economic development, community enrichment, service and human development" (Biver et al. 1995, 15).

While it is unusual to identify a male leader as womanist, Ridley-Thomas represents a unique brand of leadership that departs from traditional male-centered models. When asked about womanism and womanists—he quickly stated, "I am one!" and went on to quote womanist religious scholar, Katie Canon (Ridley-Thomas 2006).[26] Consistent with womanist leadership models, Ridley-Thomas's background prior to serving in elected office was in education and social service, with his ascent to political office driven much less by ambition than by the desire to serve (Abdullah 2002). He describes his decision to run for office as "a natural evolution of the work that I had done at SCLC" (Ridley-Thomas 2006). Prior to running for office, Ridley-Thomas was the executive director of the Los Angeles chapter of the Southern Christian Leadership Conference (SCLC-LA). In his various elected roles including city councilmember, state assemblymember and state senator, Ridley-Thomas prioritized both broad-based African-American issues,

---

[25] See Melina Abdullah's *Greater than the Sum of Her Parts* (2002) for a fuller discussion of contributing variables for womanist leadership. Also see Nancy Naples work on pathways to community work in *Grassroots Warriors* (1998).

[26] Katie Canon is author of *Katie's Canon* (1997).

including education, civil rights, and job training as well as issues that are more directly associated with women. Co-founded with his wife, Avis Ridley-Thomas, he worked to develop and secure funding for the Rosa Parks Sexual Assault Crisis Center, recognizing that South Los Angeles had the highest rate of sexual assault in the city but had virtually no service availability (Matthews 1989, 534). Prior to heading the SCLC-LA, Ridley-Thomas served as a high school teacher at Immaculate Heart High School, a girls' college-preparatory institution.[27] He also earned his Ph.D. in social ethics and policy analysis, with a concentration in social criticism and social change, from the University of Southern California. As an undergraduate, Ridley-Thomas spent time studying feminist history and liberation theology, which helped to shape his womanist vision and leadership style.

Additionally, his commitment to employing a collectivist leadership model, as reflected by the initiation of the Empowerment Congress—a forerunner to Los Angeles's Neighborhood Councils that were mandated by the city's 1999 Charter Reform—is core to the womanist approach to leadership. Drawing from his background with the SCLC and following the direction of Ella Baker, Ridley-Thomas has demonstrated his commitment to shared leadership by drawing his legislative and political priorities from the communities that he serves.

> [M]y belief in the necessity and value of forming citizen/constituent-driven organizations . . . is firmly rooted in the precept of true participatory democracy—where everyone has a voice and a corresponding responsibility in the way in which we govern. . . . I can say, without reservation, that if I occupy an elected office, the civic engagement model will be alive and well, and will be an integral part of how I discharge the duties of *any* office to which I am elected. . . . I [do] not view this job as mine to accomplish alone. I [view] myself as a catalyst for a progressive agenda driven and fueled by democratic principles and creative partnerships. . . . [E]ach partner must know his/her/their role. . . . [T]he citizen's role as teacher/student/activist, is no less important, and requires no less attention [than that of an elected official] (Ridley-Thomas 2005, 1–2).

Membership in the Empowerment Congress is open to all district stakeholders and is comprised largely of individuals who serve as informal neighborhood leaders, as well as members of neighborhood councils, local business owners, and recognized community activists. Through quarterly Congress Summits, as well as monthly meetings, Ridley-Thomas has balanced the solicitation of input from members on issues ranging from land use to public higher education with the presentation of pending legislation to garner community support. Such actions clearly

---

[27] Immaculate Heart, where Ridley-Thomas was trained by the order of nuns, has a long history of social justice and commitment to liberation theology. The Immaculate Heart Mary Sisters (IHM) order of nuns went up against Cardinal James Francis McIntyre in an effort to provide asylum to the Barrigan brothers who were protesting the Vietnam War. For more on IHM, see Anita Marie Caspary (2003). Ridley-Thomas continues to maintain relationships with several of the nuns, including Alexis Navarro, Helen Kelly, Mary Jane Pugh, and Marie Egan.

go beyond traditional constituent service models depended upon to deliver votes on Election Day. This sort of leadership model, while rarely utilized, actually won Ridley-Thomas a much stronger base of support than most mainstream politicians. As an elected official, Ridley-Thomas has acknowledged the role of a mobilized constituency in his political success. "I have enjoyed much greater success than I would have going it alone (*ibid.*, 2)," suggesting that his level of community connectedness has served both philosophical and pragmatic purposes.

A third element of the womanist leadership model that we introduce here is reflected in Ridley-Thomas's commitment to coalition politics. Departing from the strategy of deracialization, Ridley-Thomas recognizes his African-American constituency as a base that must be publicly addressed, cultivated, and appreciated, as reflected in his work as chair of the African American Voter Registration, Education and Participation Project (*ibid.*, 3). However, this recognition of his own racial identity as well as that of a great percentage of his constituency does not come at the expense of other nonBlack coalition partners. Since 1982 Ridley-Thomas has worked to identify the common challenges facing Black, Latino, and Asian Angelinos, and developing solutions that collectively empower people of color through the Black-Latino Roundtable, the Black-Korean Alliance, the Black-Jewish Youth Experience and the New Majority Working Group (Katz et al. 1992; Ridley-Thomas 2006).

Ridley-Thomas's view of the system he is a part of reflects Black power era insider/outsider strategies.

> It does not give me discomfort to critique the prevailing political economy. I'm prepared to argue for more equitable distribution of resources and primary social goods. I'm willing to advance the cause of justice rather than simple accommodation (Ridley-Thomas 2006).

Another womanist leader who emerged in the post-1992 era, Karen Bass, serves as the second contemporary case study in womanist leadership. Elected to the California state Assembly in 2004, representing the 47th Assembly District she became its first Black woman member in more than a decade.[28] Selected as majority leader in 2007 by Assembly Speaker Fabian Núñez, Bass is the first Black woman in California's history to hold the post. In 2008, Bass was elected to succeed Núñez as Speaker, becoming the first Black woman in the nation to hold more than a symbolic post as head of a legislative chamber (Williams 2008).[29] Like Elaine Brown of an earlier era in Oakland, Bass never thought she would run for political office, much less serve as majority leader of the Assembly. She was recruited to run, rather than running out of some sense of political ambition. She

---

[28] Hill, Angela. "California Lawmaker Works to Improve Her Community," *Crisis*, Vol 12, Issue 2 (2005): 8.

[29] In Washington, Rosa Franklin serves as Senate President pro tem, a largely honorary title (Williams 2008).

has often stated, "I am an activist. Being a member of the state Assembly is just my current occupation."[30]

Prior to taking her seat in the Assembly, she served as executive director of Community Coalition. Since its founding in 1990, the coalition has grown to address a broad range of issues, employing a model of leadership and an agenda for transformation that is consistent with a womanist model. In 1999, Community Coalition, based in South Los Angeles, worked to organize and mobilize high school students[31] to protest the conditions of inner-city schools and the disparities between public schools attended by Black and Latino students and those with a majority white student population. Rather than following traditional methods of leadership where power rests with a single leader and methods are limited to electoral participation and lobbying, Bass worked within the community, encouraging students to recognize their own oppression, form a movement, and participate in outside agitation that eventually led to the allocation of $2.4 billion in additional funding for schools in impoverished neighborhoods.[32]

Bass, a self-described lifelong activist, began her political and community involvement as an adolescent when a family friend encouraged her to participate in integration work in the Los Angeles area. At age 14, she began volunteering on political campaigns, serving as precinct captain for Robert Kennedy's presidential race. For her, Kennedy's assassination marked a turning point, where she moved away from liberalism and towards "leftist politics" (Bass 2003).

Bass's engagement as a womanist leader has been informed by her progressive world vision. Her emphasis on social change and societal transformation rather than liberal reform, elicits a sort of collective leadership that is indicative of a womanist model. For Bass, the most effective means of achieving more progressive agendas has been through a community-connected, coalitional model that utilizes both inside and outside methods. Further, her role as a BEO has served as one piece of the work that needs to be done.

> I've never looked at politics as elected office. Elected office is a small part of politics. I view politics as the movement for social change . . . I don't believe in the notion of the single change agent. . . . I don't believe that is the primary way change happens. Historically, change happens through social movements. I don't think the change lasts very long if it's done by one person (*ibid.*).

---

[30] Los Angeles African American Women's Public Policy Institute. "Black Women Leaders," public address, February 24, 2006.

[31] High school students from South Central Los Angeles serve as what is perhaps Community Coalition's most active and visible project—South Central Youth Empowered through Action. The mission of the project is to "recruit and train high school students to become the next generation of leaders" (Community Coalition 2002). This sort of organizing, where groups are empowered to address their own oppressions and leadership is shared, inherits the organizing principles utilized by Ella Baker, Lugenia Hope, and early African-American womens leaders.

[32] Community Coalition. Official Newsletter. April 2002.

Her leadership model has utilized both inside and outside methods. While electoral politics continue to play an important role, perhaps more important is the development of institutions that serve as "pressure agents."

> Our problem, community-wise, is once we gained the right to vote; we thought it was all done. That's why I believe that elected office is one arena of politics, but you have to have all of it in place. . . . You can be a good elected official, but if there is not an organization that is pressuring you—you need that pressure for cover, you need that pressure for focus, you need that pressure for strength. . . . [Outside methods] are frankly more important than traditional ones. I don't think the inside methods work in any kind of sustained way without outside methods continuing to push. I also believe that outside should define what's inside (*ibid.*).

This assertion that outside methods and grassroots organizing are essential to empowerment contrasts sharply against Black elected officials who view mobilization beyond voting and elections as nonpriorities or who view independent mobilized constituencies as threats to their leadership.

Conclusion

What is made apparent through the examples of Mark Ridley-Thomas and Karen Bass is the continuance of a tradition of insider/outsider partnerships for empowerment in California Black politics. Early Black elected officials in the state were compelled to pay attention to and seek approval from grassroots constituents largely because of demands made by grassroots leaders.[33] However, in the current era, where there is an absence of an independent mass political movement, mobilization is less prevalent. While there are clear examples of community-connected leaders who have proven successful in their bids for electoral seats, more traditional trajectories that embrace personal ambition, nepotism, and endorsements from incorporated Black leaders have gained popularity. Although such traditional forms of leadership are much more prevalent, they do not translate into broader-based Black empowerment. We suggest that it is not an accident that by most indicators, Black life chances have declined even as BEO numbers have been stable or increased.[34] The numbers of Blacks in office do not tell the whole story, as incorporation does not equal empowerment and the distancing of BEOs from community connections means that they are less inclined to challenge existing norms. Elected leaders like Bass and Ridley-Thomas explicitly resist this path as they seek to create ties outside the formal electoral arena. Their womanist leadership requires them to proactively seek out

[33] For example, Lionel Wilson recognized that the Black Panther Party could mobilize for him or against him. This led him to form a partnership with them in order to secure and maintain his position.

[34] California Legislative Black Caucus, 2007. *The State of Black California.*

the interests of the grassroots and prioritize those interests in their process of political agenda setting.

However, it must be recognized that as elected officials, they operate within the confines of the existing political system and they should not be counted on as being primary community mobilizers. Money is often raised from contributors who expect that the favor be returned at some future point in the legislative career of the candidate once elected. Such interests are rarely in line with the interests of the community—especially working-class and poor people. Both Ridley-Thomas and Bass have accepted campaign contributions from large corporations. Ridley-Thomas's list of contributors range from the Los Angeles Police Protective League and the California prison guards union to pharmaceutical corporate PACs, subprime mortgage lenders and large construction companies (Secretary of State 2007). Bass has recently accepted contributions from the pharmaceutical industry and the prison guards union as well as the insurance industry (Secretary of State 2007). In addition to the conflicting interests of large contributors and the voters that elect them, legislation must be passed with majority legislative buy-in. As a result, favors are doled out to liberals, moderates, and even conservatives within the legislature, both within and outside of the Democratic Party. Finally, because of the incremental nature of the legislative process, policy change is often slow to come. Thus, the limitations of womanist elected officials are clear.

In the absence of a rekindled broad-based social movement, there is still a need for a push of the pendulum of Black politics further in the direction of outside strategies. As Adolph Reed asserts, the current climate requires a return to "a functional division of labor or, what was more likely, a creative tension between new Black public officialdom and attentive Black constituencies" (Reed 1999, 152).

For electoral victories to translate into collective Black empowerment the development and maintenance of an independent strong outsider force is imperative. The position of Bass, Ridley-Thomas, and others as womanist insiders is dependent on a mobilized group that stands outside the electoral system. Grassroots leadership must stand to (1) convey their interests to electeds, (2) hold insiders accountable, and (3) serve as a looming "threat" of what might happen if the existing system is too rigid to comply with their demands. Finally, though progressive insiders might prime the pump for systemic change, such transformation cannot take place solely through the system targeted by the movement. While progressive elected officials can introduce legislation, soften liberal and moderate colleagues, and encourage the politicization of their constituencies, revolutionary transformation targets the system that insiders are a part of. Thus, while they are a vital part of the movement, they are never the movement itself—the people are.

References

Abdullah, Melina. 2007. "The Emergence of a Black Feminist Leadership Model: African American Women and Political Activism in the 19th Century." In *Black Women's Intellectual Traditions: Speaking Their Minds,* ed. Carol Conaway et al. Lebanon, N.H.: University Press of New England.

———. 2003. "Self-Defined Political Leadership among Black Women: Proactive, Group-Centered Activism beyond the Confines of Liberal Reform." American Political Science Association Annual Conference. Philadelphia.

———. 2002. "Greater than the Sum of Her Parts: A Multi-Axis Analysis of Black Women and Political Representation" (diss.). Los Angeles: University of Southern California.

Aleshire, Robert A. 1972. "Power to the People: An Assessment of the Community Action and Model Cities Experience." *Public Administration Review,* Vol. 32. Special Issue: Citizens Action in Model Cities and CAP Programs: Case Studies and Evaluation, 428–43.

Anderson, Susan. 1996. "Rivers of Water in a Dry Place—Early Black Participation in California Politics." In *Racial and Ethnic Politics in California,* ed. Byran O. Jackson and Michael B. Preston. Berkeley, Calif.: Institute of Governmental Studies Press.

Bass, Karen. 2003. Personal Interview.

Biver, Dan, and Jan Rothschild. 1995. "Mark Ridley-Thomas." *Planning,* Vol. 61, No. 4.

The Black Scholar. 1984. Vol. 15, No. 5 (September/October).

Brown, Elaine. 1992. *A Taste of Power: A Black Woman's Story.* New York: Anchor Books.

Brown, Scot. 2005. *Fighting for U.S.: Maulana Karenga, The U.S. Organization and Black Cultural Nationalism.* New York: New York University.

Browning, Rufus P., Dale Rogers Marshall, and David H. Tabb. 1990. "Can Blacks and Latinos Achieve Power in City Government? The Setting and the Issues." In *Racial Politics in American Cities,* ed. Rufus Browning, Dale Rogers Marshall, and David H. Tabb. New York: Longman.

———. 1990. "Minority Mobilization in Ten Cities: Failures and Successes." In *Racial Politics in American Cities,* ed. Rufus Browning, Dale Rogers Marshall, and David H. Tabb. New York: Longman.

Bush, Rod. 1984. *The New Black Vote: Politics and Power in Four American Cities.* San Francisco: Synthesis Publications.

California Legislative Black Caucus. 2007. *The State of Black California.*

California State Assembly. 2007. *Official Biography of Mervyn Dymally.* http://democrats.assembly.ca.gov/members/a52/biography.htm (accessed Mar. 15, 2007).

Canon, Katie. 1997. *Katie's Canon: Womanism and the Soul of the Black Community.* New York: Continuum International.

Caspary, Anita Marie. 2003. *Witness to Integrity: The Crisis of the Immaculate Heart Community California.* Collegeville, Minn.: Liturgical Press.

Covin, David. 1993. "Reflections on the Dilemmas of African American Leadership." In *Dilemmas of Black Politics: Issues of Leadership and Strategy,* ed. Georgia Persons. New York: HarperCollins College Publishers.

Crenshaw, Kimberle, and Richard Delgado (eds.). 1995. *Critical Race Theory.* New York: New Press.

Fikes, Robert. 2007. "Biography of William Byron Rumford." *Online Encyclopedia of African American History.* Quintard Taylor (ed.) Seattle: University of Washington. http://www.Blackpast.org/?q=aaw/rumford-william-byron-1908-1986. Accessed February 26, 2007.

Freer, Regina. 2004. "L.A. Race Woman: Charlotta Bass and the Complexities of Black Political Development in Los Angeles." *American Quarterly.* September, Vol. 56, No. 3, 607–32.

Gottlieb, Robert, Regina Freer, Mark Villianatos, and Peter Dreier. 2005. *The Next Los Angeles: Struggle for a Livable City.* Berkeley, Calif.: University of California Press.

Governor's Commission on the Los Angeles Riots (McCone Commission). 1965. "Violence in the City: An End or a Beginning?" (Sacramento, December). In *The Los Angeles Riots,* Robert M. Fogelson. Salem, N.H.: Ayer Company, 1988, 3.

Guinier, Lani. 2005. *Tyranny of the Majority: Fundamental Fairness in Representative Democracy.* New York: Free Press.

Halisi, CRD. 2006. Personal Interview (June 6).

Hill-Collins, Patricia. 2000. *Black Feminist Thought: Knowledge, Consciousness, and the Politics of Empowerment.* New York: Routledge.

Katz, Cindi, Neil Smith, and Mike Davis. 1992. "L.A. Intifada: Interview with Mike Davis." *Social Text.* No. 3.

Matthews, Nancy A. 1989. "Surmounting a Legacy: The Expansion of Racial Diversity in a Local Anti-Rape Movement." *Gender and Society.* Vol. 3. No. 4.

Mfume, Kweisi. 1998. *No Free Ride.* New York: Random House.

Miller, Jim, and Massiel Ladron de Guevara. 2006. "Carter's Victory a Landmark." *The Press Enterprise*, June 7.

Mitchell, John L. 2007. "Racial Issues Take a Back Seat in 37th: Multiracial Support has Laura Richardson Poised to Represent a Largely Latino District." *Los Angeles Times*, July 3, B3.

Mollenkopf, John. 1983. *The Contested City.* Princeton, N.J.: Princeton University Press.

Naples, Nancy. 1998. *Grassroots Warriors: Activist Mothering, Community Work, and the War on Poverty.* New York: Routledge.

Persons, Georgia. 1993. "Black Mayoralties and the New Black Politics: From Insurgency to Racial Reconciliation." In *Dilemmas of Black Politics: Issues of Leadership and Strategy,* ed. Georgia Persons. New York: HarperCollins College Publishers.

Piven, Frances Fox, and Richard A. Cloward. 1979. *Poor People's Movements: Why They Succeed, How They Fail.* New York: Vintage Books.

Reed, Adolph, Jr. 1999. *Stirrings in the Jug: Black Politics in the Post Segregation Era.* Minneapolis: University of Minnesota Press.

Ridley-Thomas, Mark. 2006. Personal Interview.

Secretary of State. Campaign Contributions. www.ss.ca.gov. Accessed March 10, 2007.

Self, Robert O. 2003. *American Babylon: Race and the Struggle for Postwar Oakland.* Princeton: Princeton University Press.

Smith, Jennifer B. 1999. *An International History of the Black Panther Party.* New York: Garland Publishing.

Smooth, Wendy. 2002. "African American Women State Legislators: The Impact of Gender and Race on Legislative Influence" (diss.). Silver Spring, Md.: University of Maryland.

Sonenshein, Raphael J. 1993. *Politics in Black and White: Race and Power in Los Angeles.* Princeton: Princeton University Press.

———. 1990. "Biracial Coalition Politics in Los Angeles." In *Racial Politics in American Cities,* ed. Rufus Browning, Dale Rogers Marshall, and David H. Tabb. New York: Longman.

———. 1990. "Biracial Coalitions in Big Cities: Why They Succeed, Why They Fail." In *Racial Politics in American Cities,* ed. Rufus Browning, Dale Rogers Marshall, and David H. Tabb. New York: Longman.

Stone, Clarence. 1989. *Regime Politics: Governing Atlanta, 1946–1988.* Lawrence, Kan.: University of Kansas Press.

Vogel, Nancy. 2006. "Black Democrats Expected to Take 3 Assembly Seats." *Los Angeles Times,* June 8.

Walker, Alice. 1993. *In Search of Our Mothers' Gardens.* New York: Harcourt

Walters, Ronald W., and Robert C. Smith. 1999. *African American Leadership.* Albany: State University of New York Press.

Williams, Juliet. 2008. "First Black Woman Elected to Lead Assembly." *San Diego Union Tribune*, February 29.

POLITICS

Chapter 6

Initiatives as Catalysts for Racial Politics

Terry Christensen
Larry N. Gerston

> "No man is better to govern than all others. No man is better to govern than any other man." — Hiram Johnson
>
> "The people are the ones who wield the power. . . . It is from the people that democracy gets its strength." — Arnold Schwarzenegger

Introduction

Initiatives are a central element of the public policymaking process in California. Long described as mechanisms of direct democracy,[1] initiatives are proposed legislation put before the electorate by a process of gathering the signatures of registered voters. Some are placed before the voters by interest groups or individuals with particular axes to grind; others get there when the legislature refuses or fails to resolve thorny questions.

---

[1] Elisabeth R. Gerber, Arthur Lupia, Mathew D. McCubbins, and D. Roderick Kiewiet, *Stealing the Initiative* (Upper Saddle River, N.J.: Prentice-Hall, 2001), 1.

Initiatives are a part of California's past and present, first introduced by reformer-turned-governor Hiram Johnson and the Progressives in 1911.[2] Although initiatives are employed in 23 other states,[3] the process is used with greater frequency in California than almost any other state.[4]

Aside from serving as agents of public policy, initiatives have little in common with state legislatures. Compared to the complex legislative process, initiatives are simple in design. We all know from charts that tell us "How a Bill Becomes a Law," that the legislative process is lengthy and complicated, including initial proposals, formal drafting, multiple committee hearings, amendment and more amendment, approval—and then the whole process starts over in the other house of the legislature. Most legislation doesn't survive the process, but that which does has usually—but certainly not always—been thoroughly reviewed and sometimes radically changed. Through this process, legislatures function as filtering mechanisms, contending with competing demands en route to determining policies; because they are the vortex of conflict, legislatures often fail to resolve pressing problems. Initiatives contain no such political colander; rather, voters decide policy without the benefit of committee hearings, constituent mail, meetings with various interests, or other sources of information. Nor may the proposals be amended or modified. Instead, voters-turned-policymakers give thumbs up or thumbs down relying on their own instincts and sources of information, mostly from the campaigns via direct mail or television ads.[5]

But initiatives are not only mechanisms for making public policy. They are also used to score political points, sometimes to force an issue into the public debate and sometimes as wedge issues to divide constituencies within electoral coalitions or to gain advantage for particular interests or political parties. As such, they may have significant effects on electoral outcomes and politics far beyond the issues addressed by the initiatives themselves.

Getting on the Ballot

In California, there are two types of initiatives: statutes (general laws), and constitutional amendments. Proposed initiative statutes may qualify after organizers gather signatures of 5% of the number of votes cast in the most recent gover-

---

[2] For a history of the Progressive movement in California, see George E. Mowry, *The California Progressives* (Chicago, Ill.: Quadrangle Paperbacks, 1951).

[3] Twenty-one states, including California, employ the direct initiative, which allows people to make policy directly. Three states use the indirect initiative, an approach that requires the state legislature to first consider the proposal before it is submitted to the voters.

[4] Shaun Bowler and Todd Donovan, "The Initiative Process," in *Politics in the American States*, ed. Virginia Gray and Russell L. Hanson, 8th edition (Washington, D.C.: CQ Press, 2004), 132.

[5] See Alan Rosenthal, *The Decline of Representative Democracy* (Washington, D.C.: CQ Press, 1998), 32–35.

nor's election, or about 444,952 as of 2007. Proposed constitutional amendments qualify for the ballot with 8% (711,924) of the number of votes cast in the most recent governor's election. These requirements are among the lowest found in initiative states.[6]

Low thresholds notwithstanding, few initiatives qualify for the ballot in California. Of the more than 1,200 that have been circulated for signature support, only 319, about one-fourth, have made it to the ballot. Of those on the ballot, only 105 have actually passed—and the courts have ultimately declared some of those unconstitutional. Table 1 shows the increased frequency of this policymaking tool.

Expanded Uses of Initiatives

These data obscure the fact that use of the initiative in California has grown dramatically in the past quarter century. Particularly in recent years, initiatives have emerged as the tool of groups, organizations, and ambitious individuals with extraordinarily narrow objectives who seek to legislate outcomes for a few rather than broad-based public policy. In addition, because the threshold for lawmaking via the legislature is one of the highest in the nation, elected officials sometimes turn to the initiative as a relatively speedy way of securing approval of their policy objectives.[7]

Over the past hundred years, the subject matter of initiatives has varied from arcane topics to broad themes. Sometimes, efforts have focused on narrow economic payoffs, such as taxation of oil (Proposition 87, 2006), Indian gaming (Proposition 1, 2004), workplace conditions (Proposition 97, 1988), or insurance regulation (Proposition 103, 1988). In other instances, initiatives have been proposed to create social policy. Examples include topics such as restricting abortions by teenagers (Proposition 73, 2005), medical marijuana (Proposition 215, 1996), and victims' rights (Proposition 8, 1982).

As Table 1 demonstrates, the sheer volume of initiatives has increased dramatically since the 1970s. Perhaps the watershed initiative was Proposition 13 in 1978, an extremely popular but problematic measure that strictly regulated property taxes and greatly altered public finance at all levels of government. Since 1978, interest groups, individual political leaders, reformers, corporate interests, and campaign consultants have participated in a direct democracy binge with no end in sight. But unlike past decades, in recent times money has become the crucial ingredient for a success. Grassroots support and citizen volunteers aren't enough any more. Virtually no initiative has achieved ballot status since the 1970s

---

[6] Bowler and Donovan, *op. cit.*, 138.

[7] See Peter Schrag, *Paradise Lost* (Berkeley: University of California Press, 2004), 195.

Table 1. The Track Record of Initiatives in California

Time Period	Number	Number Adopted	Number Rejected
1912–1919	31	8	23
1920–1929	34	10	24
1930–1939	37	10	27
1940–1949	20	7	13
1950–1959	11	1	10
1960–1969	10	3	7
1970–1979	24	7	17
1980–1989	52	25	27
1990–1999	50	20	30
2000–2007	50	14	36
Totals	319	105 (33%)	214 (67%)

Source: California Secretary of State.

without substantial funds to pay for signature gathering and the campaign. "We have legislation by initiative," says Ronald George, chief justice of the California Supreme Court, "and if you pay enough—and they often pay one or two dollars per signature—you can get anything on the ballot. You pay a little bit more and you get it passed."[8]

Race and Initiatives

Racial and ethnic tensions have been a part of California politics from the founding of the missions to the anti-Chinese Workingmen's movement after the Gold Rush and onward. Not surprisingly, race and ethnicity have become the subjects of several important initiatives over the years. Although few and far between, such measures go back to the early days of direct democracy. In 1920, voters approved a constitutional amendment forbidding land ownership by Japanese who were not citizens. In 1946, voters rejected Proposition 11, which would have barred employment discrimination on the basis of color or national origin. In the midst of the civil rights struggle in 1964, Californians passed Proposition 14, which repealed a new fair housing act and in 1972, they approved a ban on busing for purposes of racial integration of schools.

But demographic change in California spawned new attention on the initiative as a way of dealing with the state's challenges and perhaps as a way of introducing

[8] "Promoting Judicial Independence," *The Commonwealth* (magazine), February 2006, p. 9.

wedge issues, particularly with respect to the increased population of immigrants in California.

In 2007, immigrants comprised 27% of California's population, compared with 12% nationwide. Although California comprised about 12.5% of the nation's population, immigrants in the state—both legal and illegal—amounted to one-third of all the immigrants in the United States.[9] About half of the immigrants coming to the state were from Mexico and points south. Altogether, the massive influx of immigrants presented challenges to the state and national governments in providing public education, social welfare services, and job training. Meanwhile, although the national government maintained authority over immigration policy, federal authorities saw little reason to help California absorb its new residents, thereby requiring the state to dedicate precious resources to a controversial group.[10] Indeed, in 2006 and 2007, Congress attempted and twice failed to enact substantive immigration reform legislation.

While many have appreciated the contributions of immigrants to the California economy and the diversity of cultures and values, others have viewed these new Californians as a threat. This division of opinion about immigrants has sparked numerous initiative efforts. Some have attempted to deny basic benefits to illegal immigrants, while others have attempted to peel back opportunities afforded to nonwhites of lower economic standing or historical persecution. Much of the debate has taken place in the shadow of California's economy. A series of recessions and budgetary shortfalls have led some to point their fingers at immigrants as a drain on state revenues.[11] As the demographics of immigration intersected with volatile economics beginning in the 1980s, the frequency of race-related initiatives increased and their focus expanded to include issues of language and culture. More recent initiatives, significantly, have had the potential to pit racial and ethnic minority groups against one another. More and more, the initiative has become a battleground for the resolution of key issues in California's multicultural society. Table 2 lists major initiatives relating to race and the vote on these measures.

Proposition 63, 1986

As California grew during the 1980s, the demographic make-up of the state changed. In 1970, Latinos accounted for 12% of the state's population. Fifteen

---

[9] "Just the Facts: Immigrants in California," Public Policy Institute of California, April 2007, 1.

[10] This contradiction is summarized in Larry N. Gerston, "Immigration in California: Conflict, Confluence and Controversy," *Mediterranean Quarterly,* Vol. 15, No. 4 (Fall 2004): 68–70.

[11] Mark Baldassare discusses these parallel developments in his *A California State of Mind* (Berkeley: University of California Press, 2002), 49.

Table 2. California Propositions Related to Race and Ethnicity

Prop.	Topic	Year	Yes Vote	No Vote
1	Alien land ownership banned	1920	75	25
14*	Repeal Fair Housing Act	1964	67	33
21	Ban on school busing	1972	63	37
38	Voting material in English only	1984	71	29
63	English as official language	1986	73	27
187	No public services for illegals	1994	59	41
209	Affirmative action banned	1996	54	46
227	Bilingual education restricted	1998	61	39
54	Ban classification by race, etc.	2003	36	64

*Proposition 14 was a referendum (repealing an existing law) rather than an initiative; referenda are also placed on the ballot by petition.

Source: Secretary of State Kevin Shelley, *A History of California Initiatives*, December 2002, <http://www.ss.ca.gov/elections/init_history.pdf> (February 5, 2006).

years later, Latinos amounted to more than 20% of the state's population. These numbers and the increasing visibility of immigrants threatened the image of the "Golden State" held—or clung to—by many. As other Californians had done in the past, they worried that "their" state would be dominated by the new arrivals—who differed in race, language, and culture from the Anglo majority. In fact, in 1995, less than a decade after Proposition 63, ethnic minorities became a majority in the state's public schools[12] and soon thereafter minorities became the majority in California.

These fears were manifested in a series of ballot measures, the first of which raised the issue of language. America is a nation of immigrants, and most immigrants acculturate within a generation, adopting English as their common language. Latinos, particularly those from Mexico, have been somewhat slower to do so because their native land is so near and there are so many immigrants from Mexico in California concentrated in communities and neighborhoods, where their traditional culture thrives. That doesn't necessarily prevent them from participating fully in the culture of their new country, but some others who came here earlier concluded that more recent immigrants were resisting acculturation and living in separate societies.

The first shot in the language war was Proposition 38 in 1984 requiring publication of election ballots only in English. The initiative passed, but federal election law superseded state policy and prevented Proposition 38 from taking effect. Proposition 63, making English California's official state language, followed just two years later. Among its staunchest supporters was S. I. Hayakawa, a Japanese

[12] "In School, a Minority No Longer," *Los Angeles Times*, December 26, 1995, A1, A30.

American who had been interned during World War II and rose to become the president of San Francisco State University before winning election to the United States Senate. Hayakawa and his allies argued that only a single language, English, could unify the state's increasingly diverse population. Supporters of the initiative gathered more than one million signatures, four times the number required to qualify the initiative for the November 1986 ballot. The initiative carried with an astounding 73% of the vote.

Although proponents hoped that Proposition 63 would lead to English as the only language in public schools and other public settings, the new law turned out to be more symbolic than substantive. One study notes that because liberals in state government were in charge of implementation and because the language was so vague, "Proposition 63 was, in fact, all but ignored by state officials."[13] Rather than quell concerns, however, this attitude only stoked the flames of those who believed that California was not confronting racial issues.

Proposition 187, 1994

During the early 1990s, immigration surged in California. At the same time, the state was attempting to cope with economic recession. During this period, Governor Pete Wilson was forced to ask the legislature to raise taxes to help the state meet its basic needs. So frustrated was Wilson over the state's immigrant costs that he sued the federal government to cover costs associated with incarcerating illegal immigrants,[14] although the suits were soon rejected by federal courts. Out of this setting emerged the call to control the seemingly uncontrollable influx of immigrants who, Wilson claimed, cost the state three billion dollars in extra public education funds alone.

Frustrated over stretched state resources and the lack of federal response to the growth of immigration, political conservatives pointed to immigration as a magnet for unnecessary expenditures. In 1994, the state Republican Party joined with political conservatives to qualify the "Save Our State" initiative. Under the terms of this proposal, illegal immigrants would be denied access to public schools, public-financed health care, and virtually all public services. Locked in a tough election battle with Treasurer Kathleen Brown, daughter of former governor Pat Brown, Wilson seized Proposition 187 as a way of consolidating his conservative base and distinguishing himself from his opponent. Additional support came from former Ronald Reagan staffers who argued that Democratic President Bill Clinton was not enforcing federal legislation designed to reduce border crossings.

---

[13] Gerber, *et al., op. cit.*, 63.

[14] See "Experts Say Suit Over Immigrant Costs Will Fail, *Los Angeles Times*, April 29, 1994, A3, A33; and "Wilson Suit Affects State but Targets Nation," *Los Angeles Times*, August 11, 1995, A3, A22.

The issue and its exploitation were vividly illustrated by an inflammatory television ad showing swarms of people apparently streaming across the border. The proposition carried by a landslide of nearly three-to-two, angering Latinos, leading Democrats, and civil libertarians.

Almost immediately after passage, opponents launched nine different lawsuits against the proposition. The cases languished in federal courts during Wilson's second administration. Much of the law was declared unconstitutional by a U.S. District Court judge in 1997,[15] but some parts withstood the initial challenge. Matters changed only marginally in 1999, when newly elected Democratic Governor Gray Davis dodged the issue by offering to put the matter in the hands of a federal mediator. The new governor's response incensed his lieutenant governor, Cruz Bustamante, setting up a chasm that would haunt Davis years later during the 2003 recall election.[16] But soon after, yet another ruling declared virtually the entire proposition unconstitutional, and Davis agreed not to pursue further appeals.

Proposition 209, 1996

Two years after Proposition 187, conservatives attacked affirmative action through Proposition 209. In response to charges of discrimination against minorities and women by the civil rights and women's movements, all levels of government and most public institutions initiated affirmative action programs in the 1960s and 1970s. Special policies were introduced to assure fair hiring practices and to increase the employment of women and minorities in public sector jobs. Similar programs were introduced at institutions of higher education, including the University of California, not only for hiring of university faculty and staff, but also for admission of students. Proponents of affirmative action argued that such programs provided redress for past discrimination, increasing both fairness and diversity in public employment and public services. Greater diversity, they asserted, would assure public workers who would be representative of the increasingly diverse public they served and more sensitive to that diversity. Affirmative action in college admissions was supposed to redress similar grievances as well as to make student bodies more reflective of the state population and to expose all students to the diversity that would be part of their lives as Californians. Race and gender became crucial attributes for decisions about employment, college admissions, and more.

But there was resistance to affirmative action from the very beginning. Entrenched bureaucracies resisted changing hiring practices. Some white males argued reverse discrimination. Others insisted that race and gender trumped more substantive qualifications in hiring and admissions under affirmative action—so

---

[15] See "Judge rejects most of Prop. 187," *San Jose Mercury News*, March 19, 1998, 1A, 6A.

[16] Larry N. Gerston and Terry Christensen, *Recall! California's Political Earthquake* (Armonk, N.Y.: M. E. Sharpe Publishers, 2004), 41.

that a person who was actually less qualified by standard measures would be awarded a position over a more qualified person because of race or gender rather than the ability to perform the job.

Ward Connerly, an African-American businessman, and a regent of the University of California, became a leading spokesman for the opponents of affirmative action. Although he conceded that affirmative action programs might once have been necessary, Connerly argued that that time had passed and the continuation of affirmative action programs only served to designate persons of certain races, ethnicities, and genders as inferior. He opposed affirmative action as a form of discrimination, arguing that all should be treated equally, regardless of race or other factors. As an African American, Connerly's arguments had special resonance, offending many minority and liberal activists but giving solace to white, male critics of affirmative action. In 1995, Connerly, with the support of Governor Pete Wilson, won a close vote of the Regents of the University of California to mandate an end to race and gender preferences in admissions, an action that stunned many—especially on University of California campuses.

But Connerly wasn't finished. He soon became a leader of an initiative campaign to abolish state and local government affirmative action programs, the so-called Civil Rights Initiative of 1996, which became Proposition 209. The brainchild of a couple of academics, the initiative quickly qualified for the ballot with the support of Connerly, Governor Wilson, and the California Republican Party. A tendentious campaign followed, but the measure passed with a comfortable 54% yes vote.

The vote put California on a collision course with recent national laws and court decisions, and soon ended up in court itself. Affirmative action supporters sued to have Proposition 209 overturned on the grounds that it collided with two previous U.S. Supreme Court decisions. After several rounds in lower federal courts, the U.S. Supreme Court declined a review of an appellate court ruling upholding Proposition 209, and the initiative went into effect as state law, much to the chagrin of minority and feminist activists. Although a major victory for Connerly and Wilson, federal affirmative action programs continued and many private and public entities in California operate with some form of affirmative action guidelines that at least ensure broader outreach in hiring programs. Despite such outreach efforts, however, minority enrollment in the University of California dropped almost immediately and continued to slide.[17]

---

[17] "Less Diversity, 3K Fewer Freshmen Admitted to U.S. System," *San Francisco Chronicle*, April 20, 2004.

Proposition 227, 1998

Language and culture were soon back on the ballot with Proposition 227, titled "English for the Children." By 1998, Latino and Asian-American students accounted for 40% and 11% of California's school populations respectively. Schools faced the challenge of teaching many students who did not begin their education speaking English and who did not speak English at home. Rather than just letting them (and their teachers) struggle through the transition to a new language and culture—and because the scale of the problem was so large—many school districts introduced "bilingual" education, with instruction in both Spanish and English for several years, as students adapted to their new language. Otherwise, it was thought, teachers would be forced to focus on language rather than other subjects or, alternatively, teach the other subjects to hundreds of thousands of students who could not understand the language of instruction.

Critics argued that this system segregated students by language and relegated Spanish speakers to an inferior education. They challenged the efficacy of the system for teaching English, asserting that many students never transitioned from one language to the other. Ron Unz, a high-tech entrepreneur and millionaire, led the critics and funded signature gathering and much of the campaign, while Gloria Matta Tuchman, a Mexican-American teacher from southern California gave the critics a voice of experience. Their initiative limiting bilingual education for non-English speaking students to one year became Proposition 227 on the June 1998 ballot. As with Propositions 187 and 209, support was provided by Republican Governor Pete Wilson and the California Republican Party. Unlike earlier race-based measures, minority leaders and communities, including Latinos, were divided on Proposition 227. Bilingual teachers and many in the Latino community were adamant in their opposition, but others argued that accelerated mastery of English was essential for success in an English-speaking country. Presumably because of this division, Proposition 227 passed by 61%, an even larger margin than 187 or 209, albeit less than the 73% yes vote for Proposition 63 in 1986.

The impact of Proposition 227 is unclear even several years after its passage. California students still score low on reading tests compared to students in other states, and experts are still unable to agree on whether Proposition 227's attempts to mainstream immigrants into English instruction has been helpful or harmful to the children of California's public schools.[18]

---

[18] See Ron Unz and Catherine Snow, "Tongue Tied: Bilingual Education in the Nation of Immigrants," transcript of a debate sponsored by the Harvard Graduate School of Education, April 1, 2002, available at gsweb.Harvard.edu/news/urbaned/index08022002.html.

Proposition 54, 2003

Ward Connerly returned with another controversial ballot measure in 2003. Still concerned about racial and gender stereotypes and perhaps enjoying the limelight of campaigning, he promoted an initiative to prohibit the collection and use of race-related information by state and local governments in California (except where this would contradict federal law and in a few other specified areas). The "Racial Privacy Initiative" would still have allowed collection of race-related information in education, contracting, and employment if such classification were approved by a two-thirds majority of the legislature and by the governor as a "compelling state interest."

Once again, Connerly's proposal quickly qualified for the ballot, but while the advocates of the proposition had expected to campaign in the 2004 primary election, they ended up on the October 2003 ballot that included the recall of Governor Gray Davis. When an initiative qualifies for the ballot, it is automatically scheduled to the first available statewide election—in this case a special recall election, which greatly reduced the time available for the proponents of the initiative to raise money and organize a campaign.

Connerly and his allies argued that labeling people by race or ancestry is a form of discrimination and that state law forbids such discrimination. In addition, they asserted that racial labeling is an invasion of privacy, since people are often labeled without knowing—and since many would not identify themselves by such racial labels. Opponents of the initiative—led by the state's many active minority groups—condemned Connerly and associates as racists for proclaiming a color-blind society when discrimination still exists and for proposing to suppress data that demonstrates such discrimination and which could help reduce it.

On Election Day, Proposition 54 was defeated with a massive 64% "no" vote—the first race- and ethnicity-focused initiative to be defeated. Perhaps the tide had finally turned against these ballot measures. But this time the battle was different. Ward Connerly himself declared that being placed on the recall ballot rather than at a regular election "doomed" his proposal.[19] No initiative campaign, he insisted, could compete with the high profile recall campaign and the candidate who dominated it, Arnold Schwarzenegger. It didn't help that Schwarzenegger opposed the initiative. But the "blow that began to cripple Prop. 54," Ward Connerly wrote, "was the decision by Lieutenant Governor Cruz Bustamante [another candidate on the ballot to replace Governor Gray Davis] to hijack the 'No on 54' campaign" by channeling nearly $3.8 million in campaign contributions from tribal gambling interests into ads featuring Bustamante and opposing Proposition

---

[19] Ward Connerly, "Not a Chance," *National Review Online*, October 15, 2003 (www.nationalreview.com).

54.[20] The courts soon ruled this use of campaign funds a violation of the Political Reform Act, but only after most of the money had been spent.

Yet another key factor was voter turnout in the recall election. At more than 60%, the turnout reflected a more diverse and representative electorate than might have been expected in a normal primary election. Proposition 54 did not benefit from the antigovernment tone of the recall election. Voters rejected Governor Davis 55.4% to 44.6%, but rejected Proposition 54 by an even larger margin. Proposition 54 faced a more unified, effective, and well-funded opposition campaign than its predecessor propositions had. A coalition of groups that included minorities, women, and gays and lesbians as well as labor, teachers, and education leaders formed early on to fight the initiative and attempt to stop the trend in race- and ethnicity-related ballot measures. They worked with the anti-recall and Bustamante campaigns. Altogether, they spent over $12 million compared to $2 million by the pro-54 campaign.[21] In addition to television advertising, they mounted a massive voter contact campaign through precinct walking and phone banking. In short, they outspent and out-campaigned Connerly and his supporters.

After a stunning series of defeats—from Proposition 187 to 227—they beat back the most recent attack. But while they may have hoped to put an end to such ballot disputes, given California's diversity and continuing immigration, that seems unlikely. The outcomes of such contests may have changed, however, not only because of the efficacy of the No on 54 campaign, but also because of a secret weapon in that election: the rising number of Latino and Asian voters in California. Ironically, this increase in minority voters is partly the result of the perceived attacks on racial and ethnic minorities and immigrants in earlier ballot measures. Those who attacked won short-term victories, but ultimately may have turned the tide against themselves—forever.

Race and Plebiscites in California

In their definitive 2001 study of race, ethnicity and the initiative process, Zoltan Hajnal and Hugh Louch conclude that on the vast majority of initiatives "every racial, ethnic and demographic group . . . wound up on the winning side of direct democracy almost as often as every other group. . . . The probability that blacks and Latinos voted for the winning side was 59%. The comparable figures for Asian-Americans and whites were 60% and 62% respectively." All groups were

[20] *Ibid.*

[21] The pro-54 campaign failed to disclose $1.7 million of its $2 million in contributions until over a year after the election when Connerly and allies were forced to do so by the Fair Political Practices Commission. The belated report revealed that media magnate Rupert Murdoch, conservative brewer Joseph Coors, and others each gave $100,000 to $400,000 to Ward Connerly's American Civil Rights Coalition which in turn funded the initiative campaign. *San Francisco Chronicle*, May 19, 2005.

about equally likely to obtain the outcome they preferred, although Latinos were slightly less successful.[22]

In other words, Californians across the racial and ethnic spectrum tend to agree on ballot measures overall. That's not true, however, on propositions that directly address issues of race, ethnicity, and immigration. According to Hajnal and Louch, on these propositions (187, 209, 227), "nonwhites fared poorly compared to whites." The chances of voting for the winning side were 32% for Latinos, 48% for Asian Americans, 57% for African Americans, and 64% for whites.[23] Moreover, the authors found that, "most Asian-American voters sided with the white majority on Proposition 38 [voting materials in English only] and 227 [bilingual education]; most blacks voted with the white majority on Proposition 38. Over half of Latino voters sided with the white majority on Proposition 63 [English as official language]. In short, there was no consistent 'minority' position. . . ."[24] But Propositions 38 and 63 were put before the electorate in the 1980s, when there were far fewer Asian and Latino voters. Ultimately, Hajnal and Louch found the trend of nonwhites losing on these issues worsening rather than improving over time (Propositions 187, 209, 227), but their study ended before the defeat of Proposition 54. Only future ballot measures can confirm or repudiate the trend.

We know that racial and ethnic minority voters—especially Latinos—have opposed ballot measures focusing on race, ethnicity, and immigration, albeit with varying degrees of intensity. Hajnal and Louch demonstrate that, for the most part, however, minority votes are in synch with majorities on other sorts of ballot measures. But a closer look at selected initiatives suggests some variation within that trend. In the March 2000 primary election, for example, a majority of white, black, Latino, and Asian voters supported Proposition 22, defining marriage as between a man and a woman (as opposed to same sex partners); 65% of Latino voters supported the measure as compared to 62% of blacks, 59% of Asians, and 58% of whites.[25] On the other hand, in the March 2004 primary, Latino, black, and Asian voters were more likely to support public education by lowering the threshold for voter approval of school bonds. A majority of whites (52%) opposed the measure, while 65% of Latinos, 68% of blacks, and 55% of Asians supported it.[26] In the November 2004 election, minority voters supported stem cell research more

---

[22] Zoltan Hajnal and Hugh Louch, *Are There Winners and Losers? Race, Ethnicity, and California's Initiative Process* (San Francisco: Public Policy Institute of California, 2001), vi–vii. Also available online at www.ppic.org. Hajnal and Louch based their conclusions on data from exit polls by the Field Institute and the *Los Angeles Times* for elections from 1978 to 2000.

[23] *Ibid.*, vii.

[24] *Ibid.*, 22.

[25] *Los Angeles Times* Poll, March 9, 2000. <http://www.latimes.com/news/custom/timespoll/> (accessed February 6, 2006).

[26] *Los Angeles Times* Poll, March 2004. <http://www.latimes.com/news/custom/timespoll/> (accessed February 6, 2006).

strongly than white voters and overwhelmingly supported a health insurance proposal that went down to defeat because of white opposition.[27] In the 2005 special election, Latino voters opposed all of Governor Schwarzenegger's initiatives (teacher tenure, restrictions on political uses of union dues, state spending limits, and redistricting) by huge margins ranging from 68 to 76%, while the "no" vote among white voters ranged from 49% to 57%, according to PPIC polls.[28]

These figures suggest that while minority voters are usually on the winning side of ballot measures except where the measures relate directly to issues of race, ethnicity, and immigration—as Hajnal and Louch report—they tend to vote differently than the white majority across a range of issues. White voters are generally more conservative on these issues while Latino, African-American, and Asian-American voters are generally more liberal.

Race, Ethnicity, Initiatives and the Changing California Electorate

In the long run, the most significant impact of the series of initiatives relating to race and ethnicity in California may not be on the particular policies they addressed but on the composition and disposition of the California electorate. Perceiving themselves under attack, hundreds of thousands of Latinos and Asian Americans became politically engaged. Many became citizens and many more registered to vote. And increasingly, when they registered, they chose the Democratic Party over Republicans—and voted accordingly.

For decades, Latinos and Asians Americans have constituted a far lower proportion of voters than of the total population of California. To some extent this may be due to socio-economic status, especially for those most recently arrived from Mexico and Vietnam, or to apathy or alienation, but two other factors are probably more significant: youth and citizenship status. Many more Latinos and Asian Americans are too young to vote, while black and white populations are older and so continue to dominate the electorate. Many Latinos and Asian Americans have not yet attained citizenship status, so many who are old enough cannot vote. Political scientists Jack Citrin and Benjamin Highton report that just 27% of immigrants from Mexico who have been in the United States for 10 years or longer have become citizens—clearly slow progress towards political incorporation. But "Latino and Asian immigrants do become politically incorporated over time," they write. "The longer they live in the United States, the more likely they are to become citizens, and the longer foreign-born citizens have been in the

---

[27] *Los Angeles Times* Poll, November 2004. <http://www.latimes.com/news/custom/timespoll/> (accessed February 6, 2006).

[28] "Just the Facts: Special Election Voter Profiles," Public Policy Institute of California, November 2005 <www.ppic.org> (accessed February 6, 2006).

United States, the more likely they are to vote."[29] The same is true for Asian-American immigrants (and for earlier immigrants from Europe).

Thus, perhaps inevitably, citizenship, eligibility to vote, registration, and active participation by minorities have steadily increased over the past decade. But the initiatives that were perceived as antiminority and anti-immigrant were surely a significant spur to organizing and engagement. Minorities were just 21% of the California electorate in 1992. But the number of Latino voters alone nearly doubled in the 1990s, and by 2004 minorities were 33% of the voters, with virtually all of the increase coming from Latino and Asian-American voters.[30] The Latino electorate alone nearly doubled in the 1990s. Minorities were over 54% of the California population in 2004, but age, citizenship, and socio-economic status still resulted in underrepresentation, despite these significant gains.

What produced the gains? The normal process of the political incorporation of immigrants is a partial explanation. But increased participation in California was stimulated and accelerated by perceived antiminority and anti-immigrant ballot measures and public policy. Proposition 187 in 1994 was seen as a direct attack on their communities by many Mexican Americans and Asian Americans. They reacted by mobilizing, on college campuses and in barrios and neighborhoods. They lost the fight in 1994, but Proposition 187 was a prime mover in their increased political incorporation. Then in 1996, the U.S. Congress passed a welfare reform bill that excluded even legal immigrants from public services, a further affront (later remedied at the urging of President Bill Clinton). Propositions 209, 227, and 54 followed. Although California's varied minority groups reacted somewhat differently to these measures, all were perceived as part of a sustained attack on minorities, particularly Latinos, and Proposition 54 eventually produced a broad coalition of minority groups and their allies in successful opposition. During the 1990s alone, over a million Latinos registered to vote. Over half of Latinos now registered have done so since 1994 (Proposition 187). Asian-American registration and participation also increased dramatically.

The initiatives stimulated registration and participation, which may change electoral outcomes in California to the extent that Latino and Asian-American voters are more favorably disposed towards government spending on education, for example. But the initiatives did not simply increase registration and participation; they drove new minority voters directly into the welcoming arms of the Democratic Party and may have alienated them from California's Republican Party forever.

Vietnamese and Chinese voters, for example, have traditionally been inclined to register Republican, reflecting that party's anti-Communist stance in support of the Vietnam War and of Taiwan. But Proposition 187 and the 1996 welfare re-

---

[29] Jack Citrin and Benjamin Highton, "Latino Political Integration Follows European Pattern," *Public Affairs Report* (Winter 2002), 7.

[30] Field Poll Release #2150, January 20, 2005 "Recapping the State's 2004 Vote."

forms drove many Asian voters away from the Republican Party, even as younger Asian voters focused more and more on issues unrelated to their ancestral homelands. Partly as a consequence of the series of race- and ethnicity-related initiatives, increasing numbers of Asian-American voters are registering as Democrats or decline-to-state, and in some parts of the state, Democrats have taken the lead among Vietnamese and Chinese-American voters.[31] Overall, 39% of Asian-American "likely voters" report that they are registered as Democrats, with 31% as Republicans and 30% "decline to state" or "other."[32] Other estimates of Asian-American partisan preferences put the Democratic percentage higher.

Meanwhile, Latinos have been even more strongly aligning with Democrats, with a solid majority of about 60% consistently identifying with that party[33] and even larger majorities supporting Democratic candidates. In 1998, for example, exit polls reported that Democratic candidate for governor Gray Davis won 78% of the Latino vote (as well as 83% of the black vote and 67% of the Asian vote).[34] Al Gore, the Democratic candidate for president in 2000 won 68% of the Latino vote.[35] Democrat John Kerry did a little less well (66%) with Latinos voters in California in 2004, but still trounced his Republican opponent, who won a larger share of the Latino vote nationally than any previous presidential candidate. Percentages in the 2003 recall election were weaker, with only 53% of Latinos voting to oppose the recall of the governor they had so enthusiastically supported previously and only 55% voting for Cruz Bustamante, the state's highest ranking Latino elected official, as his replacement.[36] As noted above, in the 2005 special election, Latino and other minority voters overwhelmingly cast their ballots against Governor Schwarzenegger's initiatives and in support of the Democratic Party line.

In short, California has witnessed the steady alignment of its minority voters with the Democratic Party. While black voters overwhelmingly register and vote Democratic across the nation, Latinos and Asian Americans do not. Democrats elsewhere may do well with these voters, but Republican candidates often split the vote or win pluralities. That's not the case in California because the enthusiastic support of the Republican Party and Republican Governor Pete Wilson for Propositions 187, 209, and 227, has led many members of minority communities to conclude that Republicans are unfriendly to minorities or even racist. The California Republican Party, dominated by conservatives, has done little to dispel this perception, despite the election of an immigrant as governor in 2003.

---

[31] *San Jose Mercury News*, September 19, 1999, 1A.

[32] "Just the Facts: Latino Voters in California," Public Policy Institute of California, August 2005. <www.ppic.org> (accessed February 6, 2006).

[33] *Ibid.* The PPIC reports 56% of Latinos who are "likely voters" say they are registered as Democrats, with 23% reporting registration as Republicans and 21% claiming other parties or "decline to state."

[34] California Opinion Index (The Field Institute).

[35] "Just the Facts: The November Election" Public Policy Institute of California, November 2000. Gore won 86% of the black vote and was about equal to Republican George W. Bush among Asians and whites in California.

[36] See Gerston and Christensen, *Recall*, fn. 17, 136.

This doesn't mean the instant or total transformation of California politics. Whites are projected to remain a majority of voters until 2040,[37] and recently Latinos and Asian Americans have shown a somewhat greater inclination to register "decline to state" rather than Democratic. But it does mean that the current California electorate is strongly Democratic and that as more Latinos and Asian Americans participate it will only become more so. Can Republicans win these voters back? The verdict is split, if the 2006 gubernatorial election is any guide. According to exit poll data gathered by the *Los Angeles Times*, 33% of the state's Latinos and 31% of African Americans voted to re-elect Republican Arnold Schwarzenegger; 57% of all Asian Americans, however, voted for Schwarzenegger.[38] Beyond Schwarzenegger, the Republican Party is still dominated by conservatives who are not perceived as friendly to minority communities or their interests, which often require government spending. Perhaps more significantly, decades of political science research tells us that once a person commits to a party (by registration and by voting), switching to another party is rare. By supporting a series of initiatives that were perceived to be race baiting, Republicans may have doomed their party into the foreseeable future, bartering that future in exchange for short-term victories. The fate of Proposition 54 suggests that such victories may be at an end, but only when a broad-based minority coalition can be built around opposition to such measures. The next test could come on the issue of driver's licenses for illegal immigrants.

Race, Ethnicity, and California Politics

Controversies about race, ethnicity, and immigration are as old as California—from the conflict between missionaries and native Californians to the Yankee takeover, the Gold Rush, the importation of Chinese workers and the anti-Chinese campaigns to the Los Angeles police patrols sent out to turn back Okie and Arkie immigrants from the Midwest Dust Bowl in the 1930s and the Minute Men on the state's borders today. California draws more immigrants than any other state and perhaps any other place in the world. California is more diverse than any other state and perhaps any other place in the world. Conflict is inevitable and perhaps even healthy. And because California is unique among states and nations in the extent to which it practices direct democracy, that conflict will inevitably be expressed through the initiative process. But as we have seen, the initiatives themselves are not necessarily the end of the process.

---

[37] See Jack Citrin and Benjamin Highton, *How Race, Ethnicity, and Immigration Shape the California Electorate* (San Francisco: Public Policy Institute of California, 2002), 69.

[38] *Los Angeles Times* Poll, November 2006. <http:www.latimes.com/news/custom/timespoll/> (accessed July 28, 2007).

Chapter 7

Labor, Minorities, and Voter Initiatives: The Search for Diversity and Social Justice

Kenneth C. Burt[1]

Ethnic and racial politics in California have long reflected both the interests of working-class minorities and the influence of organized labor. The relationship has been surprisingly durable largely because of a shared membership in the Democratic Party. As a result, the greatest gains for minorities and unions—in terms of electoral victories, political appointments, and the enactment of public policy—have come through Democratic Party membership. For example, the 2007–08 California State Legislature is one of the most prolabor legislatures in history and one of the most diverse. As a result of this labor-backed diversity, there are 26 Latinos, eight African Americans, and seven Asians among the Democratic ranks. There is also a sizeable number of gays and lesbians, Jews, and women who are likewise part of the Democratic mosaic. In contrast, the Republican caucuses include only two Asians and two Latinos. Among the ethnically diverse Asian population, the two Republicans are of Japanese and Vietnamese heritage, while the seven Democrats hail from Chinese, Japanese, and Korean backgrounds and at least one is an immigrant.

Surprisingly, there is little scholarship focused specifically on the political interaction between labor and minorities. Minorities are mentioned in books on la-

[1] The author thanks Jaime Regalado for reviewing this essay and for his insights.

bor, and, conversely, labor is discussed in a few books about ethnic and racial minorities. This is true for Philip Taft's *Labor Politics American Style: The California State Federation of Labor* (1968), the lone study on the state's labor politics. In her new book, *L.A. Story: Immigrant Workers and the Future of Labor Movement* (2006), Ruth Milkman talks about politics in the context of organizing new workers. Three works include labor in the context of multiracial politics. Raphael Sonenshein's *Politics in Black and White: Race and Power in Los Angeles* (1993) examines the fabled coalition supporting Los Angeles Mayor Tom Bradley. My book, *The Search for a Civic Voice: California Latino Politics* (2007), explores the coalition behind Congressman Edward Roybal, the first Latino elected to the Los Angeles City Council in modern times. Robert Gottlieb, Mark Vallianatos, Regina M. Freer, and Peter Dreier use history to outline progressive policy in *The Next Los Angeles: The Struggle for a Livable City* (2005).[2]

This chapter examines the labor-minority relationship through the lens of that peculiar California institution, the initiative, with a focus on labor's response to four efforts by conservative business interests to use the initiative in reducing the economic and political influence of unions. The first two initiatives, in 1938 and 1958, were designed to weaken labor's collective bargaining power. The second pair of initiatives, in 1998 and 2005, would have made it more difficult for labor to spend its money for politics. Labor successfully reached out to minority voters in each of the four campaigns.

Another aspect of the labor-minority relationship is the relative strength of the two groups. The continuum of minorities in political engagement will be divided into three categories: participant, potentially pivotal, and partner in the political process. Let's define these terms. In the participant period, minority voters were engaged in the political process, but they represented a nominal number of voters and had few elected officials. In the potentially pivotal period, the total number had grown sufficiently to decide an election only if it was close. The partner period represents almost a paradigm shift because minority voters could affect the election and/or their leaders were central to developing strategy from the start of the campaign.

There is yet another political overlay to the four initiative campaigns: ideology and the perceived "future value" of a relationship. This is essential to understanding motivation as well as behavior. Within organized labor, there has always been a group of progressives that identifies minorities as historically downtrodden and in need of assistance. Although this has been rooted in ideology, there has also

---

[2] Kenneth C. Burt, *The Search for a Civic Voice: California Latino Politics* (Claremont, Calif.: Regina Books, 2007); Robert Gottlieb, Mark Vallianatos, Regina M. Freer, and Peter Dreier, *The Next Los Angeles: The Struggle for a Livable City* (Berkeley: University of California Press, 2005); Ruth Milkman, *L.A. Story: Immigrant Workers and the Future of the U.S. Labor Movement* (New York: Russell Sage Foundation, 2006); Raphael Sonenshein, *Politics in Black and White: Race and Power in Los Angeles* (Princeton, N.J.: Princeton University Press, 1993); Philip Taft, *Labor Politics American Style: The California State Federation of Labor* (Cambridge, Mass.: Harvard University Press, 1968).

been some self-interest as well because these union leaders have often sought to organize workers within these communities. For minority group leaders, some have developed a positive view of unions based on past experiences, based on labor's ability to raise wages and fight discrimination. Likewise, a minority politician might believe that an alliance with labor is essential to winning in a Democratic Party primary. Labor might see the primary election choice as being between a labor-oriented candidate and a "business Democrat." The choices in these individual legislative races are reflected in statewide candidate and voter-initiative campaigns. Statewide institutional political leaders calculate future value to relationships and demographics trends the same way Wall Street investors value a stock. The next election, like the next quarterly statement, is highly valued, but so too is the long-term investment in individual careers and coalitions.

The 1938 Election

The first antilabor initiative appeared on the November 1938 ballot along with candidates for governor and the state legislature. Proposition 1 was designed to limit the tools available to unions to organize workers and negotiate collective bargaining contracts. The election provided the first open contest between labor and capital in the state at a time when class was the dividing line nationally between the realigned Democratic and Republican parties. Two years earlier, President Franklin D. Roosevelt had won reelection by bringing union members, African Americans, and the foreign born and their children into the Democratic Party.

At that time there was only a small number of minority voters in the state and labor was a significant but not dominant institutional force. It had been only four years since voters elected the black Democrat, Augustus Hawkins, to the state legislature from Central Los Angeles. Large numbers of black voters would not move into the state until the beginning of World War II in 1941. The limited number of Latino voters tended to be transplants from New Mexico and other states or the children of refugees escaping the violence of the Mexican Revolution.

Assemblyman Hawkins' election as a prolabor legislator followed the increased labor militancy exhibited by a left-wing labor leader, Harry Bridges, and the International Longshoremen's and Warehousemen's Union. The union had shut down West Coast ports in 1934; the killing of a striker had led to the 1934 San Francisco general strike. The following year, President Roosevelt and Congress created the National Labor Relations Board.

The California Federation of Labor, the state affiliate of the American Federation of Labor (AFL), decided to remain neutral in the governor's race to focus their attention on mobilizing their members, Democratic and Republican, to vote against Proposition 1.

The inchoate Congress of Industrial Organizations (CIO), led by Bridges, took a different tack. It mobilized its more radicalized members to reach out to minorities and other community groups to build a progressive coalition to defeat

Proposition 1 and elect Culbert Olson, who promised to bring Roosevelt's New Deal to California as governor. In this effort, Assemblyman Hawkins and Benjamin Rosenthal, who represented Yiddish-speaking Jews in the Boyle Heights section of Los Angeles, helped rally their respective communities. Latinos did not have a legislator, but ethnic community organizations were able to obtain the attention of political leaders and encourage voting. The CIO, the Olson campaign, and the Democratic Party all reached out to African Americans, Jews, and Latinos, particularly in Los Angeles.

The ultimate defeat of Proposition 1 and the victory for Olson in November 1938 elevated the political importance of organized labor and minority groups, despite their small numbers. This is underscored by postelection activities. The Olson administration supported the CIO-backed First National Congress of the Mexican and Spanish-American Peoples of the United States, in Los Angeles. Speakers included Olson's son and top aide, Lieutenant Governor Ellis Patterson, and the chief of California's Division of Immigration and Housing, Carey McWilliams. Olson appointed the first Latino and the first African American to the bench, naming Mexican-born Ataulfo "A. P." Molina to the San Diego Municipal Court and Edwin Jefferson to the municipal court in Los Angeles.[3]

The CIO hired Hawkins, the part-time legislator, to help oversee the CIO political action committee (CIO-PAC). Moreover, the legislature passed, and Governor Olson signed, the first fair employment bill, authored by Hawkins, in June 1939. The 45-word bill outlawed discrimination on public works because of "race, color, or religion."[4] Olson likewise vetoed a bill that would have prohibited "relief or aid from any moneys" appropriated by state or local government for people who could not document their legal status.[5] The ideology and a desire for a relationship with the minority communities on the margins of society that drove Olson and the CIO held enormous potential for unionization and political activity.

The 1958 Election

The next big breakthrough for minorities, both in terms of appointments and policy, followed the November 1958 election when labor came from behind to defeat Proposition 18, the so-called right-to-work initiative. U.S. Senator William Knowland sought to ride the antilabor sentiment into the California governor's office. Even as organized labor began to alert its members to the perceived

---

[3] Augustus Hawkins interview, Washington, D.C., June 28, 1998; California Secretary of State, Executive Records, F3680:9, 397, California State Archives; "Molina," *Martindale-Hubbell Law Dictionary*, 1942, 70.

[4] Chapter 643, Statutes of California, 1939, California State Archives.

[5] Mario T. García, *Mexican Americans: Leadership, Ideology, and Identity, 1930–1960* (New Haven: Yale University Press, 1989), 159–60; Juan Gómez-Quiñones, *Roots of Chicano Politics, 1600–1940* (Albuquerque: University of New Mexico Press, 1994), 386.

threat, the AFL reminded the Republican Party that having its gubernatorial candidate attack unions could prove fatal: "Governor Culbert L. Olson became California's only Democratic governor of the century" by defeating the incumbent who supported an antilabor voter initiative.[6] The AFL statement was not an idle threat because Governor Earl Warren, a moderate Republican, had won re-election with AFL backing.

To rally the civil-rights community, the labor movement brought in A. Philip Randolph, the president of the Brotherhood of Sleeping Car Porters. The African-American labor leader was affectionately known as the "father of the FEPC" (the Fair Employment Practices Commission had been established by Roosevelt during World War II). Randolph provided the keynote address for a labor conference on human rights in Los Angeles in early October 1958. The Mexican-American–oriented Community Service Organization (CSO), the NAACP, and the Jewish Labor Committee cosponsored the conference with the AFL's L.A. Central Labor Council. Speakers included Assemblyman Hawkins and L.A. City Councilman Edward Roybal, the state's highest-ranking African-American and Latino elected officials, respectively. The labor-minority coalition reaffirmed labor's commitment to push for the enactment of fair employment legislation and emphasized the stake minority voters had in preserving collective bargaining in the state. A strong labor movement contributed to raising wages and ensuring equal treatment on the job; union resources were also central to the ongoing campaign for a state and local "FEPC." According to Tony Ríos, the steelworker who headed CSO statewide, the implication from the conference was clear: labor, with its future on the line and in need of a massive voter turnout by minority voters, was committing itself to going all out to ensure passage of the state FEPC should the Democrats win the election.[7]

Labor and minority activists took the campaign to their respective neighborhoods. On Los Angeles's East Side, labor formed the Eastside Committee of the Committee to Save Our State. James Cruz, who chaired the group, had served as a business agent for the AFL Brick and Clay Workers and was a member of the L.A. Democratic Central Committee and CSO's Labor Advisory Committee. The group kicked off its election outreach with a Saturday afternoon car caravan that snaked through the working-class neighborhoods, raising awareness of the election and stopping at major shopping centers to distribute information to voters. Three days later the group sponsored a rally at the local Carpenters Hall in the Boyle Heights district. Activists and elected officials organized yet another rally a few days later to inaugurate a new headquarters on Brooklyn Avenue, which

---

[6] "State AFL Launches Fight against 'Right-to-Work' campaign," *Los Angeles Citizen*, January 17, 1958, 5; Totton James Anderson, "The 1958 Election in California," *Western Political Quarterly*, Vol. XII (March 1959); Philip Taft, *Labor Politics American Style*, quote on p. 241.

[7] "Speakers Set for Human Rights Meet," *Los Angeles Citizen*, September 12, 1958, 1; "Praises Labor as Champion of Civil Rights, *Los Angeles Citizen*, October 17, 1958, 1.

served as the dispatching center for the massive precinct-walking operation against Proposition 18 and for the Democratic Party ticket.[8]

Gubernatorial candidate Edmund G. "Pat" Brown made a commitment to the black and Latino communities, as did labor. He pledged himself to support a fair employment law, as was then in effect in 14 states. Moreover, he pledged to initiate "within thirty days of becoming governor" a meeting of "leaders in business, in labor, in government and in all aspects of our lives" to find solutions to challenges in the "field of human relations." The Democratic candidate reached out to minority voters through the auspices of the minority-led "Community Groups for Pat Brown."[9]

For its part, organized labor oversaw the most extensive field campaign in the history of the media-driven state. The campaign also invested more than half its $2.5 million war chest in billboard, radio, and television commercials. Ultimately, labor outspent the gubernatorial candidates and drove the agenda in an election that saw Proposition 18 decisively defeated, Pat Brown elected the second Democratic governor in the century, and both houses of the legislature taken by the Democrats for the first time in the century. The new legislature would include Byron Rumford, an African American from Oakland.[10]

By 1958 labor's ranks had grown dramatically since 1938, peaking with about a third of the private sector organized and embraced by moderate Republican governors Earl Warren and Goodwin Knight. So, too, had the number and sophistication of minority voters increased in 20 years. While Hawkins remained the sole African-American legislator, Los Angeles City Councilman Edward Roybal provided leadership for the Mexican-American community. This growth in total voters and elected leaders gave minority voters the capacity to play a pivotal role in a statewide election between two evenly matched candidates. There was also a growing number of AFL and CIO leaders committed to civil rights and a growing statewide network of Latino and black leaders. The labor leaders were driven by ideology as well as the practical benefits of coalition politics. A. Philip Randolph, father of the FEPC, and William Becker, chief lobbyist for the Fair Employment Practices Commission in California, shared roots in the old Socialist Party.[11]

On assuming office in January 1959, Governor Brown and organized labor kept their commitment to make the creation of a state fair employment practices commission a top priority. Becker emphasized the importance of the liberal-labor coalition in passing this landmark civil rights bill in a legislature with only two

---

[8] "Eastside Rally Against 18 Saturday," *Los Angeles Citizen*, October 17, 1958, 1; "Eastside Leaders Told Evils of Proposition 18," *Los Angeles Citizen*, October 24, 1958, 1.

[9] Brown, Statement on Civil Rights, 1958, b. 56, f. Minority Group Data, Pat Brown Papers, Bancroft Library, University of California, Berkeley.

[10] Totton James Anderson, "The 1958 Election in California," 299; Philip Taft, *Labor Politics American Style*, 241.

[11] Author's interview with William Becker, St. Helena, Calif., September 8, 1993.

African Americans and no Latino or Asian members.[12] Brown appointed a record number of blacks and Latinos, as well as Asians, to state posts; Asians and Latinos won seats in the state legislature for the first time during his tenure. Brown's appointments reflected both a reward for past support and the perceived future value of the relationship. This helps explain why the number of Latino appointees increased along with the growth of the Latino electorate, some of which was paid for by the AFL-CIO. CSO used labor money, for example, to register 140,000 new Latino voters for John Kennedy in 1960.[13]

The 1998 Election

Forty years after the historic 1958 campaign, the issue of labor's role in state politics once again assumed center stage. The rematch occurred in yet another political environment. Labor's percentage of the workforce had fallen with the decline in state manufacturing. Within organized labor, the largest and most politically engaged unions represented the state's public-sector workers, who won collective bargaining rights in the 1970s, along with California farmworkers. The minority communities had grown numerically but were still a small presence at the ballot box. This was particularly true among Latinos. Worse yet, in 1994 Republican Governor Pete Wilson had won reelection by backing Proposition 140 to deny education and health care to children without documentation, winning in a campaign seen by most analysts as anti-Latino. For its part, the California Democratic Party consisted of a coalition of racial and cultural minorities, blue- and white-collar union members, and well-educated professionals.

Grover Norquist, the central figure in a web of conservative organizations in Washington, D.C., teamed up with the state's outgoing governor, Pete Wilson, to sponsor Proposition 226. It would have eliminated the right of unions to spend money collected from union dues on politics unless each member agreed in writing on an annual basis. The state's unions, led by the California Teachers Association (CTA) and the Service Employees International Union (SEIU), undertook a campaign emphasizing that Proposition 226 would "silence the voice" of working families. The initiative ultimately failed despite starting out with a two-to-one lead in the polls. The initiative was defeated as a result of overwhelming opposition by labor-union members and racial and ethnic minorities. Latinos, who for the first time were becoming a significant percentage of the statewide vote, were still angry with Governor Wilson for Proposition 187; local leaders such as Los Angeles County Federation of Labor head Miguel Contreras helped mobilized union and

---

[12] Becker interview. See also Marty Schiesl, "The Struggle for Equality," in *Responsible Liberalism: Edmund G. "Pat" Brown and Reform Government in California,* ed. Martin Schiesl (Los Angeles: California State University, Los Angeles, Edmund G. "Pat" Brown Institute of Public Affairs, 2003), 103, 105.

[13] Becker interview.

community activists. African Americans and others were upset with Wilson's support of Proposition 209, which ended affirmative action at state colleges and for government employment.

On Election Day, Proposition 226 lost at the ballot box because of high turnout by union members, Democrats, and minorities, according to an *L.A. Times*/CNN poll. Union family members constituted 23% of the vote, and 67% voted no. A greater number of Democrats (72%) voted no. Broken down by race, whites voted yes by a 10-point margin while minorities, who composed 29% of the total, killed it owing to overwhelming opposition. African Americans (14% of the total) voted no 69% of the time. Latinos (12% of the total) voted no 75% of the time, while Asians (only 3% of the total) voted no at 52%, and Jews (5%) voted no at a 63% rate.[14]

Proposition 226 drew labor closer to minorities by teaching a new generation of political leaders the importance of coalition politics in a state where minorities were a growing share of the electorate. A series of recent conservative-driven voter initiatives had targeted the right of unions to participate in politics, affirmative action, and immigrant access to health and education services. Minority voters had opposed the antilabor initiatives, and liberal unions had provided a large share of the resources to oppose the antiminority propositions. And they would do so again in 2004 when Proposition 54 would have prevented the state from collecting racial data, even for use in fighting disease. In this expensive and largely media-driven campaign, SEIU, CTA, and the California Federation of Teachers (CFT) were major donors, while the California Labor Federation has used its slate cards to successfully oppose this racially divisive measure.

It was yet an earlier conservative, Republican-backed proposition that was to have the most impact in the state Capitol. Proposition 140 imposed legislative term limits and was designed at least in part to force Assembly Speaker Willie L. Brown, Jr., a long-serving African American, out of office. Minority advocates and academics worried that the small number of minority elected officials would decline further. The concern spread as cities looked at term limits. "A significant question, especially for political incorporation theorists, is whether the incorporation of communities of color will be more difficult to achieve, and sustain, under term limits," wrote Jaime Regalado, director of the Pat Brown Institute at California State University, Los Angeles in 1998. "It seems likely that, since mass-based electoral and community coalitions have historically been difficult to maintain over time, it would be difficult to consistently create and/or maintain electoral coalitions to replace 'termed' councilmembers."[15]

The dislodging of incumbent politicians, as it turned out, provided a unique opportunity as labor and minority groups worked together to increase the number

---

[14] "Profile of the Electorate," *Los Angeles Times*, June 4, 1998, A30.

[15] Jaime Regalado, "Minority Political Incorporation in Los Angeles: A Broader Consideration," in *Racial and Ethnic Politics in California,* ed. Michael B. Preston, Bruce Cain, and Sandra Bass (Berkeley: Institute of Governmental Studies Press, 1998), 393.

of elected prolabor and minority officials. This had a dramatic affect, starting in Los Angeles, with the election of progressive, Latino, former union leaders such as Gilbert Cedillo, Fabian Núñez, and Antonio Villaraigosa. The new labor and community alliance extended beyond empowering Latinos and beyond Los Angeles, although developments in L.A. County represent the most visible successes. The L.A. Federation of Labor was instrumental in electing activist-oriented African Americans, most notably Karen Bass and Mark Ridley-Thomas. The unions also helped elect Judy Chu, a community college professor and American Federation of Teachers member. Organized labor was also central to electing the legislature's first acknowledged lesbian, Jackie Goldberg, a former union leader, who had authored the Los Angeles Living Wage Ordinance. The impact of these new legislators, many from labor's ranks, has resulted in a change of leadership, with Villaraigosa becoming assembly speaker—then mayor of Los Angeles—and Núñez being elected assembly speaker in his freshman year. These elected officials shaped the response to Governor Arnold Schwarzenegger's assault on public-employee unions in 2005.

Schwarzenegger Takes On the Teachers, Nurses, Firefighters, and Police Officers

Governor Arnold Schwarzenegger entered office with a popular mandate following the recall of Governor Gray Davis in 2003. His polling numbers reached stratospheric proportions as voters placed their hopes in his ability to provide bold leadership that would bring the state together in a forward-looking, bipartisan approach. His initial efforts only enhanced his image. He got the legislature to roll back the car tax, further heightening his image as a populist and demonstrating bipartisanship (the legislature was afraid to go against perceived popular will). He had, however, deepened the state budget deficit by some $4 million.

The CTA then cut a deal with the governor. They agreed to give back the $2 billion that was owed public schools under Proposition 98, but it would have to be repaid the subsequent year. Likewise, the California Labor Federation and their legislative allies were forced to accept a compromise on workers' compensation that primarily benefited employers when the governor threatened to take an even more distasteful measure directly to the people in the form of a ballot initiative. Driven by similar pragmatism (and to prevent massive cuts in social programs), the legislature agreed to help the governor by supporting propositions on the November 2004 ballot increasing bonded indebtedness.[16]

Following the November 2004 election, the governor and his advisors, mostly veterans of Pete Wilson's administration, began to prepare for an even more ambitious agenda. Stating that 2005 would be his "year of reform," Schwarzenegger used his state of the state address and subsequent statements to advocate for per-

[16] In terms of full disclosure, the author served as a participant-observer in these events as political director of the CFT.

manently shrinking the state's budget and to severely limit future growth. He emphasized he was not open to any compromise that might include revenue enhancement. As part of this effort, he made it clear that he had no plans to repay the money owed to the public schools. Schwarzenegger announced that he was determined to end pensions for newly hired teachers, firefighters, police officers, and other employees of state and local government. The governor proclaimed that if the legislature did not do his bidding, he would go over their heads to the people, who would pass his proposal as voter initiatives. The threat had worked with the seemingly intractable issue of workers' compensation; it might work again.

The public employees undertook a multitrack strategy. The CTA reached into its media budget and began airing television commercials educating the public about the governor's "broken promise" to pay back the money he had borrowed from the schools. The ads had legitimacy because they reinforced news accounts coming out of the Capitol. The *Los Angeles Times*'s George Skelton, for example, started a column this way: "Governor Arnold Schwarzenegger may be confused. Perhaps he's in denial. Or maybe he's being disingenuous. Or just parsing words. Or even lying."[17]

The broken promise cast a pall over the governor's dealings with legislators. A commitment had to be honored. How could anyone else, legislator or union leader, make a future deal if they were not sure it would be honored? The whole political system depended on honor among adversaries. Moreover, the CTA ads were resonating with the public, which supported greater educational funding and thought the governor should pay back the schools what he owed. More damaging to the governor's long-term interests, however, was the growing sense that he did not keep his promises.

The Pension Coalition, an established and long-functioning group composed largely of legislative advocates representing employee groups, set out to defeat the governor's pension privatization bill. Soon the bill's Achilles' heel was discovered. By eliminating funds for a pension, Schwarzenegger was eliminating the funding source for state-provided disability insurance. The police and firefighters unions went public, attacking the governor for trying to take away benefits from widows and orphans.

The message was communicated through press conferences and in a pair of radio ads that were aired more heavily in rural and conservative regions. The governor denied the charge. But the police and firefighters were adamant; Schwarzenegger was seeking to hurt the families of those who made the ultimate sacrifice. The governor's advisors came to understand that it was an argument they could not win. The legislature killed the bill and the governor was forced to abandon his fatally flawed voter initiative because there was not enough time to begin anew on signature collecting to qualify for the forthcoming special election.

---

[17] George Skelton, "Governor Is Digging Himself Deeper with Denial of School Funding Deal," *Los Angeles Times*, May 19, 2005.

During this same period the unions met and formed a new umbrella organization, the Alliance for a Better California.[18] Joe Nuñez chaired the alliance and often served as its public face. The director of governmental relations for CTA, Nuñez (no relation to the speaker) had grown up modestly in Santa Maria, an agricultural community on the state's Central Coast. The coalition started with the assumption that the governor's popularity must be lowered to increase their chances in a special election, but voters would ultimately judge each proposition on its own merits. The group realized that events over the next several months would create the context for the election. The alliance soon hired a large and bipartisan team of consultants and undertook an "inside" and an "outside" strategy, seeking to discourage the governor and other conservative groups from submitting signatures for a host of ballot initiatives, including one that would effectively remove public-sector unions from state politics.[19]

Schwarzenegger formally called the special election for November 2005 and announced support for his so-called reform package, which included Proposition 75, to require unions to get individual members' permission for specific political expenditures. This would effectively take public-employee unions out of politics. Union leaders viewed this as the governor's use of the "nuclear option." Labor could compromise on public policy, just as it did not get everything it wanted in its collective-bargaining agreements. But to severely reduce or eliminate labor's ability to engage in politics in the future was unacceptable. Organized labor mobilized its resources for the fight, seeking yet another dramatic, come-from-behind victory.[20]

Yet this election was different. The governor had called the special election precisely because it would produce a smaller turnout, with more conservative voters predisposed to support his positions. In order to have a chance of winning, labor needed to run a campaign aimed at "likely voters," and one that would also motivate "low-propensity voters (those less likely to vote)" to either vote by mail or go to the polls. It was a tall order.

The unions ultimately spent close to $100 million on issue ads, member-to-member communication, the Alliance campaign, and to oppose the governor's four initiatives; these included efforts to make it easier to fire teachers and to shrink the state budget, leading to funding cuts for schools, health care, and public

---

[18] The alliance consisted of the American Federation of State, County, and Municipal Employees; Association of California School Administrators; California Correctional Peace Officers; California Faculty Association; CFT; California Labor Federation, AFL-CIO; California Professional Firefighters; California School Employees Association; CTA; Peace Officers Research Association of California; SEIU; and SEIU Local 1000. The California Nurses Association declined to join.

[19] The consulting team included Gale Kaufman, McNally Temple, Larry Grisolano (lead on Proposition 75), and Phil Giarrizzo. See "Walking the Tightrope: GOP Warrior Takes on Own Party: Republican Political Guru Ray McNally Quarterbacks TV Campaign Aimed at Schwarzenegger Agenda," *Capitol Weekly*, August 18, 2005, 1.

[20] For information, including numerous links, go to www.igs.berkeley.edu/library/htUnionDues.html.

safety. This massive expenditure allowed the unions to run almost nonstop TV ads featuring teachers, nurses, police officers, and firefighters from January to November 2005. The campaign also established a grassroots structure.

The governor hurt his cause by picking fights with too many groups, raising millions from corporate special interests, and appearing disconnected from ordinary people. During the epic confrontation, Democratic legislative leaders refused to compromise on other issues, thus denying the governor the opportunity to appear bipartisan or to claim any policy achievements.[21]

The role of minorities in this campaign differentiated it from labors' three previous defensive campaigns. Joe Nuñez led the alliance and represented the most powerful union in the state. From the beginning, the coalition committed itself to incorporating members of minority groups into the campaign at all levels. This included an allocation of resources to mobilize minority voters, starting with focus groups to better understand black, Latino, Korean, Chinese, and Vietnamese voters. In addition to targeted outreach, plans were made to use African Americans, Asians, and Latinos in TV advertising on network and cable programs. A priority was placed on working with the chairs of the legislative caucuses representing these groups. The meetings provided an opportunity to discuss ways the groups could work together to win the election. This included recommendations for staff hiring and support for campaigning and get-out-the-vote (GOTV) efforts in various parts of the state. The campaign ultimately spent more than $5 million on minority media and outreach.[22]

The recognized importance of minority voters corresponded to the changes in the state legislature and the labor movement and reflected the needs of the campaign and of ideology. The 1998 campaign had been the first wherein labor lost the white vote and won because of strong support among minority voters. Alliance polling indicated that members of minority groups were included among the millions of low-propensity voters whom the campaign sought to motivate. Some of these potential voters were union members but others were not. Moreover, labor had spent a decade electing a more diverse legislature. Reaching out to legislative leaders for help demonstrated respect and provided a way to transform a "labor issue" into a "minority issue." This would be important to minority voters who look to their elected officials for political signals on how to vote and, most important for this election, the importance—the urgency—of voting.

The alliance's work in the emerging Asian community, which received minor attention in 1998, illuminated labor's expanded outreach effort, even as the cam-

---

[21] For a contemporary view of the governor's problems, see Dan Walter's 10-part series, "Arnold's Errors," *Sacramento Bee*, December 14–23, 2005, 3.

[22] Internal campaign documents in author's files. For an examination of the drop in the governor's approval among Latinos, see "Schwarzenegger Battles to Regain Favor with California Latinos: Polls Show Support Plunging as Arnold Promises Visit with Mexican President," *Capitol Weekly*, September 22, 2005, 1. See also "Spanish Language Commercials Now Standard for Statewide Campaigns: A Niche Market Has Gone Mainstream; Soaring Ad Revenues Triple in Two Years," *Capitol Weekly*, November 24, 2005, 1.

paign focused greater resources on African Americans and Latinos (and the all-important Spanish television).

The campaign tapped into the expanding network of Asian elected officials for support, including Assemblywoman Judy Chu in Monterey Park and Assemblyman Leland Yee in San Francisco (whose district included Daly City Filipinos). The campaign lined up support from the Asian Law Alliance, Chinese Progressive Association, Filipinos for Affirmative Action, and National Korean American Service and Education Center. The campaign used these political and organizational leaders as messengers to make the defeat of Proposition 75 salient to the Asian community. The multilanguage Asian press played a central role.

These efforts had a tremendous impact, according to Northern California Asian Outreach Coordinator Alicia Wang, because most Asian-elected officials are Democrats, and a large number of Asians—like Latinos—were newer voters. "It's the first generation, new voters and new citizens, that get all their information from the ethnic press," said Wang. It helped that Wang, a community-college professor, was herself a longtime activist in the Asian community, the Democratic Party, and organized labor.[23]

The campaign used mail, phoning, paid advertising, and flyers (including materials in Hmong and Cambodian) to reach small groups that together constituted a sizeable block of voters. So, too, did the unions. For example, the California Labor Federation oversaw, for the first time, Vietnamese-language phone banks calling union members in Orange County and San Jose, and then statewide to great effect. These efforts were layered on top of an avalanche of mail and worksite conversations.[24] They were reinforced by the presence of an Asian schoolteacher in a long-running TV ad. And on Election Day, the Asian groups were listed on GOTV door hangers along with other coalition partners.[25]

On Tuesday, November 8, 2005, California voters decisively defeated four voter initiatives sponsored by Governor Schwarzenegger, including Proposition 75, designed to effectively remove labor from state politics. The scale of the victory and size of the voter turnout surprised pundits and government officials alike. Special elections without statewide candidates on the ballot typically draw small turnouts with voters that tend to be white, older, and more conservative than the electorate as a whole. Yet in this election more than half the registered voters went to the polls and one in four were minorities. The *Los Angeles Times* emphasized that the more than 61% turnout exceeded voter participation rates in every statewide election for the last 22 years.[26] These highly motivated voters helped defeat Proposition 75 by a seven-point margin—53.5% to 46.5%.[27]

---

[23] Author interview with Alicia Wong, by phone, November 18, 2005.

[24] Author interview with Bryan Blum, by phone, November 19, 2005.

[25] Door hanger, "If You Don't Vote, He Wins," author's files.

[26] "Voters Rejecting Schwarzenegger's Bid to Remake State Government," *Los Angeles Times*, November 9, 2005, 1, with sidebar, "Election Turnout," 1.

[27] Secretary of State, Statement of the Vote, November 8, 2005, with comparative data back to 1910, certified December 15, 2005, Secretary of State web site.

According to the Public Policy Institute of California's postelection survey, the initiative failed because of opposition from three overlapping groups: union members, Democrats, and minorities. This included opposition from 68% of Latinos, who constituted 15% of the electorate, with combined Asians and blacks making up a slightly smaller number.[28] Not surprisingly, postelection polling for the California Labor Federation showed that the strongest opposition came from union members who were also Democrats and minorities.[29]

The 2005 Special Election represents, on one level, a continuation of a string of defensive battles by organized labor over a 70-year period. But on another level, it represents the culmination of a demographic and political transformation. It was the first time that the statewide labor coalition was led by a Latino and that the role of minority elected officials and minority outreach efforts were central to the campaign's design and operation. This reflects the dramatic growth in the number of minority voters as well as in the number of minority legislators. But it also reflects the "future value" that organized labor places on its alliance with minority groups. This relationship is rooted in the mutual self-interest of public employees providing public services that benefit minorities, but that conservatives want to eliminate or reduce. There is an ideological overlay because the unions are committed to enacting public policy to uplift workers and minorities into the middle class.

Conclusion

Organized labor and minority communities have been aligned within the California Democratic Party since the 1930s. In this context, the unions sought—and succeeded—in animating minority-voter anger with antilabor initiatives on the basis of both race and class. The relationship has evolved along with the growth in the number of nonwhite voters. In 1938, minorities participated in the political process, but Assemblyman Augustus Hawkins was the sole elected official, and the total number of voters was small. By 1958, Hawkins and City Councilman Edward Roybal represented African Americans and Latinos, respectively, and the number of voters had grown enough to be potentially pivotal. In contrast, minorities accounted for a quarter of the electorate in 1998. Labor came to view minority communities as a political partner. The relationship evolved, and by 2005 the labor-community alliance had reached a more mature relationship. Latino leaders such as Miguel Contreras and Joe Nuñez symbolized the fact that labor had become an organization increasingly representative of and, at times,

---

[28] Public Policy Institute of California, 2005 Special Election Voter Profile and other material distributed at postelection briefing, "The Future of Policymaking in California," in Sacramento, December 5, 2005. *Los Angeles Times* poll showed 72% of Latinos disapproved of governor's handling of his job, in "The Times Poll: Voters Dislike 3 of Governor's Propositions," *Los Angeles Times*, November 2, 2005, 1.

[29] Final Results, CLF Post Election Member Survey, November 9–23, 2005, David Binder Research.

politically led by minorities. The election of state legislators such as Gilbert Cedillo and Judy Chu likewise showed that minority legislators were unionists. These developments contributed to greater labor-minority cooperation and understanding. This relationship will require attention, however, as conflicts among allies are inevitable and, in a term-limited environment, future legislators might not share these same values or coalition orientation.

Chapter 8

Political Incorporation in California's Central Valley and Central Coast

Kim Geron

This chapter will focus on the efforts of racial minorities to achieve political incorporation in California's San Joaquin Valley and the central coast region. Specifically, after an overview to the region's demographics, we will explore political incorporation efforts in three communities in three different counties. Using political incorporation theory, we will explore if the tenets of this urban based multiracial coalition politics are applicable in valley cities and less populated areas. Political incorporation refers to the extent to which group interests are represented in policymaking either on their own as a majority that can substantially influence local issues or as participants in a governing coalition that can shape decision-making to benefit the community. For racial minorities, this has meant historically replacing conservative governing coalitions with new coalitions that changed institutions and the distribution of policy benefits so that those historically excluded were able to obtain them.[1] Yet, achieving office may not result in full political incorporation for racial minority communities.[2] Can

---

[1] Rufus P. Browning, Dale R. Marshall, and David H. Tabb, *Racial Politics in American Cities*, 3d ed. (New York: Longman Press, 2003).

[2] Jaime A. Regalado, "Minority Political Incorporation in Los Angeles: A Broader Consideration," In *Ethnic and Racial Politics in California*, Vol. II, ed. Michael B. Pre-

racial minorities in two of California's fastest growing regions, the Central Valley and Central Coast, achieve substantive and not just descriptive representation, incorporated into the dominant political coalitions that shape the politics and economics of these two important regions of California?

A Brief Overview of the Central Valley and Central Coast Regions

The Central Valley of California runs from Shasta County in the north to Kern County in the south, it contains 6.6 million residents and is one of the fastest growing areas of the state. By the year 2025, the population is expected to surge to 9.3 million people.[3] Agriculture is the dominant industry in the region. Issues such as the impact of urbanization of farmland, air quality, transportation, education, and affordable housing are major concerns in the region. The Central Valley is a large geographic area that is socially, politically, and economically varied and public opinion in this region is very diverse.

The San Joaquin Valley, which forms a major portion of California's four hundred mile Central Valley, includes eight counties: Kern, Fresno, Madera, Tulare, San Joaquin, Stanislaus, Merced, and Kings; and the Central Coast of California is comprised of Santa Barbara, San Luis Obispo, Monterey, and Santa Cruz counties. Large portions of both these regions are tied to agricultural production. In addition to their contributions to the state's economy, these regions can be viewed as a series of multi-ethnic communities with changing demographics and levels of political incorporation for racial minorities.

While the predominant racial and ethnic groups are white and Latino, there are concentrations of African Americans and Asian and Pacific Islanders in some communities as well. This racial diversity is reflected in the composition and levels of political incorporation in local government and other county and state-level positions based in the region. In Browning, Marshall, and Tabb's study of 10 northern California cities in the 1960s and 1970s, two of the cities they studied, Sacramento and Stockton, are located in the Central Valley.[4] In the late 1960s, African Americans and Latinos were a small part of the city of Sacramento's population; yet, they forged an alliance with liberal whites that successfully challenged the dominant conservative group by building an electoral coalition that helped elected racial minorities into office.[5] In Stockton, an entrenched conservative coalition dominated city hall. A coalition of African Americans, Latinos, and

---

ston, Bruce E. Cain, and Sandra Bass (Berkeley: Institute of Governmental Studies Press, 1998).

[3] "Special Survey of the Central Valley in Collaboration with the Great Valley Center," PPIC Statewide Survey," Public Policy Institute of California, June 2006, 3.

[4] Rufus P. Browning, Dale R. Marshall, and David H.Tabb, *Protest Is Not Enough* (Berkeley: University of California Press, 1984).

[5] *Ibid.*, 60.

white liberals, rather than attempting to win office citywide first, changed the electoral structure from at-large to district elections in 1971. This led to the election of two African Americans to the city council. Racial minorities in these two cities engaged in protests similar to efforts in urban communities in the Bay Area.

Since the period of the Browning, Marshall, and Tabb study, the Central Valley and Central Coast regions of California have gone through dramatic demographic changes; the Latinization of rural California has substantively impacted local politics, and other nonwhite communities have faced continuing challenges in rural communities of California. What path to political incorporation has been used by racial minorities and immigrants, and how successful have their efforts been as they have become the majority population in many communities over the past 40 years?

Central Valley Demographics and Political Incorporation

The Central Valley is perceived as politically conservative, however this is slowly changing as demographics and politics combine to change the region's politics. Within a conservative political environment there are pockets of liberal voting patterns, mostly among communities of color. The Central Valley region has historically more self-identified conservative voters on social issues;[6] yet, the growth in Latino voters, while still relatively small, and the differences they hold on key issues with white Central Valley voters based on social and economic disparities are significant

Historically, nonwhites were forced to live in segregated communities. In cities with district electoral structures, Latinos and other racial minorities have utilized residential concentrations to carve out districts with high concentrations of minorities to achieve political success. In instances where Latinos, in particular, become the majority population, they have come to dominate local politics, although not necessarily to achieve local economic power.

An analysis of San Joaquin Valley demographics indicates in Fresno County Latinos are 44% of the county population compared to nearly 40% for whites, 5% for African Americans, and 8% for APIs. Looking more closely at the city level, in Parlier, San Joaquin, Huron, Mendota, and Orange Cove, Latinos are 90% or more of the population. In Kern County, which is 38.4% Latino, the largest city is Bakersfield, and there are two cities, Arvin and McFarland, that are greater than 85% Latino. In one Central Coast county, Monterey, the cities of Gonzales, Greenfield, King, and Soledad are 80% or greater Latino.

In several of these Latino majority cities, Latinos have become the dominant political players, such as Parlier in Fresno County. In 1972, Mexican Americans organized to win the majority of the city council seats after organizing a grass

---

[6] "Special Survey of the Central Valley." PPIC Statewide Survey, Public Policy Institute of California, April 2004.

roots campaign to wrest power from the dominant Anglo business interests.[7] They have held a majority of the council seats ever since. In other agricultural communities, the process of political transition from Anglo to Mexican-American dominance has been much slower. In nearby Firebaugh, where eight of 10 residents are of Mexican descent, until 2004 there had only been four times in the city's 90-year history when a Mexican American had been elected to office. Similarly, in Coalinga with a Latino population of nearly 50% there were no Latinos on the city council in 2004,[8] and only one Latino on the city council in 2007.[9] The slower growth at the municipal level is in contrast to more rapid growth on school boards. While the number of Latino elected officials in the state has increased from 796 in 1994 to 1,080 in 2005 and 1,163 by 2007, much of this progress has come at the school board level where Latinos increased their numbers more than 43%, whereas at the municipal level, they increased less than 16% in the same time period (see Table 1).

The growth of Latino political influence can be observed in Fresno County. In 2007, seven of the 15 cities in Fresno County were headed by Latino mayors, and they were a formidable influence on Council of Fresno County Governments (COG) that determines how monies will be distributed within the county for major countywide projects such as transportation. There were a total of 101 Latino elected and appointed officials in this county, or 11.5% of the total number of Latino officials in the state, second only to Los Angles County. Latinos hold two of the five board of supervisors positions, and two state Assembly and one state Senate position along with numerous judgeships and school board seats throughout the county.[10] Despite this overall growth, Latinos are a majority or near majority of the population in many agricultural communities in Fresno County; yet they have not achieved political representation comparable to their population in several local areas. This is due to a number of factors including low U.S. citizenship rates, voter registration, and voter turnout. Many of the residents of these agricultural communities have limited experience voting. Because Latinos are assumed to be low-turnout voters, they are not approached to register and participate in the electoral process:[11]

---

[7] Sosa Riddell Adaljiza and Robert Aguallo, Jr., "A Case of Chicano Politics: Parlier, California," *Aztlan: International Journal of Chicano Studies Research,* University of California Los Angeles, Vol. 9 (1979).

[8] Donald Coleman, "Hispanics join city council contests: In Firebaugh, elected officials of Mexican descent have been rare," 2004, at www.fresno.com (accessed on July 27, 2006).

[9] 2007 National Roster of Hispanic Elected Officials. National Association of Latino Elected and Appointed Officials.

[10] Author's analysis based on the 2007 National Roster of Hispanic Elected Officials. National Association of Latino Elected and Appointed Officials.

[11] Melissa R. Michelson, "Getting out the Latino Vote: How door-to-door canvassing influences voter turnout in rural Central California." A paper presented at the Western Political Science Association, Long Beach, Calif., March 22–24, 2002.

Table 1. Total Latino Elected Officials for California in 1994 and 2005

Level of Office	1994	2005
U.S. Congress	4	7
State Officials		1
State Senators	3	10
State Assembly	9	19
County	14	25
Municipal	319	369
Judicial/Law Enforcement	50	43
Education	381	547
Special District	16	59
Totals	796	1,080

Source: 1994 and 2005 *National Roster of Hispanic Elected Officials*. National Association of Latino Elected and Appointed Officials.

There is also a significant African American presence in the central and coastal valley. They are nearly 8% of the population in Fresno County and are 11% (47,136) of the City of Fresno's population. There is currently one African American on the Fresno city council, Cynthia Sterling. African Americans are 10.8% of the population of Sacramento County, due to a high concentration in the city of Sacramento (16.4% or 61,136 people). Since the late 1960s, they have had a visible presence in Sacramento politics. During 1983–1986, Grantland Johnson was a city council member, and later a Sacramento county supervisor. In 2007, Lauren Hammond, a ten-year veteran of Sacramento city council, was the first African American woman to hold this seat. In San Joaquin County, African Americans are 11% of the county's population; this number is driven by a significant Black population of 19.3% in Stockton, the highest of any Central Valley city. In Tulare County, Carlton Jones, an African American firefighter sits on the city council in the City of Tulare, where there is a 4.7% African American population.

The only other city in this region with a significant percentage of African Americans is Seaside (12.9% in 2000), in Monterey County. This city borders Fort Ord, a military processing center from World War II to the end of the Cold War in the early 1990s. Many African Americans worked on the base or lived in the surrounding working class segregated community of Seaside. African Americans have been visible in local electoral politics since the 1960s.[12] Jerry Smith was elected as a Monterey County Supervisor in 2004; he became the first Afri-

[12] Chuck Thurman, "The Power of the Pulpit: For four decades, Rev. H. H. Lusk did not hesitate to use his position to influence local politics." *Monterey Weekly*, December 6, 2001, at: www.montereycountyweekly.com (accessed on July 25, 2005).

can American to be elected in the county in 155 years. Before becoming a Supervisor, Smith served as Mayor of the City of Seaside for three terms. He was first elected Mayor in November of 1998.[13]

Asian and Pacific Islanders are not a significant proportion of the population in most San Joaquin Valley communities. They are 11.1% of the total statewide population in 2000, 8% in Fresno County, and 11.1% in the city of Fresno where there is a high percentage of Southeast Asians. In Kern County, while they are only 3.3% of the total county population, they are 15.2% of the population of Delano, home to the United Farm Workers of America (UFWA), and a large Filipino farmworker population. In Sacramento County, they are 11.4% of the population, and 17.3% of the population in the city of Sacramento. Asian and Pacific Islanders have had a less visible electoral role with very few elected officials except in cities such as Stockton and Sacramento, where they have been able to construct multiracial coalitions to win office. In one rural community, the city of San Joaquin, in Fresno County, there are two South Asians on the five-person city council (the other three are Latinas), Amarpreet Dhaliwal who is the mayor and Tehal Dhesi, a city council member, in a community with less than a 4% Asian population. Asian Americans have been elected in other rural communities over the years such as Delano in Kern County and Lodi in San Joaquin County.

In exploring the economics of the region, the per capita income for the San Joaquin Valley was $24,550 in 2002, or 26% below the state average of $32,989. There are also subregional differences with southern San Joaquin Valley counties ranking lower than metropolitan Sacramento in per capita income.[14] Agriculture remains a dominant part of the regional economy providing 20% of all jobs in the San Joaquin region in 2002 even though there were 10,000 fewer jobs than 10 years earlier due to mechanization of farm jobs and less labor intensive crops being harvested. Growing international competition for agricultural products is another concern for the regional economy with looming threats to farm jobs and industries. Wages in agriculture are extremely low, averaging $8.10 per hour in South San Joaquin Valley counties and $8.39 in North San Joaquin Valley counties in 2004.[15] Each year, more land is being taken out of farm use; for example, during 1999–2003, 283,777 acres or 3.7% of the Central Valley's irrigated land was taken out of farm use primarily for housing and other urban uses.[16] As more people move from the large urban areas on the coast to the Central Valley there will be greater pressure on transportation, the environment, and housing.

On the central coast region, the large numbers of Latinos in places such as Watsonville in Santa Cruz County, and numerous communities in Monterey County are a product of the heavy concentration of farm labor and food process-

[13] "Jerry C. Smith of Seaside, California, Recognized for His Life by PositiveBlackImage.com" at: www.PositiveBlackImage.Org (accessed on July 25, 2005).

[14] The State of the Great Central Valley of California: Assessing the Region Via Indicators: The Economy 1999–2004." 2005. Great Valley Center. page 10.

[15] *Ibid.*, 10

[16] *Ibid.*, 28.

ing. The struggle of farmworkers for decent working and living conditions remains a central theme in the central and coastal valleys of California. The economy shapes the demographics, as immigrants, mainly from Mexico come to work in the fields and food processing plants. Most of this work is low paid, dirty, and nonunion. The United Farm Workers of America (UFWA) and the International Brotherhood of Teamsters unions only represent a small fraction of the farmworkers that totaled over 1.1 million seasonal workers in 2001, or the equivalent of 388,000 year-round fulltime workers.[17] The vast majority of farmworkers in California are immigrants from Latin America. Most first-generation immigrants cannot fully participate in the political process due to citizenship status.

The Central Valley has been dominated by large-scale agribusinesses for many decades. Many family farmers lost their land to business speculators who bought out the farmers, and consolidated them into large-scale farming operations. Rural California's agricultural industry has been restructured into a complex system that integrates farms controlled by agribusiness corporations, a shift from owner-operated farms to farms now staffed by labor contractors who hire immigrant farm laborers.[18] Partly because California was never dominated by small family-operated farms, it has been in the forefront of these changes, relying on a mobile, flexible labor force.[19] Some of the remaining family farmers held onto their lands only to sell to real estate speculators who have sped up the process of paving over the valley with housing subdivisions as desperate urban dwellers move farther east to find affordable housing and better schools.

While the Central Valley appears similar to urban communities when it comes to the breadth of ethnic and racial diversity, the impact of racial minorities in most valley communities is both minimal and substantial. Their impact has been minimal in the sense racial minorities have had a limited role in the local economic and political decision-making until recently. However, their impact is substantial in the sense they are the majority population and their incomes provide the revenues to help sustain the local economy. Yet, they are not major land owners, real estate developers, or business people. They are dependent on others for their financial sustenance. The population density of large numbers of Latinos in valley communities has political implications. While the coastal areas of Monterey and Santa Cruz are known for their beach cultures and values, most outsiders are unaware that in the cities of Salinas, Watsonville, and other agricultural communi-

---

[17] M. Akhtar Khan, Phillip Martin, and Phil Hardiman, "California's Farm Labor Markets: A Cross-Sectional Analysis of Employment and Earnings in 1991, 1996, 2001." Employment Development Department, State of California, August 2003.

[18] Refugio Rochin and Elaine Allensworth, "Latino Concentration in Rural California: The Conditions of Ethnic and Economic Patchwork," Occasional Paper No. 30 (East Lansing, Michigan: The Julian Samora Research Institute, Michigan State University, December 1997).

[19] Juan Vicente Palerm, "Farm Labor Needs and Farm Workers in California 1970 to 1989," California Agricultural Studies Report #91–2 (Santa Barbara: University of California, 1991).

ties, Latino politics has evolved over the past few decades and more often than not has set the tone for local politics. According to one local Latina politician:

> Power is still in the hands of Anglo growers. . . . The ag industry has started to reach out to the Latino elected officials around development interests in the community . . . what has happened is that the more conservative powers that be have recognized the leadership of Latinos and have begun to welcome us at the table, to discuss solving the social issues.[20]

The question that must be asked is whether the inclusion of Latino politicians is synonymous with political incorporation? We will explore this question more fully in the next section. To understand the diversity of political activity by non-white racial groups, it is essential to explore politics at a local level. The next section will explore the evolution of political incorporation efforts for racial minorities. In Browning, Marshall, and Tabb's most recent study of political incorporation of racial minorities in 10 northern California cities, they explore the incorporation of minorities onto city councils, in city government employment, and on police review boards as three measures to assess whether political incorporation has occurred.[21] They found that Stockton continues to lag behind many other northern California cities in the access and openness of the political system to political incorporation efforts. We will examine Stockton, a rapidly growing multi-ethnic city to understand how and to what extent political incorporation efforts have evolved.

Stockton, San Joaquin County

In San Joaquin County, 45 miles south of the state capitol, lies Stockton, a city of nearly 280,000, the 12th largest city in California. It is an important agricultural center of the San Joaquin Valley and is the business and commercial center of the county. The delta region surrounding Stockton makes the area one of the richest agricultural regions. Since the city was incorporated in 1850, it became home to a rich diversity of racial minorities including Asian ethnic groups, African Americans, and Mexicans. A small Chinatown enclave was built in the 1850s.[22] Japanese Americans have a long history in Stockton with strong roots in agriculture where they grew to become an influential economic force before

---

[20] Anna Caballero, "The Boomtown Chronicles: Reflections on a Changing California." An interview with Anna Caballero, mayor of Salinas, California. Recorded July 2004 by Rachel Gordon.

[21] Rufus S. Browning, Dale Rogers Marshall, and David H. Tabb, "Mobilization, Incorporation, and Policy in 10 California Cities," in *Racial Politics in American Cities*, ed. by Rufus S. Browning, Dale Rogers Marshall, and David H. Tabb (New York: Longman Press, 2003), 38.

[22] Sylvia Sun Minnick, *Samfow: The San Joaquin Chinese Legacy* (Fresno, Calif.: Panorama West Publisher, 1988).

World War II. During the war, all Japanese on the West Coast were incarcerated and lost their land.

Stockton developed a vibrant Filipino community center, known as Little Manila, which grew in the 1920s–1940s as Filipinos lived in nearby farm labor camps and in town, and spent their limited resources in Little Manila while they worked in the region.[23] With 10,000 residents living in the Stockton area at the height of the asparagus-picking season in the 1930s, 1940s, and 1950s, Filipinos claimed about a third of Stockton's population.[24] African Americans have had a continuing presence in Stockton since the 1850s working in mining, agriculture, and settling down with a small community that grew during and after WW II.[25] Yet, while minorities helped build Stockton into a thriving regional agricultural center, they were not represented in elected office. When minority groups in Stockton attempted to get a response, more often than not, they were listened to but no action was taken so minorities began to take stronger action. For example, Mexican-American organizations tried in 1970 to get the city to form a Human Rights Commission, but the council told them the city was already meeting their needs. [26]

Protests by minorities in the 1960s and 1970s demanded political representation in their local cities, but Stockton's conservative political and economic leadership refused to change. Nevertheless, racial minorities were able to win seats on the city council without removing the conservative coalition that led the city. [27]

In the late 1960s, a coalition of African Americans, Latinos, and white liberals joined together around educational issues. They chose as their strategy to change the electoral structure and set up district elections as a means to elect minorities. This measure passed in 1971. Before district elections were established, there were no African Americans or Latinos on the Stockton city council. After district elections were established, two African Americans were elected to the council and several years later a Latino was elected. Unlike other northern California cities where district elections were established after a liberal/racial minority coalition won city hall, Stockton established district elections first and then racial minorities were elected to office. By 1978 there were three council members, however, according to one account they were not part of the dominant coalition.[28]

---

[23] Lillian Galedo, Laurena Cabanero, and Brian Tom, "Roadblocks to Community Building: A case study of the Stockton Filipino community center project," Asian American Research Project Working Publication No. 4 (Davis: University of California, 1970).

[24] Julie Davidow, "A little taste of Manila in Stockton's Past," *Stockton Record*, October 21, 2002, at: http://www.littlemanila.net/.

[25] Rudolph M. Lapp, *Afro-Americans in California*, 2d ed. (San Francisco: Boyd & Fraser Pub. Co., 1987), 7.

[26] Lillian Galedo, Laurena Cabanero, and Brian Tom, "Roadblocks to Community Building: A case study of the Stockton Filipino community center project," Asian American Research Project Working Publication No. 4 (Davis: University of California, 1970).

[27] Rufus P. Browning, Dale R. Marshall, and David H.Tabb, *Protest Is Not Enough* (Berkeley: University of California Press, 1984), 42.

[28] *Ibid.*, 68

By 1994, there were three racial minority council members, one Black, one Latino, and one Asian-American member.

Since the 1971 change in electoral structure, racial minorities have been elected to the city council where previously they held no seats. Currently, a Mexican American, Edward Chavez, serves as mayor of Stockton. He is the first Mexican American to serve in this capacity even though racial minorities are more than 62% of the city's population. Each minority group built varying levels of political incorporation over the next several decades.

A number of Asian Americans have served in elected and appointed offices including Victor Mow, former Stockton city council member and currently a San Joaquin County supervisor. Gloria Nomura, a Filipina American, recently served as vice mayor of Stockton. There are also Asian Americans on local school boards. The highest ranking Asian American in the region is Assemblyman Alan Nakanishi who was the former mayor of Lodi, located in nearby San Joaquin County. Today Filipinos are the largest Asian minority in Stockton, with 15,219 residents, or 6.2% of the population, yet they have no electoral representation.

Mexican Americans began to obtain political office in the late 1980s. They are the largest minority group and are almost equal to the white population in numbers. The current mayor of Stockton, Ed Chavez, is the former police chief of the city. In addition, Leslie Barranco Martin is the city council representative for District 3 in Stockton. Steve Gutierrez, the supervisor for District 1, has served as county supervisor since 1996.

African Americans were instrumental in waging battles to change the electoral structure to district elections, leading to the election of the first racial minorities in the city. They fought for affirmative action in government hiring and school desegregation. Ralph White was instrumental in the early fights to make Stockton more inclusive. He became a city council member from 1971–1987. Currently, city council member Rebecca Nabors represents District 6.

In the mid-1980s, tensions among rivals in city politics led to an effort to curb the types of candidates elected through the district election structure that had enabled racial minorities to win seats on the city council. Measure C was put forward by future mayor Joan Darrah and others, who felt that district elected candidates were only accountable to their own district. They proposed a change in the electoral structure whereby in a June primary candidates would compete in a district-wide election, with the top two vote getters competing in a citywide runoff, thereby allowing those outside a district to determine the victory. After Measure C won at the polls, it was challenged by MALDEF as disenfranchising Hispanic voters. The measure was upheld by the court and went into effect in 1990. According to former Mayor Joan Darrah, "from 1971 to 1989, there were either two or three minority members on a council of nine, except for 1985 to 1989 when there were four out of nine. The four councils immediately after Measure C went into effect have included either two or three minority members out of a total of seven."[29]

Stockton's city council and mayor are all elected citywide, with nominations for council seats held in the district first. The ability to win and retain seats and to have a near majority of the council seats is an indication of medium level of political incorporation. The extent of political incorporation is characterized by racial minorities being able to get elected consistently, at least in certain districts that were drawn to enhance the opportunity for electoral victory by minorities, yet they are not yet full partners in the governing coalition that makes the critical economic decisions for the city. According to one local analyst's assessment, Stockton while seemingly an example of diversity and political inclusion remains dominated by real estate and downtown business interests that have held economic power for decades.[30] Meanwhile the nonwhite communities that comprise the majority of the city have yet to receive the full benefits of the political incorporation efforts.

Orange Cove, Fresno County

In Fresno County, 11 of the 15 cities have a majority Latino population. One of these cities is Orange Cove, established in 1948. The town is primarily an agricultural community with an economic base tied to growing and processing oranges in packing houses. Recently it has seen a rapid population jump; it has grown from 6,000 in 1989 to 9,255 in 2004. It is predominantly an extremely poor community. In 2000, the median household income was $22,357, per capita income was $7,125, and the percentage of people living below poverty was 44.5% with an annual unemployment rate of 24.9%, four times more than the statewide average. The demographics of the city are: Latino 90.6%, white 6.8%, Native American .6%, and African American .19%. Orange Cove's population is overwhelmingly Latino and more than half of those working are employed as seasonal agricultural laborers or packing shed workers.

For decades while Latinos were the majority population, they had no political influence in the city. This began to change in the early 1970s. When an all-white city council refused to consider the pleas of farmworkers to establish child care services in 1974 after numerous incidents in the fields, Victor Lopez, a farmworker activist ran for city council. He won by organizing every Latino voter in the community to vote by using a sophisticated get-out-the-vote operation using absentee ballots.[31] Although successful, he was the only Latino on the council for four years and had to battle the entrenched old guard of business and agricultural interests. He has held office ever since. In 1978, he ran for mayor along with two other Latinos. Again, they were successful in turning out their votes and won all

---

[29] Joan Darrah with Alice Crozier, *Getting Political: Stories of a Woman Mayor* (Sanger, Calif.: Quill Driver Books, 2003).

[30] Interview with community activist Nelson Nagai, June 15, 2005.

[31] Interview with Mayor Victor Lopez, August 25, 2005.

three seats. As Roy Rodriguez, one of the three council members elected remarked in 1989:

> we did come into the city council in 1978, not because we wanted to be city council members, but because there were needs. . . . We came into this position because we would like to have the people who are providing the services and at City Hall and at public works represent the people that live in the city and even speak the language if necessary.[32]

Latinos have been the majority of the city council ever since and today hold all five seats. Mayor Lopez, a former farmworker, aligned himself closely with Cesar Chavez and the UFWA in numerous campaigns and boycotts. Unlike the previous city leaders who were aligned with agricultural business interests, the city leadership is now focused on bringing resources to the farmworkers and packing shed workers who are the majority of the city's population. For example, the region weathered two severe freezes that ruined the orange crop and threw thousands out of work in 1991 and 1998 and both times Mayor Lopez was able to utilize his connections with state and federal officials to gain desperately needed supplies.

While some of the political actors have changed, Victor Lopez continues to provide leadership to this growing Fresno County town. He has held office for more than 31 years, 27 years as mayor making him the dean of Latino politicians in the San Joaquin Valley. Today, Lopez and the other city leaders are vocal advocates for more funding for affordable housing for the farmworkers who dominate the local economy yet cannot afford to rent or purchase homes in the area due to low wages. There are currently several affordable housing developments under construction. Orange Cove has been designated as a federal renewal community by the Housing and Urban Development (HUD) in 2002, one of only 40 rural communities designated as such in the nation. It enables Orange Cove to offer economic incentives to businesses to create jobs in the city. With Orange Cove's high seasonal unemployment rate and low level of job skills, this has enabled the city to build a small industrial park and recruit a Korean business to develop a manufacturing plant in the city for high-end televisions. This will provide steady employment and an alternative to working in the agricultural industry for the town's population. Another indication of the city addressing local population needs is the construction of its first high school, Orange Cove High School; previously students were bussed to a neighboring town as part of the King's Canyon Unified School District.

Orange Cove is an example of how a small, isolated agricultural town has been able to generate badly needed resources for its working poor population through the efforts of a unified Latino political leadership that has staffed its key

---

[32] Roy Rodriguez, Orange Cove City Council member. Participant in roundtable discussion on "Latino Political Participation in Rural California." California Institute for Rural Studies, Working Group on Farm Labor and Rural Poverty, Working Paper 8, February 1989.

administrative positions with committed and competent Latino administrators and has brought business to the table to negotiate deals that have directly benefited the majority Latino population. While the Latino community does not control the economic wealth of the area, their political influence is very strong through the electoral arena, and elected representatives are generally able to negotiate with business interests for mutual satisfactory gains including job creation, improved educational opportunities, and affordable housing. Orange Cove is an example of a high level of political incorporation by Latinos in a small town in the midst of grinding poverty of San Joaquin Valley immigrant workers.

Watsonville, Santa Cruz County

Watsonville is a rapidly growing agricultural community on the southern border of Santa Cruz County across the Pajaro River from Monterey County. Watsonville is a Latino majority city with a Latino majority city council. However, unlike towns like Parlier and Orange Cove in Fresno County that elected Latinos to office in the 1970s, the process was much slower for Latinos in Watsonville. The at-large electoral system prevented Latinos from being elected to office from the 1970s–1980s due to racially polarized voting with whites voting only for white candidates and Latinos voting for Latino candidates. The population growth of Watsonville, like other valley and rural towns is continuing to expand rapidly driven by the labor intensive work in strawberry and other fruits and vegetables harvested locally. In 1950, Watsonville was a small farming community with a large migrant worker population that largely went uncounted. By 2000, it had shot up to 44,265 with 75% Latino population (see Table 2). The growth in the primarily Mexican population was stimulated by the growing agricultural economy and the need for a more stable work force that enabled more agricultural related workers to settle permanently.[33]

The watershed event in the political evolution of Watsonville politics occurred in 1985, when the Mexican American Legal Defense and Education Fund (MALDEF) filed suit charging the at-large system discriminated against Latinos.[34] In 1989, the federal appeals court ruled in favor of the plaintiffs and for the first time an at-large system was overturned in the western region of the U.S.

The decision affects cities in all nine states within the 9th circuit.[35] In 1989, under the new district election rules, there were two majority Latino districts

---

[33] Ruben Donato,. "In Struggle: Mexican American in the Pajaro Valley Schools, 1900–1979," Ph.D. dissertation, Stanford, Calif., 1987.

[34] Paula Cruz Takash, "A Crisis of Democracy: Community Responses to the Latinization of a California Town Dependent on Immigrant Labor," Ph.D. dissertation, University of California, Berkeley, 1989.

[35] Paula Cruz Takash and Joaquin Avila, "Latino Political Participation in Rural California," California Institute for Rural Studies, Working Group on Farm Labor and Rural Poverty, Working Paper 8, February 1989.

Table 2. Watsonville Population 1950 – 2000

	General Population	Latino Pop. & % of total pop.
1950	11,374	1,001 – 8.8%
1960	13,929	2,259 – 17.0%
1970	14,561	5,069 – 44.0%
1980	23,543	11,509 – 49.0%
1990	31,099	18,551 – 60.0%
2000	44,265	33,254 – 75.1%

Sources: 1950, 1960, 1970, 1980, 1990, and 2000 Census' of Population and Housing Summary

drawn, and Oscar Rios was elected to the city council becoming the first Latino elected under district elections. His electoral victory was a culmination of a historic cannery workers strike in 1985–1987 by more than 1,000 workers, mostly Latinas, who fought for almost two years to keep their jobs and retain a union contract. Their fighting spirit galvanized the Mexican community throughout northern California and inspired many to elect new leadership to the city council that would be more responsive to the Latino majority population.

The Maturation of Local Latino Politics:

In Watsonville, there have been three distinct periods of political incorporation. The first period can be characterized by weak political incorporation for Latinos, the majority of the town's population since 1980, with none or only one Latino elected to the city council. This period began in the late 1960s and lasted until 1991. Before 1987, Latinos were effectively excluded from political representation. In 1987, Tony Campos became the first Latino elected to city council. In 1989, Oscar Rios became the first Latino elected in district elections, while Tony Campos lost his bid to win in his own district. While Latinos remained weak politically, other liberal elements were elected in 1989 and helped move Watsonville in a more inclusive direction.

The second period can be characterized as weak-medium political incorporation. In 1991, two additional Latinos were elected to the council, Campos who won the seat he lost in 1989, and Al Alcala who won in a heavily Latino downtown district. There were now three Latinos on a council of seven members. However, the agendas of the three Latinos were divided between business economic development by Campos and Alcala and concern for working people and the poor advocated by Rios. While they voted similarly on most issues that came before the council, they had different political and economic agendas. They were all Democrats, but their class interests, not their party affiliation, guided their decision-making and kept them unable to forge a unified Latino empowerment agenda.[36]

During this period, Latinos attempted to seek higher office. In 1994, Oscar Rios ran for the Santa Cruz County Board of Supervisors seat that encompassed Watsonville and lost to the incumbent. A local Chicana assistant district attorney attempted to win the local Assembly seat and also lost in 1994 and 1996. In these elections, when the majority Anglo electorate in Watsonville voted citywide for elected positions, they overwhelmingly voted against the Latino candidates and for conservative white candidates.

This pattern of defeats could be attributed to weak Latino candidates. It could be attributed to strong white candidates. It also could be blamed on continuing anti-Latino sentiments by the majority of white voters. While these interpretations all have some validity, an alternative perspective is that in order to elect a Latino candidate for citywide office, even in a majority Latino town, it was necessary to put up a candidate who could appeal to both Latino and Anglo communities and not be viewed as a threat to challenge the Anglo power structure that dominates the local economy. This type of crossover candidate must rely on Anglo voters in order to win citywide office. Even though Latinos are the majority population, with the small number of Latinos registered to vote and mobilized to get to the polls, this remained a large obstacle to greater political incorporation efforts. The reality that two of the three council seats held by Latinos were business owners was an indication that local political incorporation favored those elements in the Latino community that could receive the support and backing of the local business community with minimal inclusion of the Latino community.

By 1998, this situation began to change, as a 3rd period of medium-to-strong political incorporation by Latinos was beginning to take shape. Latinos were now part of the governing coalition that ruled the city. This period marked the rise of growing local internal conflicts among Latinos over representation. Starting with the election of two new members of the Watsonville City Council. In District 5, Ramon Gomez defeated a well-known incumbent in a major upset. Equally significant was the election in District 4, where Ana Ventura Phares, an attorney, mother, and community activist, became the first Latina elected to city office. Ventura Phares won in a district that was 65% Anglo and 45% Latino; she defeated a conservative "law and order" white male candidate who ran on a platform of cleaning up the neighborhoods of gangs and graffiti without offering any alternatives.[37]

These elections signaled a new day in Watsonville politics, particularly for young Latinos. The Gomez and Ventura Phares victories signaled a "changing of the guard" transition in political leadership to the second generation of Mexican Americans, who had grown up in the Pajaro Valley, were educated in Watsonville schools, obtained higher education degrees, and returned to the community to bring new leadership and ideas that were rooted in local traditions. The

---

[36] Interview with Councilmember Rios, June 8, 2005.

[37] Interview with Councilmember Ventura Phares, July 15, 2005.

election of two more Latinos meant for the first time, Latinos were now the majority of the city council, and a Latino was now city manager. Latinos were now in leadership positions of city government for the first time in the city's history.

In addition, Latinos began to move up into higher local elected office. In 1998, Santa Cruz Supervisor Ray Belgard retired and supported Watsonville City Council member Tony Campos for this seat. Campos easily won the election, as the Anglo and Latino communities united behind Campos to elect the first ever Latino county supervisor. Campos's victory appeared to culminate a dramatic shift in power in South County from Anglo to Latino and strengthened the voice of Latinos at the city and county level.[38]

The addition of three new city council members and a Latino elected as county supervisor appeared to be a golden opportunity for the Latino community to finally receive serious consideration from local government of long-standing problems. However, a series of events made it difficult to build consensus among Latino council members and the Latino community around a Latino empowerment agenda. Over the next several years, instead of greater unity, competing values and different priorities limited the ability of the Latino community to unite around a common program to advance the needs of the Latino community, and divisions emerged among the key players. In an environment where there are multiple interests vying for political and economic influence and opportunities for moving up politically are available, no one group or faction was able to consolidate a unifying vision for all the Latino political actors.[39]

In 2000, 24-year-old Richard de la Paz, Jr., was elected to the city council after a hotly contested race with a 26-year-old Latina opponent. Watsonville's youthful population was now reflected in its council, with several young Latinos on the council. In 2002, another electoral contest highlighted the changing dynamics in the Latino community over who should represent the community when Watsonville City Council member Ramon Gomez ran against incumbent Santa Cruz County Supervisor Tony Campos. During Campos's first campaign for the supervisor's seat, he received the support of the Latino community. However, criticisms had arisen about his failure to deliver more policy benefits to the Latino community.

The youthful Gomez gathered endorsements from labor organizations including the UFWA, while seeking to appeal to business interests, both political parties, and Latino residents. Campos, on the other hand, relied on his traditional base of support within the Democratic Party and business interests. Interestingly, the more senior candidate, Tony Campos received the endorsement of council member Oscar Rios and many other local Latino leaders. They opposed the Gomez candidacy because in seeking to widen his support base, Gomez had

---

[38] In 2000, Simon Salinas was elected as state assembly member for the Watsonville-Salinas area marking another first for the local Latino community.

[39] Kim Geron, "The Political Incorporation of Latinos: Symbolic or Substantive Changes at the Local Level," Ph.D. dissertation, University of California, Riverside, 1998.

sought the support and endorsement of not only the Democratic Party but the Republican Party, which angered many local Democrats.

In the county supervisor's race, Campos won a surprisingly close contest against Gomez; Campos received 55.5% of the vote, a margin of 600 votes. Gomez had strong labor support, with the UFWA actively walking precincts on his behalf. Gomez carried five of the seven council districts in Watsonville, demonstrating the strength of his GOTV efforts. The competitive races for Watsonville city council seats, mayor, and Santa Cruz County supervisor's seat indicate that Latino politics has grown increasingly more sophisticated, with different points of view. The existence of differences in the Pajaro Valley among Latinos is a healthy sign that internal diversity will be a part of the political landscape as Latino political power grows in the coming years.

There are several other political forces that have an influence on the shape of local politics. There is a weak Democratic Party apparatus in the South County area and a low-key Republican Party presence in liberal Santa Cruz County. The influence of community-based grass roots organizations has grown in the past few years. Interest groups including environmental, no-growth advocates, organized labor such as the Service Employees International Union (SEIU), which represents the city and county workers, the Teamsters Union, which represents local cannery and other workers, and the UFWA, which represents strawberry and other agricultural workers are all players in local politics. Other local Latino community groups have a presence in specific issues related to farm workers, housing, education, civil rights, and immigration rights. Together, community, labor, and politicians in the Latino community have built electoral coalitions to achieve electoral and political gains.

Following the election of the first Latino to office under the district election system at the end of 1989, this city has made progress in incorporating Latinos into the political structure and in redistributing limited local resources towards social service programs, parks, recreational centers, and youth activities. City resources support cultural events that were previously nonexistent or poorly supported.[40] Anti-Latino attitudes on the part of city officials were no longer tolerated; those that resisted change were removed from their positions or left their positions.

Watsonville is a city that has transitioned from rural agricultural community into part-bedroom community for commuters and part "strawberry capital" agricultural center. A vision of the city's future continues to be a work in progress because of conflicting opinions of how the city should develop, who should benefit from this growth, and what form this will take. The political incorporation of Latinos cannot be fully realized without greater community involvement in, and control over, the politics of land use and development in the area. This will require a joint effort by differing class interests within the Latino community to achieve common goals, not solely individual accomplishments. The internal diversity among Latino political leadership has allowed longstanding eco-

---

[40] *Ibid.*

nomic interests to maintain their economic and political influence. This dynamic of a newly emerging Latino leadership and a more weakened, but still formidable Anglo economic and political leadership will continue in the coming years. The traditional Anglo agricultural and economic development interests will continue to retain much of their influence in city politics but will have to share their power with the Latino majority represented by those in office and holding key appointed positions.

Conclusion

The Central Valley and coastal communities are in a process of demographic change that foreshadows a political transformation in the region from a predominantly white political leadership to a more diverse political leadership with varying levels of political incorporation by racial minorities. The cities that form the basis of this study are transitioning from a time when agricultural and other business interests dominated local and regional politics to a contemporary environment where the changing demographics of the valley and the ongoing political organizing efforts in the Latino and other racial minority communities are diversifying local politics. In the three cities examined in this chapter, it is evident that political incorporation is well underway. In rural communities, such as Orange Cove, Latinos have been elected to office, appointed to all the major posts in the city, and held majority political power for almost 30 years. Political incorporation of Latinos has resulted in meaningful and significant advances in policy benefits not only for the Latino community but for the city as a whole. In agricultural coastal communities such as Watsonville, Latino political incorporation took longer to evolve and the relationships among Latino leaders has been more contentious and less unified as different political actors seek to implement differing agendas in the midst of strong local interest group politics. Yet, after an initial period to establish a visible and consistent political presence, Latino politics has matured and grown as evidenced by 2006 Democratic Party primary race for the 38th Assembly seat between two strong Latinas from the Central Coast, Salinas Mayor Ana Caballero and Watsonville City Council member Ana Ventura Phares. Latino local politics is now stable and sophisticated with numerous high quality candidates running and winning office in this region. In the city of Stockton, African Americans, Asians, and Latinos have been involved in the political incorporation process for nearly 40 years. Racial minorities have held political office in this city since the early 1970s and have built multiracial coalitions to achieve electoral empowerment. Progress in constructing a strong multiracial governing coalition that would enhance significant policy benefits for the majority nonwhite population has been slow but the impact of racial minority politics is evident in the political leadership for the city.

In each of these local areas, political incorporation has grown from weak to varying levels of influence in the political decision-making process for local government as part of a local governing coalition. In each of the three cities, racial minorities hold multiple elected offices, including mayor, and significant appointed high-level positions. Thus according to political incorporation theory, racial minorities have achieved a visible level of incorporation. The larger question of whether the myriad number of social problems confronting minority communities has been addressed and alleviated remains a work in progress for all three communities.

The addition of numerous state-level elected officials can enhance policy benefits for the local communities that elected them. The cadre of nonwhite state assemblymembers and state senators from the valley region helps shape the larger political and economic context for local politics. This is a significant step forward for racial minorities in rural and agricultural regions of the state where they have had limited or weak representation for a long time.

The growth of Latino and other racial minority elected officials and growing numbers of voters may in the long run neutralize the growth in conservative white voters moving into the region seeking lower home prices, and reduced crime and traffic congestion. This process of changing demographics, population growth, and contested politics and economics will continue to play out in the cities and counties explored in this study. As Anna Caballero, at the time, the mayor of the city of Salinas, in Monterey County said recently:

> In many ways Salinas is the face of California for the future. Sixty-five percent of our residents are Latino, a large percentage are young families, we have a very large illiteracy rate, we have a high teen drop out rate, which then causes all the social issues like teen pregnancy, and gang violence and drugs. California is moving to a Latino majority state . . . we need to be careful because those are the families that are going to support us in our old age. They are going to be the economy. That's the challenge that Salinas faces, and I think it's the challenge for California's future as well. [41]

There is a challenge and an opportunity for progress to be made to address longstanding social and economic inequalities and the political incorporation of Latinos and other racial minorities in agricultural and rural areas of the state; it is possible and desirable for traditionally powerful agribusiness interests to join together with the new political leadership to solve the massive social and economic problems confronting the region such as how to educate immigrant agricultural workers and the children of farmworkers in order for them to fully participate in society. These and a myriad of related issues will continue to confront rural California in the coming decade.

[41] Anna Caballero, "The Boomtown Chronicles: Reflections on a Changing California." An Interview with Anna Caballero, mayor of Salinas, California. Recorded July 2004 by Rachel Gordon.

Chapter 9

Nonprofit Organizations and the Urbanized Politics of Immigrant Representation in San Francisco

Els de Graauw

Introduction[1]

San Francisco, the fourth largest city in the state of California with just under 800,000 residents in 2000, has been and continues to be a city of immigrants. According to the U.S. Census, 37% (285,541) of San Francisco's population was foreign born in 2000. This number was up from 28% (192,204) in 1980 and 34% (246,034) in 1990. About 50% of the city's foreign born in 1980 and 1990 (89,806 and 118,292, respectively) and 37% (106,200) in 2000 were recent immigrants who had arrived to the United States in the previous 10 years. As a result of continued immigration in recent decades, San Francisco's foreign-born population today is diverse in terms of its national origins. However, Asian im-

[1] Selections of this chapter also appear in: Els de Graauw, "Nonprofit Organizations: Agents of Immigrant Political Incorporation in Urban America," in *Civic Hopes and Political Realities: Immigrants, Community Organizations, and Political Engagement*, ed. S. Karthick Ramakrishnan and Irene Bloemraad (New York: Russell Sage Foundation Press, 2008).

migrants are in the majority and about 60% (175,302) of the city's foreign born in 2000 came from Asia (and mostly China). Hispanics form the second largest foreign-born group and about 20% (60,569) of immigrants in San Francisco in 2000 came from Latin America (and mostly Mexico). San Francisco also counts many noncitizens—in 2000, 43% (122,115) of San Francisco's immigrants were not naturalized citizens of the U.S.—and an estimated 40,000 undocumented immigrants (Olvera 2007). Furthermore, many of the city's immigrants are of low socio-economic status: they have low levels of formal education and limited English skills, and they constitute a large part of the low-wage workforce in the city's service sector and garment industry (Association of Bay Area Governments; Young Workers United).

Immigrants (and particularly newcomers, noncitizens, undocumented immigrants, and immigrants with low socio-economic status) are likely to hold distinct views on a number of local issues that are central to their lives, but which are of tangential interest to most Americans. It is therefore important—for the city of San Francisco where more than a third of city residents are foreign born, but also for other California cities with sizeable immigrant populations—that immigrants' views on such issues as language rights, housing, policing, English as a Second Language education, labor rights, and drivers' licenses and health care for undocumented immigrants are known to public officials and that their needs are adequately met through government policies. Representation of immigrants' interests in the political process is even more important for immigrants whose voices are less likely to be heard, including noncitizen immigrants who are excluded from the American electoral process and limited-English proficient immigrants who experience a language barrier that hampers their participation in civic and political life in the U.S. (Jones-Correa 1998; Rosenstone and Hansen 1993; Verba et al. 1995). Those more critical of immigrants and continued immigration to the U.S. might grumble at providing non-naturalized and undocumented immigrants, who are not (yet) full members of the American polity, with representation in the American political process. Such ideological objections, however, are difficult to maintain when the on-the-ground reality is that immigrants make up a proportionately large share of San Francisco's (as well as California's) population and they actively participate in various aspects of city life, regardless of their citizenship or immigration status. As immigrants send their children to local schools, use government services locally, are part of the local workforce and operate small businesses, pay taxes, and bring multicultural vitality to slumped city neighborhoods, local government officials need to pay attention to their concerns and interests and devise and implement public policies that lay the foundation for a productive local economy and healthy community for all.

Throughout American history, a variety of collective political actors—including yesteryear's urban machines, local political parties, and labor unions—have acted as institutional representatives of immigrants' interests and concerns in local politics and policymaking. However, with political machines largely vanished, local party organizations uninterested in reaching out to the new immigrants *en masse*, and labor unions divided on the immigration issue, a new type of urban organization has stepped into the representation void. In this chapter, I argue that the religious, charitable, and educational organizations that constitute the category of 501(c)(3) nonprofit organizations have emerged in recent decades as important new actors in local politics advancing the collective interests of the immigrant community *vis-à-vis* government institutions and actors. My data on San Francisco-based nonprofit organizations catering to immigrants ("immigrant nonprofits" hereafter) reveal the important ways in which these nongovernmental institutions increase local government's responsiveness to the concerns of immigrants and, by doing so, they help build a more democratic system of governance that is inclusive of the interests and needs of immigrants who reside in our midst. This chapter describes and analyzes the strategies and tactics immigrant nonprofits use to bring the voice of the immigrant community to the attention of San Francisco government officials while coping with regulations and restrictions on the political activities of organizations with the 501(c)(3) tax-exempt status. My chapter also explores which types of concerns animate the public policy advocacy work of immigrant nonprofits, which government officials these organizations interact with, and where in the policymaking process these organizations are most active and most effective. Finally, the chapter concludes with reflections on what immigrant nonprofits' participation in the local political process means for governance in multi-ethnic urban settings other than San Francisco.

The Representational Potential of Immigrant Nonprofit Organizations

Nonprofit organizations that enjoy the 501(c)(3) tax-exempt status are more commonly known as public charities that provide services to poor and other disadvantaged populations in American society. This is a diverse group of organizations that includes not only local soup kitchens for the homeless, but also large public hospitals and private universities (Salamon 1999). I focus on San Francisco-based 501(c)(3) nonprofit organizations that provide a variety of social services to the city's immigrant population. I conducted interviews with the staff of 45 of these immigrant nonprofits between 2005 and 2007 to learn about their service provision and advocacy activities, their clientele, and their interactions with members of the San Francisco political establishment as well as other types of community organizations. The 45 organizations I studied do not constitute a random or representative sample of nonprofits serving San Francisco's newcomers. Instead, they are the most visible and most active organizations of San Francisco's immigrant nonprofit sector, which counts about 300 organizations in total.[2] The organizations I surveyed share a number of characteristics:

[2] I base my estimate of 300 immigrant nonprofit organizations in San Francisco on a directory of immigrant nonprofits I put together in the course of my research. My directory brings together information from existing nonprofit databases and referrals from immigrant nonprofits I contacted. Databases and directories I consulted include the San

they are officially incorporated as 501(c)(3) tax-exempt entities, they provide programs to benefit immigrants, they have annual budgets over $25,000, at least 40% of the organizations' clientele consists of first-generation immigrants, they have multilingual staff, and many of the organizations' staff and volunteers are first- or second-generation immigrants to the U.S. They simultaneously differ from each other in size (in terms of budget and number of paid staff), the range of immigrant nationality groups they cater to, the range and nature of services they offer, the extent to which they combine service provision with political advocacy, their age, and their sources of income. In this chapter, I focus on what unifies these 45 nonprofits as institutions that mediate immigrants' political representation at the local level, and I do no discuss variation in their political activism based on different organizational characteristics.

Immigrant nonprofits provide a host of services to the city's newcomers: they provide educational, legal, immigration, health, employment, and other social services to immigrants, but also native-born ethnic and racial minorities. Increasingly, though, these organizations combine service provision with advocacy campaigns and political activism. Some nonprofits voluntarily choose to enter politics as they believe that service provision and public policy advocacy are two interrelated activities that need to be pursued in unison to fulfill the organizations' mission to serve the needs and interests of the immigrant population. Other immigrant nonprofits, however, have entered local politics more reluctantly and often out of fear of losing their public funding. Retrenchment of government spending in recent decades has forced these immigrant nonprofits—many of them had grown accustomed to receive grants and contracts from state and local government to provide public services—to advocate for public funding with government officials in efforts to secure the survival of their organizations. Regardless of whether immigrant nonprofits actively pursue or reluctantly accept a greater involvement in local political affairs, the reality is that these organizations are more aptly described as hybrid organizations that merge the provision of public services with political activism (Hasenfeld and Gidron 2005; Minkoff 2002).

It is because of their hybridity that immigrant nonprofits are in a good position to affect the representation of immigrants' collective interests with local government officials. Through service provision and daily interaction with immi-

---

Francisco Community Services Directory (San Francisco Public Library), HelpLink (United Way of the Bay Area), the California Database of the Institute for Nonprofit Organization Management (University of San Francisco), California Charitable Trust, and databases at the National Center for Charitable Statistics (Urban Institute in Washington, D.C.). Included in my directory are immigrant nonprofit organizations that officially incorporated as 501(c)(3) tax-exempt entities and a few organizations that are fiscally sponsored by a 501(c)(3) nonprofit organization (the latter is an indication that they themselves are likely to become an independent 501(c)(3) organization). This directory, like my sample of organizations surveyed for this chapter, is biased towards the more formally organized groups catering to immigrants in San Francisco and is most likely an under-count of the actual number of nonprofit organizations catering to the city's foreign-born population.

grants, immigrant nonprofits collect valuable information about the people they serve, which puts them on the frontline of developing, assessing, and articulating immigrants' needs in the public sphere. Nonprofits' expertise on the immigrant community translates into a source of power *vis-à-vis* local government officials, who would struggle to learn about the needs and interests of a large portion of the city's residents without these nonprofit allies in the immigrant community. As recipients of public monies to provide services to immigrants, these nonprofits frequently enter into communications with city agencies and elected officials and they have many opportunities to bring the needs and interests of a politically controversial and economically vulnerable population to the attention local government officials. These government-nonprofit contractual relations consequently set in motion a policy feedback loop (Pierson 1993) that provides immigrant nonprofits with opportunities to advocate on immigrants' behalf with the San Francisco Board of Supervisors (the city's legislators), the mayor, city departments, and various other local government agencies. In sum, as hybrid organizations combining service provision with political advocacy, immigrant nonprofits are strategically positioned to have both presence and influence in the local politics of immigrant representation.

A Distinct Type of Actor in Urban Politics

The representation of immigrants' needs *vis-à-vis* government officials by intermediary organizations is certainly not a new phenomenon and throughout American history different types of political actors have intervened as institutional representatives of immigrants in the local political process. Immigrant nonprofits, however, are distinct from these other types of urban institutions in a number of important ways. For example, like social movement organizations, immigrant nonprofits want to challenge the political status quo and bring about social change. However, unlike social movement organizations, immigrant nonprofits are more heavily reliant on conventional political tactics and strategies, their work is proactive and planned rather than reactive and spontaneous, they work with local government officials rather than around them, and they provide a variety of socioeconomic services in addition to their political activism. Immigrant nonprofits, furthermore, are similar to yesteryear's urban machines in that they also emphasize a reciprocal relationship with those who receive nonprofit (or machine) services. However, San Francisco-based immigrant nonprofits are not distinctly partisan organizations, they are less involved in electoral politics, and they do not operate on a vote maximization rationale like the urban machines of the past did. Finally, nonprofits are not quite like civic organizations either. Civic organizations are mostly member-serving organizations and nonprofits are largely client-serving. While both types of organizations need to maintain good relations with their donors, the key relationship for nonprofits is not one with their members, but rather one with the larger immigrant community and other disadvantaged city residents. This client or public orientation finds expression in nonprofits' communitarian pursuits and advocacy for policies benefiting public—rather than special or "members only"—interests.

Arguably, immigrant nonprofits most closely resemble interest groups as both types of organizations are motivated to speak for, act for, and look after the interests of their clients or constituents in the political process (Berry with Arons 2003). However, differences in federal tax status give nonprofits and interest groups different standings in the governmental process. Nonprofit organizations receive a more favorable tax treatment from the federal government than do interest groups and as a result nonprofits are subject to more government restrictions and regulations on their political activities than are interest groups. Nonprofits with the 501(c)(3) status do not pay income tax on their revenue and donor contributions are tax-deductible. As a result of these financial incentives, federal tax law bars these organizations from partisan politics at any level of government and places restrictions on nonprofits' lobbying activities. Legally, 501(c)(3) nonprofits are allowed to lobby, but their lobbying must be an "insubstantial part" of their organizations' overall activities (Harmon et al. 2000; Lunder 2006).[3] In contrast, interests groups—registered under sections 501(c)(4), 501(c)(5), and 501(c)(6) of the tax code—are ineligible for tax-exempt contributions, but they have fewer restrictions on their political activities and they may be actively involved with political campaigns to influence elections to public office. According to Berry and Arons (2003), the relatively stricter government regulations of 501(c)(3) nonprofits help explain why these organizations are more reluctant than interest groups to engage in public policy advocacy and other overly political activities for fear of losing their tax-exempt status.

Under federal law, though, lobbying has a narrow meaning and only advocacy before a legislature is subject to limitations. Consequently, many forms of

[3] There is a second standard that 501(c)(3) organizations can use to ensure that their lobbying activities are in compliance with federal law. This second standard is known as the "section 501(h) expenditure test" and was added to the Internal Revenue Code in 1976. If 501(c)(3) nonprofit organizations elect for the 501(h) status, they are covered by clearly defined lobbying rules and benefit from more generous limits on lobbying. To date, only a very small percentage (about 2.5%) of 501(c)(3) nonprofits nationwide have elected to become 501(h) entities (Berry with Arons 2003). Section 501(h) was enacted to clarify the much-criticized and ambiguous "insubstantial part" test. The 501(h) rule is sometimes referred to as "the 20% rule" and establishes specific dollar limits that are calculated as a percentage of a nonprofit's total budget. With the 501(h) status, a 501(c)(3) nonprofit can use up to 20% of the first $500,000 of its budget for legislative lobbying. For organizations with larger budgets, these dollar amounts slide upward until they reach a $1 million cap on lobbying expenditures. Cost-free lobbying activities (such as legislative advocacy by volunteers) do not count toward an organization's lobbying limit under the 501(h) expenditure test. However, organizations with the 501(h) election that exceed their lobbying limit will initially receive a steep fine and repeat offenders will lose their 501(c)(3) tax-exempt status (Harmon et al. 2000). Seven of the 45 San Francisco-based immigrant nonprofits I surveyed told me they have the 501(h) election. My interview data, however, do not show a clear difference in the amount and type of political activism between immigrant nonprofits with and those without the 501(h) election.

political activity by nonprofits are not limited under federal law. These unrestricted political activities include advocacy with the executive and judicial branches of government, nonpartisan and unbiased analysis and research on all sides of a policy or legislative issue, invited public testimony before any government body, and instances where a nonprofit organization engages with stakeholders in discussions of broad social, economic, and political problems (Harmon et al. 2000; Lunder 2006). With the legal constraints on nonprofits' political activism generally overstated, in reality there are many safe and unrestricted opportunities for immigrant nonprofits to undertake political work at the local level. Later on in the chapter, I discuss the various strategic ways in which immigrant nonprofits in San Francisco take part in local politics and policymaking in ways allowed by federal law.

This brief comparison of immigrant nonprofits with other types of organizations active in urban politics suggests that immigrant nonprofits form a distinct type of urban political actor likely to make a unique contribution to local power dynamics and political outcomes. First, as 501(c)(3) tax-exempt entities with government restrictions on their political activism, immigrant nonprofits experience pressures to direct their advocacy claims to political actors other than local legislators and to frame and package these advocacy claims in nonpartisan terms. Second, as organizations more exclusively dedicated to advance the welfare of the immigrant population, they are likely to bring to the attention of local government officials a variety of ethnic and cultural diversity issues of particular concern to immigrants that otherwise might not become part of the public agenda, such as language access and local sanctuary for undocumented immigrants. Third, in advancing an immigrant-friendly local agenda that fits with the restrictions on nonprofits' partisan activities, immigrant nonprofits are likely to travel a route of nonpartisan collaboration with government officials emphasizing the practical need for concrete immigrant-friendly local policies. Finally, as staff members often share in the immigrant experience of the people they serve and have strong commitments to advance the welfare of the city's newcomers, it is difficult for public officials to ignore these organizations. Immigrant nonprofits have a clear presence in local political affairs and they are not easily co-opted by other local governmental and nongovernmental institutions for whom immigrant issues are often of short-lived or secondary importance.

Advocacy for Symbolic and Material Immigrant Issues

Immigrant nonprofits in San Francisco concern themselves with a variety of public policy issues that directly affect the city's immigrant population. While there are a number of nonprofits that advocate for more just immigrant admission policies with federal government officials, most of the 45 organizations I surveyed focus on the increasingly localized dynamics of immigrant integration and consequently direct their advocacy efforts in that area at government officials at the municipal and state levels. Additionally, immigrant nonprofits are interested in policy issues of symbolic as well as material relevance to the immigrant community. While the organizations have good track records in advocating for both types of integration policies, it has been more challenging for nonprofits to advocate for material policies, which often necessitate collaborations with different types of organizations and result in greater pushback from city officials because they tend to be more complicated and costly for the city to implement and enforce.

Little Saigon, Victoria Manalo Draves Park, and Sanctuary for Undocumented Immigrants

With regards to symbolic policies inclusive of newcomers' interests, immigrant nonprofits in San Francisco have successfully advocated with local government officials for such measures as getting part of the Tenderloin district—a poor San Francisco neighborhood home to about 250 Vietnamese American-owned businesses and 2,000 of the city's 13,000 Vietnamese immigrants and Vietnamese Americans—officially designated as "Little Saigon" in 2004 (Estrella 2004). In 2005, immigrant nonprofits convinced local legislators to name a park in the south of Market district after Victoria Manalo Draves, to date the only woman of Filipino ancestry to win an Olympic gold medal (Werner 2006). Additionally, since 2005—in response to federal immigration reform proposals that would criminalize undocumented immigrants and Bay Area workplace raids by U.S. Immigration and Customs Enforcement (ICE) to enforce sanctions against employers who knowingly hire undocumented immigrants—various immigrant nonprofits have successfully put pressure on San Francisco officials to reaffirm the city's status as a sanctuary city and its commitment to a "don't ask-don't tell" policy where city employees (including local law enforcement officers) are not required to report undocumented city residents to federal immigration officials.[4] Even if these measures are only symbolic in nature and do not produce clear substantive benefits to immigrants, they are important in that they are likely to create a local context where immigrants feel welcomed, appreciated, and safe. With research demonstrating that immigrants' individual civic and political participation increases in such welcoming contexts (Bloemraad 2003, 2006), immigrant nonprofits are important as organizational vehicles that prod government officials to pass policies of symbolic importance that in turn create an environment that is inviting of immigrants' participation in civic and political affairs.

---

[4] In 1989, the San Francisco Board of Supervisors adopted the City of Refuge Ordinance, a "noncooperation policy" that bars local officials from collaborating with federal immigration authorities in all but a few explicit circumstances. The ordinance also forbids the use of any city resources to enforce federal immigration laws. To further strengthen its commitment to sanctuary for undocumented immigrants, the city recently created (2007) the position of Immigrant Rights Administrator, who supervises city departments to make sure they follow the sanctuary policy (Buchanan 2007). The City of Refuge Ordinance, however, has no real legal meaning and cannot stop federal authorities from enforcing U.S. immigration laws and arresting San Francisco residents who violate those laws.

Multilingual Government and a Local Minimum Wage

In recent years, San Francisco-based immigrant nonprofits have also been able to move local government officials to adopt and implement local laws with material significance for the city's immigrant population. These include a language-access ordinance benefiting the city's 100,000 limited-English proficient residents and a local minimum wage resulting in wage increases for 54,000 low-wage workers, many of whom are immigrants (Reich and Laitinen 2003).[5] I classify these policies as material policies because they provide tangible resources to immigrants and impose costs on those adversely affected by them (the city in the case of language access and employers in the case of the local minimum wage).

With regards to language access, immigrant nonprofits played an instrumental role in getting the Equal Access to Services Ordinance (EASO) enacted by the San Francisco Board of Supervisors in 2001. This ordinance removes language barriers that limited-English speakers may have in accessing city government and public services. As a result of EASO, public information and government services in San Francisco need to be offered in English, Chinese, and Spanish city-wide. In certain supervisorial districts with a high concentration of Russian, Filipino, and Vietnamese immigrants, branch offices of city departments are also required to offer city services in Russian, Tagalog, and Vietnamese. What is remarkable about this ordinance—which in effect created multilingual government at the local level—is that it was and continues to be a policy issue dominated and monopolized by immigrant nonprofit organizations. A small group of immigrant nonprofits dominated the policymaking process from beginning to end: they identified the need for EASO, put the policy on the city's legislative agenda, drafted the text of the law, advocated for its passage, monitored the implementation of the ordinance since its enactment in 2001, and is currently (2007) negotiating with local government officials to amend the law. Immigrant nonprofits were also the only organizations that looked at language access as a policy issue in its diverse nature. Language accessibility is an issue that cuts across different policy areas—including health care, education, employment, community safety, and political participation—and consequently affects a number of different community institutions that interact with immigrants, including labor unions and churches. While labor unions and churches with an immigrant membership deal with language barriers all the time,

[5] While I do not discuss these policies in this chapter, immigrant nonprofits in San Francisco also campaigned for passage of the Paid Sick Leave Ordinance (2006). Legislated via initiative with 61% of the vote, this San Francisco law mandates sick days for those who work in the city, including undocumented immigrants. Immigrant nonprofits also advocated for the Health Care Security Ordinance (2006). Unanimously adopted by the San Francisco Board of Supervisors in 2006, this ordinance provides comprehensive health care for the city's 82,000 uninsured adult residents, among whom are many immigrants. Finally, immigrant nonprofits also supported passage of the Municipal Identification Cards Ordinance in 2007. This ordinance requires the county clerk to issue municipal identification cards to all residents of San Francisco and helps immigrants previously without government-issued identification to open a bank account, for example, or to obtain a library card.

they have other goals to accomplish and other priorities that guide their work and as a result they have been only tangentially interested in language access as a policy issue.

Immigrant nonprofits were also part of the campaign to pass the Minimum Wage Ordinance, which was legislated via initiative and passed with 60% of the vote in 2003. Compared to language access, this policy raising the minimum wage city-wide[6] is less exclusively an "immigrant issue." Consequently, immigrant nonprofits had to share the advocacy spotlight with labor unions, worker centers, religious institutions, and other organizations speaking for low-wage workers spanning different ethno-racial and demographic groups, including blacks, the working poor, the elderly, single-parent households, and immigrants. Immigrant nonprofits worked alongside these organizations in the San Francisco Minimum Wage Coalition, a diverse and vibrant coalition that campaigned for passage of this progressive policy. While labor unions played a dominant role in this campaign, immigrant nonprofits certainly pulled their weight. For example, they helped collect the signatures that placed the issue on the ballot and paid to have their arguments in favor of the ballot measure included in the city's official voter guide (San Francisco Department of Elections). They shared stories with the local media of immigrants' hardships of living on the state minimum wage in the high-cost city of San Francisco. They also mobilized immigrants to attend rallies in support of the ballot measure and help with door knocking and leafleting to convince San Francisco voters of the merits of the ballot measure. Perhaps most importantly, in discussions with other members of the Minimum Wage Coalition about the content of the ordinance, immigrant nonprofits made sure that protections for immigrant workers were written into the ordinance. As a result of immigrant nonprofits' insistence on securing protections for immigrant workers, the Minimum Wage Ordinance prohibits employers from retaliating against employees who file wage complaints. This protection is especially important for undocumented immigrants.

Participation in the Minimum Wage Coalition was advantageous to immigrant nonprofits as it enabled them to incorporate the concerns of the immigrant community into public discussions about a city-wide minimum wage. It also gave them the opportunity to educate voters, policymakers, and immigrants alike about the importance of a city-wide minimum wage to the immigrant community. Additionally, the coalition served as cover for immigrant nonprofits' political work and it made less visible to the outside world nonprofits' electioneering activities. However, immigrant nonprofits also had to contend with a number of challenges in collaborating with labor unions in particular. Labor unions have more resources and enjoy fewer restrictions on their election activities, which allowed them to

---

[6] The San Francisco minimum wage is adjusted yearly based on the previous year's Consumer Price Index for urban wage earners in the San Francisco-Oakland-San Jose metropolitan area. For 2008, the city's minimum wage is set at $9.36 per hour. In 2008, the California state minimum wage is $8.00 per hour and the federal minimum wage is $6.55 per hour (effective July 24).

prevail in the coalition's campaign endeavors. Labor unions had money to pay for the initiative campaign and a large membership base to help them to mobilize and turn out voters in support of the ballot measure. In contrast, immigrant nonprofits lacked the resources to finance the cost of the ballot campaign. Additionally, most immigrant nonprofits have clients, who are less easily mobilized than dues-paying union members are. Finally, immigrant nonprofits cater to immigrants, many of whom are not citizens of the United States and who cannot vote in American elections. While the nonprofits could convince immigrants that the Minimum Wage Ordinance was a policy to their benefit and one that needed to pass, they could not turn them out as voters on Election Day. Finally, as the Minimum Wage Ordinance was perceived by many to be the pet issue of Tom Ammiano and Matt Gonzalez, who at the time were both on the board of supervisors and ran for mayor of San Francisco when the minimum wage issue was on the 2003 ballot, some immigrant nonprofits were reluctant to spend money on the campaign or step up their voter mobilization activities for fear that these might be mistaken for nonprofits' illegal political campaign interventions.[7]

Immigrant Voting Rights

While immigrant nonprofits have had a number of important local legislative and electoral successes in San Francisco, sometimes achieved in collaboration with other types of institutions with a progressive urban agenda, there are also instances where their advocacy on behalf of the immigrant population met with greater resistance and was less successful. Proposition F from 2004, the narrowly defeated (with 51–49% of the vote) ballot measure that would have allowed noncitizens with children in the San Francisco school district to vote in school board elections, serves as an example. The measure was placed on the ballot by nine members of the San Francisco Board of Supervisors, but it enjoyed strong campaign support among labor unions, education advocates, and a large nonpartisan coalition of immigrant nonprofits that emphasized the practical benefits of alien suffrage and argued that parents' participation in school affairs and noncitizen voting would benefit children's education and inspire immigrants to become active and responsible American citizens. While a handful of municipalities across the U.S. allow noncitizens to vote in local elections today, enfranchisement of noncitizens remains a highly contentious issue and arguably calls into question the value of American citizenship. In San Francisco, opposition to Proposition F came from both liberals and conservatives, demonstrating the contentious nature and ideological complexity of the issue even in this progressive "left coast" city.

---

[7] In 1999 and 2000, Tom Ammiano was the lead champion of San Francisco's Living Wage Ordinance (officially called the Minimum Compensation Ordinance), the law mandating that city contractors who provide services and tenants at the San Francisco Airport pay their covered employees a minimum wage higher than the state and federal minimum wages and provide employees with a certain number of paid and unpaid days off per year. In 2003, Matt Gonzalez publicly supported the Minimum Wage Ordinance and identified low-wage worker rights as one of the key issues in his mayoral platform.

Prominent city and state officials[8], an opposition group backed by the business community, and the editorial board of the *San Francisco Chronicle* all opposed the measure (Hayduk 2006). Among other things, they emphasized that Proposition F was in violation of the California State Constitution and they argued that noncitizen voting would cost the city a minimum of $700,000 per election (San Francisco Department of Elections). Opponents further complicated the issue by emphasizing their support for legal immigrants' acquisition of American citizenship and their simultaneous opposition to voting rights for noncitizens and undocumented immigrants in particular. They also attempted to divide the immigrant community on the ballot measure by pitting legal immigrants—who, through naturalization, had earned the right to vote—against undocumented immigrants—who had broken the law and arguably did not deserve the suffrage (Hayduk 2006). The San Francisco ballot measure also drew opposition from around the country from such right-of-center groups like the Federation for American Immigration Reform (FAIR) and conservative politicians, who feared that noncitizen voting in San Francisco could instigate noncitizen voting in other municipalities and bring about an undesired change in the political status quo (Hayduk 2006). Given the controversy and the amount of public debate that this issue generated in San Francisco and elsewhere in the U.S. and given the fact that supporters of Proposition F were outspent by opponents by a ratio of 1:6, it is actually an accomplishment that proponents were able to convince 49% of San Franciscans to vote "yes" on the ballot measure in the short, six-month span of the initiative campaign (Hayduk 2006).

In considering these different policy issues and how they were translated into local law or became part of public debate, it is clear that immigrant nonprofits have acted as important institutional representatives of the San Francisco newcomer community by advocating for various immigrant-friendly policies. Immigrant nonprofits appear to be most effective as agents of group representation when they do not need to compete for policymakers' attention with other urban political actors, if it concerns an issue that more exclusively affects the city's immigrant population, and when the policy issue can be framed in straightforward practical terms that are acceptable to policymakers and voters of a variety of ideological persuasions.

Strategic Response to Federal Restrictions on Nonprofits' Political Activities

Immigrant nonprofits employ a number of tactics and strategies of influence that make them strategic actors in the local politics of immigrant representation. What makes them strategic is that they take part in the local policymaking process

[8] They included Ed Harrington (the city controller), Louise Renne (the former city attorney), Dianne Feinstein (former mayor of San Francisco and current Democratic U.S. senator), and Bill Jones (the former Republican California secretary of state) (San Francisco Department of Elections; Hayduk 2006).

while navigating and negotiating a number of government restrictions and regulations on their political activities. While federal tax law creates limits on immigrant nonprofits' political undertakings, they also present opportunities for these organizations' input in local politics in creative, innovative, and perhaps unexpected ways. It is true that compared to labor unions and other types of interest groups with immigrant members—which have fewer restrictions imposed on the amount and type of politicking they can legally do—immigrant nonprofits have a relatively limited repertoire of political resources to draw from in the governmental process. However, they certainly are not the politically passive and incompetent organizations they are often made out to be, and they have the goodwill, motivation, and capability to address immigrant issues that other types of urban institutions and actors often lack.

Immigrant nonprofits, for example, are legally allowed to lobby as long this constitutes an "insubstantial part" of their organizations' overall activities. However, the line between lobbying activities—which are restricted and defined by federal law as advocacy targeted at the legislature with the goal of influencing the passage or defeat of a specific piece of legislation—and the education of policymakers—which often is nonpartisan in character, invited by government officials, and not restricted by law—is thin and often vague. The immigrant nonprofits I surveyed certainly advocate for policy change, but emphasize that their political activities are efforts to educate policymakers on issues affecting immigrants. Also, nonprofit advocacy targeted at the executive and judicial branches of government are not limited by law and many immigrant nonprofits stand out for their frequent interactions and collaborations with various city departments with which many have contracted for years to provide services to the city's immigrant population. Immigrant nonprofits will also challenge local laws or practices by taking issues to the district attorney, city attorney, or the local court system, but this type of judicial activism is more likely to happen when the city is not the party being challenged. For example, a number of immigrant nonprofits continue to monitor the implementation of the city's Minimum Wage Ordinance and have challenged noncompliant employers in court to make sure they pay low-wage immigrant workers the minimum wage mandated by San Francisco law. However, in efforts to maintain amicable relations with city officials, immigrant nonprofits have been less willing to seek legal recourse for the city's partial noncompliance with the Equal Access to Services Ordinance.

Immigrant nonprofits also have to cope with the restriction that bars them from partisan politics, which means they cannot endorse or directly campaign for a candidate or party, donate money to a candidate or party, or distribute materials aimed at influencing the outcome of an election to public office. With these restrictions, immigrant nonprofits are barred from participating in many aspects of the electoral process. However, these restrictions on nonprofits' electioneering do not apply to the initiative process or issue campaigns and immigrant nonprofits can (and many of them do) take positions on city ballot measures, as was the case with the Minimum Wage Ordinance in 2003 and Proposition F in 2004. Additionally, leaders from the immigrant nonprofit sector do endorse candidates running for local and state office. While they do this in their capacity as concerned citizens without stating their nonprofit affiliation, the public endorsements of these well-known leaders in the immigrant community do signal where an immigrant non-profit stands on particular candidates and their platforms.

In efforts to get around the restriction that immigrant nonprofits cannot engage in partisan politics, they also tend to take a pragmatic approach to policymaking. Immigrant nonprofits frame issues in practical rather than more ideological language and this resonates well with many local policymakers who like to legislate concrete things that improve the way the city runs. While the nonprofits advocating for immigrant-friendly local policies are certainly motivated by social justice and civil rights goals and nonprofit staff often privately favor the more progressive members on the board of supervisors, their interactions with San Francisco government officials tend to be free from such ideological language and do not demonstrate a clear favoritism toward legislators of a particular political leaning. This mismatch between nonprofits' internal ideology and their practical public face when advocating with local government officials indicates that these organizations are adept at switching codes or discourses and creates situations where nonprofits can cooperate and build congenial, rather than adversarial, relations with local legislators of different political views.

The federal restrictions specifying both the amount and type of political work that immigrant nonprofits are permitted to do consequently affect these organizations' standing in the local political process. Compared to labor unions and interest groups that can influence government officials of a particular partisan persuasion with a combination of votes, campaign contributions, and information, nonprofits have fewer political resources at their disposal and they experience greater challenges in accessing local decision-making arenas. However, in advocating for immigrant-friendly policies from outside City Hall, immigrant nonprofits have successfully teamed up with strategically positioned officials inside the San Francisco political establishment. There are a number of high-ranking public officials with roots in San Francisco's immigrant nonprofit sector who form natural allies for nonprofit organizations that want in on local policymaking. For example, the City Administrator Ed Lee and Assessor-Recorder Phil Ting both used to work for a San Francisco-based nonprofit organization providing legal services to the low-income Asian Pacific Islander community. In recent years, both Lee and Ting have been key supporters of the city ordinance providing linguistically accessible and culturally competent services to limited-English city residents. With immigrant nonprofits advocating for immigrant-friendly policies from outside government and with nonprofit-trained public officials advancing immigrant integration from inside city hall, there are two different ways in which the immigrant non-profit perspective is incorporated into the local policymaking process.

Compared to other urban political institutions, however, immigrant nonprofits also have a keen knowledge or expertise on the local immigrant population that they can leverage with local policymakers. As direct service providers firmly rooted in the communities they serve, immigrant nonprofits know the city's immigrant population well and they can easily identify new concerns that should be addressed with new legislation or updated administrative rules and procedures. This knowledge on the immigrant population serves as an important political resource in a city where more than a third of the population is foreign born and where local legislators, who—with two legislative aids each—are admittedly understaffed, gladly avail themselves of nonprofits' expertise on the immigrant community to enable them to develop policies that better serve the city's diverse population. Other types of organizations, whose core constituency is not comprised of immigrants, do not have this expertise with which to influence the local policymaking process.

A final strategy that immigrant nonprofits employ in attempts to maximize their political input and raise the voice of the immigrant community in local policymaking is through collaboration with other types of organizations (such as labor unions) on issues that affect immigrants. While these coalitions can function as covers for nonprofits' political work and allow politically active nonprofits to go unnoticed to those concerned about their politicking, they also come with the challenge of working alongside organizations that have a different constituency base and a different organizational structure, that are guided by different goals, and that often have more political resources and fewer restrictions on their political activities. Immigrant nonprofits with public policy aspirations, but without the financial and staff resources to take part in politics, have also joined larger regional coalitions of immigrant organizations (such as the Bay Area Immigrant Rights Coalition, located in Oakland), which dedicate themselves exclusively to community education and public policy advocacy and do not provide direct social services to the immigrant community.

Immigrant Nonprofits and Policy Implementation

San Francisco-based immigrant nonprofits advocate for immigrant-friendly policies with all three branches of local government and they take part in various stages of the policymaking process. However, they stand out for their frequent and successful interactions with various city departments and administrative agencies in the period after the enactment of local ordinances. As bureaucratic advocates, immigrant nonprofits not only monitor immigrant-friendly policies to ensure that they are implemented to the letter of the law, but also advocate for regulatory or procedural changes so local policies are implemented with maximum benefit to the city's immigrant population.

With regards to the Equal Access to Services Ordinance (EASO) I discussed earlier, nonprofit organizations have regularly checked in with city departments to learn about their progress in providing language access to the city's limited-English residents. When they learned that the Immigrant Rights Commission[9]—

[9] The Immigrant Rights Commission was created by the San Francisco Board of Supervisors in 1997 and functions as a consultative body whose primary duty it is to pro-

the government body officially responsible for monitoring and facilitating compliance with EASO and charged with the duty to resolve disputes arising under the ordinance—was only providing minimal monitoring of EASO and city departments were not (fully) complying with the law, immigrant nonprofits took on a more active implementation role, which was welcomed by the commission and other city officials. Immigrant nonprofits had many meetings with department heads to educate them about the requirements of EASO and help them determine which documents needed translation and which positions should be staffed by bilingual personnel. In short, these organizations got city departments engaged with the language issue and provided the technical assistance to increase the city's capability to offer linguistically accessible and culturally competent information and services to foreign-born residents.

Immigrant nonprofits have played an equally important role in implementing the city's Minimum Wage Ordinance (MWO). In particular, they have assisted the city's Office of Labor Standards Enforcement (OLSE)—the local government body that enforces labor laws adopted by the San Francisco Board of Supervisors and the city's voters—in going after noncompliant employers. Most, if not all, violations of the MWO involve immigrant workers, many of whom are undocumented. Immigrants, however, are not always aware that OLSE can help them recover their wages and they are often afraid to ask for help from a government agency. As a result, immigrant workers often take their wage concerns to local nonprofit organizations instead. With longstanding relationships and experience in providing linguistically and culturally appropriate education and outreach to the immigrant community, immigrant nonprofits have the unique ability to build trust and case-manage vulnerable immigrant workers in a way that government agencies cannot. With their up-to-date and on-the-ground knowledge of what is happening at the worksite, immigrant nonprofits have emerged as important intermediaries registering immigrant workers' complaints and relaying them to city officials, enabling OLSE to investigate these cases and possibly start administrative procedures against noncompliant employers. OLSE is well aware of the important role that immigrant nonprofits play in their enforcement work and in 2006 the Minimum Wage Implementation and Enforcement Ordinance was passed with the aim of strengthening the enforcement mechanisms of the MWO and developing a multifaceted outreach and education program that includes a collaborative of local immigrant nonprofits.

Immigrant nonprofits' presence and effectiveness as policy implementers should not come as a surprise. Their strength in policy implementation results from federal restrictions on nonprofits' political activities, which encourage these organizations to aim their advocacy energies at the executive branch and the city's administrative agencies. However, I believe that another explanation for immigrant nonprofits' prominence in policy implementation can be found in the hybrid nature of the work they do. Immigrant nonprofits mount advocacy campaigns

---

vide advice and make recommendations to the board of supervisors and the mayor on issues affecting the city's immigrant population.

aimed at policy enactment and they provide services that in turn focus on policy implementation. As a result, these organizations have experienced firsthand that policy implementation is not automatic and that there often exists a gulf between policy enactment and policy implementation. As social service providers that often work on contract with city departments, immigrant nonprofits get constant feedback from their immigrant clients about city policies that work and those that do not. As such, these organizations are not only among the first to hear about implementation issues and shortcomings, but they also have connections with city departments to address these problems. Labor unions, in contrast, work with contracts and are less experienced with using public enforcement to ensure a policy or agreement sticks.

Urbanized Politics and the Promise of Inclusive Governance

Immigrant nonprofit organizations in San Francisco play an important role in bringing the needs and interests of the city's immigrant population to the attention of government officials. They certainly have a political presence in San Francisco and have been quite effective in advocating for local policies that many immigrants have benefited from, such as language access and a city-wide minimum wage. Immigrant nonprofits in other established gateway cities are likely to play a similarly important role as local institutions representing the immigrant population, even though the issues that animate their political activism and their success as policy advocates are likely to vary with the composition of the local immigrant population and the specifics of the political context in which they operate. There is support for this statement in the research of other scholars concerned with the organizational mediation of immigrants' political incorporation in such cities as Boston, Los Angeles, Chicago, and New York City (Bloemraad 2006; Cordero-Guzmán 2001, 2005; Wong 2006).

I also expect immigrant nonprofits' political activism in other locales as a result of a confluence of developments that have created both opportunities and pressures for all nonprofit organizations to play a more active role in local politics today. Privatization of the American welfare state and continued immigration to America's urban centers have stimulated the growth in recent decades of nonprofit organizations that cater to America's newcomers (Hung 2007). Simultaneously, more extensive government contracting with nonprofits during the 1960s and 1970s, followed by devolution of government responsibilities to municipalities and curtailments of government spending during the 1980s and 1990s, have created pressures for immigrant nonprofits to influence allocation decisions made by local government officials (Grønbjerg 1993, 2001; Marwell 2004; Smith and Lipsky 1993). Additionally, while the municipality remains the true locus of immigrant integration, more recently immigration policy has undergone a shift and as a result of stalled immigration reform at the federal level, government officials in various states and localities are making decisions related to the implementation of immigration policies.[10] This increased localization and urbanization of immigrant and immigration policies shifts the development and implementation of these policies down to the local level where nonprofits operate and creates opportunities for these organizations to play a more active role in the local politics of immigrant representation.

While occupying a more prominent role in service provision and public policy advocacy at the local level at a time when the political process related to immigrant issues is increasingly urbanized, immigrant nonprofits today are in a good position to shape a system of governance that is more equitable and includes the diverse voices of the immigrant community. Not only do immigrant nonprofits serve as watchdogs educating local officials about the changed needs and interests of the immigrant population, they also intervene as agenda setters that share their knowledge of the immigrant population and propose concrete policies to benefit the local immigrant community. They also play a key role in monitoring policy implementation to maximize immigrants' benefits from enacted policies. Immigrant nonprofits' efforts to shape public policy are not always successful. However, as they interact with a variety of local policymakers, immigrant nonprofits are adding an important channel through which immigrants' concern can trickle up to the radar screen of local officials and they help bring about a system of governance that is more democratic, more accountable, and perhaps more efficient. Nonprofits' role in the local politics of immigrant representation, furthermore, comes at a time when the tasks of local governments are becoming more complex and polities are growing larger and more heterogeneous (Fung and Wright 2001). As a result, nonprofits' interventions in the political process might be a welcome development as they can enhance local government's capacity to respond to the diversity challenges of multi-ethnic urban areas with large immigrant populations, in California as well as the rest of the U.S.

---

[10] An example of this localization and urbanization of immigration policy is the federal government's calls upon local police agencies to become involved in the enforcement of federal immigration laws in the aftermath of the terrorist attacks of 2001. Additionally, a number of localities across the U.S. (including Escondido, California) have adopted laws forbidding landlords to rent to undocumented immigrants. Such discriminatory local policies not only have questionable constitutional legitimacy (and they are being challenged in court), but also leave to local officials the decision of whether a person is residing in the U.S. legally or not, a determination that only the federal government can make. Also, the National Conference of State Legislatures (NCSL) provides evidence of the increased localization of immigrant and immigration issues nationwide. A 2007 NCSL report documents that, as a result of the federal gridlock on immigration reform, state governments have introduced about two and a half times more bills addressing immigrant issues in 2007 than they did in 2006.

References

Association of Bay Area Governments. http://www.abag.ca.gov/

Berry, Jeffrey M. (with David F. Arons). 2003. *A Voice for Nonprofits*. Washington, D.C.: Brookings Institution Press.

Bloemraad, Irene. 2003. "Institutions, Ethnic Leaders, and the Political Incorporation of Immigrants: A Comparison of Canada and the United States." In *Host Societies and the Reception of Immigrants*, ed. Jeffrey G. Reitz. La Jolla, Calif.: Center for Comparative Immigration Studies, UCSD, 361–401.

_____. 2006. *Becoming a Citizen: Incorporating Immigrants and Refugees in the United States and Canada*. Berkeley, Calif.: University of California Press.

Buchanan, Wyatt. 2007. "ID Card Plan Would Help Immigrants Get Basic Services." *San Francisco Chronicle*. September 19, B1.

Cordero-Guzmán, Héctor R. 2001. "Immigrant Aid Societies and Organizations." In *Encyclopedia of American Immigration*, ed. James Ciment. Armonk, N.Y.: Sharpe Reference, 334–40.

_____. 2005. "Community Based Organizations and Migration in New York City." *Journal of Ethnic and Migration Studies* 31(5): 889–909.

de Graauw, Els. 2008. "Nonprofit Organizations: Agents of Immigrant Political Incorporation in Urban America." In *Civic Roots and Political Realities: Immigrants, Community Organizations, and Political Engagement*, ed. S. Karthick Ramakrishnan and Irene Bloemraad. New York, NY: Russell Sage Foundation Press.

Estrella, Cicero A. 2004. "S.F.'s Little Saigon: Stretch of Larkin Street Named for Vietnamese Americans." *San Francisco Chronicle*. February 16, B1.

Fung, Archon, and Erik Olin Wright. 2001. "Deepening Democracy: Innovations in Empowered Participatory Democracy." *Politics & Society* 29(1): 5–41.

Grønbjerg, Kirsten A. 1993. *Understanding Nonprofit Funding: Managing Revenues in Social Services and Community Development Organizations*. San Francisco, Calif.: Jossey-Bass.

_____. [1998] 2001. "Markets, Politics, and Charity: Nonprofits in the Political Economy." In *The Nature of the Nonprofit Sector*, ed. J. Steven Ott. Boulder, Colo.: Westview Press, 217–31.

Harmon, Gail M., Jessica A. Ladd, and Eleanor A. Evans. [1991, 1995] 2000. *Being a Player: A Guide to the IRS Lobbying Regulations for Advocacy Charities*. Washington, D.C.: Alliance for Justice.

Hasenfeld, Yeheskel, and Benjamin Gidron. 2005. "Understanding Multi-Purpose Hybrid Voluntary Organizations: The Contributions of Theories on Civil Society, Social Movements and Non-Profit Organizations." *Journal on Civil Society* 1(2): 97–112.

Hayduk, Ron. 2006. *Democracy for All: Restoring Immigrant Voting Rights in the United States*. New York, N.Y.: Routledge.

Hung, Chi-Kan Richard. 2007. "Immigrant Nonprofit Organizations in U.S. Metropolitan Areas." *Nonprofit and Voluntary Sector Quarterly* 36(4): 707–29.

Jones-Correa, Michael. 1998. *Between Two Nations: The Political Predicament of Latinos in New York City*. Ithaca, N.Y.: Cornell University Press.

Lunder, Erika. 2006. "Tax-Exempt Organizations: Political Activity Restrictions and Disclosure Requirements." *Congressional Research Service* (RL33377; 20 April). http://www.ombwatch.org/npadv/PDF/CRSReportonTaxexempt organizationsRestrictions.pdf, last accessed December 4, 2007.

Marwell, Nicole P. 2004. "Privatizing the Welfare State: Nonprofit Community-Based Organizations as Political Actors." *American Sociological Review* 69: 265–91.

Minkoff, Debra. 2002. "The Emergence of Hybrid Organizational Forms: Combining Identity-Based Service Provision and Political Action." *Nonprofit and Voluntary Quarterly* 31(3): 377–401.

NCSL Immigrant Policy Project. 2007. "Enacted State Legislation Related to Immigrants and Immigration." Washington, D.C.: National Conference of State Legislatures. http://www.ncsl.org/print/immig/2007immigrationfinal.pdf, last accessed December 4, 2007.

Olvera, Javier Erik. 2007. "San Francisco Supervisors OK ID Cards for Undocumented Immigrants." *San Jose Mercury News*, November 20, Local, 7B.

Pierson, Paul. 1993. "When Effect Becomes Cause: Policy Feedback and Political Change." *World Politics* 45: 595–628.

Reich, Michael, and Amy Laitinen. 2003. "Raising Low Pay in a High Income Economy: The Economics of a San Francisco Minimum Wage." *Institute for Research on Labor and Employment. Institute for Research on Labor and Employment Working Paper Series*. http://repositories.cdlib.org/iir/iirwps/iirwps-099-03, last accessed December 4, 2007.

Rosenstone, Steven J., and John Mark Hansen. 1993. *Mobilization, Participation, and Democracy in America*. New York, N.Y.: Macmillan Publishing Company.

San Francisco (California). 2006. "Report Concerning the Status of San Francisco's Equal Access to Services Ordinance." City and County of San Francisco, CA: Immigrant Rights Commission.

San Francisco Department of Elections. http://www.sfgov.org/site/elections_index.asp

Salamon, Lester M. 1999. *America's Nonprofit Sector: A Primer*. 2d ed. New York, N.Y.: Foundation Center.

Smith, Steven Rathgeb, and Michael Lipsky. 1993. *Nonprofits for Hire: The Welfare State in the Age of Contracting*. Cambridge, Mass.: Harvard University Press.

U.S. Census Bureau. 1990, 2000. Census of Population and Housing, Summary File 3 (SF-3) –Sample Data. http://factfinder.census.gov.

Verba, Sidney, Kay Lehman Schlozman, and Henry E. Brady. 1995. *Voice and Equality: Civic Voluntarism in American Politics*. Cambridge, Mass.: Harvard University Press.

Werner, Ken. 2006. "Grand-opening of Victoria Manalo Draves Park: First New Park in a Decade." *BeyondChron*, October 30. http://www.beyondchron.org/news/index.php?itemid=3845, last accessed December 4, 2007.

Wong, Janelle S. 2006. *Democracy's Promise: Immigrants and American Civic Institutions*. Ann Arbor, MI: University of Michigan Press.

Young Workers United. http://www.youngworkersunited.org/.

Chapter 10

Elections, Economics, and Coalitional Politics: Investigating California's Future(s)

Manuel Pastor[1]

Introduction

The last several elections in California have produced a series of both surprising victories and stunning defeats for both conservative and liberal forces. Underlying the wild swings in the state's political mood has been a series of shifting coalitions, particularly by race, class, and economic philosophy.

In October 2003, for example, California voters removed Governor Gray Davis from office in a special recall election and replaced him with Arnold Schwarzenegger. The electoral triumph was convincing: Schwarzenegger won nearly half the vote despite a crowded field that included three main contenders. Moreover, support was across the board—despite the presence of a moderate Latino Democrat, Lieutenant Governor Cruz Bustamante, competing to replace Davis, Schwarzenegger was able to secure 31% of the Latino vote (more than the 18% he secured of the African-American vote, with the latter still remarkably high for a Republican in a multicandidate election). Schwarzenegger also scored 40%

[1] The author gives thanks to Rachel Rosner, Justin Scoggins, and Christian Martinez for research support and to the MacArthur Foundation's Building Successful Regions pilot network for inspiring and supporting several of the ideas informing this work.

of voters with household incomes below $40,000, only six points shy of the edge he had with voters making between $40,000 and $75,000.[2] Republican pollsters were rightly thrilled with the gains and beneath the celebration was a confidence that perhaps a center-right rainbow coalition—one that focused on how a pro-business and progrowth alliance could benefit all—might have salience in California.

Yet the basis for this center-right coalition seemed shaken only two years later. In the November 2005 elections, every one of the propositions supported by now-Governor Schwarzenegger went down in defeat—along with a few supported by other interests, partly because of voter fatigue at legislating through the ballot box. From the point of view of coalitional politics, however, one of the more significant facts was that Latino support for the governor's key proposition—an effort to limit government spending—stood at only 25%, and class and racial divisions were very sharply drawn in the voters' response to another Schwarzenegger-supported proposition, one that sought to limit the ability of unions to utilize member-generated resources in political campaigns. While the usual account of the election has rightly focused on the diminution of the governor's power and popularity, partly due to a sort of overreaching via strong-arm reform, an equally important feature was the erosion of the nascent Republican rainbow, particularly with regard to the low-tax, anti-union aspects of the economic philosophy. And, of course, the next chapter in the story starred a newly coalitional and bipartisan governor, as Schwarzenegger publicly acknowledged his errors in calling for the special election and began to make his way closer to the middle and back to the more widespread support he had once enjoyed.

Meanwhile, in Los Angeles, a new rainbow has been emerging, this in the form of the March 2005 election of Antonio Villaraigosa. The new mayor won over 60% of the overall vote, a result helped along by a very strong 84% share of the Latino electorate—but what was most striking was that Villaraigosa also garnered 50% of the white vote, 48% of the black vote, and 44% of the Asian vote.[3] Strikingly, the support was also wide across the income board: about two-third of those in the income bands below $60,000 in household income voted for Villaraigosa while his share of those with household incomes above $60,000 was still a healthy 55%.[4] This was the Democratic rainbow—one reaching across the geography of a fragmented Los Angeles and across the various racial and class lines that usually divide—and it has seemed to hang together even as Villaraigosa's stature

---

[2] Data from a *Los Angeles Times* exit poll available at http://www.igs.berkeley.edu/library/htRecall2003.html#Topic4.

[3] Data taken from the *Los Angeles Times* exit poll. The Center for the Study of Los Angeles at Loyola Marymount University's exit poll suggests an even stronger showing: 57% of the white vote and 58% of the black vote. http://www.lmu.edu/csla/press/releases_2005/Runoff.html.

[4] Equally interesting, particularly in light of the ethnic "generation gap" we stress below, is that Villaraigosa was estimated to have received 77% of the voters aged 18–29 and 70% of those aged 30–44.

has been diminished by a struggle with the school board over mayoral control and the political spillover from marital difficulties.

Will Antonio's coalition hold—and will Arnold pull his back together? Much, we would argue, depends on the nature of the economic model employed and the economic results obtained. After all, while each of these two coalition-forgers promised new strategies and new leadership that could reach across ethnic lines, there was also an explicit and implicit focus on economic strategies that could bridge the gap between business, labor, and community. Undergirding the Schwarzenegger appeal was the promise to restore the state's economy from a brutal recession and to right the fiscal ship through business-friendly governance. The Villaraigosa campaign, while addressing a much broader range of local issues, also promised to resurrect the Los Angeles economy and address the widening divides of income that had plagued the city for nearly two decades.[5]

In our view, to understand the possibilities for coalition-building for a new California, it is necessary to step back from the immediate concerns of elections and polls and take up a series of underlying challenges, particularly economic, that must be faced by any political force seeking a place in the state's landscape. These include a full recognition of what I have termed the three "news": the new demography, the new economy, and the new inequality. Essentially, the changing racial landscape of California has made coalitions both more necessary and more difficult, and triggered a new sort of "generation gap"—one in which the demography of the older population in the state is very different from that of the younger population and hence investments in the future have diminished.

This failure to invest is all the more important because of the other "news": the changing economy and the rise in income inequality. From a state that once prided itself on the broad opportunities for economic advancement and personal transformation afforded those who arrived here, California seems to have become a state marked by deep economic chasms. Addressing these will require a combination of robust economic growth, steady improvements in education, and policies focused on lifting labor and community standards. This is a combination that both cuts across and runs against traditional party lines as well as the usual gap between business and community agendas—and putting it in place to secure the future of California will require new coalitional skills.

Below, I focus on these big underlying economic challenges to coalition formation. I begin by first sketching the new trends in California, pointing out the ways in which the new demographics call out for new coalitions and the ways in

---

[5] Indeed, it was exactly that widening divide that seemed to derail the coalition builder role model Villaraigosa has sought to imitate, former Mayor Tom Bradley. While his early years of governance brought great opportunity in public employment, his eventual economic development strategy relied on a downtown-based strategy that seemed to leave aside the neighborhoods. The growing opposition, stalemated economic development, and Bradley's growing lack of leadership on economic issues was signaled most strongly by his decision after the 1992 riots to turn over the recovery effort for poor neighborhoods to Peter Uberroth, a businessman from Orange County who had successfully organized the 1984 Olympics.

which the new inequality shifts both material interests and economic imperatives. I then turn to coalition politics *per se*, noting how material interests, shared ideologies, and dynamic leaders can undergird new alliances. I close by discussing one potential source of encouragement: the new attention to regional economies, politics, and collaboratives. This new level of action in which mutual understandings are being built across the usual divides of race, class, and geography suggests that both researchers and political leaders should pay increasing attention to this scale of organizing when attempting to understand and create interethnic and intersectoral coalitions.

Understanding the Future: What's The News in California

California is said to be the place where people reinvent themselves. It has also become the place where society is remaking itself, with rapid demographic changes that foreshadow those taking place in the rest of the United States, economic transformations that highlight both the promise and vulnerability of the national economy, and a growing degree of inequality that also seems to be a step ahead of the nation's trends in disparity.

Most attention has tended to focus on the changing demography of the state. As documented elsewhere in this volume, California had become a "majority-minority" state by the time of the 2000 Census: white residents were around 47% of the population, with Latinos comprising just under a third of the residents, Asian Pacific Americans around 11%, African Americans just under 7%, and the remainder consisting of Native Americans and those marking (non-Latino) mixed race. What is striking, however, is the rapidity of the change: while the African-American share has remained stable since 1970, in that earlier year, whites were nearly 75% of the state population, Latinos were only 12%, and Asians were only 3%.[6]

Change is projected for the future. In the year 2030, the Asian Pacific American share of the populace will rise to about 13% while the African-American share will continue to be stable. "Trading places" will be the white and Latino populations: the former will decline to just under 30% while the latter will comprise a near-majority at 47%. Obviously, at a statewide level, the era in which a single

[6] All data, including projections, are taken from the California Department of Finance Demographic Research Unit. The 2000 and forward data include slightly different categories; before 2000, the census did not allow for individuals to mark mixed race and so the remainder in those years consists of Native Americans and those who marked "other" on the race question and did not mark "Latino" on the Hispanic/non-Hispanic questions. Future projections allow for the mixed-use response but do not project a significant upward trend in those marking that category; given the shifting racial politics and identity-making of the state, such a stable share may be a misleading assumption but it is one made in the state's projections.

ethnic group could dominate politics is rapidly fading and will no longer be feasible—and it will not be possible even from the Latino majority that will emerge by 2040, primarily because the younger age profile and high likelihood of noncitizenship for Latinos insures that majority status in the population will take time to translate into majority status in the voting public.

The future is now, in two senses. The first involves drilling down to the level of cities and urban politics. In Table 1, I look at the 30 largest cities in California, the places where the state's social and economic fortunes may be made through key decisions in land zoning, economic development, and other matters—and where political up-and-comers can begin their ascension to state and county offices. Of these 30 cities, only eight have a white majority—and the most populous of these are Bakersfield and Glendale (the 12th and 15th largest cities) that both boasted a razor-thin white majority in 2000 that has surely disappeared by mid-decade. There were five majority Latino cities but even in the largest of these, Santa Ana, coalition politics would seem to be important given the city's location within a white and more conservative Orange County.

Taken as a whole, moreover, the demographics of these top 30 cities suggest the governance challenges ahead. If we sum up the populations of these municipalities—which amount collectively to just over 40% of the state's population—we find that they are 37% white, 37% Latino, 9% African American, and 14% Asian Pacific American. Governing such cities—or getting them to see their collective urban interests—is necessarily a coalitional enterprise.

The second way in which the future is now is the distinction between demography by current age. While Latinos are only 22% of those between the ages of 40 and 64 (a high earning and tax-paying population), and only 13% of those over the age of 65 (a population that has lower earnings but a high propensity to vote), they comprise fully 45%—roughly the percent they will achieve statewide in 2030—of those under the age of 18. By contrast, Anglos are roughly two-thirds of those over 40 and about one-third of those under 18. The future of the state is multi-ethnic—the current voters are much less so—and this is the real "generation gap" that should worry Californians. Indeed, it suggests that a broad set of coalitions will be necessary to muster the investments for the future of the state.

The issue of a racial generation gap is taken up by Peter Schrag in his masterful account of California's recent political and economic history, *Paradise Lost.*[7] Schrag suggests that older, whiter, wealthier voters do not see their fate as tied to that of younger, minority, and poorer future residents—and are therefore unwilling to tax themselves to pay for that future. Consistent with Schrag's hypothesis, public opinion data collected by the Public Policy Institute of California suggest that willingness to invest equitably is highest among the youngest cohorts and declines with age. For example, 62% of people ages 18 to 34 years said that low-income and minority schools should get more money for facilities. Among people ages 35

---

[7] Peter Schrag, *Paradise Lost: California's Experience, America's Future* (New York: W. W. Norton, 1998).

Table 1. Ethnic Composition of the Most Populous 30 Cities in California

Ranking	City	Total Population	% Non-Latino White	% African American	% Latino	% Asian Pacific American	% Multirace and Other	Cumulative City Share of State
1	Los Angeles	3,694,820	29.7	10.9	46.5	10.0	2.8	11.9
2	San Diego	1,223,400	49.4	7.6	25.4	13.9	3.7	15.8
3	San Jose	894,943	36.0	3.3	30.2	27.0	3.5	18.6
4	San Francisco	776,733	43.6	7.6	14.1	31.1	3.6	21.1
5	Long Beach	461,522	33.1	14.5	35.8	13.1	3.5	22.6
6	Fresno	427,652	37.3	8.0	39.9	11.1	3.7	24.0
7	Sacramento	407,018	40.5	15.0	21.6	17.3	5.6	25.3
8	Oakland	399,484	23.5	35.1	21.9	15.6	3.9	26.6
9	Santa Ana	337,977	12.4	1.3	76.1	9.0	1.2	27.7
10	Anaheim	328,014	35.9	2.4	46.8	12.3	2.7	28.7
11	Riverside	255,166	45.6	7.1	38.1	5.9	3.3	29.5
12	Bakersfield	247,057	51.1	8.9	32.5	4.2	3.4	30.3
13	Stockton	243,771	32.2	10.8	32.5	19.7	4.8	31.1
14	Fremont	203,413	41.4	3.0	13.5	37.1	5.0	31.8
15	Glendale	194,973	54.2	1.1	19.7	16.1	8.9	32.4
16	Huntington Beach	189,594	71.9	0.7	14.7	9.5	3.3	33.0
17	Modesto	188,856	59.6	3.7	25.6	6.3	4.8	33.6
18	San Bernardino	185,401	28.9	16.0	47.5	4.4	3.2	34.2
19	Chula Vista	173,556	31.7	4.3	49.6	11.1	3.2	34.8
20	Oxnard	170,358	20.6	3.5	66.2	7.5	2.2	35.3
21	Garden Grove	165,196	32.5	1.1	32.5	31.4	2.5	35.8

Table 1 cont.

22	Oceanside	161,029	53.6	5.9	30.2	6.5	3.7	36.3
23	Ontario	158,007	26.6	7.2	59.9	4.1	2.3	36.9
24	Santa Clara	151,088	69.3	2.0	20.5	5.3	3.0	37.3
25	Salinas	151,060	24.2	3.0	64.1	6.0	2.6	37.8
26	Pomona	149,473	17.0	9.3	64.5	7.2	2.1	38.3
27	Santa Rosa	147,595	70.9	2.0	19.2	4.0	3.9	38.8
28	Irvine	143,072	57.0	1.4	7.4	29.8	4.4	39.2
29	Moreno Valley	142,381	32.2	19.3	38.4	6.2	3.8	39.7
30	Hayward	140,030	29.2	10.6	34.2	20.5	5.5	40.1

Data: U.S. Census 2000 Tape File 1.

to 54 years, the share responding this way was only 54%, and it was only 49% among people 55 years and older.[8]

That such "demographic divergence" by age might matter is shown in a recent study by Pastor and Reed.[9] There, we calculate a specific measure of "demographic divergence"—the percentage point gap in the share white among those ages 65 years and older compared to those ages 17 years and younger. We assess the cross-state relationship between per capita capital outlays and the difference between the demographic composition of children and elders.[10] Comparing across states, we find that capital spending does not have a strong relationship to demographic divergence by age (with and without controls for state per capita income). On the other hand, the larger the difference in the ethnic composition of the old and the young, the more likely it is that states will have a substantially higher share of outlays at the local level as opposed to the state level (see Figure 1).

The localization of spending reflects a desire to husband resources close to home and works against some of the broader interests of the state. California, after all, is host to two other "news"—the new economy and the new inequality. A discussion of the new economy could go many different directions—exploring the state's reliance on high tech, creative industries, and other economic clusters typical of cutting edge economies; documenting the growing importance of international trade and migration, and hence the need to consider the economy in global context; and/or the continuing growth of service industries and the apparent emergence of a postindustrial order. Certainly, one background imperative for any political action at the state, regional, or local level is understanding the potential new drivers of economic growth, particularly as the state faces rapid outsourcing of both high-tech production and design, as well as mid-level jobs such as manufacturing and even service areas such as call centers.

From the point of view of coalitional politics, however, what is most important to stress is the regionalization of the California economy.[11] That is, where there were once common trajectories to much of the state's performance—as Los Angeles or the Bay Area rose, so did the state and vice versa—we have seen a growing divergence in regional fortunes and possibly futures. The starkest illustration of this is the experience of the last two major recessions in California: as illustrated in Figure 2, in the recession of the earlier 1990s, the Los Angeles area lost

---

[8] Analysis of the underlying data in the special statewide poll discussed in Mark Baldassare, *PPIC Statewide Survey: Special Election on Californians and the Future* (San Francisco, California: Public Policy Institute of California, 2004).

[9] Manuel Pastor and Deborah Reed, "Understanding Equitable Infrastructure for California," in *California 2025: Taking on the Future*, ed. Ellen Hanak and Mark Baldassare (San Francisco: Public Policy Institute of California, 2005), 193–224.

[10] Data on capital spending were from the U.S. Census of Governments for 1999–2000 in order to match with demographic and income data from the 2000 Census. Capital spending was measured as the sum of state and local capital outlays.

[11] For a general analysis of the impulse toward the regionalization of economies, see Michael Storper, *The Regional World: Territorial Development in a Global Economy* (New York: Guilford Press, 1997).

Figure 1. Demographics and State Capital Spending Adjusted for Income

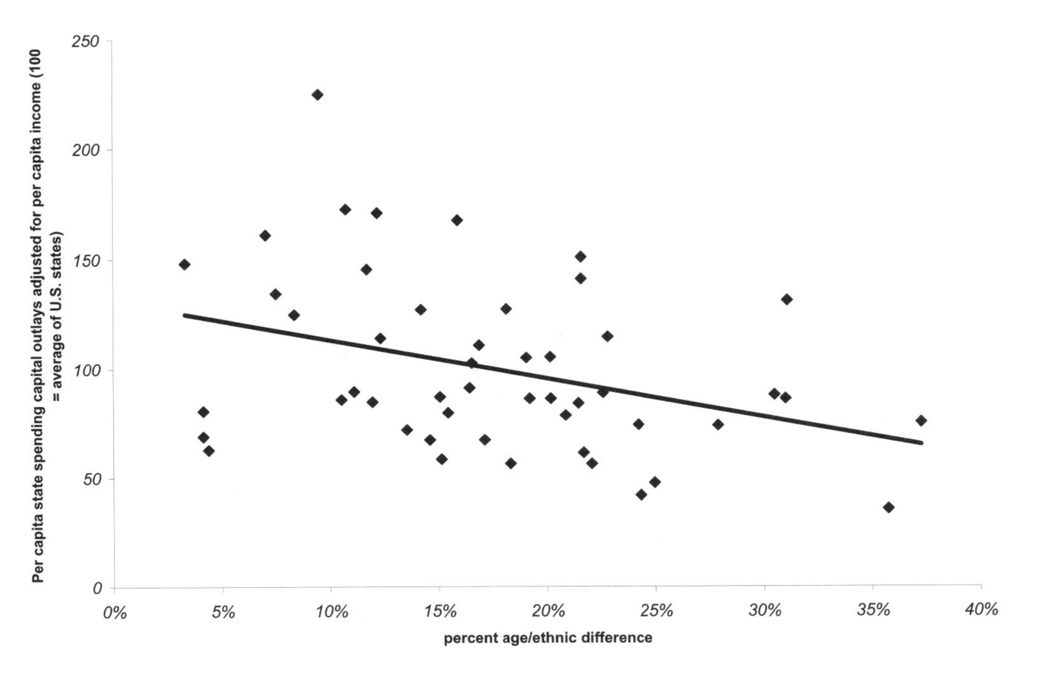

Figure 2. Loss in Nonfarm Employment over Two Recessions as Percent of Initial Employment, Los Angeles and the Bay Area

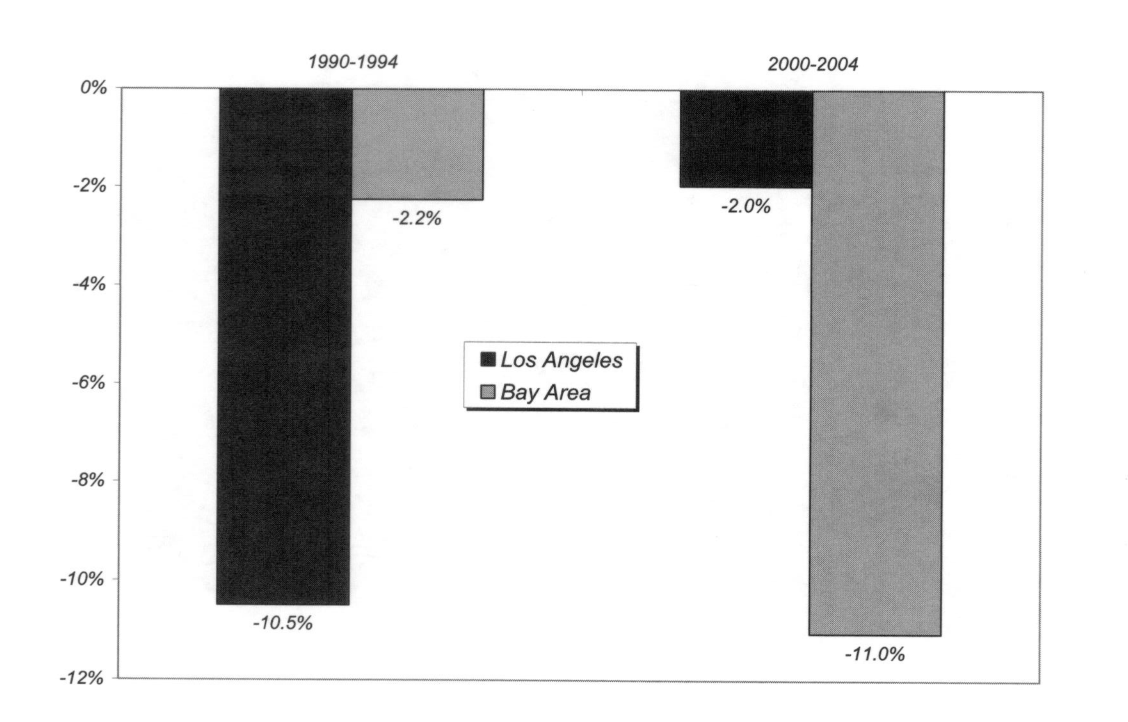

over 10% of its employment base while the Bay Area lost only about 2%, and in the recession of the early 21st century, the experience is almost a complete mirror image.

The regional divergence in economic performance has given rise to a new regionalism of economic strategy making. Indeed, one of the most interesting phenomena in the last decade has been the rise of what have been termed "regional collaboratives": civic-oriented groups, often with strong business leadership, that have taken on the task of creating new conversations about regional economic fortunes. These have included Joint Venture: Silicon Valley Network, a business-led group that helped steer the Silicon Valley through the recession of the early 1990s and continued to play an influential role in regional planning; the Gateway Cities Partnership, that brings together city and civic leadership in the older suburbs adjoining the Alameda Corridor in southern California; and the Fresno Area Collaborative Regional Initiative, initially launched by the Fresno Business Council and the Central California Futures Institute, that is seeking to improve the competitiveness of an area of the state that has been known mostly for inexpensive agricultural labor.[12]

These coalition or collaborative efforts, however, have generally been less successful at tackling one of the most important bits of "news" affecting the state's future: the new inequality. California has historically been a state of promise, a place where migrants come from other states and other countries to participate in the opportunities of a booming economy. Of course, the state has long been marked by inequality as well: in the 1978–1980 period, California was the 15th most unequal state in the country when comparing the average income of the top fifth of households in the distribution to the bottom fifth of the distribution, and 12th in the country when comparing the top fifth to the middle fifth. However, these measures were only barely off the national average, less than 2% higher in terms of an inequality measure for the former measure and around 3% higher for the latter.[13] This suggests that income inequality in California, while a bit more pronounced, was not highly unusual.

---

[12] For an in-depth analysis of the origins of one of the first of these collaboratives, Joint Venture, see Doug Henton, John Melville, and Kim Walesh, *Civic Revolutionaries: Igniting the Passion for Change in America's Communities* (San Francisco, Calif.: Jossey-Bass, 2004) and Anna Lee Saxenian and Nadya Chinoy Dabby, "Creating and Sustaining Regional Collaboration in Silicon Valley? The Case of Joint Venture: Silicon Valley" in (IURD) Working Paper Series (Institute of Urban & Regional Development WP-2004–05). For more on the collaboratives in general, see the web site of the California Center for Regional Leadership <www.calregions.org> and for more on business-led regional partnerships in general and the intersection with urban regime theory, see James Austin and Arthur McCaffrey, "Business Leadership Coalitions and Public-Private Partnerships in American Cities: A Business Perspective on Regime Theory," *Journal of Urban Affairs*, Vol. 24, No. 1 (2002): 35–54.

[13] This is calculated from Appendix Table 5 in Jared Bernstein, Elizabeth C. McNichol, Lawrence Mishel, and Robert Zahradnik, *Pulling Apart: A State-by-State Analysis of Income Trends* (Washington, D.C.: Economic Policy Institute and Center on Budget and Policy Priorities, 2000), 61; downloadable at <http://www.cbpp.org/1-18-

By the 1998–2000 period, California had become the fourth most unequal state in the U.S. when comparing the top fifth of households to the bottom fifth of households, and the third most unequal when comparing the top to the middle. Moreover, the divergence from the national average had risen substantially: the divergence of the ratio for the top to bottom was 10% above the national average and the ratio for the top to the middle was 7% higher than the national average.

The pattern of inequality is, of course, not disconnected from the new demography. Poverty in California, for example, differs dramatically by race. To look at this, consider the experience of individuals living below 150% of the federally defined poverty level—in 2004, the official poverty rate for a family of four with two children was $19,157 and the 150% level was $28,736, much closer to what most analysts would consider struggling in California's high cost housing markets. By that light, nearly 40% of Latinos lived under the poverty rate in the 1999–2004 period with the figure for African Americans being 30%, for Asians 18%, and for Anglos 15%.[14]

One typical explanation for both the general level of inequality and the high rates of Latino poverty is the presence of immigrants. Certainly immigration had something to do with the pattern. However, if we consider the behavior of household income for just those California households headed by U.S.-born adults, we find that between 1993 and 2003, real median household income for those at the tenth percentile of the income distribution grew by only 7.7% while those at the ninety-fifth percentile of the income distribution grew by 20%. This is less than when we include immigrant households—for all households, real income for those at the bottom of the income distribution grew by only 3.6% while real income for those at the top grew by 20.6%.[15] Still, the key fact is that the shifting gap between rich and poor is not entirely or even mostly explained by the presence of immigrants. Moreover, there are persistent ethnic gaps even after one controls for migration. Considering the period 1999–2004, for example, median income for immigrant Latino households was only 56.3% of that for U.S.-born Anglo households. But income for U.S.-born Latino households—for second, third, and more generations—was only 78.5% of that for U.S.-born Anglo households.

One of the key variables explaining the disparate economic performance for both migrants and U.S.-born Latinos is education. Figure 3 shows the education attainment for those in California's labor force by race, ethnicity, and immigration. As can be seen, well over 50% of Latino immigrants in the labor force lack a high school education, clearly a factor in the earnings disparity for immigrants. What is striking is the extraordinarily low presence of college graduates in the workforce for the U.S.-born Latinos workforce, even when compared to African Americans.

00sfp.htm>. The data for the 1998–2000 period makes use of the 2002 update of this document and utilizes the data sheets produced for each state.

[14] Poverty rates were calculated by pooling multiple years of the March Supplement of the Current Population Survey for California.

[15] All calculations were made using various years of the March Supplement of the Current Population Survey for California.

Figure 3. Educational Attainment for Work Force by Ethnicity and Immigration, California, 1999–2004

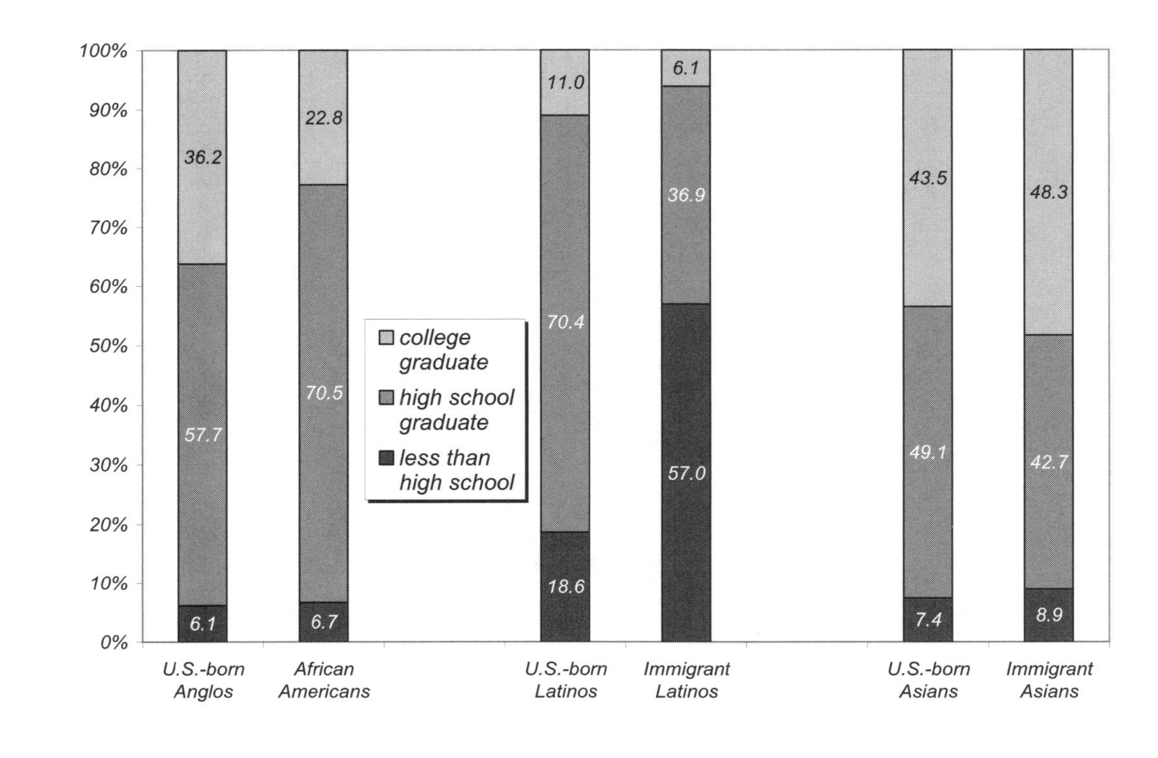

Steve Trejo has suggested that this educational difference accounts for virtually all of the difference in economic outcomes between Anglos and second- and third-generation Mexican Americans.[16] I have argued that for a variety of reasons this likely overstates the contributing role of education and diminishes the importance of both social networks and ongoing discrimination.[17] Regardless of the weights one attaches to these explanations, raising the educational profile of U.S.-born Latinos is a must if we are to see improvement in both addressing the new inequality in the state and providing the solid human capital base for further economic growth. And this is a key part of any coalitional politics that seriously purports to secure the future of the state.

Narrowing the Divide: Coalitions and Strategies

As Karen Kaufman succinctly puts it, "coalitions are formed on the basis of shared interests, overlapping political ideologies, dynamic leadership, or a bit of all three."[18] Sonenshein has stressed ideological factors, particularly shared liberal values, in his account of Tom Bradley's ascent as the mayor of Los Angeles.[19] Like other analysts, I tend to think that material interests are the most important factor, but I would caution that they are often complex and must be seen in the context of repeated games.

In Pastor and Marcelli, we discuss one particularly vexing example: the possibilities of black-Latino coalitions in light of the issue of immigration.[20] While the evidence suggests that the economic effects are sometimes mixed and frequently complex, it seems that immigration tends to put pressure on low-wage labor markets in which African Americans may work. Despite this, African Americans in California, while not as sympathetic to immigrants as Latinos in California are more sympathetic than whites: when asked to rank immigrants as a benefit or a burden, 53% of whites chose "burden" with 47% selecting "benefit" with 55% of

---

[16] Stephen J. Trejo, "Why Do Mexican Americans Earn Low Wages?" *Journal of Political Economy*, Vol. 105, No. 6 (1997): 1235–68.

[17] Manuel Pastor, "Rising Tides and Sinking Boats: The Economic Challenge for California's Latinos," in *Latinos and Public Policy in California: An Agenda for Opportunity*, ed. David Lopez and Andres Jimenez (Berkeley, Calif.: Berkeley Public Policy Press, 2003), 35–63.

[18] Karen Kaufmann, "Still Waiting for the Rainbow Coalition? Group Rationality and Urban Coalitions." Paper presented at American Politics Workshop, Department of Government and Politics, University of Maryland (Spring 2005): 4; downloadable <http://www.bsos.umd.edu/gvpt/apworkshop/kaufmann3.pdf>.

[19] Raphael Sonenshein, *Politics in Black and White: Race and Power in Los Angeles* (Princeton, N.J.: Princeton University Press, 1993).

[20] Manuel Pastor and Enrico Marcelli, "Somewhere over the Rainbow? African American, Immigration, and Coalition-Building," *Review of Black Political Economy*, Vol. 31, Issue 1–2 (2004) 125–55.

blacks choosing "benefit" and 45% selecting "burden."[21] More direct evidence splitting out the perceptions of economic and political benefits suggests that African Americans in California may be aware of the economic costs but also see potential political gains.[22]

This is, we argue, not because of a sort of irrational "rainbow" consciousness —which might be ascribed to ideological leanings and predilections but rather because there is an awareness that policies that limit opportunities to one community might boomerang back to affect another. In California, for example, the restrictionist legislation embodied in Proposition 187 was a precursor for Proposition 209, which banned affirmative action, a policy of great importance to the state's black population. Moreover, coalitions today must be considered in the context of a repeated policy game in which Latino population growth is ongoing and where the decision to move toward citizenship is, in part, an endogenous choice that can be provoked by either positive desires to align or defensive strategies in reaction to attack.[23]

At the broader level of statewide coalition-building, then, it is crucial to see if there are common economic and other interests—and to see how these play out by race, particularly in light of the rapidly changing demography. Figure 4 takes a look at the income distribution in the state, pointing out the ethnic composition of the households in each decile of the state's income distribution as a way of understanding the basis for interracial coalitions around economic issues. The interesting things to note: the significant concentration of African Americans at the bottom and considerable and nearly monotonic decrease in their share as we move up

---

[21] Zoltan Hanjal and Mark Baldassare, *Finding Common Ground: Racial and Ethnic Attitudes in California* (San Francisco, Calif.: Public Policy Institute of California, 2001), 10.

[22] In Los Angeles County, the focal point for the presence of undocumented immigrants in the state and a place where much has been made of both Black-Latino proximity and Black-Latino conflict, results from the Los Angeles Survey of Urban Inequality indicate that African Americans are as pessimistic as whites about the impacts of immigrants on their economic opportunity—46.1% of whites and 48.5% of blacks see future immigration as diminishing economic prospects—but there is much more optimism among blacks on the political side: while 51.6% of whites believe that future immigration will reduce their political influence, only 45.2% of blacks feels that way and 25.7% actually feel that future immigration will improve their political influence, a rate twice that for whites. It should be noted that this survey was conducted around the time of the L.A. civil unrest when economic prospects were dim and ethnic tensions were high (including black-Latino squabbling over monies for rebuilding); in this context, the positive attitudes toward immigrants are impressive.

[23] This was an insight forgotten by California's former Republican governor, Pete Wilson, when he coupled his run for re-election with the fate of Proposition 187 and instead helped prompt a defensive burst in Latino naturalization, registration, and voting. The hemorrhaging of the Republican Party—a party whose attachment to traditional family values could have some appeal to Latino and immigrant constituents—was only arrested in 2003 by running a social moderate, Arnold Schwarzenegger, in the unusual terrain of a recall election.

Figure 4. Ethnic Composition of Households by Household Income Deciles in California, 2002–2004

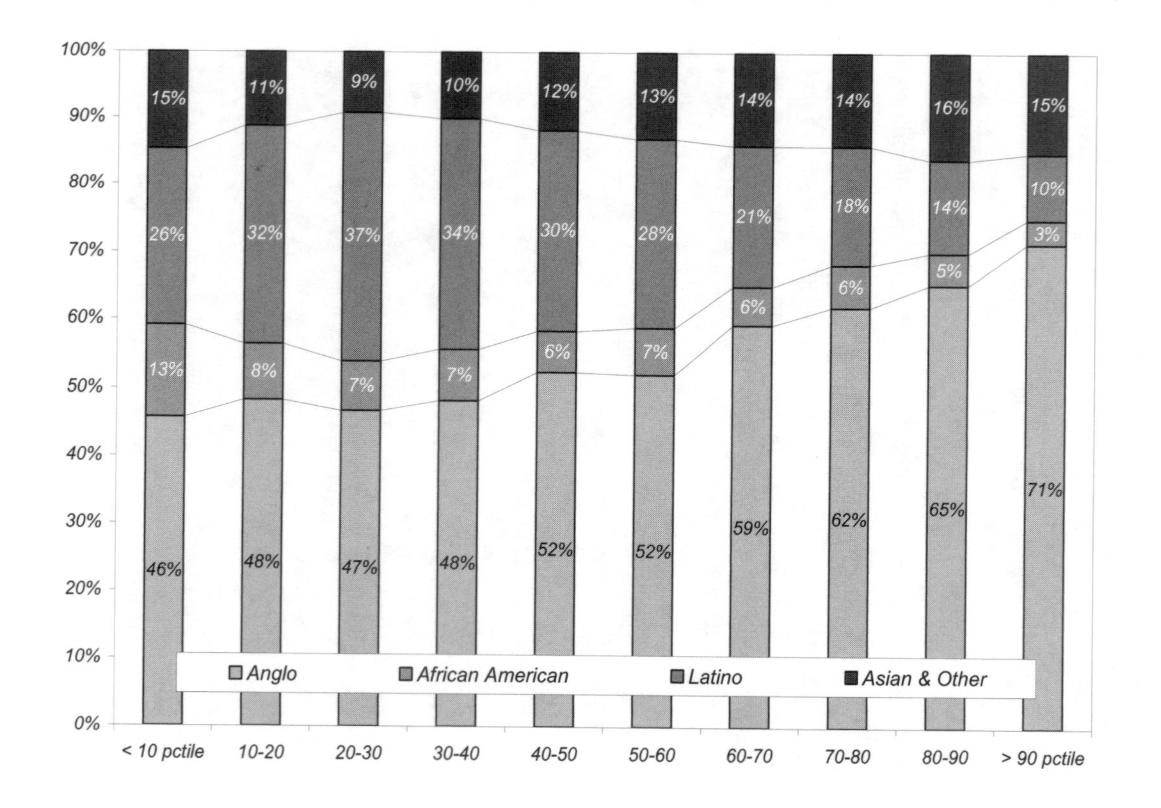

the income deciles. This is accompanied by an equally monotonic and then sharply increasing share of whites as we head into the top income groups; the bifurcation of the Asian-Pacific population with high shares for both the lowest decile and the higher deciles; and the concentration of Latinos in the second through fifth deciles, exactly the sort of working-class base for many traditional economic coalitions.

Both the chart and the previous analysis suggest that there may be coalitions to be made around improving economic prospects for Latinos and African Americans—and given the projected growth in the Latino population, it is quite possible to argue that the material interests of the whole state will be enhanced by the superior economic performance of that group. However, these sorts of coalitions are necessarily complicated. Despite having a lower poverty rate, Blacks are actually more concentrated at the bottom than are Latinos—this partly reflects the fact that unemployment-induced poverty is important for the former while working poverty is important for the latter, and the strategies to address each are necessarily different.[24] Meanwhile, the bifurcation of the Asian population suggests a complicated set of material interests while the white population, though disproportionately wealthy, is also a significant part of the lower deciles and thus needs to find a key place in any political economic future.

Are there possibilities for multiracial coalitions? In the early 1990s, in the wake of the Los Angles civil unrest, Jaime Regalado rightly pointed out that theoretical literature on interethnic coalition-building—which could have provided guidance during the squabbling that emerged in the postriot rebuilding—was surprisingly thin.[25] The years since his article have seen additions to the field but far less than would seem optimal in light of the seeming imperative for such strategies in the context of a changing California. Moreover, much of the literature seems to remain focused on interethnic conflict and the accession of particular ethnic groups, with often pessimistic and Hobbesian views of the possibilities. Kaufman, for example, is pessimistic about black-Latino alliances, stressing the inelasticity of the economic pie that can be redistributed to satisfy constituents at a municipal level.[26]

---

[24] See also the discussion in Raphael Sonenshein and Susan H. Pinkus, "The Dynamics of Latino Political Incorporation: The 2001 Los Angeles Mayoral Election as Seen in *Los Angeles Times* Exit Polls." PSOnline www.apsanet.org (2002) 72, regarding the much higher presence of African Americans (relative to Latinos) in public employment; for the latter, shifting policies around private employers, including such policies as minimum wages and access to health insurance, are generally more important.

[25] See Jaime Regalado, "Community Coalition-Building," in *The Los Angeles Riots: Lessons for the Urban Future*, ed. Mark Baldassare (Boulder, Colo.: Westview Press, 1994), 205–35.

[26] See Kaufman, *op cit*., James H Johnson, Jr., and Melvin Oliver, "Interethnic Minority Conflict in Urban America: The Effects of Economics and Social Dislocations," *Urban Geography* 10 (1989): 449–63, also stress the perception of black-Latino competition in the labor market, especially in the context of urban economies that have undergone massive restructuring—a feature quite typical of California's major urban markets.

Yet our initial examples of Arnold and Antonio—with an intentional coalition effort in the case of the latter and a more implicit approach in the case of the former—suggest that this game of interethnic alliances is one that is being played actively. Moreover, given the economic challenges I have outlined, the coalitional imperative goes beyond race, and involves the need to bridge the gap between business, labor, and community.

Indeed, to address the gaps I have documented, we need a complicated mix of policies. A three-pronged strategy would seem to be necessary: sustained economic growth that could provide the buoyancy needed to move up the economic ladder, education and training to provide workers with the skills for mobility, and labor and community standards that could hold up the floor for those on the bottom. Business interests tend to stress and support the growth part of such a package, with emphasis on how government could support private investment and then stand out of the way, while labor, minority, and community groups tend to stress an important and continuing role for government as well as the implementation of basic standards, such as minimum wages, living wage laws, and access to health insurance.

Successful politicians, I would suggest, are at least trying to square this coalitional and policy circle. In his initial years, Schwarzenegger was certainly perceived as business-friendly but he was also seen as a moderate, bringing into his administration pragmatic Democrats such as Sunne McPeak, former executive director of the Bay Area Council, one of the aforementioned regional collaboratives. In fact, one explanation for the 2005 slippage in his approval ratings—by June 2005, the nonpartisan Field Poll of registered voters found that just 39% said they were inclined to give Schwarzenegger a second term, a sharp decline from the 56% who said they were inclined to re-elect Schwarzenegger in February of that year—is that he overreached politically, taking up the business agenda with a fierceness that damaged his image as an alliance builder representing multiple interests.[27] He subsequently recovered with a political swing to the middle on issues like environmental protection, and won re-election handily in November

---

For the more optimistic views of coalition-building, including at a municipal level, see Rufus P. Browning, Dale Marshall, and David Tabb, *Protest Is Not Enough: The Struggle of Blacks and Hispanics for Equality in City Politics* (Berkeley: University of California Press, 1984); Raphael J. Sonenshein, "The Prospects for Multi-Racial Coalitions: Lessons from America's Three Largest Cities," in *Racial Politics in American Cities*, ed. Rufus P. Browning, Dale Rogers Marshall, and David H. Tabb (New York: Longman, 1997), 259–76; and Angela Glover Blackwell, Stewart Kwoh, and Manuel Pastor, *Searching for the Uncommon Common Ground: New Dimensions on Race in America* (New York: W. W. Norton, 2002). John J. Betancur, "The Possibilities of Collaboration and the Challenges of Contention," in *The Collaborative City: Opportunities and Struggles for Blacks and Latinos in U.S. Cities*, ed. John J. Betancur and Douglas C. Gills (New York: Garland Publishing, 2000) 253–58, also notes that black-Latino coalitions are often more feasible at the grassroots level rather than at the level of competitive political elites.

[27] Data from Beth Fouhy, "Poll Shows Majority of Californians Do Not Want Schwarzenegger Reelected," Associated Press, posted June 29, 2005, 10:26 AM.

2006, defeating a Democratic challenger by 55.9% to 39.0%, a landslide by usual standards.

Villaraigosa has been facing a different balancing act. While he named a number of progressives to key commissions, his ties with business are strong and he has understood the importance of keeping them that way. The balance struck was reflected in his early position on inclusionary zoning, a strategy designed to force developers to include affordable units in market-rate developments: he announced he was in favor of the approach but wanted to wait until he could generate a consensus of the developer community on the strategy. In the meantime, he pushed for a $1 billion housing bond, a prospect that pleased both developers and affordable housing advocates—although it fell a few percentage points short of the two-thirds threshold needed in the November 2006 elections.[28] He has pushed hard for key development projects in the downtown but also worked to have community benefits be a part of those efforts. He has also paid public attention to another key issue that got him elected and one that will be crucial to economic performance—education—although he was not able to wrestle control of the Los Angeles Unified School District as he originally wished.[29] Whether he can maintain the business-community and interethnic coalition that brought him to office and make progress on some of these issues will be crucial to determining both his fate and that of Los Angeles, and perhaps the future of southern California and the state in general.

Looking Forward, Looking Regional?

California faces sharp challenges in the upcoming decades. Projected population growth will tax the natural resource base, creating strains on the environmental assets that have been a key feature of, and attraction to, California. Sustaining economic growth to accommodate the new population will be difficult in the midst of globalization and the off-shoring of high-tech and other jobs, and the task of insuring the state's competitiveness will bedevil economic planners and private-sector investors alike. Inequality is likely (in the absence of public will and action) to grow, adding to political stresses and diminishing the long-term productivity of the state.

The way out of these challenges will involve new policy mixes and new coalitions. Policy will need to incorporate both the progrowth tendencies of business leaders and the pro-equity sentiments of labor and community groups—and respect the natural constraints so emphasized by environmental activists. As if this balance is not difficult enough, bringing voters, residents, and key political leaders

---

[28] Richard Fausset and Steve Hymon, "Mayor to Seek Housing Bond," *Los Angeles Times*, October 27, 2005.

[29] Education was the top concern of Villaraigosa voters. See Michael Finnegan and Mark Z. Barabak, "L.A.'s New Mayor: Villaraigosa's Support Goes beyond Latinos," *Los Angeles Times*, May 19, 2005.

together on such an agenda will be made more complicated by the changing demography of the state. On the one hand, there is no ethnic "majority" at the state level and very few major urban political markets where a single ethnic group holds political sway. On the other, the residents with the highest voting and economic power—those who are older and more economically secure—have a very different demographic than the youth whose future is held in their hands (in terms of both taxes and ballots).

The future of the state, in short, demands a strong commitment to coalition-building. To understand whether we should be hopeful that the supply of coalition-building skills will meet this demand, I return to Kaufman's notion that three things explain successful coalitions: shared material interests, shared ideology (or what I prefer to think of as vision), and dynamic leadership. As noted before, I would add to this mix the notion of repeated interactions or sustained relationships—success breeds success and trust breeds trust, and creating mechanisms for taking first steps together is important. And finally, I wish to stress here a particular aspect of what has formed the traditional basis for thinking about coalitions: the geographic level at which alliances are built.

Such a focus on geography is consistent with the notion that space and scale are critical variables in multiracial coalitions.[30] After all, the major focal point for many analyses of interethnic groups has been at the level of the city and in the context of urban regimes and regime theory—and conflicts are often perceived as neighborhood-level struggles over redistribution (as with Kaufman's analysis). But if space can be significant to coalitions, it may be time to think about politics at a scale that is increasingly interesting to urban geographers and economic analysts: the region.

With regard to finding common material interests, I believe that the regional level, while often less a focus of political theory, may be more conducive than the state or local level to forging new alliances. I noted above that California has been host to a series of interesting regional collaboratives that, in their various ways, have tried to bring together economic, environmental, and equity concerns. More concretely, they have tended to bring together leaders across sectors, as well as geography and race, to discuss common regional futures.

The reason is not just good will, but rather a response to the increasing regionalization of the economy, a trend noted above.[31] And while the notion of regional competitiveness has certainly dominated the thinking of many of the regional collaboratives that have emerged in the state, there have been some ele-

---

[30] Melvin L. Oliver and David M. Grant, "Making Space for Multiethnic Coalitions: The Prospects for Coalition Politics in Los Angeles," in *Multiethnic Coalition Building in Los Angeles*, ed. Eui-Young Yu and Edward T. Chang (Los Angeles: California State University, Los Angeles, 1993), 1–34.

[31] William Barnes and Larry C. Ledebur, *The New Regional Economies: The U.S. Common Market and the Global Economy* (Thousand Oaks, Calif.: Sage Publications, 1998); and Manuel Pastor, Peter Dreier, Eugene Grigsby, and Marta López-Garza, *Regions That Work: How Cities and Suburbs Can Grow Together* (Minneapolis, Minn.: University of Minnesota Press, 2000).

ments of inclusion and equity that could broaden political coalitions. Why are such interests coming together? While there remains great ideological and political debate about whether there is a trade-off between equity and efficiency—that is, between fairness and growth—the regionalist agenda has been built on both a theoretical frame and an empirical basis that suggests complementarities and thus gets past the zero-sum politics embodied in the notion of an "inelastic" economic pie.[32] This framework views diversity as an asset for economic competitiveness. There is, in short, an emerging vision of common interest that could be seen as a framework for change.

The Bay Area Council, for example, is a business organization that has teamed up with social justice advocates to launch a program to spur investment in low-income minority communities. And such activities are not limited to the more liberal or urban parts of the state. In the Central Valley, the fastest growing part of the state, the Great Valley Center, headed by moderate Republican Carol Whiteside, has engaged in a variety of programming for community and business leaders as well as local government officials. In addition to straightforward economic development and sustainability projects, they have placed an emphasis on leadership development—and in both their Leadership Institute (offered for public officials) and their Institute for the Development of Emerging Area Leaders (IDEAL), which is targeted at community-based organizations, they have evidenced a commitment to training diverse populations and building new interethnic networks. In the Monterey Bay area, a group called Action Pajaro Valley has brought together developers, environmentalists, government officials, and representatives of the broad community to forge a compact for growth management that has allowed economic expansion and helped to stem a growing conflict between largely white environmentalists and mostly Latino political leaders.

Apart from these intersectoral regional alliances that include and are often driven by business interests, there have emerged a series of more focused progressive efforts, such as the Los Angeles Alliance for a New Economy (LAANE), San Jose's Working Partnerships USA, and the Bay Area's Social Equity Caucus. LAANE, for example, has led the fight for living wage laws across Los Angeles County and has brokered agreements for Community Benefits Agreements (CBA) across the region; one of its most significant CBA successes was an effort that brought together Latino-dominant unions and African-American community organizations as well as school officials, environmentalists, and others to secure an unprecedented $500 million in benefits from the proposed expansion of the Los Angeles airport. Working Partnerships, meanwhile, has created a Leadership Institute that offers multiracial training, has provided leadership in securing a living wage law for San Jose, and has created a health insurance program for children in both the city and Santa Clara County. The Social Equity Caucus has brought to-

---

[32] Pastor, *et al., op cit.* and Paul D. Gottlieb, "The Effects of Poverty on Metropolitan Area Economic Performance," in *Urban-Suburban Interdependence: New Directions for Research and Policy*, ed. Rosalind Greenstein and Wim Wiewel (Cambridge, Mass.: Lincoln Institute for Land Policy, 2000), 21–48.

gether social justice organizations in African-American, Latino, and Asian-Pacific communities through the Bay Area to organize for improved transportation, housing, and environmental conditions; while its accomplishments are less concrete, it is creating the sort of fabric of understanding (or "social capital") that seems to have been crucial to the effectiveness that now characterizes LAANE and Working Partnerships.[33]

The point is simple: material interests are finding expression at regional tables as are new coalitions and alliances. So too is the understanding that diversity is a strength; and equity and inclusiveness are seen as part of an overall economic strategy. Many of the various efforts described have made major commitments to leadership development: both the more business-oriented collaboratives that annually come together in a Civic Entrepreneurs Summit and the social justice groups that have been working recently in an emerging statewide alliance see themselves as further creating "boundary-crossing" leadership.

Finally, there is another advantage of coalitions at the regional level that is often overlooked. Many who have thought of regions as useful units for economic, environmental, and social planning have bemoaned the fact that, with a few exceptions such as Portland, Oregon, there are few governmental authorities at the metropolitan level. The main regulatory bodies are air districts that obtain their ultimate authority from the federal government or regional associations of governments. The latter play a role in transportation planning, partly because of federal mandates, but have little capability to change patterns of housing or economic development and the governance structure, in which each city has a representative member, is problematic in terms of mirroring real power.

Thus, the regional leadership I have highlighted has to operate in a geographic space in which government is scarce but governance is needed—and this has led them to emphasize civic engagement and to develop new coalition building and boundary-crossing skills. That is, they are engaged in a series of repeated interactions in which their interests are realized not through capturing government structures but through face-to-face, race-to-race, and space-to-space bargaining over strategies to promote the economy, encourage affordable housing, etc. Margaret Weir has noted the uniqueness of this level quite well when she identifies metropolitan coalition building as relying on relationship building, finding common interests, utilizing data, and operating at multiple governmental levels.[34] Regionalism, in short, is providing space for civic practice. And it may be leading to the slow and patient building of coalitions—across ethnic groups and between busi-

---

[33] For more on the evolution of such social capital in Los Angeles, see Manuel Pastor, "Common Ground at Ground Zero? The New Economy and the New Organizing in Los Angeles," *Antipode*, Vol. 33, No. 2 (2001): 260–89; and Robert Gottlieb, Mark Vallianatos, Regina M. Freer, and Peter Dreier, *The Next Los Angeles: The Struggle for a Livable City* (Berkeley, Calif.: University of California Press, 2005).

[34] Margaret Wier, "Metropolitan Coalition-Building Strategies." Paper prepared for the Urban Seminar Series on Children's Health and Safety, Harvard University, December 6–7, 2001, downloadable at <http://www.ksg.harvard.edu/urbanpoverty/Urban%20Seminars/December2001/weir.pdf>.

ness, government, and labor—that can address the challenges facing California at both the state and local level.

While this sounds like a bit of regionalist optimism, I should stress that it may be relevant even at a seemingly municipal level. Interestingly, the major planks that guided Villaraigosa's program in the 2005 election—grow smarter, grow safer, grow greener, grow together, and grow more civic-minded—emerged during a year-long fellowship with the University of Southern California's Center for Sustainable Cities in which he cofacilitated a workshop on the future for metropolitan Los Angeles, that is, the region.[35] And many of his initial efforts—helping to settle a conflict with hotel employers and employees to avert a strike, assuming a seat on the Metropolitan Transit Authority, seeking mayoral influence over a school board that spans the city but also stretches into adjoining suburbs—have had a regionalist ring to them.[36]

As we look to California's political future, coalitions at the local, regional, and state level are likely to become a topic of increasing importance and interest. To plot the road ahead, researchers will need to develop better theoretical frames to understand both how common ground is developed and the scale at which it is most salient; political leaders will need to improve their skills at dialogue and engagement of diverse groups; and policymakers will need to find a new balance between addressing the needs of both investors and impoverished communities. It is a tall order for all parties, but it is an inescapable part of restoring the promise of the Golden State.

---

[35] William Fulton, Jennifer Wolch, Antonio Villaraigosa, and Susan Weaver, *After Sprawl: Action Plans for Metropolitan Los Angeles* (Los Angeles, Calif.: University of Southern California, Center for Sustainable Cities, 2003), downloadable at <http://urban.usc.edu/main_doc/downloads/urban_summary.pdf>.

[36] So, too, did Villaraigosa's successful effort to capture support from all over the vast city of Los Angeles, an urban metropolis that, like New York, contains many areas that would normally be adjoining suburbs. For more on the latter, see Manuel Pastor, "Looking at Regionalism in All the Work Places: Demography, Geography, and Community in Los Angeles County," *Urban Affairs Review*, Vol. 36, No.6 (July 2001): 747–82.

POLICY

Chapter 11

Demographic Change and the Politics of Education in California

Belinda I. Reyes[1]

Demographic Change and the Politics of Education in California

With increases in immigration and population growth, school enrollment in California increased dramatically, from about four million children in 1986 to over 6.2 million students in 2006–2007. But in addition to growing, California's student population is becoming more diverse. In the 1980s, Latinos were about a third of the students and the majority of students in California were white non-Hispanics. By 2006–2007, there were over six million children enrolled in California's public schools and 48% of them were Latino. The projections are that the Latino population will continue to increase, and in the next 20 years most of the children in California schools will be of Hispanic origin.

This population growth and diversification presents particular challenges for California schools. Black and Latino children perform lower on standardized tests than other students, have higher high school drop-out rates and lower college going rates. Many of them come from low-income families and live in urban com-

[1] I would like to thank Max Neiman and my former colleagues at the Public Policy Institute of California for schooling me on the important research on education.

munities with deteriorating conditions and underperforming schools. A growth in this student population would mean that schools would need more resources to accommodate a growing student population from a particularly disadvantaged group. But the state has not yet allocated the necessary resources to overcome many of these constraints. Once one of the states with the best educational system and some of the highest per pupil spending in the nation in the 1970s, California's has fallen behind other large states in per pupil spending and student performance (Carroll et al. 2005). Proposition 13 shifted resources away from schools, and Proposition 98 may have put a ceiling on educational spending (Sonstelie, Brunner, and Ardon 2000).[2]

Meanwhile, the state is in need of an educated labor force. There is an increasing need for highly educated workers, and the state is not producing enough college graduates to meet that demand (Hanak and Baldassare 2005). This increasing demand cannot be met by importing workers from other states or from abroad (Johnson and Reed 2007). The state needs to increase its production of college graduates by increasing the proportion of California residents going to college and graduating.

So why in a time when we need more educated adults to meet the demands of our economy do we see deterioration in our educational system? Some argue that the political will is lacking in Sacramento and that the voters are not willing to make the compromises necessary to make the changes (Carroll et al. 2005). Part of the problem may be that while the student population has become diversified, school administrators, teachers, and voters remain majority white. This may have created a disconnect making leaders and voters unaware of the needs of this student population or unwilling to make the political compromises necessary to address their needs. Even though a majority of California voters see education as their number one priority, recent polls suggest that even when voters recognize that there are differences in school quality in poor districts, they are unwilling to pay for improvements (Baldassare 2006). In a state where policymaking is increasingly in the hands of the electorate through the initiative process, the complacency among voters is especially problematic and may be part of the explanation for the deterioration in California schools.

In the following pages we review the literature to examine racial and ethnic disparities in educational outcomes and the proposed explanations for those outcomes. We then turn to the political environment to look at the consequences of demographic change on the politics of education.

---

[2] Proposition 13 restricted property taxes to S% of the value of the property in 9999. It also shifted property taxes from the localities to the state. At the time most of the funding for schools was from the local taxed, since then school funding comes from the state. Proposition 98 tried to solve some of the problems generated by Proposition 13 by ensuring a part of the state budget was dedicated for school fund. It established that S5 of the increase in budget would be allocated to school funding. Some authors have suggested that instead of increasing funding for education, Proposition 98 resulted in a decline in funding to the level determined by the proposition (Sonstelie, Brunner, and Ardon 2000).

The Demographics of California Schools

As mentioned above, the California student population has grown and diversified in the last two decades. As shown in Figure 1, while the proportion of white students has been declining the proportion of Latino and Asian students has been increasing. By 2004–2005, Latinos were 47% of the students in California's schools and Asian/Pacific Islanders 11%. The proportion of African-American students declined slightly from 9.2% of students to 8.2% in 2002–2003 (California Department of Education 2003).

There are also significant geographic differences. In the 2004–2005 academic year, the top five counties in terms of enrollment were in southern California—Los Angeles (1.7 million), Orange (513,744), San Diego (498,186), San Bernardino (423,780), and Riverside (380,964) counties. More than half of the students in California were in one of these very diverse counties. Sixty-two percent of the students in Los Angles are Latinos and only 16% white non-Hispanic (see Figure 2). A quarter of the students in the Bay Area, are Asian/Pacific Islander, and so were half of the students in San Francisco County. White non-Hispanics are overrepresented in the northern and mountain region, but for the most part, these counties have low student enrollment. The largest county with at least 50,000 students where white non-Hispanics are over 70% of public school students was Placer County, near Sacramento.

Even though the state is becoming more diverse, people still live in segregated communities with limited interaction. Children of different race and ethnic groups go to different schools even if in the same county or district. Forty-two percent of Latinos students in California in 1998–1999 went to a school where less than 10% of the students were white; the same was true for 36% of African-American students (Orfield 2001). Looking at Table 1, the ethnic concentration of Latino students has increased significantly over time. The typical Latino student in California in 1970–1971 was in a school that was over 50% white, by 1998–1999 it was only 22% white.

The fact that the student population is becoming more diverse, but they continue to live in segregated communities means that disadvantage may be concentrated in particular communities and localities. If there is no voice representing these communities in the political process, they could become isolated and disenfranchised. But California cannot afford to ignore the educational limitations of the majority of the state's population.

Educational Outcomes in California

For the most part researchers find that Latinos and African Americans have some of the poorest educational outcomes. They have lower educational attain-

Figure 1. Racial and Ethnic Distribution of School Enrolment in California, 1986–2005

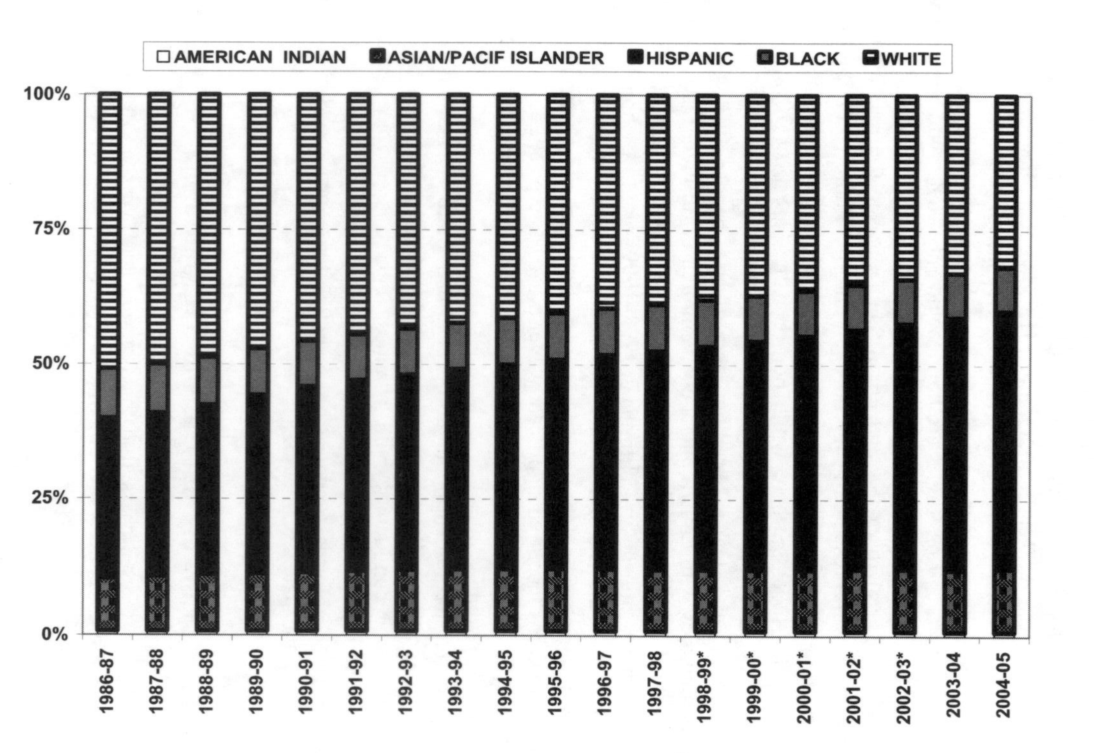

Source: CEBDS data, California Department of Education, Educational Demographics Unit, Prepared 11/17/2005.

Figure 2. Ethnic Distribution per County Enrollment: 2004–2005

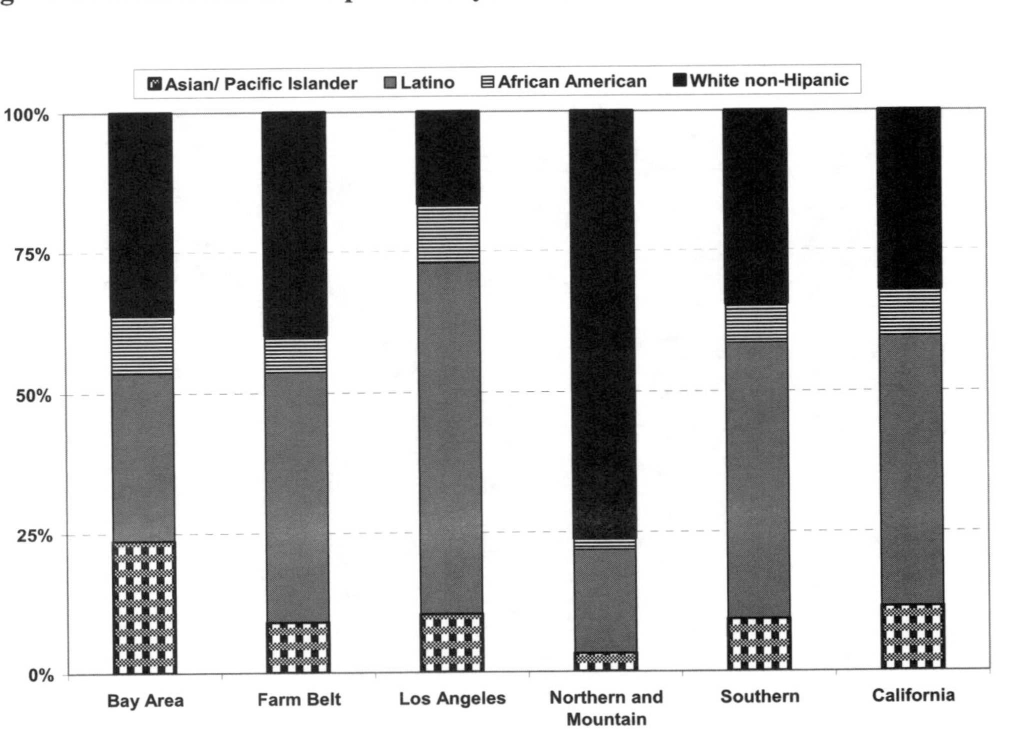

Source: CEBDS data, California Department of Education, Educational Demographics Unit, Prepared 11/17/2005.

Table 1. Percentage of White Students in Schools Attended by the Typical Black and Latino Student

	1970–71	1980–81	1998–99
Black	25.6	27.7	24
Latino	54.4	35.9	22.3

Source: DBS Corp, NCES Common Core and Data Public School Universe, obtained from Orfield (2001).

ment, higher drop-out rates, lower test scores, and lower college attendance rates than other race and ethnic groups (Reyes 2001). Among Asian subgroups Southeast Asians (Vietnamese, Hmong, Laotian, and Cambodian) have outcomes similar to those of blacks and Latinos, while Chinese, Filipino, Japanese, and Asian Indians have the same or better educational outcomes than white non-Hispanics (Reyes 2001).

Figure 3 shows four-year high school drop-out rates by race and ethnicity in California. One of every four African Americans and one in every six Latinos and Pacific Islanders enrolled in school between 9th and 12th grade were estimated to have dropped out of school by 2003–2004. On the other hand, 8% of white non-Hispanics, 7% of Filipinos, and 6% of Asians dropped out in this four-year period. This is a decline from prior years, especially for Hispanic students (see Figure 4). Drop-out rates declined significantly throughout the 1990s, and increased again in the early 2000s. In 1992–1993, 27% of African-American and Latino children dropped out of school between 9th and 12th grade.

Not only are Latino and African-American children more likely to drop out of high school, they are less likely to complete college than other children. In Table 2, we present the college completion rate for the four major race and ethnic groups, and then we look at subgroups of Latinos and Asians. In 2000, 39% of whites between the ages of 25 and 29 had a college education, compared to 8% of Latinos. Looking at Latino subgroups, low educational attainment is more of a problem among foreign-born Latinos who emigrated with low levels of education and may have had no contact with U.S. educational institutions—only 4% of foreign-born Mexicans and 6% of Central American immigrants between the ages of 25 and 29 graduated from college. But even U.S.-born Latinos have lower college graduation rates than whites and Asians. In 2000, only 13% of U.S.-born Mexicans between the ages of 25 and 29 graduated from college. The exception is Latinos of Caribbean decent who have graduation rates similar to other groups.

These patterns, especially the low educational attainment of Latinos, present particular challenges for California. In less than 20 years, Latinos will outnumber

Figure 3. Estimate of the 4-Year Dropout Rate by Race and Ethnicity, 2003–2004

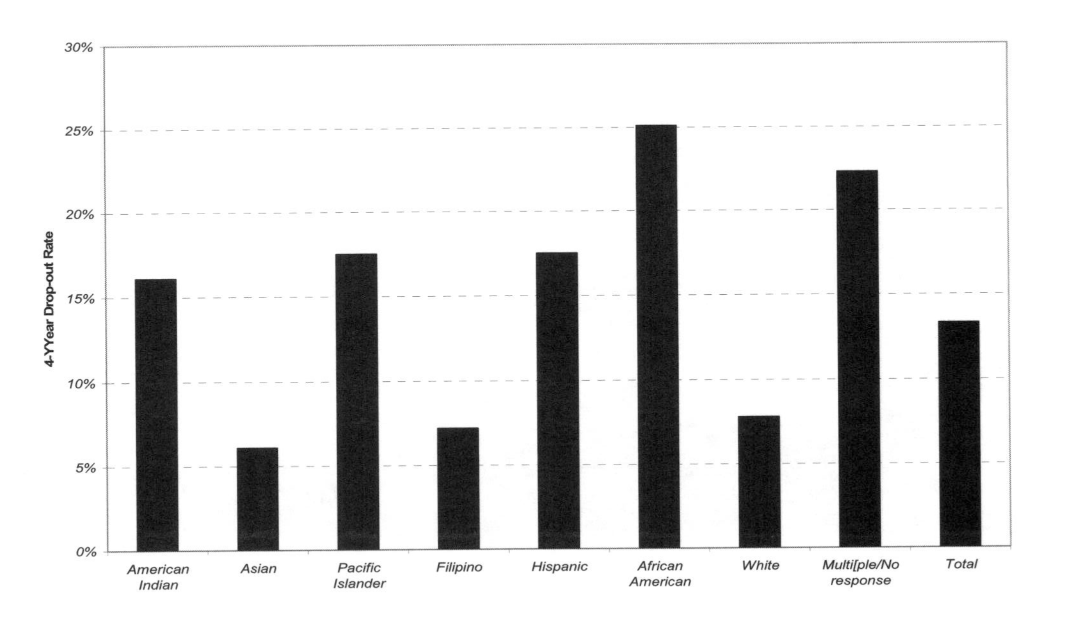

Note: The 4-year rate is an estimated percentage of students who will drop out during a four-year period, calculated using the dropout rate for each grade (9–12).

Source: Estimate Generated from California Department of Education, Educational Demographics Unit–CBEDS for 2003–2004 Academic Year.

Figure 4. Trends in 4-Year Dropout Rates by Race and Ethnicity, 1992–2004

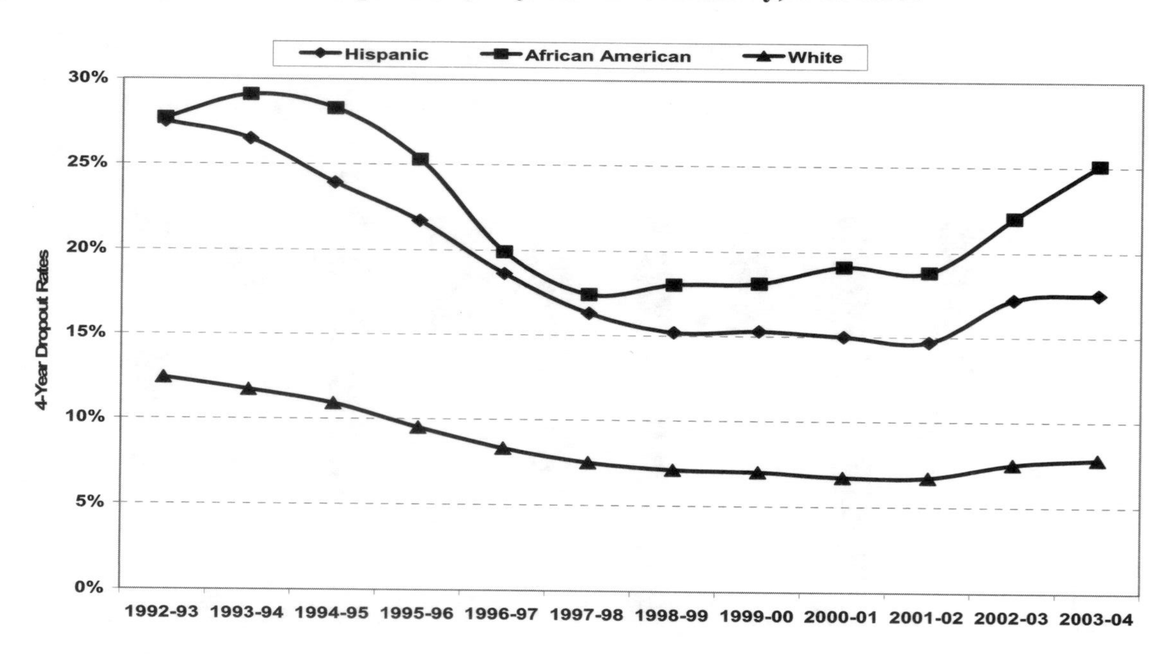

Note: The 4-year rate is an estimated percentage of students who will drop out during a four-year period, calculated using the dropout rate for each grade (9–12).

Source: Estimate Generated from California Department of Education, Educational Demographics Unit–CBEDS for 2003–2004 Academic Year.

Table 2. College Completion Rates for Young Adults 25 to 29 Years Old, 2000

		College Completion
White		39%
Black		18%
American Indian		15%
Multirace		34%
Hispanic		8%
Mexican	U.S. Born	13%
	Foreign Born	4%
Central American	U.S. Born	25%
	Foreign Born	6%
Caribbean	U.S. Born	41%
	Foreign Born	24%
Asian and Pacific Islanders		51%
Chinese	U.S. Born	73%
	Foreign Born	66%
Japanese	U.S. Born	62%
	Foreign Born	46%
Asian Indian	U.S. Born	72%
	Foreign Born	80%
SE Asian	U.S. Born	39%
	Foreign Born	31%
Filipino	U.S. Born	43%
	Foreign Born	34%
Korean	U.S. Born	71%
	Foreign Born	57%

Source: Estimates generated from the 2000 micro sample of the U.S. Census.

whites in the state of California, and by 2040 they will be the majority (Reyes 2001). Not addressing these disparities could reduce economic opportunities for a growing proportion of the state's population, reduce economic growth, reduce resources for state coffers, and contribute to economic and social inequality. A recent study by the RAND Corporation estimated that doubling the number of Latino college graduates could bring a $13 billion windfall to the state on reductions in public spending and increases in revenues, not including the private benefit in consumption and production (Mizell and Vernez 2001). The cost of doing nothing could be disastrous.

Alternative Explanations for Poor Outcomes

There are three basic explanations for the performance gap: one emphasizes the conditions of the families, the other the conditions of the neighborhoods, and the last one the conditions of schools and school programs. First, difference in education attainment is attributed to differences in family background characteristics, such as income, family structure, parents' education, and parents' involvement in schools (Phillips et al. 1998; Mayer 1997). Families with limited income cannot afford to live in good neighborhoods with better schools. Parents may have multiple jobs and may not have the time to help children with homework or participate in school activities. Parents with low levels of education and/or language limitations may not be able to help their children with homework or participate in school activities. Figure 5 shows the correlation between socio-economic conditions of families and student performance. Compared to students who are better off, a smaller proportion of students from socio-economic disadvantaged backgrounds were at or above proficient levels in English for their grade level. Similar patterns occur in math scores or other standardized tests (Reed 2005).

Neighborhood and peers appear to have a detrimental effect on student performance (Betts et al. 2000; Cook and Ludwig 1997; Farkas, Lleras, and Maczuga 2002; Fordham and Ogbu 1986; Rose et al. 2003). Some researchers argue that because they see no connection to the broader society, lack role models, and experience dilapidated crime-ridden neighborhoods, poor black and Latino children in central cities to develop an oppositional culture that lowers aspirations and discourages educational success (Fordham and Ogbu 1986; Cook and Ludwig 1997; Farkas et al. 2002; Ogbu 1991). But the behavior is also linked to family resources (Kao and Tienda 1998; MacLeod 1987). Family resources have been found to influence the perceived feasibility of a continuing education, children's aspirations, and outcomes.

Lastly, the schools that Latinos and African-American children attend have fewer school resources, lower-quality teachers and more overcrowded and deteriorating facilities than the schools of most white children. This in turn affects student performance (Hanushek 1997, 2003; Ferguson 1998; Phillips et al. 1998; Holland

Figure 5. Students Scores in English Standardized, Stanford 9 Test by Socio-Economic Disadvantage

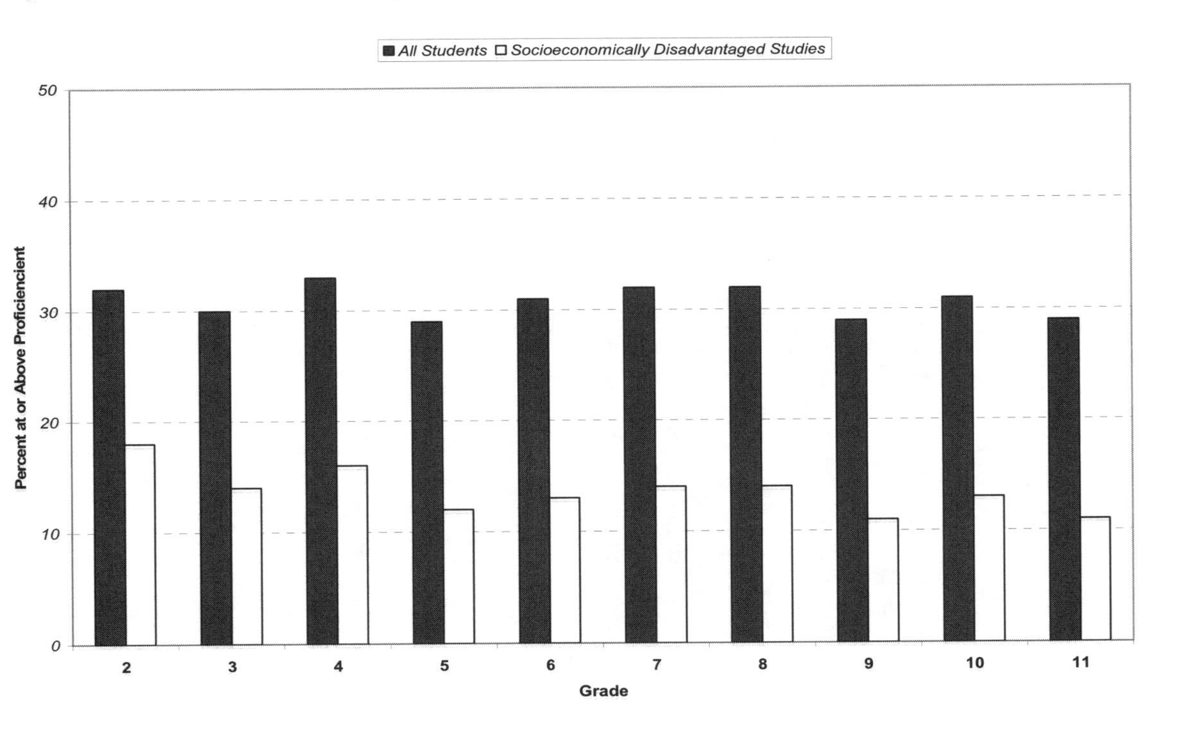

Source: Data from the California Department of Education. Results obtained from EdSource, "California Student Achievement: Multiple Views of K-12 Progress," Report, June 2002.

1989; Leake and Leake 1992; Polite 1993b; Adler, Kless, and Adler 1992; Davis and Jordan 1994). Urban schools that many poor Latino and black children attend have more teachers with emergency credentials or waivers and less experience and education. Table 3 shows teacher credentials, experience and education, level of overcrowding, and performance of California schools. Fifty-two percent of Latino and 43% of African-American elementary school students attended a low performing school. Only 10% of white elementary school students attended a low-performing school. There are also more low-income students in the schools attended by most Latino and black students. There are slightly fewer fully-credentialed teachers in schools attended by Latinos and African-American students, but the differences are not dramatic.

These factors explain most of the educational gap. Poor families live in deteriorated neighborhoods with poor quality schools. This creates limited expectations, which influences children's aspirations and educational progress. At the same time, school resources cannot compensate for family and neighborhood conditions to mediate the impact of poverty and isolation and improve the chance of success for many children. But why is this the case in the sixth largest economy? At play may be the state's willingness or ability to tackle these issues and do what is necessary to improve the schools and neighborhoods and provide adequate programs for black and Latino children. In recent years the state has reduced class size in particular grades and has enhanced teacher training and facilities (Carroll et al. 2005; Reed 2005; Rose et al. 2003). Still, the allocation of resources has not been large enough to significantly improve outcomes (Carroll et al. 2005; Rose et al. 2003). In the next section we discuss the political factors that may lead to an unwillingness or lack of ability on the part of voters and school administrators to address the problems facing these children.

The Political Environment

In a state where policymaking is increasingly in the hands of the electorate through the initiative process, complacency among the voters can have serious consequences for schools. Part of the explanation for this complacency may be a mismatch between students and voters. Table 4 shows the demographics in California schools and the electorate. Of the 6.3 million students in California's public schools in 2004, 47% were Latino, 31% white, 11% Asian/Pacific Islander, and 8% African American. On the other hand, California voters are overwhelmingly white non-Hispanic (70%). And although segregation may have declined slightly in California, it is still persistent. In 2000, almost 60% of whites lived in neighborhoods that were either segregated or somewhat segregated, so did 51% of Latinos (Sandoval, Johnson, Tafoya 2002). Segregation may isolate whites from the problems facing nonwhite children in schools. This may make them less supportive of programs to improve conditions for nonwhite children.

Table 3. School Resources of California Elementary Students, by Race and Ethnicity (by percentage)

	Share of Students	Low-Performing Schools	Low-Income Students	Teachers without a Full Credential	Teacher Less than 3+ Years Experience	Teacher Master's Degree	Overcrowded Schools
American Indian	1	29	55	4	10	26	7
Hispanic	49	52	72	9	11	29	27
Black	8	43	64	10	12	28	24
Pacific Islander	1	26	54	6	11	29	12
White	30	10	34	3	9	31	4
Filipino	2	16	48	6	12	31	12
Asian	8	15	42	4	11	30	14
All	100	34	56	7	11	29	18

Sources: Deborah Reed, "Educational Resources and Outcomes in California, by Race and Ethnicity," *California Counts*, Public Policy Institute of California, 6(3), February 2005.

Table 4. The Ethnic Distribution of the California Electorates and California Students

	Total Number	White	Latino	Asian/Pacific Islander	African American
Students in Public Schools 2004–05	6.3 million	31%	47%	11%	8%
California Voters 2000	7.8 million	70%	14%	7%	8%

Source: Data on students and schools were generated from the California Department of Education CBEDS files. The data on board members were provided by the California School Board Association.

If we look at recent initiatives with implications for education, for instance the vote on propositions 227, 229, and 187, a majority of white voters imposed their political will on the rest of the population (Hajnal, Gerber, and Louch 2002; Haznal and Baldassare 2001).[3] As shown in Table 2, 76% of Latinos, 74% of African Americans, and 61% of Asians opposed Proposition 209, but it passed with 51% of the votes because the majority of white voters (63%) supported the initiative (Haznal and Baldassare 2001; Baldassare 2000). Proposition 187 passed by a comfortable margin, but divided the state. The vast majority of Latinos (77%), African Americans (53%), and Asians (53%) opposed the measure. However, because white voters were strongly in favor of the proposition (63%), Proposition 187 ultimately passed (Haznal and Baldassare 2001). The same was true, although less dramatically for Proposition 227. Although the exit polls shows that 63% of Latinos and 52% of African Americans voted to maintain bilingual education programs, because 67% of whites and 57% of Asians voted in favor of the initiative, it won by a 20% margin (Haznal and Baldassare 2001).

We observe similar patterns in the votes for school bonds. Whites are less likely to vote for school bonds while Latinos are more likely to support them. Proposition 26 in March of 2000 tried to reduce the vote requirement from a two-thirds majority to a simple majority. Eight months later, Proposition 39 would reduce it to 55% of the votes. *Los Angeles Times* exit polls show that over 60% of Latinos voted in favor of each measure, but since only 48% of whites voted for Proposition 26 the measure failed. Proposition 39 passed by capturing 50% of white voters. In 1998, Proposition A1 proposed a $9 billion bond to improve educational facilities and fund class-size reduction. This measure passed with a wide margin (63% of the votes) because it had broad support. Regardless, whites were less supportive of the initiative than Latinos—86% of Latinos planned to vote for the initiative, while only 60% of whites were going to do the same (Baldassare 2000).

The fact that we see different voting propensities does not necessarily mean that the ethnic distribution of school children has an influence on white voters. It could be that whites are less likely to vote for school bonds no matter the ethnic composition of the student population. Social scientists have examined the effect of the age and ethnic composition of voters on school expenditures (Brunner and Balsdon 2004; Poterba 1998; Colburn and Horowitz 2003). Researchers argue that voters decide which expenditure program to support on the basis of their individual self-interest. Therefore voters may be less likely to support programs if they do not see a direct benefit from (Poterba 1998). Having children in local schools has a positive and significant effect on whether a household head supports higher spending on education (Rubinfeld 1977; Wyckoff 1984). Elderly

---

[3] Proposition 227 passed in 1998, practically put an end to bilingual education programs. Proposition 209, a 1996 initiative, sought to end government affirmative action programs. And Proposition 187 of 1994 would have restricted access to schools for undocumented children.

voters, who tend not to have children in school, are less likely to vote for increases in school expenditures (Poterba 1998).

Some academics go beyond the neoclassical type argument about individual self-interest and argue that the unwillingness to support policies that favor minorities stem from a new form of racism (Bobo and Kluegal 1997; Sears 1988; Sears and Kinder 1971; Sears et al. 1997; Kinder and Sears, 1981; McConahay 1982; Kinder and Sanders 1996). The symbolic racism theory argues that old fashioned explicit forms of racism declined in the United States, but that a new form of racism involves a set of beliefs "including the sense that discrimination is no longer an obstacle for blacks, that their current lack of upward social mobility is caused by their unwillingness to work hard, that they demand too much of government, and that they have received more than they deserve" (Hutchings and Valentino 2004).

But some critics, such as Sniderman et al. (2000), argue that although racism has not disappeared, the affect on blacks is not the most important factor predicting white policy preferences. Critical for the affect of demographics on voting is the level of interaction and political fragmentation in the locality. Brunner and Balsdon (2004) find that older adults are more likely to support local expenditures than statewide increases in expenditure, suggesting the importance of the local context on policy preferences. But looking at historical data, Crimmins and Ingegneri (1990) found that elderly voters were more likely to support increases in expenditures in the past than in recent years, which could be the result of demographic changes. In a politically fragmented environment, a high proportion of African Americans decreased the likelihood that whites would vote for increases in educational spending (Colburn and Horowitz 2003; Kinder and Mendelberg 1995). This is also supported by Alesina, Baqir, and Easterly (1997), who find that in cities with more diversity there is less spending on education. However, Carsey (1995) found that white voters who live *in the same neighborhoods* as blacks are more likely to vote for African-American candidates. Hence, the more critical issue may not be whites' unwillgness to support programs that benefit minorities, but the level of interaction among racial and ethnic groups. Social scientists, such as Dixon (2006) and Branton and Jones (2005), argue that the social context, the level of interaction, and the conditions of the community in which people live have an effect on attitudes and policy preferences (also see Oliver and Wong 2003). However, as discussed above, groups continue to be segregated and increasingly the courts are reversing desegregation efforts of the past.[4]

The willingness of voters to advocate for children is also critical for policy development and implementation. There is an extensive literature of how interest groups affect local policymaking and how to make policymakers accountable to voters (Roberts 2004; Martin 2003; Hajnal and Trounstine 2005, among others). In these studies, civic participation and dialogue are critical to make policymakers

[4] In late June 2007, the United States Supreme Court invalidated voluntary school desegregation plans, making it more difficult for schools to deal with issues of diversity.

responsive to the needs of a particular interest group (Martin 2003; Hajnal and Trounstine 2005). In California, Latinos participate at very low rates, see Figure 6. The most important reason why they do not participate is that the majority of Latinos in California are not eligible to vote. In 2002 only 35% of Latinos in California were eligible to vote—either because they have not been in the country long enough, they are not old enough, they have not yet naturalized or they are undocumented (Reyes 2003). They are also less likely to participate in other forms of civic engagement (Ramakrishnan and Baldassare 2004). Latinos are less likely to sign petitions, contribute to political campaigns, or write to public officials. Nevertheless, they are more likely to attend local meetings, especially those related to school issues. Only 38% of Latinos say they vote regularly in elections, but 43% participate in local meetings (Ramakrishnan and Baldassare 2004). Local meetings may be more accessible for people without citizenship, and they may be more willing to participate at a level where they see more influence. But some cities have gone beyond allowing noncitizens to vote on local elections. New York City and Boston allow noncitizens to vote in school board elections, and recently San Francisco considered doing the same. This approach recognizes the potential political disconnect between those with the right to vote and those influenced by the policy decisions and enfranchises everyone affected by the policy decisions.

If representation of a group on a governing board enhances the policy responsiveness of that body to such groups, then underrepresentation might deprive particular groups of needed programs and benefits. Even if voters in California wanted to be responsive to the troubles facing schools, they may not know how best to address the problem because the education leadership may not be responsive to the needs of nonwhite students. Looking at Table 5, 72% of teachers, 70% of school administrators, and 68% of school board members who selected a racial/ethnic category are white non-Hispanic. Latinos are one of every seven teachers and administrators and one of every 10 board members in the state.

Political scientists have examined the possible consequences of underrepresentation of particular groups on local policymaking, although it is a contested issue (Leal, Meier, Martinez-Eber 2004; Polinard et al. 1994; Meier, Gonzalez-Juenke, Wrinkle, and Polinard 2005; Reyes and Neiman, forthcoming). Leal, Meier, Martinez-Ebers (2004) find not only that at-large election affects Latino representation, but that this in turn affects the hiring of Latino administrators and teachers. Although also contentious, there is some evidence that teacher's race and ethnicity have a positive impact on children of the same ethnicity (Dee 2004; Clewell and Villegas 1998; Evans 1992; Hess and Leal 1997). For instance, black students are less likely than other race and ethic groups to enroll in advanced math courses, and rigorous math has been found to affect future earnings and college success (Adelman 1999; Rose and Betts 2001). Klopfenstein (2005) finds that increasing the number of black math teachers has a positive impact on the likelihood that black students will enroll in rigorous math courses. Dee (2004) finds a strong positive impact of the ethnicity of the teacher on test scores using randomized experiments. Ehrenberg, Goldhaber, and Brewer (1995) find no impact on

Figure 6. Estimate of the Eligible Population by Race and Ethnicity in California

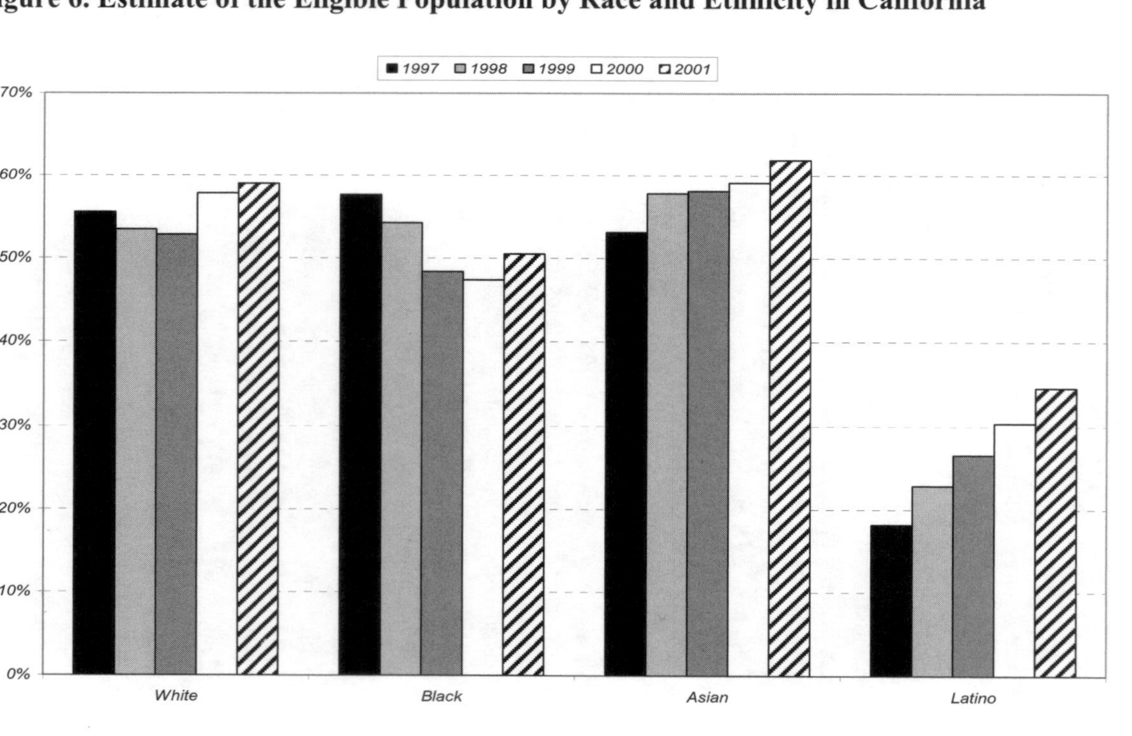

Source: Reyes (2003).

Table 5. The Ethnic Distribution of California Students, Teachers, and Administrators

	Total Number	White	Latino	Asian/Pacific Islander	African American
Students in Public Schools 2004–2005	6.3 million	31%	47%	11%	8%
School Teachers 2004–2005	306,548	72%	15%	6%	4.5%
School Administrators 2004–2005	26,523	70%	15%	4%	8%
Board Members 2005	5,143	68%	9%	2%	2%

Source: Data on students and schools was generated from the California Department of Education CBEDS files. The data on board members were provided by the California School Board Association.

test scores, but a difference on teacher perceptions or evaluations of students. However, teachers' perceptions have been found to have an impact on student outcomes (Ferguson 1998; Oates 2003).

Recent lawsuits have challenged systems of elections in California in order to increase minority representation on school boards. For instance, in July 15, 2004, Latino voters filed a lawsuit in Kings County Superior Court claiming that the Hanford Joint Union High School District's at-large system of electing school board members violates the California Voting Rights Act of 2001. The school district, which as of the 2000 Census, was 39% Latino, has not had a Latino representative among the five-member board of trustees for the past 20 years. For the most part, the argument of the case is supported by academic evidence that shows underrepresentation by types of election systems (Canon 1999; Davidson and Grofman 1994; Heileg and Mundt 1983; McDonald and Engstrom 1992; Meier and England 1984; Polinard, Wrinkle, and Longoria 1990, 1991; Fraga, Meier, and England 1986). Researchers generally find at-large election methods to be detrimental to nonwhite representation (Welch 1990; Davidson and Korbel 1981; Taebel 1978; Polinard, Wrinkle, and Longoria 1991; McDonald and Engstrom 1992; Bezdek, Billeaux, and Huerta 2000). Still today, about two-thirds of California school districts have at-large elections, 20% have area-at-large elections, and 15% have district elections (California School Boards Association Survey; Leal, Meier, and Martinez-Ebers 2004).

These findings suggest that a mismatch between the demographics of students and the political leadership in California could have serious consequences on the educational progress for African-American and Latino children, as voters and political leaders are not aware of or are unwilling to make the political compromises that are essential to make real improvements in education in California.

V. Policy Implications

No Child Left Behind set a standard of accountability for schools, and students of every racial and ethnic group are expected to realize particular levels of achievement. Given the demographics in California schools, these new standards demand close attention to the educational progress of nonwhite children, especially Latino children who soon will be the overwhelming majority of school age children in California.

When compared with their white counterparts, black and Latino students made substantial educational progress. They reduced the test score gap in mathematics and reading (Berends et al. 2005). There have also been increases in high school graduation and college completion rates. But differences across racial and ethnic groups persist. In general, the educational literature highlights the importance of socio-economic conditions of families and school and neighborhood characteristics in predicting student achievement. Improvements in the condition of families have as much or more of an impact on education achievement than improvements in school conditions (Berends et al. 2005). But the increase in segregation of Latinos and African Americans in underperforming schools is worsening conditions for children. School policies may have a limited impact if they are not accompanied by policies that address the conditions of families and communities. In addition to improving teacher training, decreasing class size, and increasing accountability, increasing parental involvement in schools, and improving conditions for families through occupational training, English classes, and other adult educational programs could have a strong positive impact on student achievement. Increasing bridge programs and access to secondary education, perhaps by reinstating affirmative action programs, could change expectations and aspirations. It is also critical to continue to address the increasing racial isolation of students in predominantly minority schools. One needs to address school funding issues, not just by equating funding, but by providing adequate funding for the needs of students. Developing regional approaches to school finance, where wealthier districts share the financial responsibility for these children, or increasing racial balance through busing or school choice programs, could affect social isolation. School choice, vouchers, and charter schools have been brought up as ways to diversify schools (Goldring and Smrekar 2002; Kahlenberg 2001), but there is no evidence thus far that these policies reduce racial isolation or contribute directly to closing achievement gaps (Gill et al. 2001; Zimmer et al. 2003).

Finally, California needs to address the potentially politically difficult issue of a leadership that no longer represents the state's population. Increasing Latino and African-American participation and voting could have consequences on school policy. Efforts to increase naturalization, registration, and voting are critical for California's local communities. Another alternative is to consider noncitizen resident voting for local offices, so as to engage many immigrant parents unable to vote on local government, bringing their voice to the debate and enfranchising them locally.

Finally, changes in the ethnic composition of board members, administrators, and teachers could have positive impacts on student performance. This could be achieved with a change in the system by which school board members are elected from at-large to district elections. Nonwhite board members are more likely to gain office in this type of election system and once in office they are more likely to bring in nonwhite teachers and administrators.

These compromises are critical for the future of the state. As the nonwhite population continues to increase, an educational system capable of engendering ever larger proportions of skilled workers would not only allow for increasing productivity but for a more flexible economy and a labor force better able to achieve the economies of scale required for such flexibility. Improvement in education can reverse some of the deterioration in the state's distribution of income in addition to generating more tax revenue for infrastructure improvements and to maintaining a social safety net. Improving educational opportunities for all racial and ethnic groups is the main challenge for California's educational system and a crucial focus for policymakers looking to ensure a better future for the state's economy and the welfare of its population.

References:

Adelman, C. 1999. "Answers in the Tool Box: Academic Intensity, Attendance Patterns, and Bachelor's Degree Attainment." Washington, D.C.: U.S. Department of Education, Office of Education Research and Improvement.

Adler, P. A., S. J. Kless, and P. Adler. 1992. "Socialization to Gender Roles: Popularity among Elementary School Boys and Girls." *Sociology of Education* 65: 169–87.

Alesina, A., R. Baqir, and E. Easterly. 1997. *Public Goods and Ethnic Divisions.* Working Paper 6009, Cambridge, Mass.: National Bureau of Economic Research.

Baldassare, Mark. 2000. *California in the New Millennium: The Changing Social and Political Landscape.* Jointly published by the Public Policy Institute of California and the University of California Press, San Francisco, Calif.

———. 2006. PPIC Statewide Survey: Special Survey on Education, April.

Berends, Mark, Samuel R. Lucas, Thomas Sullivan, and R. J. Briggs. 2005. *Examining Gaps in Mathematics Achievement among Racial-Ethnic Groups, 1972–1992.* Santa Monica: RAND Corporation.

Betts, Julian R, Kim S. Rueben, and Anne Danenberg. 2000. *Equal Resources, Equal Outcomes? The Distribution of School Resources and Student Achievement in California.* San Francisco, Calif.: Public Policy Institute of California.

Bezdek, R. R., D. M. Billeaux, and J. C. Huerta. 2000. "Latinos, At-Large Elections, and Political Change: Evidence from the 'Transition Zone.'" *Social Science Quarterly* 81(1): 207–25.

Bobo L. D.,and J. R. Kluegel. 1997. "Status, Ideology, and Dimensions of Whites' Racial Beliefs and Attitudes: Progress and Stagnation." In *Racial Attitudes in the 1990s: Continuity and Change,* ed. S. A. Tuch and J. K. Martin. Westport, Conn.: Praeger, 93–120.

Branton, R P., and B. S. Jones. 2005. "Reexamining Racial Attitudes: The Conditional Relationship between Diversity and Socioeconomic Environment." *American Journal of Political Science* 49(2): 359–72.

Brunner, Eric, and Ed Balsdon. 2004. "Intergenerational Conflict and the Political Economy of School Spending." *Journal of Urban Economics* 56: 369–88.

California Department of Finance. 2004. *California Public K-12 Enrollment and High School Graduate Projection by County–2004 Series.* Available online: www.dof.ca.gov/HTML/DEMOGRAP/K12Grads04.xls.

Canon, David T. 1999. "Electoral Systems and the Representation of Minority Interest in Legislation." *Legislative Studies Quarterly* 24(3): 331–85.

Carroll, Stephen J., Cathy Krop, Jeremy Arkes, Peter A. Morrison, and Ann Flanagan. 2005. *California's K–12 Public Schools: How Are They Doing?* Santa Monica, Calif.: RAND Corporation.

Carsey T. M. 1995. "The Contextual Effects of Race on White Voter Behavior—The 1989 New York City Mayoral Election." *Journal of Politics* 57 (1): 221–28.

Casteel, Clifton A. 1998. "Teacher-Student Interactions and Race in Integrated Classrooms." *Journal of Educational Research* 92: 115–20.

Citrin J., D. P. Green, and David Sears. 1990. "White Reactions to Black Candidates: When Does Race Matter?" *Public Opinion Quarterly* 54: 74–96.

Clewell. Beatriz Chu, and Ana Maria Villegas. 1998. "Diversifying the Teacher Force to Improve Urban Schools." *Education and Urban Society* 31(1): 3–17.

Colburn, Christopher, and John B. Horowitz. 2003. "Local Politics and the Demand for Public Education." *Urban Studies* 40(4): 797–809.

Cook, Philip J., and Jens Ludwig. 1997. "Weighing the "Burden of 'Acting White'": Are There Race Differences in Attitudes toward Education?" *Journal of Policy Analysis and Management* 16: 256–78.

Crimmins E. M., and D. G. Ingegneri. 1990. "Interaction and Living Arrangements of Older Parents and Their Children—Past Trends, Present Determinants, Future Implications." *Research on Aging* 12(1): 3–35.

Darling-Hammond, Linda, 2002. "Research and Rhetoric on Teacher Certification: A Response to 'Teacher Certification Reconsidered.'" *Education Policy Analysis Archives* 10(36).

Davis, James Earl, and Will J. Jordan. 1994. "The Effects of School Context, Structure, and Experiences on African American Males in Middle and High School." *Journal of Negro Education* 63(4): 570–87.

Davidson, Chandler, and Barnard Grofman, eds. 1994. *Quiet Revolution in the South: The Impact of the Voting Rights Act, 1965–1990*. Princeton, N.J.: Princeton University Press.

Davidson, Chandler, and George Korbel. 1981. "At-Large Elections and Minority-Group Representation: A Re-examination of Historical and Contemporary Evidence." *Journal of Politics* 43: 982–1005.

Dee, Thomas, 2004. "Teachers, Race, and Student Achievement in a Randomized Experiment." *The Review of Economics and Statistics.* 86(1): 195–210.

Dixon, Jeffrey C. 2006. "The Ties That Bind and Those That Don't: Toward Reconciling Group Threat and Contact Theories of Prejudice." *Social Forces*, Vol. 84, No. 4: 2179–2204.

EdSource. 2002. California Student Achievement: Multiple Views of K-12 Progress, Report, June 2002.

Ehrenberg, R. G., D. D. Goldhaber, and D. J. Brewer. 1995. "Do Teacher's Race, Gender, and Ethnicity Matter? Evidence from the National Educational Longitudinal Study of 1988." *Industrial and Labor Relations Review* 48(3): 547–61.

Esch, Camille E., and Patrick M. Shields. 2002. *Who Is Teaching California's Children?* Center for the Future of Teaching and Learning, Santa Cruz, Calif.

Evans, M. O. 1992. "An Estimate of Race and Gender Role-Model Effects in Teaching High School." *Journal of Economic Education* 23(3): 209–17.

Farkas, G., C. Lleras, and S. Maczuga. 2002. "Does Oppositional Culture Exist in Minority and Poverty Peer Groups?" *American Sociological Review* 67: 148–55.

Ferguson, Ronald F. 1998. "Teachers' Perceptions and Expectations and the Black-White Test Score Gap." In *The Black-White Test Score Gap,* ed. C. Jencks and M. Phillips. Washington, D.C.: Brookings Institution Press.

Fordham, Signithia, and John Ogbu. 1986. "Black Students' School Success: Coping with the Burden of 'Acting White.'" *Urban Review* 18: 176–206.

Fraga, Luis, Kenneth Meier, and Re England. 1986. "Hispanic Americans and Educational-Policy—Limits to Equal Access." *Journal of Politics* 48(4): 850–76.

Hanak, Ellen, and Mark Baldassare (eds.). 2005. *California 2025: Taking on the Future*. San Francisco, Calif.: Public Policy Institute of California.

Hanushek, Eric A. 1997. "The Economics of School Resources and Student Performance: An Update." *Educational Evaluation and Policy Analysis* 19(2): 141–64.

———. 2003. "The Failure of Input-Based School Policies." *Economic Journal* 113: F64–F98.

Hanushek, Eric A., John F. Kain, Jacob M. Markman, and Steven G. Rivkin, "Does Peer Ability Affect Student Achievement?" *Journal of Applied Econometrics* 18(5): 527–44.

Haycock, Kati. 1998. "Good Teaching Matters: How Well-Qualified Teachers Can Close the Gap." *Thinking K–16*, Vol. 4, No. 2.

Haznal, Zoltan, and Mark Baldassare. 2001. *Finding Common Ground: Racial and Ethnic Attitudes in California*. San Francisco, Calif.: Public Policy Institute of California.

Haznal, Zoltan, Elizabeth Gerber, and Hugh Louch. 2002. "Minorities and Direct Legislation: Evidence from California Ballot Proposition Elections." *Journal of Politics* 64(1): 154–77.

Haznal, Zoltan, and J. Trounstine. 2005. "Where Turnout Matters: The Consequences of Uneven Turnout in City Politics." *Journal of Politics* 67(2): 515–35.

Heileg, Peggy, and Robert Mundt. 1983. "Changes in Representational Equity: The Effect of Adopting Districts." *Social Science Quarterly* 64: 393–97.

Hess, Frederick M., and David L. Leal. 1997. "Minority Teachers, Minority Students, and College Matriculation: A New Look at the Role-Modeling Hypothesis." *Policy Studies Journal* 25(2): 235.

Holland, S. 1989. "Fighting the Epidemic of Failure: A Radical Strategy for Educating Inner-City Boys." *Teacher Magazine* (September/October): 88–89.

Hoxby, Caroline. 2000. "Peer Effects in the Classroom: Learning from Gender and Race Variation." National Bureau of Economic Research Working Paper 7867, Cambridge, Mass.

Hutchings, Vincent L., and Nicholas A. Valentino. 2004. "The Centrality of Race in American Politics." *Annual Review of Political Science* 7: 383–408.

Johnson, Hans P., and Deborah Reed. 2007. "Can California Import Enough College Graduates to Meet Workforce Needs?" *California Counts: Population*

Trends and Profiles 8(4). San Francisco, Calif.: Public Policy Institute of California.

Kao, Grace, and Marta Tienda. 1998. "Educational Aspirations of Minority Youth." *American Journal of Education* 106(3): 349–84.

Kinder, Donald, and Tali Mendelberg. 1995. "Cracking in American Apartheid: The Political Impact of Prejudice among Desegregated Whites." *Journal of Politics* 57: 402–24.

Kinder, Donald, and L Sanders, 1996. *Divided by Color: Racial Politics and Democratic Ideals.* Chicago: University of Chicago Press.

Kinder, Donald, and David Sears. 1981. "Prejudice and Politics: Symbolic Racism Versus Racial Threats to the Good Life." *Journal Personality and Social Psychology* 40: 414–31.

Klopfenstein, K. 2005. "Beyond Test Scores: The Impact of Black Teacher Role Models on Rigorous Math Taking." *Contemporary Economic Policy* 23(3): 416–28.

Krueger, Alan B. 2003. "Economic Considerations and Class Size." *Economic Journal* 113: F34–F63.

Leal D. L., V. Martinez-Ebers, K. J. Meier. 2004. "The Politics of Latino Education: The Biases of At-Large Elections. *Journal of Politics* 66(4): 1224–44.

Leake, D. O., and B. L. Leake. 1992. "Islands of Hope: Milwaukee's African American Immersion Schools. *Journal of Negro Education* 61(1): 4–11.

MacLeod, J. 1987. *Ain't No Makin' It: Leveled Aspirations in a Low-Income Neighborhood.* Boulder, Colo.: Westview Press.

Mayer, Susan E. 1997. *What Money Can't Buy: Family Income and Children's Life Chances*. Cambridge, Mass.: Harvard University Press.

Martin, Paul. 2003. "Voting's Rewards: Voter Turnout, Attentive Publics, and Congressional Allocation of Federal Money." *American Journal of Political Science* 47(1): 110–27.

McConahay, J. B. 1982. "Self-Interest versus Racial Attitudes as Correlates of Anti-Busing Attitudes in Louisville: Is It the Buses or the Blacks?" *Journal of Politics* 44: 692–720.

McDonald, Michael D., and Richard L. Engstrom. 1992. "Minority Representation and City Council Electoral Systems: A Black and Hispanic Comparison." In *Ethnic and Racial Minorities in Advanced Industrial Democracies*, ed. Anthony M. Messina, Luis R. Fraga, Laurie A. Rhodebeck, and Frederick D. Wright. New York: Greenwood Press.

Meier, Kenneth, and R. E. England. 1984. "Black Representation and Educational-Policy—Are They Related?" *American Political Science Review* 78(2): 392–403.

Meier, Kenneth, Eric Gonzalez-Juenkel, R. D. Wrinkle, and J. L. Polinard. 2005. "Structural Choices and Representational Biases: The Post-Election Color of Representation." *American Journal of Political Science* 49(4): 758–68.

Mizell, Lee, and Georges Vernez. 2001. *Increasing the Education Attainment of Hispanics: Program Effectiveness.* DRU-2714-HSF, Santa Monica, Calif.: RAND, December.

Oates GLS. 2003. "Teacher-Student Racial Congruence, Teacher Perceptions, and Test Performance." *Social Science Quarterly* 84(3): 508–25.

Ogbu, John. 1991. "Minority Coping Responses and School Experience." *Journal of Psychohistory* 18: 433–56.

Oliver, J. E., and J. Wong. 2003. "Intergroup Prejudice in Multiethnic Settings." *American Journal of Political Science* 47(4): 567–82.

Orfield, Gary. 2001. "Schools More Separate: Consequences of a Decade of Resegregation." The Civil Rights Project Harvard University.

Phillips, M., J. Brooks-Gunn, G. Duncan, P. Klebanov, and J. Crane, 1998. "Family Background, Parenting Practices, and the Black-White Test Score Gap." In *The Black-White Test Score Gap*, ed. C. Jencks and M. Phillips. Washington, D.C.: Brookings Institution Press, 103–45.

Polinard, J., Robert D. Wrinkle, and Tomas Longoria. 1990. "Education and Governance: Representational Links to Second Generation Discrimination." *Western Political Quarterly,* Vol. 43, No. 3: 631–46.

———. 1991. "The Impact of District Elections on the Mexican-American Community—The Electoral Perspective." *Social Science Quarterly* 72(3): 608–14.

Polite, V. 1993. "If We Knew Then What We Know Now: Fouled Opportunities to Learn in Suburbia." *Journal of Negro Education* 62(1): 12–23.

Poterba, James M. 1998. "Demographic Change, Intergenerational Linkages, and Public Education." *The American Economic Review* 88(2): 315–20.

Ramakrishnan, S., Karthick, and Mark Baldassare. 2004. *The Ties That Bind: Changing Demographics and Civic Engagement in California.* San Francisco, Calif.: Public Policy Institute of California.

Reed, Deborah. 2003. "*The Growing Importance of Education in California.*" Occasional Paper Series, San Francisco, Calif.: Public Policy Institute of California.

———. 2005. "Educational Resources and Outcomes in California, by Race and Ethnicity." *California Counts*, Public Policy Institute of California, 6(3), February.

Reyes, Belinda (ed.). 2001. *A Portrait of Race and Ethnicity in California: An Assessment of Social and Economic Well-Being*. San Francisco, Calif.: Public Policy Institute of California.

———. 2003. "Latinos in California: Population Growth and Diversity." In *Latinos and Public Policy in California: An Agenda for Opportunity*, ed. David Lopez and Andres Jimenez. Berkeley, Calif.: Institute of Governmental Studies Press, University of California.

Reyes, Belinda, and Max Neiman. Forthcoming. *Systems of Election, Latino Representation, and Student Outcomes in California Schools*. Berkeley: California Policy Research Center Report.

Rivkin, Steven G., Eric A. Hanushek, and John F. Cain. 2002. "Teachers, Schools, and Academic Achievement." Unpublished manuscript.

Roberts, Nancy. 2002. "Keeping Public Officials Accountable through Dialogue: Resolving the Accountability Paradox." *Public Administration Review* 62(6): 658–69.

Roberts, Nancy. 2004. "Public Deliberation in an Age of Direct Citizen Participation." *American Review of Public Administration* 34(4): 315–53.

Rose, Heather, and J. R. Betts. 2001. *Math Matters: The Links between High School Curriculum, College Graduation, and Earnings*. San Francisco, Calif.: Public Policy Institute of California.

Rose, Heather, Jon Sonstelie, Ray Reinhard, and Sharmaine Heng. 2003. *High Expectations, Modest Means: The Challenge Facing California's Public Schools*. San Francisco, Calif.: Public Policy Institute of California.

Rubinfeld, Daniel L. 1977. "Voting in a Local School Election: A Micro Analysis." *Review of Economics and Statistics* 59(1): 30–42.

Sandoval, Juan Onésimo, Hans Johnson, and Sonia Tafoya. 2002. "Who's Your Neighbor? Residential Segregation and Diversity in California." *California Counts.* San Francisco, Calif.: Public Policy Institute of California.

Sears, David. 1988. "Symbolic Racism." In *Eliminating Racism: Profiles in Controversy*, ed. P. A. Katz and D. A. Taylor. New York: Plenum, 53–84.

Sears, David, and Donald Kinder. 1971. "Racial Tensions and Voting in Los Angeles." In *Los Angeles: Viability and Prospects for Metropolitan Leadership*, ed. W. Z. Hirsch. New York: Praeger, 51–88.

Sears, David, C. van Laar, M. Carrillo, and R. Kosterman. 1997. "Is It Really Racism? The Origins of White Americans' Opposition to Race-Targeted Policies." *Public Opinion Quarterly* 61:16–53.

Sears, David, J Sidanius, and Larry Bobo. 2000. *Racialized Politics: The Debate about Racism in America*. Chicago: University of Chicago Press.

Sniderman P. M., G. C. Crosby, and W. G. Howell. 2000. "The Politics of Race." In *Racialized Politics: The Debate about Racism in America,* ed. David Sears, J Sidanius, and Larry Bobo. Chicago: University of Chicago Press, 236–79.

Sonstelie, Jon, Eric Brunner, and Kenneth Ardon. 2000. *For Better or For Worse? School Finance Reform in California*. San Francisco, Calif.: Public Policy Institute of California.

Steinacker A. 2004. "Metropolitan Governance: Voter Support and State Legislative Prospects." *Publius* 34(2): 69–93.

Taebel, Delbert. 1978. "Minority Representation on City Councils." *Social Science Quarterly* 59: 142–52.

Walsh, Kate. 2001. *Teacher Certification Reconsidered: Stumbling for Quality.* Baltimore, Md.: Abell Foundation.

Welch, S. 1999. "The Impact of At-Large Elections on the Representation of Blacks and Hispanics." *Journal of Politics* 52(4): 1050–76.

Wyckoff, James H. 1984. "The Nonexcludable Publicness of Primary and Secondary Public Education." *Journal of Public Economics* 24(3): 331–52.

Chapter 12

Cumulative Disadvantage and Racial and Ethnic Disparities in California Felony Sentencing

Elsa Y. Chen[1]

Introduction

Using the framework of cumulative disadvantage theory, this chapter examines the extent to which racial and ethnic disparities emerge and either remain steady or increase as white, black, and Latino individuals proceed through several successive stages of the California criminal justice system, including arrest, trial, conviction, and sentencing. The analysis finds that whites are underrepresented in proportion to their share of the population, while African Americans and Latinos are overrepresented, throughout the criminal justice process. However, the pattern of overrepresentation differs for blacks and Latinos. Consistent with the theory of cumulative disadvantage, the gap between African Americans and whites grows steadily from one stage to the next in the criminal justice process. In contrast, the gap between Latinos and whites remains stable, which suggests that Latinos experience continuous, rather than cumulative, disadvantage.

The analysis then turns to explanations for the observed gaps. Disparities in outcomes may actually be the result of interracial or interethnic differences in rates

[1] The author thanks Brandi-Ann Tanaka for research assistance and the Santa Clara University Faculty Development Program for funding.

and types of criminal offending. Therefore, data on individual offenders are analyzed to determine the degree to which observed disparities are explained by differences between racial and ethnic groups in variables that are regarded as "legally relevant," such as the offenses for which defendants are convicted, the number of prior offenses on their criminal records, and the type of attorney representing defendants in court. The analysis finds that disparities persist between black and white defendants in sentencing outcomes after controlling for legally relevant factors. This is consistent with the idea that discrimination remains present to some extent in the sentencing of African-American felony defendants. The findings are less clear for Latinos, who are not found to be sentenced to prison disproportionately once several legally relevant factors are controlled, but do appear to receive significantly longer sentences than whites.

The findings indicate that whites, blacks, and Latinos, in the aggregate, experience advantage or disadvantage in the criminal justice system very differently. African Americans are not only more likely to encounter worse outcomes than Latinos on a consistent basis, but in line with cumulative disadvantage theory, negative outcomes seem to lead to more severe future consequences for African Americans as well.

Theoretical Framework: Cumulative Disadvantage

The concept of cumulative advantage has its origins in the literature on the history of science. In his seminal paper published in the journal *Science*, sociologist Robert Merton describes what he terms the "Matthew Effect" in scientific careers, referring to the passage in the Biblical book of Matthew that states: "For unto every one that hath shall be given, but from him that hath not shall be taken away even what he hath" (Merton 1968). Merton finds a pattern of divergence in scientific careers: resources and recognition tend to be allocated disproportionately to researchers who are already prominent, while lesser-known scientists receive less credit and fewer rewards for comparable accomplishments (Merton 1968).

Over the past four decades, the concept of cumulative advantage or disadvantage has been applied in disparate academic fields, including labor economics, public health, medical sociology, gerontology, class and poverty research, and criminology (Dannefer 2003; DiPrete and Eirich 2006; O'Rand 1996). A common thread among the wide range of studies is the finding that existing inequalities between subsets of a cohort diverge even further over time. For example, gaps in health outcomes between individuals with high, moderate, and low levels of education grow progressively wider as members of a cohort become older (Ross and Wu 1996). Income and wealth inequalities between the well-educated and less-educated have been found to increase with age (O'Rand 1996). Recent studies find a comparable dynamic among racial groups as stratification in health status diverges over the life course: blacks experience elevated rates of hospitalization compared to whites, and these differences become amplified later in life (Ferraro et al. 2006), and black women were nearly twice as likely to die at a young age than white women (Caputo 2004), even when other important predictors are controlled.

Cumulative disadvantage theory has been cited in the criminal justice literature as well, particularly in works focusing on delinquency and life course. Sampson and Laub explain that those who engage in delinquent behavior face increasingly diminished chances of success throughout their life course: delinquency "may spark failure in school, incarceration, and weak bonds to the labor market, in turn increasing later adult crime" (Sampson and Laub 1997). A criminal record eliminates certain employment opportunities, including several that require union memberships, bond coverage, or licenses; thus, for those with few legitimate alternatives, the relative appeal of illicit sources of income may increase (Sampson and Laub 1997). Furthermore, participation in crime may lead to arrest and incarceration, which may in turn result in a wide range of consequences, such as the interruption of education, the loss of employment and earnings, discontinuity in housing, disruption of medical care and changes in health status, weakening of family ties, and diminished opportunities for marriage and parenthood (Mauer and Chesney-Lind 2002; Petersilia 2003; Travis and Petersilia 2001; Travis and Waul 2003). In short, the effects of delinquent behavior can snowball into life-altering consequences.

Furthermore, delinquency, crime, and their associated sanctions may produce greater adverse effects among lower-class individuals than among those with more "social capital," who usually possess greater resources or mechanisms to cope with "negative life events" (Sampson and Laub 1997). As Sampson and Laub (1997, 23) put it, "the probability of adolescent risks becoming transmuted into adverse adult circumstances is greatest among those in disadvantaged racial and economic situations." On the other hand, contrary to the pattern predicted by cumulative disadvantage theory, Hannon (2003) finds that delinquent behavior has a more detrimental impact on educational attainment for upper-middle-class youth than for poor youth (Hannon 2003). This supports an alternative hypothesis, "disadvantage saturation," which reasons that chances for success are already so dismal for many highly disadvantaged youth that a label of "delinquent" or "nondelinquent" makes little difference in their chances for success.

These competing hypotheses may apply not only to class disparities, but also to racial disparities. In line with the notion of cumulative disadvantage, Pager (2003) finds that the presence of a record of prior imprisonment harms employment prospects for all job applicants, but that African Americans are harmed more than whites (Pager 2003). Considering that initial job prospects for black applicants are already worse than those for whites (in fact, Pager's experimental study found that black applicants *without* criminal records had lower chances for employment than whites *with* criminal records), a criminal conviction makes it difficult for whites to secure gainful and legitimate employment, but it presents an even greater disadvantage for blacks.

Cumulative disadvantage theory proposes that disparities between groups—such as those associated with education, class, gender, or race—do not remain constant, but rather increase as cohorts advance through a temporal process such as aging. The theory can apply not only to the life course, but also to successive stages of a system or process with multiple stages, such as professional careers (Bielby and Bielby 1992; McClelland 1990; Merton 1968; Smith-Doerr 2006). The authors of *Measuring Racial Discrimination*, a report of the National Research Council Panel on Methods for Assessing Discrimination, state: "as individuals engage in sequential interactions in the labor or housing markets or within the health care, criminal justice, or education systems, discriminatory experiences may have cumulative effects" (Blank, Dabady, and Citro 2004). Although disparities may seem small or nonexistent in studies that look only at one stage of a system, they can cumulate in several ways: over successive generations; across processes within a domain, such as throughout an individual's educational experience from early childhood through high school or later; or across domains, e.g., education can affect employment, which can affect health and housing (Blank, Dabady, and Citro 2004).

Moreover, the sum of successive experiences of disadvantage or discrimination may exceed the constituent parts. This may be due to "feedback effects" such as diminished or enhanced expectations of success or failure that can lead to behavioral changes (such as not pursuing educational or employment opportunities) or perceptions (such as racial profiling by law enforcement officers or juries) and may generate self-fulfilling prophecies (Blank, Dabady, and Citro 2004).

While past studies have discussed the effects of criminal justice experiences on other aspects of ex-offenders' lives, this chapter will focus on cumulative disadvantage from one process to another *within* the criminal justice system. The theory may offer an accurate characterization of what occurs as different racial and ethnic groups proceed through the criminal justice system. Disparities are likely to be present from the earliest stages of the process, with African Americans disproportionately represented among arrestees. Then, it is possible that the gap between whites and other groups widens at each successive stage of the criminal justice process.

A finding that cumulative disadvantage or cumulative discrimination exists in the criminal justice system could have important implications for policymakers. Racial and ethnic disparity may be the product of intergroup differences in behavior (such as rates of criminal offending) or other contributing factors, or discrimination by individual participants, but it may also be caused or perpetuated by institutional or organizational policies or structures (Blank, Dabady, and Citro 2004; Blumstein 2001; Caputo 2004; Kennedy 2001). As such, public institutions can potentially play an active role in monitoring and reducing or mitigating racial and ethnic inequalities that are found to exist within their jurisdictions (Blank 2005).

Methodology and Data

The analysis in this chapter comprises two main sections. The first section seeks to quantify and map out the degree of disparity in outcomes experienced by African Americans, whites, and Latinos at several stages of the criminal justice process, to see whether observed patterns fit those that cumulative disadvantage theory would predict.[2] Statistics for each of these three racial and ethnic categories are fitted to a flowchart that diagrams each step of the process, from arrest through incarceration. A cumulative disadvantage model is also designed with progress through the criminal justice system treated as a "life course" and a comparison of the trajectories of blacks, whites, and Latinos as they move through the system.

In the second section, regression analyses are used to determine the extent to which the disparities observed in the flowchart are explained by racial and ethnic differences in legally relevant factors such as the severity of the crime and the defendant's prior criminal record. The analyses in this section test some of the prevailing hypotheses that have been offered to explain racial and ethnic disparities in sentencing outcomes.

The analyses are performed on data from several stages of the criminal justice system in a single state, California. As Auerhahn notes in her 2003 study of incarceration in California, the United States criminal justice "system" can, and should, be thought of as "fifty-one independent systems (i.e., the states and the federal system)," each carrying out its own laws and the policy decisions of its own legislators (Auerhahn 2003). Significant state-to-state variation also exists in racial and ethnic composition of populations, race relations, and rates of arrest and imprisonment (Hawkins and Hardy 1989). In the analyses here, state-level statistics allow for a broad understanding of the extent to which racial and ethnic disparities emerge throughout the California criminal justice system, while individual level data enable rigorous hypothesis testing using regression models that include key control variables.

The data used in this chapter are gathered from a variety of sources. The State Court Processing Statistics (SCPS) data collection program, administered by the United States Department of Justice, Bureau of Justice Statistics, is the source of the data used for most of the cross tabulations and regression analyses. The SCPS data include criminal case adjudication type and outcome, attorney type, current offense category, the number and nature of prior convictions, and sentence type and length, as well as defendants' race and Hispanic/Latino origin. This program "tracks felony cases filed in May of even-numbered years until their final disposition or until one year has elapsed from the date of filing" (U.S. Department of Justice 2004). The year 2000 SCPS dataset for Felony Defendants in Large Urban Counties provides individual offender-level judicial processing statistics for a

---

[2] Data were also available for a fourth category, labeled "other." Many of the individuals categorized as "other" are Asians or Pacific Islanders, but the category also includes Native Americans and persons whose race is not determined or recorded. Because it is not particularly instructive to draw conclusions about "other," this category is excluded from the analyses in this paper.

stratified sample of 40 of the 75 most populous counties in the United States, including nine California counties (U.S. Department of Justice 2004).[3]

Additional data on arrests, including the race and ethnicity of arrestees statewide, are obtained from the *Crime in California* reports, compiled by the Criminal Justice Statistics Center within the California Department of Justice (Criminal Justice Statistics Center 2005). These statistics are collected and submitted annually by local police departments and most of the information is eventually incorporated into the FBI's Uniform Crime Reports. Data on the size and racial and ethnic composition of California's prison population are obtained from reports published by the Data Analysis Unit, Offender Information Services Branch, of the California Department of Corrections and Rehabilitation (California Department of Corrections and Rehabilitation 2005).

Limitations of the Data

The optimal dataset for a rigorous test of cumulative disadvantage theory would be longitudinal, consisting of multiple observations, recorded at specific time intervals, for a large cohort of individuals (Blank 2005; Blank, Dabady, and Citro 2004). However, data on cohorts moving through the criminal justice system are rare. In the absence of appropriate longitudinal data, multiple successive cross-sections are sufficient for initial tests to determine whether real-world observations yield findings consistent with what cumulative disadvantage theory would predict (Blank 2005). A second limitation pertains to the findings' generalizeability. The analyses here are conducted on data from the state of California. Because each state's criminal justice system operates separately from those of other states, conclusions based on any single state may not be applicable to other states. California is one of the most racially and ethnically diverse states in the nation, with the second-highest Latino population and the third-lowest proportion of residents reporting their race as white in the 2000 census (Grieco 2001; Guzman 2001). Although this makes the state unrepresentative of the rest of the nation, it provides a "natural laboratory" well-suited to the study of racial and ethnic dynamics. Furthermore, California is the most populous state in the U.S., with about 36.5 million residents, representing about 12% of the United States' population (United States Census Bureau 2006). Only five nations (including the United States) have gross national products exceeding California's gross state product (Office 2004). With over 166,500 inmates in 2005, California is home to the nation's second-largest prison population (Harrison and Beck

[3] The nine counties are Alameda, Contra Costa, Los Angeles, Orange, Riverside, San Bernadino, San Diego, San Mateo, and Santa Clara counties. Details on the process of selecting counties for the stratified sample can be found in the Bureau of Justice Statistics report, "Felony Defendants in Large Urban Counties, 2002," Thomas H. Cohen and Brian A. Reaves. 2006. Felony Defendants in Large Urban Counties, 2002. Washington, D.C.: U.S. Department of Justice, Bureau of Justice Statistics.

2006). Thus, an analysis of California is important on its own. Furthermore, criminal justice policy innovations adopted in the state, such as "Three Strikes and You're Out," "Truth in Sentencing," and drug treatment diversion programs (e.g., "Proposition 36"), often spread to other parts of the nation (Austin et al. 1996; Rinaldo and Kelly-Thomas 2005; Turner et al. 2001).

Findings and Discussion

The Flow of Disparity throughout the California Criminal Justice System

An examination of the entire criminal justice system helps to shed light on how and where sentencing disparities develop. Figure 1 below offers a systemic view of the extent to which African-American, white, and Latino individuals experience certain outcomes at different rates throughout the criminal justice process. The percentages presented in the diagram indicate the proportions of whites (W), blacks (B), and Latinos (L) advancing from each stage of the criminal justice system to the subsequent step. It is clear from this flow chart that racial and ethnic disparities surface at every major stage, starting with arrests, and proceeding through the filing or dismissal of charges, guilty plea, or trial for those against whom charges are filed, conviction or acquittal, and sentencing, including jail and prison. The percentages are calculated using the data on California from *State Court Processing Statistics, 1990–2000: Felony Defendants in Large Urban Counties* (U.S. Department of Justice 2004). This evidence demonstrates that ethnic and racial disparities are prevalent throughout the California criminal justice system, rather than isolated in any one stage of the process.

Table 1 below is a complement to Figure 1; it summarizes the proportions of African Americans, Latinos, and whites represented in the state population and at several stages of the California criminal justice system.

Disparities in Arrest

The criminal justice process illustrated in Figure 1 begins upon arrest of a suspect. Blacks and Latinos in California are arrested in disproportionate numbers compared to their share of the population. As shown in Table 1, African Americans represent about 6.2% of the adult population in California, but they make up over 21% of the adult felony arrests. Latinos, who constitute about 28% of the adult population, make up about 38% of the adult felony arrestees. These disproportionalities may exist for several reasons. First, arrests may be higher for certain populations because they may offend at higher rates. Alternatively, some law enforcement officers may be more prone to arrest minority suspects due to personal biases that lead them to be more suspicious of minorities. Sus-

Figure 1. Flowchart of Criminal Justice Process with Conditional Percentages of White (W), Black (B), and Latino (L) Adult Felony Arrestees Experiencing Each Outcome

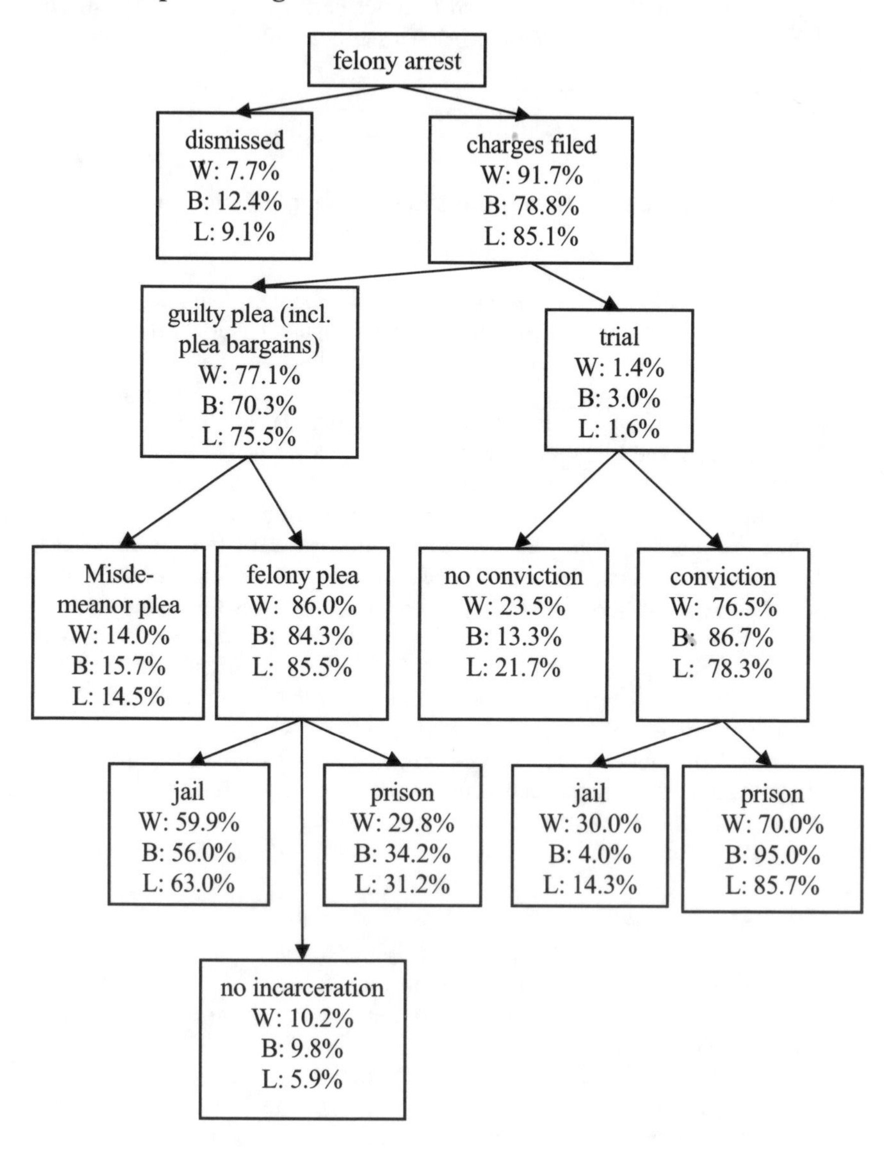

Data from State Court Processing Statistics, 1990–2000, California subsample.

Table 1. Representation of Blacks, Whites, and Latinos at Different Stages of the Criminal Justice System

	% Black	% White	% Latino
Adult population[1]	6.2	51.1	28.1
Adult felony arrestees[2]	21.2	35.5	38.1
All trials[†]	25.2	31.0	37.8
Jury trials[†]	47.5	19.7	31.1
Defendants convicted at trial[†]	31.4	24.1	34.6
Defendants sentenced to incarceration[†]	23.9	31.3	39.4
Defendants sentenced to prison[†]	27.8	30.5	38.5
Adult prison population[3]	28.9	28.4	37

[†] Calculated using State Court Processing Statistics data.

[1] United States Census Bureau, 2004. *Resident Population by Race, Hispanic or Latino Origin, and State: 2003,* 2003 [cited September 30, 2004].

[2] Criminal Justice Statistics Center, California Department of Justice. 2005. Crime in California, Table 31: Gender and Race/Ethnic Group of Felony Arrestees, 2003. Sacramento, Calif.: California Department of Justice, Division of California Justice Information Services, Bureau of Criminal Information and Analysis, Criminal Justice Statistics Center.

[3] California Department of Corrections and Rehabilitation. 2005. Prison Census Data as of June 30, 2005, Table 4: Total Institution Population, Offenders by Ethnicity and Gender. Sacramento, Calif.: California Department of Corrections and Rehabilitation, Offender Information Services, Estimates and Statistical Analysis Section, Data Analysis Unit.

pects who commit certain types of crimes may also be easier targets for the police. For example, street criminals like drug dealers may be easier to detect and arrest than white-collar criminals. To the extent that racial groups are represented disproportionately among crime types, these would be reflected in arrest rates.

Disparities in Case Filings and Dismissals

Charges are filed against 92% of white felony arrestees, as compared to 79% and 85% of black and Latino arrestees, respectively. Charges are least likely to be dismissed for white arrestees (8%), and most likely to be dismissed for black arrestees (12%). Latino arrestees fall in between; 9% of their arrests result in dismissed charges.

Studies have found that criminal charges are more likely to be dismissed for African-American arrestees than for white arrestees (Free 2003; Petersilia 1983; Petersilia 1985). The present study corroborates these findings. As seen in Figure 1, cases are dismissed with no charges filed for 12% of black felony arrestees, compared with 9% of Latino arrestees and 8% of white arrestees. At first, elevated numbers of dropped charges may appear to be an indicator of leniency. However, many researchers cite statistics like these as evidence that the police are more willing to arrest innocent minorities despite insufficient grounds to file charges or as a result of racial profiling (Batton and Kadleck 2004; Cole 1999; Free 2003). Using prison inmates' self-reports of crimes committed and past arrests, a 1985 RAND survey found that the probability of arrest for any given criminal offense was extremely low, and that there was no significant difference between blacks, Latinos, and whites in their likelihood of arrest relative to the number of crimes they actually committed, except in the case of personal robbery. For that offense, black and Latino offenders were more likely to be arrested (Petersilia 1985). For other offenses, however, elevated arrest rates for African Americans may represent some degree of "overarresting" by the police.

On the other hand, some scholars find no evidence of systematic discrimination against African Americans by law enforcement officers. They conclude that high arrest rates for blacks are primarily a reflection of disproportionately high rates of criminal offending among African Americans, which may, in turn, result from a variety of social factors such as economic deprivation, family structure, or segregation (D'Alessio and Stolzenberg 2003). A vast literature exists on the correlation between race and violence (Gabbidon, Greene, and Young 2002; Hawkins 2003; McNulty and Bellair 2003; Peterson and Krivo 2005; Velez, Krivo, and Peterson 2003), but a thorough discussion of this issue is beyond the scope of the present investigation.

An alternative or additional explanation is that victims or witnesses may be less able or willing to describe or identify minority suspects, which makes it difficult for prosecutors to gather sufficient evidence to proceed with criminal charges (Petersilia 1985). This may be particularly true when victims live in the same neighborhoods as the offenders. Fear of retaliation, combined with a sentiment of disdain for "snitches," or informers who cooperate with the police, may silence potential witnesses (Heredia 2006; Miller 1996; Walker 2005).

Without data on underlying rates of criminal offending by race and ethnicity, it is not possible to draw detailed conclusions about the extent to which the disparities in arrest are linked to differences in criminality. However, the overrepresentation of African Americans, and to a lesser degree, Latinos, among the adult felony arrestee population indicates that disparities at the arrest stage account for some of the disproportionality between blacks, whites, and Latinos that is eventually observed in sentencing outcomes, and the comparatively high proportion of dismissed charges for black and Latino arrestees is consistent with the idea that individuals in these groups get "overarrested" by law enforcement authorities.

Disparities in Guilty Pleas, Trials, and Convictions

Among arrestees against whom charges are filed, 77% of white felony defendants plead guilty, in comparison with 70% of black defendants and 76% of Latino defendants. Among those who enter a guilty plea, the proportion of those pleading guilty to a felony is roughly the same among whites (86%), blacks (84%), and Latinos (86%). The remainder of the defendants who pleaded guilty did so to misdemeanor charges, indicating that they had negotiated plea bargain terms.[4] Very few cases proceed to trial, but the proportion of black defendants who proceed to a jury or bench trial (3%) is more than double the proportion of white defendants who do so (1.4%), and nearly twice the percentage of Latino defendants who go to trial (1.6%).[5] Among defendants who opt for a trial, black defendants have the highest rate of conviction (87%), compared to Latinos (78% convicted) and whites (77%).

African Americans may experience more punitive sentencing outcomes because they are more likely than whites to be tried before juries than to plea bargain (Sidanius 1988). This could be due to negative perceptions of plea bargaining among African Americans, or to prosecutors' reluctance to offer attractive plea deals to minority defendants. Disparities in the proportion of defendants who opt for jury trials are important because individuals convicted by juries tend to receive longer sentences than those who plead guilty, regardless of race. Moreover, juries may be even more punitive towards minority defendants for several reasons, including discriminatory jury selection processes or biased attitudes held by individual jurors (Kennedy 2001).

Disparities in Sentencing

African Americans who are convicted by trial are more likely to be sentenced to prison (95%) than Latinos (86%) or whites (70%). A less severe sentence of jail time, with or without probation, was imposed on only 4% of black felons who were convicted by trial, as opposed to 14% of the Latino convicted felons and 30% of whites who were convicted.[6] Felony defendants who plead guilty tend to receive more lenient sentences than those who are convicted by trial. Even among those who plead guilty, however, African Americans are more likely to receive prison sentences (34%) than Latinos (31%) or whites (29%), and they

[4] Some of the defendants who pleaded guilty to felony charges may also have accepted plea bargains; the data do not provide sufficient detail to determine the proportion of defendants who did so.

[5] The percentages of trials and dismissals do not total 100% because other outcomes are also represented in the data, albeit in small numbers. These include acquittal, diversion or deferral, and cases still awaiting pending results.

[6] Jail sentences are typically less than one year in length and served in a local facility, while prison terms are one year or longer and served in a state correctional facility.

are less likely than either other group to be sentenced to jail terms without prison (56% of blacks, 60% of whites, 63% of Latinos). Latino defendants who plead guilty are the least likely to receive sentences that include no incarceration (6% of Latinos vs. 10% of blacks and 10% of whites), but most likely to be sentenced to jail.[7]

The data in Figure 1 illustrate clearly that African Americans are more likely to experience harsher criminal justice outcomes than whites at several stages of the criminal justice process. Outcomes for Latinos in the criminal justice system compare unfavorably to those for whites, but are not as severe as those for blacks, at most points in the process.

Evidence of Cumulative Disadvantage

The above discussion demonstrates the consistency with which African Americans, whites, and Latinos experience disparate outcomes at multiple points throughout the criminal justice process. Next, we investigate whether the disparity experienced by African Americans and Latinos is continuous or cumulative.

A graphical illustration provides further perspective. In Figure 2 below, the X-axis tracks four major stages in the "life course" of a criminal case: arrest, trial, conviction, and sentencing (to imprisonment). The Y-axis represents a measure of "representativeness" or "proportionality": it is the ratio calculated by dividing the percentage of each group represented in the cross-section by the group's proportion of the general population. As shown in Table 1, for felony arrestees, African Americans represent 17% of the arrestee population, and 6% of the general population, so the Y-value for African Americans in the first cross-section is 17 divided by 6, or 2.83. Whites represent 51.1% of the population and 40% of arrestees, so their Y-value is 40 divided by 51.1, or 0.78. The lines for each group can be interpreted as trajectories of advantage or disadvantage as the groups proceed through the criminal justice system.

Two key observations can be made by examining Figure 2. First, whites, Latinos, and blacks have very different "starting points," and their trajectories remain separated as the three groups move through the system. Whites are consistently underrepresented by a factor of about one-third to one-half. Latinos are consistently overrepresented by about one-quarter to two-fifths. But the gap between whites and Latinos is far smaller than that between African Americans and either group. Blacks are overrepresented among arrestees by a factor of about three and a half, and among defendants going to trial by a factor of about four. Their share of defendants convicted of felonies is more than five times their share of the population, and their share of those sentenced to prison is about four and a half times their share of the population.

Second, the trajectories for the three groups are not parallel. Whites and Latinos have roughly flat trajectories, with whites consistently underrepresented in

---

[7] The "no incarceration" category includes probation, fines, and "other" sentences.

Figure 2. Comparison of Trajectories through the Criminal Justice System for African Americans, Whites, and Latinos

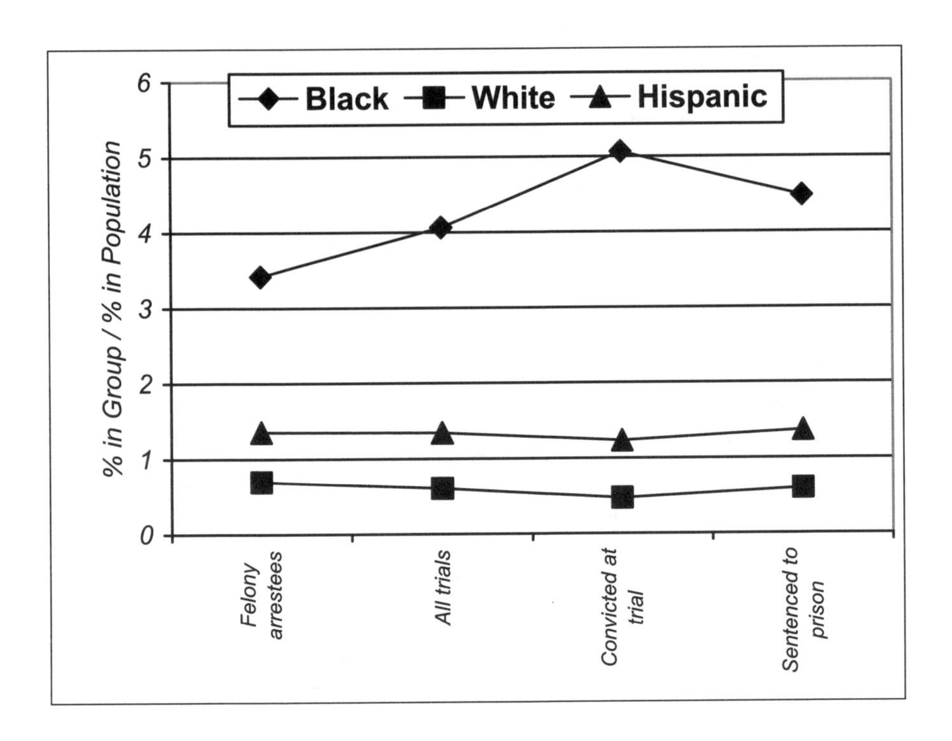

comparison to their share of the population and Latinos consistently overrepresented. Blacks start out highly overrepresented and the gap between blacks and the other groups grows from arrest to trial to conviction, shrinking slightly for the cross-section of the population of those receiving prison sentences. In the language of cumulative disadvantage theory, whites seem to experience continuous advantage as they move through the system, Latinos' path is consistent with a pattern of continuous disadvantage, and blacks follow a trajectory indicating cumulative disadvantage.

Impacts of Legal vs. Extralegal Factors

Studies by researchers from RAND recognize the apparent overrepresentation of black and Latino inmates in California's prison population, but find that with only a few exceptions, racial disparities in sentencing outcome and length disappear almost entirely when variables such as crime committed and prior criminal record are factored into analyses (Klein, Petersilia, and Turner 1990; Petersilia 1985). These findings are tested here using current data from California.

Two regression analyses are conducted to determine whether race and ethnicity still influence sentencing after current offense, prior record, and other potentially relevant variables are taken into consideration. The first model is a logistic regression in which a dichotomous dependent variable represents whether or not the defendant was sentenced to incarceration. This is known as the "in/out" variable in the sentencing research literature (Demuth and Steffensmeier 2004; Klein, Petersilia, and Turner 1990; Spohn, Gruhl, and Welch 1981–82). In the parlance of economists who study criminal deterrence theory, the "in/out" variable measures the "certainty" of punishment (Becker 1968; Cameron 1988; Ehrlich 1973; Grogger 1991; Nagin 1978; Yu and Liska 1993). The second model is a log-linear regression in which the dependent variable is the log-transformed length of the prison term to which the defendant is sentenced. In contrast to the "certainty" variable, this dependent variable measures sentence "severity." Prison sentence length is a continuous variable with values ranging from eight to 348 months. The values for sentence length in months are clustered toward the lower end of the variable's distribution, with a long tail to the right (median = 24.0 months, mean = 40.1 months with a standard deviation of 50.96, skewness = 10.92 with $p < 0.05$). Therefore, this variable is log-transformed in order to resemble a normal distribution more closely. Demuth and Steffensmeier (2004) use the same dependent variables, but different independent variables, in an investigation using a national sample of State Court Processing Statistics data from the years 1990–1996.

Each of these two models includes the following independent variables:

Legally relevant variables:

- County of conviction (dummy variables for nine California counties)[8]
- Most serious conviction charge (dummy variables for 18 separate offense categories)
- Total number of arrest charges
- Defendant's criminal justice status at time of arrest: dummy variables for arrestee on probation and arrestee on parole
- Type of attorney: dummy variables for public defender, private attorney, assigned counsel, and self-representation
- Dummy variable for pretrial detention, i.e., defendant not released on bail
- Number of prior misdemeanor convictions
- Dummy variable representing one or more prior adult felony convictions for violent offense
- Dummy variable representing bench trial (i.e., a trial before a judge)
- Dummy variable representing jury trial
- Dummy variable for plea bargain

[8] Since criminal courts are organized at the county level and the prosecutors and judges in different counties abide by different standard operating procedures, this is a legally relevant variable.

Extralegal variables:

- Dummy variable for black
- Dummy variable for Latino
- Interaction variables:
  - Dummy variable for black * Dummy variable for bench trial
  - Dummy variable for Latino * Dummy variable for bench trial
  - Dummy variable for black * Dummy variable for jury trial
  - Dummy variable for Latino * Dummy variable for jury trial
- (Reference variables for guilty plea and non-Latino white omitted)
- Dummy variable for male

Interaction variables between race or ethnicity and adjudication method are included, in addition to the main effects of race and trial type, because recent research suggests that plea bargaining and jury trials produce different outcomes for black, Latino, and white individuals (Johnson 2003).

Several conclusions can be drawn from the results of the regression analyses. First, as shown in the upper portion of Table 2, most of the legally relevant variables included in these models do exert statistically significant impacts on both the decision to incarcerate and the length of the prison sentence that is imposed upon those sentenced to prison. Variables with statistically significant impacts on both in/out decision and sentence length include conviction charge, total number of charges, criminal justice status at the time of arrest (i.e., probation or parole), pretrial detention in jail, the total number of prior misdemeanor charges, and jury trial. Defendants who are tried before judges face higher odds of being sent to prison compared to those who plead guilty, but no statistically significant increase or decrease in sentence length.

The analysis finds that the type of attorney representing a defendant has no significant bearing on either the in/out decision or the sentence length. Among the individuals included in this data sample, 61% of black defendants are represented by public defenders, compared with 56% of Latino defendants, and only 48% of white defendants. The proportion of white defendants who hire private attorneys (16%) is more than twice that for black defendants (8%), while Latino defendants fall in between, but closer to whites, with 14% represented by private attorneys. However, differences in type of legal representation matter only if the quality of representation varies commensurately. According to criminologist Coramae Richey Mann, "the quality of service provided by assigned counsel is generally thought not to be as high as that of privately retained counsel," due to factors such as the relative inexperience of assigned attorneys or the low fees generated by assigned cases (Mann 1993). This does not seem to be true among the individuals in our sample, though: conviction rates are higher for defendants who retain private attorneys (90% convicted) and those with assigned attorneys (92% convicted) than for those with public defenders (89% convicted). Unexpectedly, conviction rates are lowest (73%) for the very few defendants who represent themselves, but because only 15 individuals fell into this category, this estimate is less reliable than the others. This pattern held true for all but two of the nine California coun-

Table 2. Regression Results
Dependent Variable = Prison Sentence In/Out and Sentence Length in Months[1]

	Model 1: Logistic Regression Prison Sentence In/Out				Model 2: OLS Reg. Ln (sentence in mo.)			
	Odds ratio (e^B)	Wald χ^2	d.f.	Sig.	B	SE	Sig.	e^B
Constant	0.00	0.00	1	0.987	3.22	6.07	0.595	25.15
County	†				†			
Most serious conviction charge	†				†			
Total number of charges	1.09	14.06	1	0.000	0.03	0.01	0.000	1.03
On probation at time of arrest	1.68	22.04	1	0.000	0.14	0.03	0.000	1.15
On parole at time of arrest	0.33	46.55	1	0.000	-0.07	0.03	0.023	0.93
Type of attorney: public defender	0.56	1.91	1	0.167	-0.09	0.06	0.126	0.91
Type of attorney: private	0.87	0.10	1	0.748	0.08	0.08	0.288	1.08
Type of attorney: assigned	0.70	0.59	1	0.444	-0.09	0.08	0.258	0.91
(Reference: self-represented/other)								
Detained in jail before trial	4.89	140.47	1	0.000	0.14	0.06	0.017	1.15
Prior misdemeanor convictions	1.12	33.16	1	0.000	-0.01	0.01	0.054	0.99
Prior adult felony conviction for violent offense	0.79	55.70	1	0.000	0.01	0.01	0.489	1.01
Bench trial	8.54	3.83	1	0.050	0.41	0.32	0.189	1.51
Jury trial	8.00	2.93	1	0.087	1.04	0.32	0.001	2.82

	Model 1: Logistic Regression Prison Sentence In/Out				Model 2: OLS Reg. Ln (sentence in mo.)			
	Odds ratio (e^B)	**Wald χ^2**	**d.f.**	**Sig.**	**B**	**SE**	**Sig.**	**e^B**
Male	1.42	5.57	1	0.018	0.15	0.06	0.011	1.16
Black	1.26	2.52	1	0.112	0.11	0.05	0.023	1.12
Latino	1.02	0.02	1	0.882	0.12	0.05	0.006	1.13
(Reference: white)								
Interaction var: jury trial * black	2.71	0.36	1	0.550	1.20	0.15	0.000	3.33
Interaction var: jury trial * Hisp.	3.10	0.45	1	0.502	0.72	0.19	0.000	2.06
Interaction var: bench trial * black	$2.13*10^8$	0.00	1	1.000	0.61	0.54	0.264	1.84
Interaction var: bench trial * Hisp.	0.97	0.00	1	0.986	0.07	0.32	0.823	1.07
n	3458				884			
Cox & Snell r^2	0.37							
Nagelkerke r^2	0.55							
r^2					0.23			

[†]Individual coefficients were calculated for dummy variables representing each value of these categorical variables. Coefficients are omitted from this table.

[1]Because life sentences are difficult to quantify in months, individuals sentenced to life were not included in the data used in this analysis. Maximum sentences of life in prison were imposed on only 11 of the 925 offenders for whom maximum sentences were available.

ties included in this analysis.[9] It is possible that these results arise because defendants may choose different types of representation based on their perceived chances of success in court, and private attorneys are sought by those who face the direst consequences and lowest odds of success. Another explanation for public defenders' lower conviction rates compared to private or assigned attorneys is that, contrary to conventional wisdom, they may provide higher quality representation for many criminal cases, due to factors such as experience working with certain prosecutors, judges, and even clients on an ongoing basis (O'Connor 2006).

The county of arrest significantly influences the in/out decision, but not the sentence length. In California, district attorneys are elected at the county level and have the authority to implement internal policies regarding the charging of cases, including "wobblers," offenses that may be charged as either felonies, which carry prison terms, or misdemeanors, which carry sentences of jail, fines, or both (Legislative Analyst's Office 2005; Ricciardulli 2002). This may influence the rate of prison sentencing. Furthermore, juries may be more or less inclined to convict due to variations in local attitudes toward crime and punishment. On the other hand, sentence lengths may vary less between counties: once charges are filed, the attached sentences are constrained by the determinate sentencing system in place in California.

Another variable that does not significantly increase the odds of imprisonment or sentence length is the variable representing at least one prior adult felony conviction for a violent offense. This finding is a bit surprising, as one might expect this variable to influence sentence length. The lack of an observed effect may be the result of a high degree of heterogeneity among the repeat violent offenders for whom this variable is coded "1."

The effects of the extralegal variables are displayed in the lower portion of Table 2. The results from the logistic regression (Model 1) demonstrate that race and ethnicity do not appear to have an effect on the "in/out" decision to sentence an offender to prison, when legally relevant variables such as current offense and prior record are controlled. None of the odds ratios associated with the race and ethnicity variables is statistically significant. However, black and Latino defendants who are sent to prison tend to receive longer sentences when they are tried before juries. The variables representing interactions between jury trial and both black and Latino are significant at the $p < .001$ level. Because the dependent variable, sentence length, in the log-linear regression (Model 2) is natural-log-transformed, the antilog of the estimated coefficient represents the actual effect of a unit change in the independent variable on sentence length in months. This value is shown in the rightmost column of Table 2, labeled "e^B." With any type of adjudication, African-American and Latino defendants receive sentences that are about

[9] Conviction rates were higher for those represented by private attorneys than for public defenders in Alameda, Contra Costa, Los Angeles, Orange, and San Bernardino counties. The reverse was true in Riverside and Santa Clara counties. No defendants were represented by public defenders in San Mateo County, and data on adjudication outcomes were available for only seven defendants, all of whom were convicted, in San Diego County.

12 to 13% longer than prison terms handed down to whites. These differences help to explain why African Americans and Latinos are disproportionately represented in the prison population.

In addition to the main effects of race and ethnicity, African Americans who are convicted in jury trials receive prison sentences that are 3.3 times longer, and Latinos who are convicted by juries receive sentences that are 2.1 times as long. These findings are consistent with the possibility that either individual discrimination by jurors, or institutional discrimination in the process of jury selection, leads to more severe sentencing outcomes for minority defendants who are tried by jury. In comparison, bench trials (conducted before judges rather than juries) do not result in statistically significant disparities in either the likelihood of prison incarceration or the length of prison sentences for black defendants. Unlike juries, judges do not appear to let defendants' race or ethnicity influence their sentencing decisions.

Male defendants face approximately 42% higher odds of a prison sentence than female defendants, and the sentences that men receive are about 16% longer than those for women, even when current offense, prior record, and other factors are controlled. There are many potential explanations for this, including the perception that female offenders are less threatening, the belief that women would fare worse than men in prison, and practical considerations such as concerns regarding the care of female inmates' custodial children (Steffensmeier, Kramer, and Streifel 1993; Steffensmeier, Ulmer, and Kramer 1998).

Conclusion

A detailed flow diagram of the criminal justice process in California shows clearly that African Americans, whites, and Latinos consistently experience highly disparate outcomes from arrest through criminal charging, plea bargaining or trial, and sentencing. Criminal charges against African Americans are more likely to be dismissed, which may be interpreted as evidence of leniency, but could alternatively indicate that black suspects are disproportionately arrested without adequate evidence to proceed in court. Blacks are about twice as likely as whites or Latinos to go to trial rather than plea bargaining, and they are most likely of the three groups to be convicted. Whether they plead guilty to a felony or are convicted by a judge or jury, African Americans are more likely than Latinos or whites to be sentenced to incarceration in prison. Latinos fall in between blacks and whites in their rates of charges filed, plea bargains, trials, conviction, and incarceration in prison.

Gaps between white, Latinos, and African Americans exist from arrest onwards. A look at the degree of disproportionality experienced by the three groups as they proceed through the system indicates that Latinos and blacks experience disadvantage differently. Relative to whites, Latinos appear to experience continuous disadvantage, with a relatively constant level of overrepresentation from arrest through imprisonment, while African Americans' trajectory is consistent with a pattern of cumulative disadvantage. The gap between blacks and the other two groups, especially whites, grows from arrest through imprisonment.

When several legally relevant factors are statistically controlled, black and Latino defendants are not more likely to be sentenced to prison than whites. This suggests that some of the observed sentencing disproportionality experienced by African Americans can be attributed to differences in factors such as the types and numbers of crimes they commit, their probation or parole status, their criminal records, and their decisions to plead guilty or go to trial. On the other hand, even when current and prior offenses, criminal justice status, and adjudication type are controlled, the analysis still finds that black and Latino defendants receive significantly longer prison sentences. The disparities are particularly pronounced for defendants who are tried and sentenced by juries. African-American defendants are about twice as likely as white or Latino defendants to opt for jury trials, usually with negative results. Blacks are more likely to be convicted by juries, and once they are convicted, they receive lengthier prison terms than whites. Latinos who are convicted by juries also receive longer sentences than whites, but to a lesser extent than blacks. This suggests that bias by individual jurors or institutional discrimination (e.g., in the jury selection process) may play a role in jury sentencing. Similar disparities are not observed for bench trials, in which judges make the rulings.

Inequities that emerge from many different processes and decisions in this system add up to substantial inequalities in sentencing outcomes for Latino and especially African-American felony defendants in California. While differences in offense rates and types account for a proportion of these disparities, some degree of institutional or individual discrimination also appears to influence the composition of California's enormous criminal justice population. The integrity of the state's criminal sentencing system depends on its ability to maintain a reputation for consistency and fairness regardless of the race or ethnicity of arrestees, defendants, and inmates. The above analyses show that no single agency or organization within the criminal justice system bears sole responsibility for the racial and ethnic disparities that are observed; the flip side of this is that participants and leaders in many different agencies, organizations, and jurisdictions can contribute to efforts to reduce these disparities.

References

Auerhahn, Kathleen. 2003. *Selective Incapacitation and Public Policy: Evaluating California's Imprisonment Crisis.* Albany: State University of New York Press.

Austin, James, Michael A. Jones, Wendy Naro, and Robyn L. Cohen. 1996. National Survey of State Sentencing Structures: National Council on Crime and Delinquency.

Batton, Candice, and Colleen Kadleck. 2004. "Theoretical and Methodological Issues in Racial Profiling Research." *Police Quarterly* 7 (1): 30–65.

Becker, Gary S. 1968. "Crime and Punishment: an Economic Approach." *Journal of Political Economy* 76:169–217.

Bielby, William T., and Denise D. Bielby. 1992. "Cumulative Versus Continuous Disadvantage in an Unstructured Labor Market: Gender Differences in the Careers of Television Writers." *Work and Occupations* 19 (4): 366–86.

Blank, Rebecca M. 2005. Tracing the Economic Impact of Cumulative Discrimination. Paper read at American Economic Association annual meetings, at Philadelphia, Pa.

Blank, Rebecca M., Marilyn Dabady, and Constance F. Citro. 2004. *Measuring Racial Discrimination.* Washington, D.C.: National Academies Press.

Blumstein, Alfred. 2001. "Race and Criminal Justice." In *America Becoming: Racial Trends and Their Consequences*, ed. N. J. Smelser, W. J. Wilson, and F. Mitchell. Washington, D.C.: National Academy Press.

California Department of Corrections and Rehabilitation. 2005. Prison Census Data as of June 30, 2005, Table 4: Total Institution Population, Offenders by Ethnicity and Gender. Sacramento, Calif.: California Department of Corrections and Rehabilitation, Offender Information Services, Estimates and Statistical Analysis Section, Data Analysis Unit.

Cameron, Samuel. 1988. "The Economics of Crime Deterrence: A Survey of Theory and Evidence." *Kyklos* 41: 301–23.

Caputo, Richard K. 2004. "Women Who Die Young: The Cumulative Disadvantage of Race." *Affilia* 19 (1): 10–23.

Cohen, Thomas H., and Brian A. Reaves. 2006. *Felony Defendants in Large Urban Counties, 2002.* Washington, D.C.: U.S. Department of Justice, Bureau of Justice Statistics.

Cole, David. 1999. *No Equal Justice: Race and Class in the American Criminal Justice System.* New York: The New Press.

Criminal Justice Statistics Center, California Department of Justice. 2005. Crime in California, Table 31: Gender and Race/Ethnic Group of Felony Arrestees, 2003. Sacramento, Calif.: California Department of Justice, Division of California Justice Information Services, Bureau of Criminal Information and Analysis, Criminal Justice Statistics Center.

D'Alessio, Stewart J., and Lisa Stolzenberg. 2003. "Race and the Probability of Arrest." *Social Forces* 81 (4): 1381–97.

Dannefer, Dale. 2003. "Cumulative Advantage/Disadvantage and the Life Course: Cross-Fertilizing Age and Social Science Theory." *The Journals of Gerontology Series B: Psychological Sciences and Social Sciences* 58B (6): S327-S337.

Demuth, Stephen, and Darrell Steffensmeier. 2004. "Ethnicity Effects on Sentence Outcomes in Large Urban Courts: Comparisons among White, Black, and Hispanic Defendants." *Social Science Quarterly* 85 (4): 994–1011.

DiPrete, Thomas A., and Gregory M. Eirich. 2006. "Cumulative Advantage as a Mechanism for Inequality: A Review of Theoretical and Empirical Developments." *Annual Review of Sociology* 32: 271–97.

Ehrlich, Isaac. 1973. "Participation in Illegitimate Activities: A Theoretical and Empirical Investigation." *Journal of Political Economy* 81 (3): 521–65.

Ferraro, Kenneth F., Jr., Roland J. Thorpe, George P. McCabe, Jessica A. Kelley-Moore, and Zhen Jiang. 2006. "The Color of Hospitalization over the Adult Life Course: Cumulative Disadvantage in Black and White?" *The Journals of Gerontology Series B: Psychological Sciences and Social Sciences* 61B (6): S299–S306.

Free, Marvin D., Jr. 2003. "Race and Presentencing Decisions: The Cost of Being African American." In *Racial Issues in Criminal Justice: The Case of African Americans*, ed. M. D. J. Free. Westport, Conn.: Praeger.

Gabbidon, Shaun, Helen Taylor Greene, and Vernetta D. Young, eds. 2002. *African American Classics in Criminology & Criminal Justice*. Thousand Oaks, Calif.: Sage.

Grieco, Elizabeth M. 2001. The White Population: 2000: Census 2000 Brief. Washington, D.C.: United States Department of Commerce, Bureau of the Census.

Grogger, Jeffrey. 1991. "Certainty vs. Severity of Punishment." *Economic Inquiry* XXIX: 297–309.

Guzman, Betsy. 2001. The Hispanic Population: 2000: Census 2000 Brief. Washington, D.C.: United States Department of Commerce, Bureau of the Census.

Hannon, Lance. 2003. "Poverty, Delinquency, and Educational Attainment: Cumulative Disadvantage or Disadvantage Saturation?" *Sociological Inquiry* 73 (4): 575–94.

Harrison, Paige, and Allen J. Beck. 2006. *Prison and Jail Inmates at Midyear 2005*. Washington, D.C.: United States Department of Justice, Bureau of Justice Statistics.

Hawkins, Darnell F., ed. 2003. *Violent Crime: Assessing Race and Ethnic Differences*. Cambridge; New York: Cambridge University Press.

Hawkins, Darnell F., and Kenneth A. Hardy. 1989. "Black-White Imprisonment Rate: A State-by-State Analysis." *Social Justice* 16 (4): 75–94.

Heredia, Christopher. 2006. T-shirts Divide; "Stop Snitchin'" Stymies Police Trying to Cut Crime. *San Francisco Chronicle*, January 28, 2006, B8.

Johnson, Brian. 2003. "Racial and Ethnic Disparities in Sentencing Departures Across Modes of Conviction." *Criminology* 41 (2): 449–89.

Kennedy, Randall. 2001. "Racial Trends in the Administration of Criminal Justice." In *America Becoming: Racial Trends and Their Consequences*, ed. N. J. Smelser, W. J. Wilson, and F. Mitchell. Washington, D.C.: National Academy Press.

Klein, Stephen, Joan Petersilia, and Susan Turner. 1990. "Race and Imprisonment Decisions in California." *Science* 247 (4944): 812–16.

Mann, Coramae Richey. 1993. *Unequal Justice: A Question of Color*. Bloomington: Indiana University Press.

Mauer, Marc, and Meda Chesney-Lind, eds. 2002. *Invisible Punishment: The Collateral Consequences of Mass Imprisonment*. New York: The New Press.

McClelland, Katherine. 1990. "Cumulative Disadvantage among the Highly Ambitious." *Sociology of Education* 63 (2): 102–21.

McNulty, Thomas L., and Paul E. Bellair. 2003. "Explaining Racial and Ethnic Differences in Serious Adolescent Violent Behavior." *Criminology* 41 (3): 709–48.

Merton, Robert K. 1968. "The Matthew Effect in Science: The Reward and Communication Systems of Science Are Considered." *Science* 159 (3810): 56–63.

Miller, Jerome G. 1996. *Search and Destroy: African-American Males in the Criminal Justice System.* Cambridge: Cambridge University Press.

Nagin, Daniel S. 1978. "General Deterrence: A Review of the Empirical Evidence." In *Deterrence and Incapacitation: Estimating the Effects of Criminal Sanctions on Crime Rates*, ed. J. C. Alfred Blumstein and Daniel Nagin. Washington, D.C.: National Academy of Sciences.

O'Connor, Roderick. 2006. Personal interview with Roderick O'Connor, Esq., Santa Clara County Office of the Public Defender, edited by E. Chen. Santa Clara, Calif.

Office, California Legislative Analyst's. 2007. *Cal Facts 2004: California's Economy and Budget in Perspective* 2004 [cited July 27 2007]. Available from http://www.lao.ca.gov/2004/cal_facts/2004_calfacts_econ.htm.

O'Rand, Angela. 1996. "The Precious and Precocious: Understanding Cumulative Disadvantage and Cumulative Advantage over the Life Course." *The Gerontologist* 36 (2): 230–38.

Pager, Devah. 2003. "The Mark of a Criminal Record." *American Journal of Sociology* 108 (5): 937–75.

Petersilia, Joan. 1983. *Racial Disparities in the Criminal Justice System.* Santa Monica, Calif.: Rand.

———. 1985. "Racial Disparities in the Criminal Justice System: A Summary." *Crime and Delinquency* 3 (1): 15–34.

———. 2003. *When Prisoners Come Home*. New York: Oxford University Press.

Peterson, Ruth D., and Lauren J. Krivo. 2005. "Macrostructural Analyses of Race, Ethnicity, and Violent Crime: Recent Lessons and New Directions for Research." *Annual Review of Sociology* 31 (1): 331–57.

Rinaldo, Suzanne Gelber, and Ian Kelly-Thomas. 2005. *Comparing California's Proposition 36 (SACPA) with Similar Legislation in Other States and Jurisdictions.* Berkeley, Calif.: The Avisa Group.

Ross, Catherine E., and Chia-Ling Wu. 1996. "Education, Age, and the Cumulative Advantage in Health." *Journal of Health and Social Behavior* 37 (1): 104–20.

Sampson, Robert J., and John H. Laub. 1997. "A Life-Course Theory of Cumulative Disadvantage and the Stability of Delinquency." In *Developmental Theories of Crime and Delinquency: Advances in Criminological Theory*, ed. T. P. Thornberry. New Brunswick, N.J.: Transaction.

Sidanius, Jim. 1988. "Race and Sentence Severity: The Case of American Justice." *Journal of Black Studies* 18 (3): 273–81.

Smith-Doerr, Laurel. 2006. "Stuck in the Middle: Doctoral Education Ranking and Career Outcomes for Life Scientists." *Bulletin of Science, Technology & Society* 26 (3): 243–55.

Spohn, Cassia, John Gruhl, and Susan Welch. 1981–1982. "The Effect of Race on Sentencing: A Re-examination of an Unsettled Question." *Law & Society Review* 16 (1): 71–88.

Steffensmeier, Darrell, John Kramer, and Cathy Streifel. 1993. "Gender and Imprisonment Decisions." *Criminology* 31 (3): 411–46.

Steffensmeier, Darrell, Jeffrey Ulmer, and John Kramer. 1998. "The Interaction of Race, Gender, and Age in Criminal Sentencing: The Punishment Cost of Being Young, Black, and Male." *Criminology* 36 (4): 763–98.

Travis, Jeremy, and Joan Petersilia. 2001. "Reentry Reconsidered: A New Look at an Old Question." *Crime and Delinquency* 47 (3): 291–313.

Travis, Jeremy, and Michelle Waul, eds. 2003. *Prisoners Once Removed*. Washington, D.C.: Urban Institute Press.

Turner, Susan, Terry Fain, Peter W. Greenwood, Elsa Chen, and James Chiesa. 2001. National Evaluation of the Violent Offender Incarceration/Truth-in-Sentencing Incentive Grant Program, 1996–1999. Washington, D.C.: U.S. Department of Justice, National Institute of Justice.

U.S. Department of Justice, Bureau of Justice Statistics. 2004. *State Court Processing Statistics, 1990–2000: Felony Defendants in Large Urban Counties* [Computer file] Conducted by Pretrial Services Resource Center [producer], 2004. ICPSR ed. Ann Arbor, Mich.: Interuniversity Consortium for Political and Social Research [distributor], 2004 [cited January 16, 2006, 2004].

United States Census Bureau. 2004. Resident Population by Race, Hispanic or Latino Origin, and State: 2003, 2003 [cited September 30, 2004].

———. 2007. *State & County QuickFacts* 2006 [cited July 27, 2007]. Available from http://quickfacts.census.gov/qfd/states/06000.html.

Velez, Maria B., Lauren J. Krivo, and Ruth D. Peterson. 2003. "Structural Inequality and Homicide: An Assessment of the Black-White Gap in Killings." *Criminology* 41 (3): 645–72.

Walker, Rob. 2005. Silent Treatment. *New York Times*, October 9, 2005, Section 6, Column 1.

Yu, Jiang, and Allen E. Liska. 1993. "The Certainty of Punishment: A Reference Group Effect and Its Functional Form." *Criminology* 31 (3): 447–64.

About the Authors

Melina Abdullah is assistant professor of Pan-African Studies at California State University, Los Angeles. She earned her Ph.D. and M.A. from the University of Southern California in political science and her B.A. from Howard University in African-American studies. Her research focuses on power allocation and societal transformation. Abdullah has authored several articles and book chapters, including "The Emergence of a Black Feminist Leadership Model," "Hip Hop as Political Expression," "Self-Defined Leadership Among Black Women," "Capitalistic Hands around My Throat: Corporate Control and the Erosion of Hip Hop's Womanist Roots," and "Pushing and Pulling Towards Coalition: African Americans and the Election of Antonio Villaraigosa." She is currently working on her first book, *Move the Crowd: Hip Hop and Political Mobilization*. Abdullah defines herself as a womanist, scholar-activist—recognizing that the role that she plays in the academy is intrinsically linked to broader struggles for the liberation of oppressed people.

Sandra Bass first joined the David and Lucile Packard Foundation from 2002 to 2004 and was a senior editor/policy analyst for The Future of Children. She re-joined the foundation in 2005 as program officer and is responsible for managing and monitoring the foundation's directed grantmaking funds, which include the President's and Special Opportunities funds. She also conducts research and works on special projects. Prior to joining the foundation, Bass was assistant professor of criminology and government and politics at the University of Maryland. She also served as interim associate director for the Institute for Research on Women and Gender at Stanford University. She holds a bachelor's degree in political science from San José State University and an M.A. and Ph.D. in political science from the University of California, Berkeley. She was a doctoral fellow at Rand Corporation and coedited *Racial and Ethnic Politics in California, Vol. II.*

Kenneth C. Burt is the political director of the California Federation of Teachers and a visiting scholar at UC Berkeley. He is the author of *The Search for a Civic Voice: California Latino Politics*, and has published in a number of journals and anthologies. The Historical Society of Southern California awarded Burt its 2004 Doyce B. Nunis, Jr. Award. Burt is a board member of the Edmund G. "Pat" Brown Institute for Public Affairs and previously worked for Lieutenant Governor John Garamendi and Assembly Speaker Willie L. Brown, Jr. For more information, go to www.kennethburt.com.

Bruce E. Cain is Heller Professor of Political Science at the University of California, Berkeley, and director of the University of California Washington Center. He joined the Berkeley faculty from the California Institute of Technology, where he had taught for 13 years. A *summa cum laude* graduate of Bowdoin College, he studied as a Rhodes Scholar at Trinity College, Oxford. He later received his Ph.D. in political science from Harvard University. His writings include *The Reapportionment Puzzle, The Personal Vote,* and *Congressional Redistricting.* Cain has served as a polling consultant and as a redistricting consultant, and has been a political commentator for numerous radio and television stations in Los Angeles and the Bay Area. He has received the Zale Award for Outstanding Achievement in Policy Research and Public Service, and he is a member of the American Academy of Arts and Sciences.

Elsa Y. Chen is assistant professor of political science and director of the Public Sector Studies Program at Santa Clara University. Prior to that, she worked as a policy analyst in the RAND Criminal Justice Program. Her recent publications include "Impacts of 'Three Strikes and You're Out' on Crime Trends in California and throughout the United States" in the *Journal of Contemporary Criminal Justice* and "The Liberation Hypothesis and Racial and Ethnic Disparities in the Application of California's Three Strikes Law," in the *Journal of Ethnicity in Criminal Justice.* Chen earned her Ph.D. from UCLA and has an M.P.P. from Harvard's Kennedy School of Government and an A.B. in Public and International Affairs from Princeton University.

Wendy K. Tam Cho is associate professor with appointments in the Department of Political Science and the Department of Statistics and Senior Research Scientist at the National Center for Supercomputing Applications at the University of Illinois at Urbana-Champaign. She has also been a faculty member at Northwestern University. She received her B.A. in political science and mathematics, her M.A. in political science and statistics, and her Ph.D. in political science, all from the University of California, Berkeley. Her scholarly interests lie in the areas of political methodology, American politics, racial/ethnic politics, and computational solutions to social science problems. Her work has been funded by the National Science Foundation and has appeared in the *American Journal of Political Science*, the *Journal of Politics*, the *British Journal of Political Science*, and *Political Analysis*, among others. She currently serves on the executive council for the American Political Science Association, on the editorial board of *American Politics Research*, the *Journal of Politics*, *Political Analysis*, *PS: Political Science & Politics*, and *State Politics and Policy Quarterly* and is associate editor of *Political Analysis*.

Terry Christensen specializes in state and local politics. He is the author or co-author of nine books. Local and national media regularly call on him for analysis of politics in California and Silicon Valley. His most recent book is a new edition of *Local Politics: Governing at the Grassroots* (2006), co-authored by Tom Hogen-Esch. Other works include *Projecting Politics: Political Messages in American Films*, co-authored by Peter Haas and *Recall! California's Political Earthquake* (2004), co-authored by Larry N. Gerston. Christensen's teaching focuses on local government and politics; he also directs the SJSU political science department's internship program, which he created over 30 years ago. Generations of community leaders and activists have graduated from his classes to serve in elected and administrative positions and as volunteers. He is also active in local politics, advocating policy proposals and advising and mentoring candidates for local office, including many of his former students. He has served on numerous civic committees and commissions—again, often with his former students. He chaired the Department of Political Science from 1994 to 2002. In 1998, he was named San José State University's Outstanding Professor. Most recently he served for 2.5 years as executive director of CommUniverCity San Jose, a partnership between the city of San Jose, San José State University, and the Five Wounds/Brookwood Terrace neighborhoods. CommUniverCity concentrates hundreds of students performing community service in these neighborhoods, with projects selected by residents and supported by the city.

Luis Ricardo Fraga is associate vice provost for faculty advancement, director of the Diversity Research Institute, Russell F. Stark University Professor, and professor of political science at the University of Washington. His areas of primary research interest are urban politics, politics of race and ethnicity, educational politics, and voting rights policy. He is coauthor of *Multiethnic Moments: The Politics of Urban Education Reform* (Temple 2006) and was a member of the special taskforce of the American Political Science Association that wrote *Democracy at Risk: How Political Choices Undermine Citizen Participation and What We Can Do about It* (Brookings 2005). He has also published in the *American Political Science Review, Perspectives in Politics, American Journal of Political Science, The Journal of Politics, Political Research Quarterly, Dubois Review, Urban Affairs Quarterly,* and the *Harvard Journal of Hispanic Policy.* He is a former secretary of the American Political Science Association and a former president of the Western Political Science Association. He is one of the coprincipal investigators of the Latino National Survey (LNS), the first-ever state stratified survey of Latinos in the United States. Fraga has been given 14 awards for his teaching, advising, and mentoring. He was the keynote speaker at the 2008 Teaching and Learning Conference of the American Political Science Association.

Larry Gerston is professor of political science at San José State University. His *Public Policy Making in a Democratic Society: A Guide to Civic Engagement* was heralded as a breakthrough in explaining "hands on" citizen participation. *Recall! California's Political Earthquake* (with Terry Christensen), was selected as "outstanding academic book of 2004" by the American Library Association. In his most recent research and tenth book, *American Federalism: A Concise Introduction* (2007), he seeks to demystify the unique and complex power relationships among the various levels of American government. Gerston has been the political analyst at NBC11 (the Bay Area NBC station), since 1980 and radio station KCBS since 2002. He writes "Up Front," a monthly column in *San Jose*

Magazine, and has penned more than 100 op-ed columns in newspapers including the *San Jose Mercury News*, *San Francisco Chronicle,* and *Los Angeles Times*. He has also appeared on NBC Nightly News, BBC, NPR, and CNN's Inside Politics. Previously he worked for a California legislator and Los Angeles County supervisor.

Els de Graauw is a postdoctoral fellow at the Hauser Center for Nonprofit Organizations at Harvard University where she is working towards turning her dissertation research on immigrant political incorporation in San Francisco into a book. She received her M.A. in American studies from Radboud University Nijmegen in the Netherlands and her M.A. and Ph.D. in political science from UC Berkeley. Her research interests include immigration, urban politics, public policy, nonprofit organizations, and racial and ethnic politics. She will join the faculty at CUNY-Baruch College in 2009 as an assistant professor of political science.

Regina Freer is associate professor in the politics department at Occidental College in Los Angeles. She graduated with a B.A. from University of California, Berkeley and an M.A. and Ph.D. in political science from the University of Michigan, Ann Arbor. Her research and teaching interests include race and politics, demographic change, urban politics, and the intersection of all three in Los Angeles in particular. She is a co-author of the University of California Press book, *The Next Los Angeles: The Struggle for a Livable City*, a work that examines connections between historical and contemporary progressive social justice organizing in Los Angeles. She also authored "L.A. Race Woman: Charlotta Bass and the Complexities of Black Political Development in Los Angeles" in the September 2004 issue of *American Quarterly* and "Black Korean Conflict," a chapter in the edited volume, *The Los Angeles Riots*. A scholar/activist, Freer is a committed member of several local boards and organizations. She also currently serves on the Los Angeles City Planning Commission, having been appointed by Mayor Antonio Villaraigosa in 2005.

Kim Geron is associate professor of political science at California State University East Bay. He teaches courses in public policy and public administration. His research interests include race and ethnic politics, social movements, labor, and immigrant rights. His book, *Latino Political Power*, was published in 2005 by Lynne Rienner Publishers.

Ali Modarres is the associate director of the Edmund G. "Pat" Brown Institute of Public Affairs at California State University, Los Angeles and a professor in the Department of Geography and Urban Analysis on the same campus. He specializes in urban geography, and his primary research and publication interests are community development and planning. He has published in the areas of social geography, immigration, race and ethnicity, environmental equity, and transportation planning, as they relate to the issues of access and the role of public policy in creating disadvantaged communities. His recently co-authored book (with Christopher Boone), *City and Environment*, was published by Temple University Press.

Manuel Pastor is professor of geography and American studies and ethnicity at the University of Southern California and director of the Program for Environmental and Regional Equity at USC's Center for Sustainable Cities. His research has focused on issues of environmental justice, regional inclusion, and the economic and social conditions facing low-income urban communities. He was the founding director of the Center for Justice, Tolerance, and Community at the University of California, Santa Cruz, and has received fellowships and grants from the Guggenheim Foundation, the Irvine Foundation, the National Science Foundation, and many others. Pastor's most recent book, co-authored with Chris Benner and Laura Leete, is *Staircases or Treadmills: Labor Market Intermediaries and Economic Opportunity in a Changing Economy*. He is also the co-author of *Searching for the Uncommon Common Ground: New Dimensions on Race in America* and *Regions That Work: How Cities and Suburbs Can Grow Together*. Pastor served as a member of the California Commission on Regions, and in January 2002 was awarded a Civic Entrepreneur of the Year award from the California Center for Regional Leadership. He holds an economics Ph.D. from the University of Massachusetts, Amherst.

Ricardo Ramirez is assistant professor of political science and American studies and ethnicity at the University of Southern California. His research interests include state and local politics, political behavior, and the politics of race and ethnicity. He is the coeditor of *Transforming Politics, Transforming America: The Political and Civic Incorporation of Immigrants in the United States.*

Belinda I. Reyes is assistant professor at Raza Studies in the College of Ethnic Studies at San Francisco State University. Formerly a founding faculty member at the University of California, Merced, and a research fellow at the Public Policy Institute of California, her publications include: "Holding the Line? The Effect of the Recent Border Build-up on Unauthorized Immigration"; "Taking the Oath: An Analysis of Naturalization in California and the United States"; and "A Portrait of Race and Ethnicity in California: An Assessment of Social and Economic Well-Being." These publications explore different dimensions of immigration, policy, and the social and economic progress of racial and ethnic groups in the United States. Reyes also conducted research on racial diversity on education. In "Systems of Elections, Latino Representation, and Student Outcomes in Central California" and "Faculty, Managers, and Administrators in the University of California, 1996 to 2002," she explores ethnic diversity in higher education and K-12 and the potential consequences of underrepresentation. Her research focuses on the policy issues confronting people of color in the United States. She has briefed various federal, state, and local governmental bodies and addressed numerous civic organizations. She has been a senior program associate at PolicyLink; a lecturer at the University of California, Berkeley; a research fellow at the University of Michigan; and a visiting scholar at the Federal Reserve Bank of San Francisco.